Financial Lexicon

A compendium of financial definitions, acronyms, and colloquialisms

ERIK BANKS

palgrave
macmillan

© Erik Banks 2005

All rights reserved. No reproduction, copy or transmission of this publication may be made without written permission.

No paragraph of this publication may be reproduced, copied or transmitted save with written permission or in accordance with the provisions of the Copyright, Designs and Patents Act 1988, or under the terms of any licence permitting limited copying issued by the Copyright Licensing Agency, 90 Tottenham Court Road, London W1T 4LP.

Any person who does any unauthorised act in relation to this publication may be liable to criminal prosecution and civil claims for damages.

The author has asserted his right to be identified as the author of this work in accordance with the Copyright, Designs and Patents Act 1988.

First published 2005 by
PALGRAVE MACMILLAN
Houndmills, Basingstoke, Hampshire RG21 6XS and
175 Fifth Avenue, New York, N.Y. 10010
Companies and representatives throughout the world

PALGRAVE MACMILLAN is the global academic imprint of the Palgrave Macmillan division of St. Martin's Press, LLC and of Palgrave Macmillan Ltd. Macmillan® is a registered trademark in the United States, United Kingdom and other countries. Palgrave is a registered trademark in the European Union and other countries.

ISBN 1–4039–3609–9

This book is printed on paper suitable for recycling and made from fully managed and sustained forest sources.

A catalogue record for this book is available from the British Library.

A catalog record for this book is available from the Library of Congress.

10 9 8 7 6 5 4 3 2 1
14 13 12 11 10 09 08 07 06 05

Transferred to digital printing in 2006

DATE DUE

OCT 2 4 2019	
	PRINTED IN U.S.A.

DISCARDED

Contents

Acknowledgments	*v*
The author	*vi*
Summary of colloquialisms, foreign terms, and acronyms	*vii*
Introduction	*xv*
A	1
B	26
C	50
D	96
E	120
F	136
G	159
H	170
I	177
J	197
K	199
L	201
M	219
N	236

O	250
P	260
Q	290
R	292
S	320
T	355
U–V–W	373
X–Y–Z	391
Numeric	396
Selected references	***397***

Acknowledgments

I would like to extend my thanks and appreciation to Andrea Hartill at Palgrave Macmillan for her enthusiasm, support, and guidance on this new project. Thanks are also due to the editing, production, and marketing teams at Palgrave for their work in producing the book. I would also like to acknowledge the contributions of a number of referees from the banking and insurance sectors who were kind enough to review select definitions in this book and provide input on scope and detail.

And, as always, my deepest thanks go to Milena.

EB
Redding, Connecticut
2004

The author

Erik Banks spent 16 years in the financial services industry, holding senior risk management positions at several global financial institutions, including Partner and Chief Risk Officer of Bermuda reinsurer XL Capital's derivatives subsidiary, and Managing Director of Corporate Risk Management at Merrill Lynch, where he spent 13 years managing credit risk, market risk and risk analytics/technology teams in Tokyo, Hong Kong, London and New York. He is the author of 18 books on risk management, emerging markets, governance, derivatives, alternative risk transfer, merchant banking, and electronic finance.

Summary of colloquialisms, foreign terms, and acronyms

COLLOQUIALISMS

Accelerator
Actuals
All-in
Alligator spread
Alphabet stock
Ankle biter
Asian tail
Aunt Millie
Baby bond
Back door
Back door listing
Bad bank
Bankmail
Bear hug
Bear raid
Bear spread
Bear trap
Beauty contest
Bed breakfasting
Belly of the curve
Belly up
Bellwether
Benchmark
Big Board

Big uglies
Black knight
Blank check preferred
Blowout
Blue chip
Bogey
Boiler room
Boilerplate
Bond crowd
Book-building
Bookrunner
Bootstrapping
Bottom fishing
Bought deal
Brady bond
Breaking syndicate
Bricks and mortar
Broken date
Bubble
Buck
Bucket shop
Bulge bracket
Bull spread
Bunching

Busted convertible
Buy minus
Buy the book
Cable
CAMEL
Carrot equity
Carve-out
Chapter 11
Cheap
Check kiting
Cherry pick
Chewable pill
Chinese Wall
Churning
Circle
Circuit breaker
City Code
Clawback
Clean
Clean price
Clone fund
Coat-tailing
Consol
Contagion

Contrarian
Cookie jar accounting
Cooking the books
Cooling off period
Concert party
Cornering
Crack spread
Creeping tender
Crown jewel defense
Crown jewels
Crush spread
Daimyo
Daisy chain
Dawn raid
Dead cat bounce
Dead hand clause
Dead hand poison pill
Death spiral
Dirty float
Dirty price
Dirty stock
DK [Don't know]
Dog and pony show
Double dipping
Down round
Dragon
Dry powder
Dwarf
Elbow
Elephant
Elephant hunting
Embeddo
EPS bootstrapping
Evergreen
Fallen angel
Fannie Mae
Fighting the tape
Fill or kill
Fire sale
Flash price
Flight to quality
Flip in pill
Flip over pill

Flipper
Floater
Following the fortunes
Footsie
Freddie Mac
Free rider
Freeze-out
Front door
Front running
Gather in the stops
Geisha
Ghosting
Ginnie Mae
Gnome
Goldbricks
Golden handcuffs
Golden handshake
Golden hello
Golden parachute
Good money
Grains
Granny bond
Graveyard market
Gray knight
Gray market
Greeks
Greenmail
Greenshoe
Gun jumping
Gunslinger
Haircut
Handle
Hard landing
Head and shoulders
Heavy market
High street bank
Hit the bid
Hot money
Hung deal
Incubator
Jobber
Jobbing
Junk bond

Kaffirs
Kicker
Killer bees
Kiwi
Laddering
Laundering
League table
Legging
Line
Lobster trap
Local
Locked market
Long and wrong
Long bond
Long end
Macaroni defense
Main Street
Married put
Matilda
Midget
Mini
Momo
Moneyness
Morning notes
Names
Natural
Near money
Nifty Fifty
Noming the pipes
Omnipresent specter
One man picture
OPM [Other people's money]
Over the wall
Overlined
Pac-Man defense
Painting the tape
Paris club
Parking
Penny jumping
Penny stock
People pill
Phantom stock

Piercing the corporate veil
Pig on pork
Piggy-backing
Pink sheets
Pinning the strike
Pip
Pipeline
Point
Poison pill
Poison put
Poop and scoop
Porcupine provision
Portfolio pumping
Pot
Pre-pack
Puffery
Puke point
Pump and dump
Punt
Pup company
Quiet period
QT [Questioned trade]
Raider
Rainmaker
Red herring
Red-lining
Repo
Reverse
Reverse head and shoulders
Reverse repo
Reverse tying
Revolver
Rich
Riding the curve
Rio trade
Roadshow
Roller coaster
Rolling down the curve
Round trip
Safe harbor rule
Samurai
Saturday night special
Scalper
Scorched earth defense
Seat
Selling away
Shadow calendar
Shadow stock
Shark repellent
Shoe
Shogun
Short against the box
Short end
Short squeeze
Sinker
Size
Sleeping beauty
Snowballing
Softs
Spark spread
Special
Spinning
Spring loading
Square
Squeeze
Stack and roll
Stag
Stapled stock
Sticky deal
Story paper
Street name
Stripping the yield curve
Strong hands
Stub
Stuck deal
Supersinker
Sweetener
Tag along rights
Tail
Tailgating
Take the offer
Teaser
Teeny
Texas hedge
Thin market
Third market
Tight market
Tombstone
Tom-next
Ton
Too big to fail
Torpedo stock
Toxic waste
Triple witching hour
Turkey
Twisting
Tying
Underwater
Upstairs market
Vanilla
Vulture bid
Vulture fund
War chest
Weak hands
Wet barrels
Whipsaw
Whisper numbers
Whisper stock
Whistleblower
White knight
White squire
Widows and orphans
Winding-up
Window dressing
Without
Yankee
Yard
Yield burning
Zombie

FOREIGN LANGUAGE TERMS

Ad valorem
Ajustabonos
Amakudari
Arbitrageur
Aufsichtrsrat
Bancassurance
Banque d'affaires
Bolsa
Bordereau
Borsa
Bourse
Boutique
Bund
Bundesbank
Caveat emptor
Chaebol
Conseil d'Administration
Conseil du Surveillance
Corpus
Daimyo
Entrepôt
Ex-gratia
Filz
Force Majeure
Geisha
Gensaki
Gyosei Shido
Hausbank
Keiretsu
Laissez faire
Mochiai
Nostro
Noyau dur
Pari passu
Pfandbriefe
Pro-forma
Pro-rata
Samurai
Schuldschein
Shibosai
Shikko yakuin
Shogun
Shokken
Tranche
Uberrimae fidei
Ultra vires
Vis major
Vostro
Vorstand
Zaibatsu
Zaitech

ACRONYMS

ABS	Asset-backed security	B2B	Business-to-business [exchange]
ACH	Automatic clearing house	B2C	Business-to-consumer [exchange]
ADR	American Depository Receipt	BA	Banker's acceptance
ADS	American Depository Share	BACS	Bankers' Automated Clearing Service
AGM	Annual general meeting	BBA	British Bankers Association
ALM	Asset-liability management	BIS	Bank for International Settlements
APT	Arbitrage Pricing Theory	BTF	Block trading facility
ARM	Adjustable rate mortgage	CAPM	Capital Asset Pricing Model
ART	Alternative risk tranfer	CBO	Collateralized bond obligation
ATS	Alternative trading system	CD	Certificate of deposit

ACRONYMS

CDO	Collateralized debt obligation	EBITDA	Earnings before interest, taxes, depreciation and amortization
CFD	Contract for differences		
CFTC	Commodity Futures Trading Commission	EBRD	European Bank for Reconstruction and Development
CHAPS	Clearinghouse Automated Payment System	ECB	European Central Bank
		ECN	Electronic communications network
CHIPS	Clearinghouse Interbank Payment System		
		ECP	Euro commercial paper
CIF	Cost, insurance, freight	ECU	European currency unit
CLO	Collateralized loan obligation	EFP	Exchange for physical
CMO	Collateralized mortgage obligation	EFT	Electronic funds transfer
		EMTN	Euro medium term note
COD	Cash on delivery	EMU	European Monetary Union
CP	Commercial paper		
CPI	Consumer Price Index	EONIA	Euro overnight index average
CPR	Conditional prepayment rate		
		EPS	Earnings per share
CSA	Credit support annex	ERM	Enterprise risk management
CTA	Commodity Trading Advisor		
		ESOP	Employee stock ownership plan
CTD	Cheapest-to-deliver		
D&O	Directors' and officers' [insurance cover]	ETF	Exchange-traded fund
		EURIBOR	Euro Interbank Offered Rate
DAC	Deliver against cash		
DCF	Discounted cash flow	FASB	Financial Accounting Standards Board
DIP	Debtor-in-possession		
DJIA	Dow Jones Industrial Average	FCM	Futures commission merchant
DK	Don't know [a trade]	FDIC	Federal Deposit Insurance Corporation
DPC	Derivative product company		
		FHLMC	Federal Home Loan Mortgage Corporation
DPO	Direct public offering		
DTC	Depository Trust Company	FIFO	First in, first out
		FNMA	Federal National Mortgage Association
DVP	Delivery versus payment		
		FOB	Free on board
EBIT	Earnings before interest and taxes	FOMC	Federal Open Markets Committee

FRA	Forward rate agreement	IBRD	International Bank for Reconstruction and Development
FRCD	Floating rate certificate of deposit		
FRN	Floating rate note	IDB	Inter-dealer broker
FSA	Financial Services Authority	IFC	International Finance Corporation
FTC	Federal Trade Commission	ILS	Insurance-linked security
FTSE 100	Financial Times Stock Exchange 100 [Index]	IMF	International Monetary Fund
FX	Foreign exchange	IO	Interest only [strip]
G7	Group of 7	IOI	Indication of interest
G10	Group of 10	IPO	Initial public offering
GAAP	Generally Accepted Accounting Principles	IRB	International Ratings Based [approach]
GATT	General Agreement on Tariffs and Trade	IRR	Internal rate of return
		ISDA	International Swaps and Derivatives Association
GC	General collateral		
GDP	Gross domestic product	ISMA	International Securities Market Association
GDR	Global Depository Receipt		
GDS	Global Depository Share	JGB	Japanese Government Bond
GEMM	Gilt-edged market-maker	LBO	Leveraged buyout
		LDC	Lesser developed country
GIC	Guaranteed investment contract	LEAPS	Long-term equity appreciation security
GNMA	Government National Mortgage Association	LEPO	Low exercise price option
HICP	Harmonized Index of Consumer Prices	LIBID	London Interbank Bid
HLT	Highly leveraged transaction [loan]	LIBOR	London Interbank Offered Rate
IAS	International Accounting Standards	LIFO	Last in, first out
		LIMEAN	London Interbank Mean
IASB	International Accounting Standards Board	LLC	Limited liability company
IBF	International Banking Facility	LTV	Loan-to-value
		MAC	Material adverse change [clause]
IBNR	Incurred but not reported	MBO	Management buyout

MBS	Mortgage-backed security	RAP	Receive against payment
MFN	Most favored nation	RAROC	Risk-adjusted return on capital
MOB	Municipals over bonds [spread]	REIT	Real estate investment trust
MOF	Multiple option facility	REMIC	Real estate mortgage investment conduit
MOS	Mutual offset system		
MTN	Medium term note	ROA	Return on assets
NASD	National Association of Securities Dealers	ROE	Return on equity
		ROI	Return on investment
NASDAQ	National Association of Securities Dealers Automated Quotation [System]	RPI	Retail Price Index
		RUF	Revolving underwriting facility
NAV	Net asset value	S&L	Savings and loan [association]
NCD	Negotiable certificate of deposit	S&P500	Standard and Poor's 500
NIC	Newly industrialized country	SDR	Special Drawing Right
NIF	Note issuance facility	SEC	Securities and Exchange Commission
NPV	Net present value		
NYSE	New York Stock Exchange	SNIF	Standby note issuance facility
OAS	Option-adjusted spread	SPE	Special purpose entity
OECD	Organization for Economic Cooperation and Development	SPV	Special purpose vehicle
		SRO	Self regulatory organization
OID	Original issue discount		
OPEC	Organization of Petroleum Exporting Countries	TAC	Targeted amortization class [bond]
		TBA	To be announced [security]
OTC	Over-the-counter		
P/E	Price/Earnings [ratio]	TED	Treasury–Eurodollar [spread]
PAC	Planned amortization class [bond]	TIBOR	Tokyo Interbank Offered Rate
PIK	Payment in kind		
PLC	Public limited company	TIPS	Treasury Inflation Protected Security
PO	Principal only [strip]	TOPIX	Tokyo Price Index
P&L	Profit and loss	TRIN	Trading Index
QIB	Qualified institutional buyer	TRUF	Transferable revolving underwriting facility
QT	Questioned trade	VAR	Value-at-risk

VAT	Value added tax	WI	When-issued [security, Treasury]
VIE	Variable interest entity		
VRCD	Variable rate certificate of deposit	WTO	World Trade Organization
WAC	Weighted average coupon	XD	Ex-dividend
		XR	Ex-rights
WAM	Weighted average maturity	XW	Ex-warrant
		XOL	Excess of loss [agreement]

Introduction

Financial Lexicon is a comprehensive financial reference that explains the formal and informal terminology of finance. We have structured the book much as any other dictionary so that it can be used as an easy (and hopefully frequent) guide and reference. Perhaps the hardest part in a project of this type is limiting the scope of content. Accordingly, as we set out to prepare this text we operated under two fundamental rules:

- Rule 1: Include the most commonly encountered terms in a particular field.
- Rule 2: Limit the fields to the essentials of the following:
  - securities and investment
  - corporate finance
  - commercial banking
  - investment banking
  - insurance/reinsurance
  - risk management
  - trading
  - derivatives
  - credit and equity analysis
  - business economics
  - business law

Unlike other financial dictionaries, we have decided to include some of the colloquialisms that have crept into the business vernacular over the years. We believe this is important because much of what happens in the banking, securities, asset management, and insurance industries is based to a degree on the informal language of the trade. So, when the reader hears of the "hung deal" in a securities underwriting, "stripping the yield curve" in a trading environment, or "spinning" in financial regulations, he or she is encountering the real language of finance; these terms convey concisely, efficiently, and sometimes colorfully what might otherwise take whole sentences to express. We have tried to take some care with colloquialisms by including terms that seem to have some survived for a period of time. Obviously, new phases of market development can lead to the creation of new words, and these may ultimately fall out of use when the market phase subsides or changes. We have tried to be cognizant of this by focusing on the enduring terms of the marketplace.

There are, of course, instances where a particular concept or definition is known by different terms, even in the same marketplace. Rather than repeating definitions, we refer the reader to the single source for the definition, using some judgment about which of the two, and sometimes three, words serves as the "anchor" term.

HOW TO USE THE *FINANCIAL LEXICON*

The *Financial Lexicon* contains clear, concise, easy-to-read financial definitions and descriptions, arranged in alphabetical order. Each definition ranges from 2 to 10 sentences in length (depending on topic and complexity).

- Cross-references to other terms in the Lexicon are indicated in CAPITALS.
- Foreign and colloquial terms are distinguished as follows:
    - French: FR
    - German: GER
    - Italian: ITL
    - Japanese: JPN
    - Korean: KOR
    - Latin: LAT
    - Spanish: SPN
    - Colloquial: COL
- Where relevant "Also known as" references for terms that are known by multiple names are included.
- References to additional terms within the *Lexicon* are included where we believe these can add supplementary information or points of view.
- References to external sources of information are included where we believe these may be of use to the reader.
- Examples, charts, and figures are incorporated where additional clarity

and information can be communicated. Where appropriate, we have also used very simple formulas and equations to convey certain terms, but these are non-technical and suitable for general business readers.

- In common with other dictionaries, the Lexicon ignores hyphenation when ordering entries alphabetically. As an example, the reader will notice:
    - AD VALOREM
    - ADD-ON
    - ADDITIONAL BONDS TEST.

A

A-SHARE In the United Kingdom, a share of COMMON STOCK featuring RENT RIGHTS but no CONTROL RIGHTS. The lack of control rights generally causes A-shares to trade at a discount to conventional shares.

ABANDON The act of not exercising or selling an OPTION, occurring when the contract ends OUT-OF-THE-MONEY.

ABANDONMENT (1) The voluntary surrender of right of title to real or financial property. (2) Within the INSURANCE sector, the transfer of rights to damaged or lost property from the INSURED to the INSURER.
- (2) See also ABANDONMENT CLAUSE.

ABANDONMENT CLAUSE A clause in an INSURANCE contract that gives the INSURED the right to abandon property and make a CLAIM for a full SETTLEMENT from the INSURER; the same clause also gives the insurer rights to the abandoned property.
- See also ABANDONMENT.

ABILITY TO PERFORM A COUNTERPARTY's financial capacity to perform on its contractual obligations. Strong counterparties, with high CREDIT RATINGS, have a greater ability to perform than weak, or poorly rated, ones. Ability to perform is the essence of financial credit analysis and is distinguished from WILLINGNESS TO PERFORM.

ABS See ASSET-BACKED SECURITY.

ABSOLUTE LIABILITY LIABILITY that occurs without fault, or an action deemed to be contrary to the public good that is neither negligent nor willful. A company found to be in breach of absolute liability may be required to provide restitution to injured parties.

ABSOLUTE PRIORITY RULE A legal concept indicating that if a public company DEFAULTS, shareholders are only entitled to recover their investments after creditors have been fully repaid. In most BANKRUPTCY cases shareholders receive little, if any, restitution

since they are subordinate to all other claimholders. Absolute priority also extends to the broad category of creditors, where secured creditors receive payment before senior unsecured creditors, who receive payment before junior and subordinated creditors.
- See also SUBORDINATION.

ACCELERATED DEPRECIATION A DEPRECIATION mechanism that permits faster recovery of costs than conventional STRAIGHT LINE DEPRECIATION methods, and generates greater TAX SHIELDS. Accelerated depreciation is applied to qualifying fixed assets, including those that are expected to become obsolete before the end of their economically useful lives. In the United States, the Accelerated Cost Recovery System became mandatory in the 1980s.

ACCELERATION A clause in a credit agreement, INDENTURE or MASTER AGREEMENT that requires a COUNTERPARTY'S outstanding sums to become due and payable when it triggers an EVENT OF DEFAULT or breaches a COVENANT. In some instances accelerated payments, except those related to DERIVATIVES and REPURCHASE AGREEMENTS, may be halted through an AUTOMATIC STAY, which is generally invoked in the event of a BANKRUPTCY filing.

ACCELERATOR [COL] A firm that provides start-up ventures with seed CAPITAL, administrative services, and business plan support. Accelerators often focus on start-ups that have been rejected by INCUBATORS or VENTURE CAPITAL groups because of insufficient development work. Accelerators may be compensated through fees or pre-INITIAL PUBLIC OFFERING EQUITY stakes.

ACCEPTANCE (1) In INSURANCE, an agreement to an offer of coverage that creates a binding contract; this is generally accomplished when an INSURER issues a policy and an INSURED pays a PREMIUM. (2) In banking, a BANKER'S ACCEPTANCE or BILL OF EXCHANGE.

ACCEPTING HOUSE In the United Kingdom, a financial firm (i.e., BANK, MERCHANT BANK) that guarantees that a BILL OF EXCHANGE or BANKER'S ACCEPTANCE created by a drawer will be paid to the BENEFICIARY or bearer on the due date. The accepting house charges a fee in the form of a discount on the amount of the bill for assuming the drawer's CREDIT RISK.

ACCOMMODATION LINE An agreement by an INSURER to UNDERWRITE a certain amount of business submitted by a BROKER, regardless of quality. The intent is for the insurer to develop a strong relationship with the broker, to the point where high quality business (i.e., profitable and/or low RISK) can be regularly concluded.

ACCOMMODATION PAPER A NEGOTIABLE INSTRUMENT endorsed by a party that does not receive any value in return. Accommodation paper is generally used to help another party secure financing.

ACCOUNTING VALUE An approach to financial analysis that values a company's COMMON STOCK as a function of EARNINGS PER SHARE and the PRICE/EARNINGS multiple. The higher either variable, the more valuable the stock, and thus the company.
- See also ENTERPRISE VALUE.

ACCOUNTS PAYABLE Trade credit created by a supplier when it permits a client to pay in the future for goods or services that have already been delivered by the supplier. Payables are a common source of short-term financing for many industrial and service companies. A client company is generally required to arrange payment within 7 to 180 days, though in some cases terms may extend even further. In exchange for granting the payment extension, the supplier explicitly or implicitly charges a financing cost.
- See also ACCOUNTS RECEIVABLE.

ACCOUNTS RECEIVABLE Trade credit created by a company when it permits a client to pay in the future for goods or services that have already been delivered by the company. A client company is generally required to arrange payment within 7 to 180 days, though in some cases terms may extend even further. In exchange for granting the payment extension, the company implicitly or explicitly charges its customers a financing cost. Receivables granted in the normal course of business are routinely sold to third parties on a non-recourse basis (FACTORING) or used as COLLATERAL to secure funding (ACCOUNTS RECEIVABLE FINANCING); in some cases they are repackaged and sold through a SECURITIZATION.
- See also ACCOUNTS PAYABLE.

ACCOUNTS RECEIVABLE FINANCING Short-term financing obtained by a company through a RECOURSE sale of ACCOUNTS RECEIVABLE to a third party.
- See also FACTORING, FORFAITING.

ACCREDITED INVESTOR Under the US SECURITIES AND EXCHANGE COMMISSION Regulation D, a wealthy investor with a minimum net worth of $1 million or annual income of more than $200,000 that is permitted to invest in high RISK investments that are normally intended only for sophisticated investors that can withstand large economic losses.

ACCRETING SWAP An OVER-THE-COUNTER SWAP featuring a NOTIONAL PRINCIPAL balance that increases on a preset schedule or through the triggering of a market event, generally a breach of a

defined INTEREST RATE level. Accreting swaps typically have a LOCKOUT PERIOD during which increases are prohibited.
- See also AMORTIZING SWAP, INDEX PRINCIPAL SWAP, REVERSE INDEX PRINCIPAL SWAP, VARIABLE PRINCIPAL SWAP.

ACCRETION A periodic increase in the value of an ASSET or LIABILITY originally issued, granted, or sold at a discount to FACE VALUE. In general, the contract will increase on a straight-line basis towards face value as maturity of the transaction approaches.
- See also ACCRETION OF DISCOUNT, AMORTIZATION, ORIGINAL ISSUE DISCOUNT.

ACCRETION OF DISCOUNT The process of adjusting the BOOK VALUE of a BOND purchased at a DISCOUNT to reflect the effects of a non-cash payment of COUPON interest as maturity approaches.
- See also ACCRETION, AMORTIZATION, ORIGINAL ISSUE DISCOUNT.

ACCRUAL BASIS A general accounting method that reports income when it is earned and expenses when they are incurred.
- See also CASH BASIS.

ACCRUAL BOND (1) A TRANCHE of a COLLATERALIZED MORTGAGE OBLIGATION that pays no COUPON interest or PRINCIPAL until all other tranches have been redeemed; this protects investors holding other tranches from PREPAYMENTS. The accrual bond is similar to a zero coupon bond but carries an explicit coupon rate and may ultimately pay both principal and coupons prior to final maturity. (2) A ZERO COUPON BOND.
- (1) Also known as Z-BOND.

ACCRUAL NOTE See RANGE FLOATER NOTE.

ACCRUED INTEREST The interest on a BOND or LOAN that has been earned but not yet paid. Interest payable/receivable accumulates between COUPON payment periods; once a periodic interest payment is made, accrued interest reverts to zero and begins building on a daily basis until the next payment. Accrued interest of a FIXED INCOME instrument can be computed via:

$$AI = \frac{C\,(AD)}{2\,(n)}$$

where C is the coupon, AD is the actual number of days that have elapsed since the last coupon, and n is number of days in the coupon period.
- See also CLEAN PRICE, DIRTY PRICE.

ACCUMULATED DIVIDEND A DIVIDEND that has been declared, but not yet paid, to investors holding CUMULATIVE PREFERRED

STOCK. No dividends are payable to holders of COMMON STOCK until accumulated dividends have been paid. Since accumulated dividends are contractually owed to investors, they are reflected as a LIABILITY on the issuer's balance sheet until they are fully paid.

ACCUMULATION AREA A TECHNICAL ANALYSIS charting figure reflecting a price range where buyers gradually build positions in a security, keeping the price above a minimum floor level. The steady buying interest is often interpreted as a bullish signal, and may indicate a possible BREAKOUT to the upside.

ACCUMULATION PERIOD The period of time during which the purchaser of an ANNUITY makes PREMIUM payments to an INSURER; once the accumulation period has ended, the annuity program provides the ANNUITANT (i.e., the original purchaser or a designated BENEFICIARY) with contractual payouts.

ACH See AUTOMATIC CLEARINGHOUSE.

ACID TEST See QUICK RATIO.

ACQUISITION The purchase of one company by another in order to fulfill particular strategic goals related to revenues, market share, product/service offerings, or competition. An acquisition may be structured as a stock acquisition, where the acquiring company offers investors in the target company a specific price for their COMMON STOCK, or an asset acquisition, where the acquiring company offers to buy a portion or majority of the target company's ASSETS. Stock acquisitions based on full integration require tendering of all MINORITY INTEREST shares.
   ▪ See also CONSOLIDATION, MERGER, TAKEOVER.

ACQUISITION COST The cost associated with marketing and writing new INSURANCE business, generally comprised of AGENT commissions, UNDERWRITING expenses, fees, and marketing support costs.

A portion of these costs may be charged back to INSUREDS through EXPENSE LOADING.

ACTIVE INVESTMENT STRATEGY A process of dynamically managing a PORTFOLIO of securities by analyzing the RISK factors that influence each ASSET class (such as INTEREST RATES, interest rate VOLATILITY, CREDIT SPREADS, FOREIGN EXCHANGE RATES, and corporate earnings) and allocating CAPITAL to those where risk and return appear attractive. An active strategy may require frequent rebalancing.
- See also INDEXING, PASSIVE INVESTMENT STRATEGY.

ACTUAL AUTHORITY Powers granted by a PRINCIPAL to an AGENT to deal on its behalf. Actual authority may be explicit or implicit, and actions taken by the agent are generally binding on the principal.
- Also known as EXPRESS AUTHORITY.

ACTUAL CASH VALUE The cost of replacing damaged or destroyed property, generally on the basis of new cost less DEPRECIATION. Actual cash value determination is the most common method of financial SETTLEMENT in INSURANCE contracts unless an alternative method, such as full value (new cost) is specified.

ACTUAL EXPOSURE The amount of CREDIT RISK exposure in a DERIVATIVE or financial transaction, typically reflected as a MARK-TO-MARKET valuation. If DEFAULT occurs when actual exposure is positive to the non-defaulting party, a credit loss arises; if negative, no credit loss occurs. Actual exposure is one of two components, along with FRACTIONAL EXPOSURE, in the determination of total credit exposure.
- Also known as ACTUAL MARKET RISK, REPLACEMENT COST.
- See also POTENTIAL EXPOSURE.

ACTUAL MARKET RISK See ACTUAL EXPOSURE.

ACTUALS [COL] Physical commodities, such as GRAINS, SOFTS, metals, and energy, which are traded and delivered under COMMODITY DERIVATIVE contracts.

ACTUARIAL ADJUSTMENT In INSURANCE, the process of modifying the PREMIUM rate and RESERVES to reflect actual loss experience.

ACTUARIAL EQUIVALENT In INSURANCE, a statistical measure based on the expectation that a loss will occur, and the benefits that will become payable as a result. By computing this measure, the INSURER can vary the PREMIUM it charges INSUREDS.
- See also ACTUARIAL PRICING.

ACTUARIAL PRICING In INSURANCE, the pricing of RISK based on probabilities of loss occurrence constructed from statistical distribu-

tions. Actuarial pricing is used to develop PREMIUMS that are intended to cover losses from underwritten risks and provide future benefits payable to beneficiaries.
- See also ACTUARIAL EQUIVALENT.

AD VALOREM [LAT] Literally, "according to the value." In general, a tax applied to the value of goods and services, such as a VALUE ADDED TAX.

ADD-ON A NEW ISSUE of COMMON STOCK for a company that has already completed an INITIAL PUBLIC OFFERING. The add-on increases the issuer's PAID-IN CAPITAL account, generating additional funds for operations; however, since the transaction results in the creation of new shares it is considered dilutive. The UNDERWRITING SYNDICATE allocates add-on shares to new institutional and/or retail clients; if it is only offered to existing shareholders, the transaction takes the form of a RIGHTS ISSUE.
- See also PRIMARY OFFERING, SECONDARY OFFERING.

ADDITIONAL BONDS TEST A COVENANT in an INDENTURE that limits the amount of new BONDS that an issuer can FLOAT. The test, which is intended to keep the issuer's total LEVERAGE in check, is often measured by a TIMES INTEREST EARNED ratio or a FIXED CHARGE COVERAGE ratio.

ADJUSTABLE RATE MORTGAGE (ARM) A MORTGAGE with a floating INTEREST RATE that resets every 1, 3, 6, or 12 months, and a final maturity of 5 to 30 years. In the United States, common floating ARM indexes include LIBOR, PRIME RATE, Cost of Funds Index, and the constant maturity TREASURY BOND rate. In order to protect the borrower and lender against extreme rate movements, ARMs generally feature periodic and lifetime CAPS, and lifetime FLOORS.
- Also known as VARIABLE RATE MORTGAGE.

ADJUSTABLE RATE MORTGAGE (ARM) SECURITY A MORTGAGE-BACKED SECURITY created through the SECURITIZATION of a pool of ADJUSTABLE RATE MORTGAGES rather than conventional fixed rate mortgages. As a result of the floating rate component, ARM securities are generally more complex to value and HEDGE than standard fixed rate issues.

ADJUSTABLE RATE PREFERRED STOCK PREFERRED STOCK that pays investors a floating DIVIDEND that resets periodically (generally every quarter or every 49 days); the floating dividend is typically pegged to TREASURY BILL rates or some other recognized MONEY MARKET rate.
- Also known as MONEY MARKET PREFERRED STOCK, VARIABLE RATE PREFERRED STOCK.
- See also DUTCH AUCTION PREFERRED STOCK.

ADJUSTED BASIS The base price used to determine capital gains or losses on an investment, generally including a deduction for commissions at the time of purchase or sale, along with adjustments for any STOCK SPLITS that may have occurred.

ADJUSTED BREAKEVEN A measure of the number of years it takes for an investor to recover the initial CONVERSION PREMIUM paid when purchasing a CONVERTIBLE BOND, after accounting for the fact that the investor may purchase more COMMON STOCK than represented by the CONVERSION RATIO. Adjusted breakeven is typically computed as:

$$ABE = \frac{Conv_{prem}}{C - \left(\frac{P_{CB}}{S}(DPS)\right)}$$

where $Conv_{prem}$ is the conversion premium, C is the COUPON, P_{CB} is the price of the convertible bond, S is the price of the common stock, and DPS is DIVIDENDS per share.
- See also EQUIVALENT BREAKEVEN, SIMPLE BREAKEVEN.

ADJUSTMENT BOND A BOND issued as a RECAPITALIZATION instrument by a company in FINANCIAL DISTRESS, often as an INCOME BOND that only pays investors COUPON interest as earnings permit.

ADMITTED INSURANCE An INSURANCE contract written by an ADMITTED INSURER that is authorized to do business in the state or jurisdiction where the policy is issued.
- See also NON-ADMITTED INSURANCE.

ADMITTED INSURER An INSURER that is authorized to write INSURANCE business in a particular state or jurisdiction; the contracts it offers are classified as ADMITTED INSURANCE.
- Also know as AUTHORIZED INSURER, LICENSED CARRIER.
- See also NON-ADMITTED INSURER.

ADR See AMERICAN DEPOSITORY RECEIPT.

ADS See AMERICAN DEPOSITORY SHARE.

ADVANCE See LOAN.

ADVANCE–DECLINE A TECHNICAL ANALYSIS tool that measures the number of COMMON STOCKS that advance against the number that decline over a given period of time. A rising advance–decline is a generally regarded as a bullish signal, a falling advance–decline as a bearish signal.

ADVANCE OPTION A short-term LINE OF CREDIT granted by an UNDERWRITER to an issuer of securities that can be drawn if the underwriter cannot successfully place the securities. The advance option thus guarantees the issuer access to short-term funds regardless of the relative success of the NEW ISSUE.

ADVANCE PREMIUM In INSURANCE, a PREMIUM payment by the INSURED to the INSURER prior to the due date.

ADVANCE REFUNDING An exchange of outstanding GOVERNMENT BONDS for a NEW ISSUE of securities prior to final maturity of the original issue, typically arranged to take advantage of a lower INTEREST RATE environment.

ADVANCE SETTLEMENT In INSURANCE, payment of a CLAIM by the INSURER to the INSURED prior to the settlement date.

ADVANCED METHODOLOGY A credit-based CAPITAL ALLOCATION process promulgated by the BANK FOR INTERNATIONAL SETTLEMENTS under the INTERNAL RATINGS BASED (IRB) APPROACH. BANKS use internal models to determine EXPECTED CREDIT LOSSES and UNEXPECTED CREDIT LOSSES by estimating a COUNTERPARTY'S DEFAULT RISK, RISK EQUIVALENT EXPOSURE, and LOSS GIVEN DEFAULT (as well as the impact of RISK mitigants and the relationship of counterparty exposures to other exposures in the PORTFOLIO). Capital is then allocated to cover the resulting exposure.
- See also FOUNDATION METHODOLOGY.

ADVERSE DEVELOPMENT COVER A FINITE INSURANCE CONTRACT where the INSURED shifts the timing of losses that have already occurred, as well as those that have been INCURRED BUT NOT YET REPORTED, to the INSURER. In exchange for a PREMIUM the insurer assumes losses in excess of the insured's RESERVE, providing LOSS FINANCING up to a maximum amount dictated by the POLICY CAP.
- See also LOSS PORTFOLIO TRANSFER, RETROSPECTIVE FINITE POLICY.

ADVERSE OPINION An AUDIT OPINION by an external auditor indicating that a company's financial statements do not accurately reflect its financial position and cannot be relied on as a result of omissions, errors, lack of information, or lack of conformity to accepted accounting principles.
- See also QUALIFIED OPINION, UNQUALIFED OPTION.

ADVERSE SELECTION Mispricing of RISK as a result of information asymmetries. This occurs when an INSURER cannot clearly distinguish between different classes of risks, and leads to a dearth or excess of risk coverage at a given price, i.e., charging a standard or low PREMIUM rate for a significant or UNINSURABLE RISK, or a high premium for a small or inconsequential risk.
- See also MORAL HAZARD.

ADVISED LINE A BANK LINE that a financial institution approves and maintains for a customer. The size of the line is specifically conveyed

to the customer, though availability depends on the terms of the credit agreement and/or the payment of a COMMITMENT FEE.
- Also known as CONFIRMED LINE.
- See also GUIDANCE LINE.

AFFIRMATIVE OBLIGATION One or more duties that a SPECIALIST or MARKET MAKER must undertake, including taking one side of a purchase or sale ORDER through a proprietary account when the other side cannot be immediately matched, quoting two-sided markets at all times, and reporting all executed trades within a pre-defined time frame.
- Also known as POSITIVE OBLIGATION.
- See also INTERPOSITIONING, NEGATIVE OBLIGATION.

AFTER HOURS TRADING TRADING in securities that occurs after the formal close of an EXCHANGE, through telephonic networks or ELECTRONIC COMMUNICATION NETWORKS supported by BROKER/DEALERS. In practice only BENCHMARK securities with a broad investor follow trade after hours.

AFTERMARKET See SECONDARY MARKET.

AGED ASSETS ASSETS held for resale by a BANK or SECURITIES FIRM that have been owned for a long period of time (i.e., many months). Aged assets may indicate misvaluation.

AGED FAIL A FAIL TO RECEIVE or FAIL TO DELIVER between two parties that is not settled within 30 days. In most instances the party expecting to receive securities must remove the entry from the ASSET accounts on the balance sheet until the error is resolved. Aged fails may signal increased PROCESS RISK.

AGENCY CAPTIVE A CAPTIVE, owned by one or more INSURANCE AGENTS, which is used to write insurance cover for a large number of third party clients.
- See also GROUP CAPTIVE, PROTECTED CELL COMPANY, PURE CAPTIVE, RENT-A-CAPTIVE, SISTER CAPTIVE.

AGENCY COSTS Direct and indirect costs arising from the separation of ownership (i.e., COMMON STOCK shareholders) and control (i.e., DIRECTORS and managers) that ultimately lead to a reduction in ENTERPRISE VALUE. Agency costs can include the expenses associated with implementing processes for monitoring, reporting, and auditing.

AGENCY PROBLEM A conflict based on the fundamental "mistrust" that arises between COMMON STOCK shareholders, DIRECTORS, and management. The agency problem centers on whether directors and managers always act in good faith and seek to advance the interests of shareholders.
- Additional reference: Berle and Means (1991).

AGENCY SECURITY In the United States, NOTES or BONDS issued by government-sponsored or government-guaranteed institutions (e.g., FEDERAL NATIONAL MORTGAGE ASSOCIATION, GOVERNMENT NATIONAL MORTGAGE ASSOCIATION, FEDERAL HOME LOAN MORTGAGE CORPORATION). The securities carry explicit or implicit government support related to PRINCIPAL and interest payments, and thus carry the strongest CREDIT RATINGS. Agency securities, which are issued with short- to long-term maturities and fixed or floating coupons, are exempt from REGISTRATION requirements established by the SECURITIES AND EXCHANGE COMMISSION.

AGENT A party that acts as a representative of a PRINCIPAL, carrying express or implied authority to deal on behalf of the principal. In financial services a BROKER is an agent of the employing BANK or SECURITIES FIRM and is paid commissions for client business. A bank may act as an agent for other banks in fulfilling certain duties related to arranging LOANS and NEW ISSUES. In INSURANCE, the independent agent represents at least two INSURERS and attempts to find the best possible deal for INSUREDS in exchange for a percentage of PREMIUMS charged.
- See also ACTUAL AUTHORITY, AGENT BANK, APPARENT AGENCY, EXPRESS AUTHORITY.

AGENT BANK A BANK forming part of a SYNDICATE arranging a LOAN for a borrower that is responsible for protecting the interests of all other syndicate banks. The lead bank arranging the loan is often selected as the agent bank.
- See also AGENT.

AGGREGATE DEMAND The total amount spent on final goods and services. In an open economy this is generally considered to be the sum of consumption, investment, government spending, and net exports.
- See also AGGREGATE SUPPLY.

AGGREGATE EXCESS OF LOSS REINSURANCE A REINSURANCE agreement where the REINSURER provides the CEDING INSURER with coverage on a large number of small losses arising from multiple policies, once an agreed ATTACHMENT point has been reached.

AGGREGATE INDEMNITY The total INSURANCE coverage an INSURED has against a specific RISK, generally a combination of a primary policy and one or more secondary policies.

AGGREGATE LIMIT See POLICY CAP.

AGGREGATE STOP LOSS INSURANCE An INSURANCE contract that becomes effective once a company's SELF-INSURANCE threshold has exceeded a predefined value. Once in effect, the coverage assumes the form of a standard insurance contract with defined terms and conditions.

AGGREGATE SUPPLY The total amount of goods and services enterprises are willing to provide consumers at a given ratio of prices to wages.

▪ See also AGGREGATE DEMAND.

AGM See ANNUAL GENERAL MEETING.

AJUSTABONOS [SPN] Medium-term INFLATION-LINKED SECURITIES, issued by the Mexican government, which pay a regular fixed COUPON and adjust the PRINCIPAL every quarter based on the movement of the Mexican CONSUMER PRICE INDEX. The adjusted principal accumulates over the life of the bond and is paid to investors at maturity.

ALEATORY CONTRACT A contract that can result in an unequal exchange of value between the contracting parties. INSURANCE is an aleatory contract, as the PREMIUM paid by the INSURED is generally larger or smaller than any SETTLEMENT received from the INSURER in the event of a loss and CLAIM.

ALIEN INSURER In the United States, an INSURER formed on the basis of the legal requirements of a country other than the United States. In order to qualify to write INSURANCE in the United States, the alien insurer must adhere to relevant state insurance regulations.

ALL-IN [COL] Abbreviated form of "all-included," referring to the total costs attributable to a firm's NEW ISSUE of securities or a bank's issue of DEPOSITS. The all-in generally includes the core COST OF CAPITAL plus the UNDERWRITING SPREAD and commissions; for bank funding instruments it may also include a PREMIUM for deposit INSURANCE.

▪ See also FLOTATION COST.

ALL LINES INSURANCE See MULTIPLE PERIL POLICY.

ALL-OR-ANY PORTION ORDER An ORDER to purchase or sell any, or all, of a specified quantity of securities, generally at the BROKER's discretion.

▪ See also ALL-OR-NONE ORDER.

ALL-OR-NONE ORDER An ORDER to purchase or sell securities that must be filled completely or not at all. All-or-none orders are often marked FILL OR KILL.

▪ See also ALL-OR-ANY PORTION ORDER.

ALL-OR-NONE UNDERWRITING A NEW ISSUE UNDERWRITING where the issuer has the right to cancel the entire transaction if the SYNDICATE is unable to successfully place the entire issue.

▪ See also BEST-EFFORTS UNDERWRITING, BOUGHT DEAL.

ALL-OR-NOTHING OPTION See BINARY OPTION.

ALL RISKS COVER See ALL RISKS POLICY.

ALL RISKS POLICY A broad INSURANCE policy that covers losses from all PERILS except those that are specifically excluded.
- Also known as ALL RISKS COVER.
- See also NAMED PERIL POLICY.

ALLIED LINES A PROPERTY AND CASUALTY INSURANCE policy that provides coverage for fire and associated PERILS, including water damage, demolition, and contamination.

ALLIGATOR SPREAD [COL] An OPTION SPREAD that is unprofitable even in favorable market conditions, as a result of large BROKER commissions or fees. An alligator spread is often comprised of many discrete transactions, which generate excessive costs and detract from any profits.

ALLOTMENT The share of a NEW ISSUE of securities granted by the LEAD MANAGER to SYNDICATE members (and ultimately investors). Allotment may be determined by existing relationships between the lead manager and each syndicate member, or by the perceived or proven ability of a given member to place the securities with a particular base of investors.

ALM See ASSET–LIABILITY MANAGEMENT.

ALPHABET STOCK [COL] Separate classes of COMMON STOCK issued by a company, where each class (often denoted by a letter of the alphabet) represents a different subsidiary. Investors in an alphabet stock receive the RENT RIGHTS and CONTROL RIGHTS associated with that stock, but not those of the overarching parent company.
- See also CLASSIFIED STOCK.

ALTERNATIVE RISK TRANSFER (ART) A product, channel, or solution that transfers RISK exposures between the INSURANCE and REINSURANCE sectors and the CAPITAL MARKETS in order to achieve specific RISK MANAGEMENT goals. As a result of regulatory rules and DIVERSIFICATION benefits, it is often desirable to shift INSURABLE RISKS to the financial sector and FINANCIAL RISKS to the insurance sector; ART mechanisms, such as CAPTIVES, DERIVATIVES, INSURANCE-LINKED SECURITIES, CONTINGENT CAPITAL, and ENTERPRISE RISK MANAGEMENT, make this possible.
- See also CONVERGENCE.

ALTERNATIVE TRADING SYSTEM (ATS) See ELECTRONIC COMMUNICATIONS NETWORK.

AMAKUDARI [JPN] Literally, "descent from heaven"; a Japanese practice of appointing a senior financial regulator to a senior executive position within a BANK or SECURITIES FIRM.

AMERICAN BINARY OPTION See BINARY-BARRIER OPTION.

AMERICAN DEPOSITORY RECEIPT (ADR) A negotiable certificate issued by a US BANK representing a foreign company's COMMON STOCK (shares of which are held in CUSTODY by the bank). ADRs, denominated in US dollars, are registered with the SECURITIES AND EXCHANGE COMMISSION and are traded on an EXCHANGE or OVER-THE-COUNTER. ADRs may be sponsored (approved/backed by the company) or unsponsored (not backed/approved by the company).
- See also AMERICAN DEPOSITORY SHARE, GLOBAL DEPOSITORY RECEIPT, GLOBAL DEPOSITORY SHARE.

AMERICAN DEPOSITORY SHARE (ADS) COMMON STOCK issued by a foreign company in the US marketplace. ADSs, denominated in US dollars, are registered with the SECURITIES AND EXCHANGE COMMISSION and are traded on an EXCHANGE or OVER-THE-COUNTER.
- See also AMERICAN DEPOSITORY RECEIPT, GLOBAL DEPOSITORY RECEIPT, GLOBAL DEPOSITORY SHARE.

AMERICAN OPTION An OPTION that can be exercised at any time prior to, and including, maturity.
- See also BERMUDAN OPTION, EUROPEAN OPTION.

AMORTIZATION A periodic reduction in the value of a LIABILITY or ASSET, as in a decrease in the PRINCIPAL balance of a LOAN through repayments to the lender (or payments into a SINKING FUND), or a decrease in the value of a fixed asset through periodic deductions for DEPRECIATION. Amortization may be based on constant, increasing, or decreasing payments.
- See also ACCRETION, ACCRETION OF DISCOUNT.

AMORTIZING SWAP An OVER-THE-COUNTER SWAP featuring a NOTIONAL PRINCIPAL balance that amortizes, or declines, on a preset schedule or through the triggering of a market event (commonly the breaching of an INTEREST RATE level). Amortizing swaps typically have a LOCKOUT PERIOD during which amortization is prohibited.
- See also ACCRETING SWAP, INDEX PRINCIPAL SWAP, REVERSE INDEX PRINCIPAL SWAP, VARIABLE PRINCIPAL SWAP.

AMOUNT AT RISK In INSURANCE, the lesser of a POLICY CAP on a contract and the MAXIMUM PROBABLE LOSS to the INSURED. INSURERS use amount at risk to estimate potential losses within their PORTFOLIOS.

ANGEL An investor or VENTURE CAPITAL partner that funds a private start-up company in exchange for a pre-INITIAL PUBLIC OFFERING EQUITY stake. The angel's participation in tactical and strategic decisions may be active or passive.

ANKLE BITER [COL] A SMALL CAP STOCK, i.e., one with market capitalization of less than $1 billion.

ANNUAL AGGREGATE LIMIT The maximum amount that an INSURANCE contract will pay in settlements to an INSURED over a 12-month period, regardless of the number of CLAIMS submitted.

ANNUAL GENERAL MEETING (AGM) A meeting of a public company's DIRECTORS, executives, and shareholders to review the year's financial performance and vote on specific agenda items (e.g., selection of DIRECTORS, external auditor).

ANNUAL INFLATION SWAP An OVER-THE-COUNTER SWAP involving the exchange of floating (actual) and fixed INFLATION at the end of each annual evaluation period. Annual inflation swaps, which generally reference an inflation index of consumer prices, are often structured as long-term transactions, with maturities extending to 10+ years.

 ▪ See also INFLATION SWAP, ZERO COUPON INFLATION SWAP.

ANNUITANT A person or entity entitled to receive regular ANNUITY benefits based on capital that has been contributed into an annuity program during the ACCUMULATION PERIOD.

ANNUITY An investment contract, generally purchased from an INSURER through single or multiple tax-deferred CAPITAL contributions, that guarantees fixed or variable payments to an ANNUITANT starting at some future date, and lasting for a stated period of time. The PRESENT VALUE of an annuity is given as:

$$PV_{ann} = CF \left[\frac{1}{r} - \frac{1}{r(1+r)^t} \right]$$

where CF is the stated cash flow, r is the DISCOUNT RATE, and t is the time until maturity.

 ▪ See also PERPETUITY.

ANTI-DILUTION PROVISION See PRE-EMPTIVE RIGHT.

ANTI-TAKEOVER DEFENSE A legal or structural tactic adopted by a company in order to protect it from being acquired by another company. Defenses may be used in conjunction with, or as a substitute for, ANTI-TAKEOVER LAWS.

 ▪ Also known as PORCUPINE PROVISION, SHARK REPELLENT.
 ▪ See also BLANK CHECK PREFERRED, POISON PILL, SCORCHED EARTH DEFENSE, STAGGERED BOARD.

ANTI-TAKEOVER LAWS Laws enacted in certain national systems that prohibit, or severely limit, a company from acquiring another company, primarily in instances involving HOSTILE TAKEOVERS.

 ▪ See also ANTI-TAKEOVER DEFENSE.

ANTI-TRUST Policies and regulations that restrict the formation of OLIGOPOLY or MONOPOLY power in order to promote free market competition.

ANTICIPATORY HEDGE An ex-ante HEDGE that is created to reduce the variability associated with a future ASSET, LIABILITY, or cash inflow; the hedge may be created with DERIVATIVES or a LONG POSITION or SHORT POSITION in the UNDERLYING reference.

ANY-AND-ALL BID A TAKEOVER mechanism where a company seeking to acquire a target firm agrees to pay the same price for any shares that are tendered. The any-and-all bid stands in contrast to the TWO-TIER BID, where investors receive an inducement PREMIUM for tendering their shares by an initial cut-off date.

APPARENT AGENCY Conduct by an AGENT that causes another party to believe the agent is authorized to conduct business on behalf of a PRINCIPAL, whether or not that is the case. A principal may be legally bound by apparent agency.
- See also ACTUAL AUTHORITY, EXPRESS AUTHORITY.

APPORTIONMENT The practice of dividing an INSURED's CLAIMS covered under multiple INSURANCE contracts, typically in proportion to total insurance coverage. Apportionment is generally written into a contract through a separate clause.
- See also DIVIDED COVER, OVERLAPPING INSURANCE, PRIMACY, PRO-RATA.

APT See ARBITRAGE PRICING THEORY.

ARBITRAGE An investment strategy involving the simultaneous purchase and sale of two ASSETS in order to capitalize on small price or rate discrepancies. The intent of the strategy is to generate a profit with a minimum amount of RISK; true arbitrage is risk-free.
- See also HEDGE, LONG ARBITRAGE, PURE ARBITRAGE, QUASI ARBITRAGE, SHORT ARBITRAGE, SPECULATION, YIELD ENHANCEMENT.

ARBITRAGE COLLATERALIZED DEBT OBLIGATION A COLLATERALIZED DEBT OBLIGATION (CDO) arranged by a BANK or SECURITIES FIRM to take advantage of perceived profit opportunities between assembling and managing a PORTFOLIO of credit risky securities or CREDIT DERIVATIVES and issuing TRANCHES to fund the portfolio.
- See also BALANCE SHEET COLLATERALIZED DEBT OBLIGATION, CASH COLLATERALIZED DEBT OBLIGATION, SYNTHETIC COLLATERALIZED DEBT OBLIGATION.

ARBITRAGE PRICING THEORY (APT) A financial theory posited as a testable, and more flexible, alternative to the CAPITAL ASSET PRICING MODEL (CAPM), based on the concept that multiple linear

RISK factors influence the return of a security, and the factors can be estimated through principal components/factor analysis. By understanding the risk and return contribution of each factor, an optimal portfolio can be created. APT, like CAPM, makes use of BETA as a measure of risk. The single-factor APT return is given by:

$$E(r_j) = E(r_f) + \lambda_1 \beta_{1,j}$$

where $E(r_j)$ is the expected return of security j, $E(r_f)$ is the expected RISK-FREE RATE, λ_1 is the slope of risk factor 1, and $\beta_{1,j}$ is the beta related to risk factor 1 and security j.

The equation can be expanded to multi-factor form, with z risk factors:

$$E(r_j) = E(r_f) + \sum_{l=1}^{z} \lambda_l \beta_{l,j}$$

- Additional references: Roll (1977), Roll and Ross (1980), Ross (1976).

ARBITRAGEUR [FR] An individual or institution engaged in ARBITRAGE transactions.

ARBITRATION A formal mechanism to resolve disputes between parties, widely used in the securities industry when conflicts appear between BROKERS and clients, and in the INSURANCE industry when disputes arise between INSUREDS and INSURERS. The results of arbitration are considered to be final and binding on parties choosing to participate.
- See also ARBITRATION CLAUSE.

ARBITRATION CLAUSE A clause in an INSURANCE contract stating that the INSURED and INSURER agree to ARBITRATION in the event of disagreement on a CLAIM. Similar disclosure is common in investment brokerage account agreements.

ARM See ADJUSTABLE RATE MORTGAGE.

ARMS INDEX See TRADING INDEX.

ARREARS SWAP An INTEREST RATE SWAP with a floating INTEREST RATE that is set in arrears rather than in advance; thus, the rate may be set two days before payment date, rather than six months plus two days before payment date (as on a standard semi-annual swap).
- Also known as LIBOR IN ARREARS SWAPS.

ARTICLES OF INCORPORATION A legal document filed by the founders of a company that results in the issuance of a certificate of incorporation from an authorizing government or legal entity. The articles contain details on the company's business, founders, DIRECTORS, and authorized CAPITAL. Articles of incorporation, together with the corporate CHARTER, give a company its legal form and existence.

ASCENDING TOP A TECHNICAL ANALYSIS formation that reveals repeatedly higher peaks in the price/level of a security or index, reflecting a bullish trend.

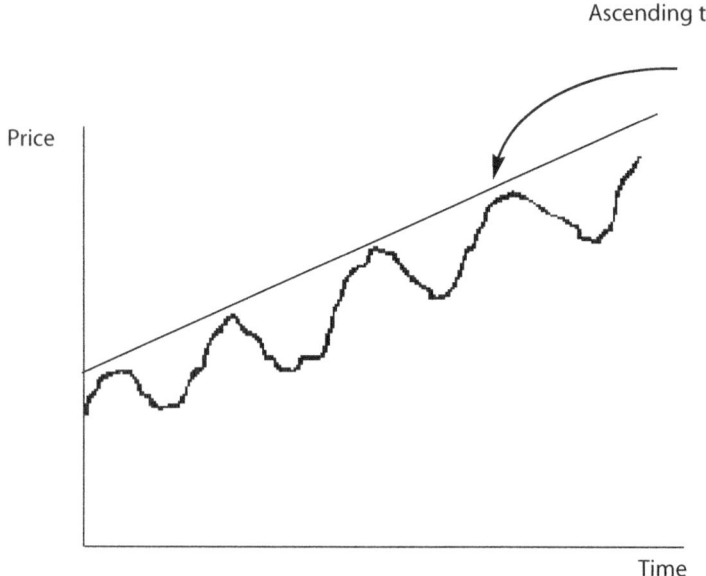

- See also DESCENDING BOTTOM, FALLING TOP, RISING BOTTOM.

ASIAN OPTION A COMPLEX OPTION that grants the buyer a payoff based on the geometric or arithmetic MEAN price of the UNDERLYING reference over a predetermined averaging period (i.e., ASIAN TAIL). The payoff can be determined by applying the average path to the price of the underlying (AVERAGE PRICE OPTION) or the STRIKE PRICE (AVERAGE STRIKE OPTION).
- Also known as AVERAGE OPTION.

ASIAN TAIL [COL] The length of the averaging period in an ASIAN OPTION.

ASK See OFFER.

ASSET A financial contract or physical object with value that is owned by an individual, company, or sovereign, which can be used to generate additional value or provide LIQUIDITY. Assets are credits to the balance sheet, and may include CASH, investments, ACCOUNTS RECEIVABLE, LOANS granted, INVENTORY, real estate, plant and equipment, and GOODWILL. Assets are characterized by varying degrees of LIQUIDITY, and may be funded through DEBT or EQUITY.
- See also LIABILITY.

ASSET ALLOCATION The process of investing CAPITAL across, or within, a specific set of ASSET classes in order to achieve a desired RISK/return profile.

ASSET-AT-EXPIRY OPTION A BINARY-BARRIER OPTION that grants the buyer a payoff at expiry equal to a fixed ASSET amount if the price of the UNDERLYING market reference breaches the BARRIER at any time during the transaction.

■ See also ASSET-AT-HIT OPTION, BINARY OPTION.

ASSET-AT-HIT OPTION A BINARY-BARRIER OPTION that grants the buyer an immediate payoff equal to a fixed ASSET amount if the price of the UNDERLYING market reference exceeds the BARRIER.

■ See also ASSET-AT-EXPIRY OPTION, BINARY OPTION.

ASSET-BACKED SECURITY (ABS) A NOTE or BOND collateralized by CASH FLOWS from a pool of ASSETS such as ACCOUNTS RECEIVABLE, LEASES, or consumer or auto LOANS. Investors in ABS have an undivided interest in the assets that have been secured; assets in the pool are transferred to a SPECIAL PURPOSE ENTITY established as a TRUST, which issues the securities that are sold to investors.

ASSET-BASED LOAN A RECOURSE or NON-RECOURSE LOAN granted by a BANK to a customer for use in acquiring INVENTORY, machinery, equipment, or other fixed ASSETS (apart from real estate). The underlying asset is often used to secure the loan.

ASSET CONVERSION LOAN See SELF-LIQUIDATING LOAN.

ASSET COVERAGE The ability for a company to use its ASSETS to cover a particular financial CLAIM or LIABILITY, such as a class of DEBT or PREFERRED STOCK. Asset coverage can be computed via:

$$AC = \frac{TA - IN - Cl - Cl_{SR}}{Cl}$$

where TA equals total assets (expressed in terms of BOOK VALUE or LIQUIDATING VALUE), IN is INTANGIBLES, Cl is the claim being covered, Cl_{SR} is any claim ranking senior to Cl.

The greater the asset coverage, the stronger the financial position and flexibility of the company.

ASSET–FUNDING LIQUIDITY RISK The RISK of loss arising from an inability to obtain unsecured funding at a reasonable economic cost, causing a forced pledge or sale of ASSETS at a loss. A sub-category of LIQUIDITY RISK.

■ See also ASSET LIQUIDITY RISK, ENDOGENOUS LIQUIDITY RISK, EXOGENOUS LIQUIDITY RISK, FUNDING LIQUIDITY RISK.

ASSET–LIABILITY MANAGEMENT (ALM) A business and RISK MANAGEMENT practice where BANKS and SECURITIES FIRMS manage the CASH FLOWS generated by ASSETS (e.g., LOANS, REVERSE REPURCHASE AGREEMENTS, investments), LIABILITIES (e.g., DEPOSITS, REPURCHASE AGREEMENTS), and OFF-BALANCE SHEET ACTIVITIES (e.g., DERIVATIVES, REVOLVING CREDIT AGREEMENTS, GUARANTEES). Depending on a bank's view of INTEREST RATES, its willingness to assume RISK, and its revenue goals, the ALM process may support a MISMATCH in the DURATION of assets and liabilities in order to take advantage of perceived profit opportunities.
- See also GAP, GAPPING, RATE SENSITIVE ASSETS, RATE SENSITIVE LIABILITIES.

ASSET LIQUIDITY RISK The RISK of loss arising from an inability to sell or pledge ASSETS at, or near, their carrying value when needed; a sub-category of LIQUIDITY RISK.
- See also ASSET–FUNDING LIQUIDITY RISK, ENDOGENOUS LIQUIDITY RISK, EXOGENOUS LIQUIDITY RISK, FUNDING LIQUIDITY RISK.

ASSET-OR-NOTHING OPTION A BINARY-BARRIER OPTION that grants the buyer a payoff equal to a fixed ASSET value if the price of the UNDERLYING market reference exceeds the STRIKE PRICE at expiry.
- See also BINARY OPTION, CASH-OR-NOTHING OPTION.

ASSET STRIPPING The process of selling corporate ASSETS acquired in a TAKEOVER or ACQUISITION. Such disposals may occur when the value of selling assets and using the proceeds to repay DEBT or invest in alternative ventures is estimated to be greater than the value of preserving them on the balance sheet.
- See also BREAKUP VALUE, LIQUIDATION VALUE.

ASSET SWAP An OVER-THE-COUNTER INTEREST RATE SWAP that exchanges BOND COUPONS from fixed rates into floating, or vice versa, creating a synthetic investment that meets an investor's specifications.

ASSIGNEE The party to whom an ASSIGNOR transfers title, CLAIM, or property, as in a SECURED DEBT transaction.

ASSIGNMENT The sale or transfer of a financial contract, such as an OVER-THE-COUNTER DERIVATIVE or LOAN, from the original COUNTERPARTY to a third party; an assignment is often arranged in order to reduce CREDIT RISK exposure and typically requires permission from the original party to the contract.

ASSIGNOR The party assigning title, CLAIM, or property to the ASSIGNEE, as in a SECURED DEBT transaction.

ASSUMABLE MORTGAGE A MORTGAGE that can be transferred from the original borrower to a new purchaser of the underlying property. The assumability feature eliminates the need for the original LOAN to be repaid and a new loan to be arranged, which reduces time and expense factors.

ASSUMED BOND A BOND issued by one company that is the legal LIABILITY of another company, such as might be found between a parent and subsidiary or two joint venture partners.

ASSUMED LOSS RATIO See COMBINED RATIO.

ASSUMPTION OF RISK See RETENTION.

ASSUMPTION REINSURANCE A REINSURANCE mechanism where a REINSURER assumes the CEDING INSURER's obligations through a wholesale transfer of hundreds, or thousands, of individual INSURANCE policies.

ASSURANCE See INSURANCE.

ASSURER See INSURER.

AT BEST ORDER An ORDER to buy or sell securities at the best price available at the time the order is placed.

AT-EXPIRY OPTION A BINARY OPTION that grants the buyer a payoff at expiry equal to a fixed ASSET or cash value if the price of the UNDERLYING market reference breaches the BARRIER at any time during the transaction.
- See also ASSET-AT-EXPIRY OPTION, AT-HIT OPTION, BINARY-BARRIER OPTION, CASH-AT-EXPIRY OPTION.

AT-HIT OPTION A BINARY OPTION that grants the buyer an immediate payoff equal to a fixed ASSET or cash value if the price of the UNDERLYING market reference breaches the BARRIER at any time during the transaction.
- See also ASSET-AT-HIT OPTION, AT-EXPIRY OPTION, BINARY-BARRIER OPTION, CASH-AT-HIT OPTION.

AT THE CLOSE ORDER An ORDER to buy or sell securities at the market closing price; if the order cannot be fully executed, it is cancelled.
- See also AT THE OPEN ORDER.

AT THE FIGURE ORDER See AT THE FULL ORDER.

AT THE FULL ORDER An ORDER to buy or sell securities at the integer closest to the BID (for a purchase) or OFFER (for a sale).
- Also known as AT THE FIGURE ORDER.

AT-THE-MONEY A condition where the STRIKE PRICE of an OPTION is precisely equal to the current price of the UNDERLYING reference ASSET. An at-the-money option has no INTRINSIC VALUE but it features maximum TIME VALUE.
- See also IN-THE-MONEY, MONEYNESS, OUT-OF-THE-MONEY.

AT THE OPEN ORDER An ORDER to buy or sell securities at the market open price; if the order cannot be fully executed, it is cancelled.
- See also AT THE CLOSE ORDER.

ATS See ALTERNATIVE TRADING SYSTEM.

ATTACHMENT (1) The economic level at which INSURANCE or REINSURANCE coverage becomes effective, i.e., the first dollar above the INSURED's DEDUCTIBLE. An INSURER's total potential liability extends from the point of attachment to the POLICY CAP. (2) An addition or amendment to an insurance contract providing explanations or additional coverages or EXCLUSIONS; the attachment is often replaced by an ENDORSEMENT or RIDER.

ATTACHMENT METHOD A process of combining several existing MONOLINE POLICIES i.e., separate INSURANCE covers for PROPERTY AND CASUALTY, general LIABILITY, and others, under a single master agreement, without redrafting to consolidate the individual components.
- See also SINGLE TEXT METHOD.

ATTORNEY-IN-FACT A party holding POWER OF ATTORNEY, and who is therefore authorized to deal on behalf of the executor of the power of attorney.

AUCTION MARKET A general market system where securities are purchased and sold through competitive BIDS and OFFERS, through DEALERS or BROKERS acting as AGENTS for clients.
- Also known as ORDER-DRIVEN MARKET.
- See also DEALER MARKET, DUTCH AUCTION, ENGLISH AUCTION.

AUCTION RATE PREFERRED STOCK See DUTCH AUCTION PREFERRED STOCK.

AUDIT OPINION An independent opinion rendered by a company's external AUDITOR after a review of financial statements and operations. The opinion generally takes one of three forms: UNQUALIFIED OPINION, meaning the financial statements are a fair and accurate representation of the company's financial position and conform to accepted accounting principles; QUALIFIED OPINION, meaning the financial statements may contain some deviations or problems; and ADVERSE OPINION, meaning the financial statements do not accurately reflect the company's financial position.

AUDITOR An independent accountant or financial expert that analyzes and verifies the nature and accuracy of a company's financial statements and renders an AUDIT OPINION that is used in the preparation of statutory financial statements. In order to arrive at a conclusion, an auditor generally reviews a company's accounting policies/processes and the transactions that are used to prepare financial statements.

AUFSICHTSRAT [GER] The SUPERVISORY BOARD of a German CORPORATION.
- See also VORSTAND.

AUNT MILLIE [COL] An unsophisticated investor.
- See also WIDOWS AND ORPHANS.

AUTARKY An economic system without any external trade, or one where trade is reduced or eliminated through barriers and quotas.

AUTHORIZATION RISK The RISK of loss that occurs when an employee or AGENT of a company commits the firm to a legally binding, but unauthorized, transaction; in most instances the firm will be required to perform as contracted. A sub-category of PROCESS RISK.

AUTHORIZED CAPITAL The maximum number of shares of COMMON STOCK a company is permitted to issue, per the terms of its ARTICLES OF INCORPORATION. Issuance in excess of authorized capital requires an amendment to the articles.

AUTHORIZED INSURER See ADMITTED INSURER.

AUTOCORRELATION A statistical measure that indicates the degree of CORRELATION of a random variable with itself; specifically, it measures the relationship between a value in a time series and those that occur before and after. Positive autocorrelation indicates that deviations from the equilibrium exist across periods, while negative autocorrelation means that deviations tend to be reversed.
- See also CORRELATION.

AUTOMATIC CLEARINGHOUSE (ACH) In the United States a national ELECTRONIC FUNDS TRANSFER network that clears and settles recurring payments between financial institutions, as well as debits and credits generated through business-to-business commerce and trade transactions.

AUTOMATIC COVERAGE An INSURANCE contract that automatically comes into effect when an INSURED acquires new property or revalues existing property. Automatic coverage eliminates the possibility of UNDERINSURANCE.

AUTOMATIC NON-PROPORTIONAL REINSURANCE Automatic REINSURANCE coverage for an INSURER that becomes effective once a defined loss limit is exceeded, often implemented through a STOP LOSS AGREEMENT or a CATASTROPHE PER OCCURRENCE EXCESS OF LOSS contract.
- See also AUTOMATIC PROPORTIONAL REINSURANCE.

AUTOMATIC PROPORTIONAL REINSURANCE Automatic REINSURANCE coverage for an INSURER that becomes effective once a defined loss limit is exceeded, generally implemented through a sharing agreement such as a SURPLUS SHARE or QUOTA SHARE.
- See also AUTOMATIC NON-PROPORTIONAL REINSURANCE.

AUTOMATIC REINSTATEMENT CLAUSE A clause in an INSURANCE contract indicating that after the INSURER has paid the INSURED on a CLAIM, the original contract limits are automatically renewed.

AUTOMATIC STAY A legal provision afforded to a debtor in BANKRUPTCY that prohibits filing of lawsuits against the company and limits the ability of creditors to dispose of COLLATERAL held as security. While creditors in general cannot sell any of the debtor's collateral, those holding security against DERIVATIVES or REVERSE REPURCHASE AGREEMENTS are permitted to do so under exemption clauses or SAFE HARBOR RULES. The delay created by the automatic stay is necessary as the bankruptcy RECEIVER must complete a thorough analysis of the value of the company's ASSETS and LIABILITIES, as well as the nature of any payments made during PREFERENCE PERIODS.

AVAILABLE RESERVES The difference between a BANK's excess RESERVE balance with the CENTRAL BANK and net funds borrowed through the central banking system or via a DISCOUNT WINDOW.

AVAL A third party GUARANTEE on a BILL OF EXCHANGE, BANKER'S ACCEPTANCE, or PROMISSORY NOTE that is intended to reinforce the creditworthiness of the obligation.

AVERAGE DOWN A strategy of buying additional securities at a lower price in order to reduce the average cost of the entire position.
- See also AVERAGE UP.

AVERAGE EXPECTED RISK EXPOSURE POTENTIAL EXPOSURE of an OVER-THE-COUNTER DERIVATIVE that is based on the average maturity of the transaction and the expected movement of the underlying market reference.
- See also AVERAGE WORST-CASE RISK EXPOSURE, TERMINAL EXPECTED RISK EXPOSURE, TERMINAL WORST-CASE RISK EXPOSURE.

AVERAGE EXPOSURE The POTENTIAL EXPOSURE of an OVER-THE-COUNTER DERIVATIVE based on the average maturity of the transaction.
- See also TERMINAL EXPOSURE.

AVERAGE OPTION See ASIAN OPTION.

AVERAGE PRICE OPTION A COMPLEX OPTION that grants the buyer a payoff equal to the difference between an average price on an UNDERLYING market reference and a predefined STRIKE PRICE.
- See also ASIAN OPTION, AVERAGE STRIKE OPTION.

AVERAGE STRIKE OPTION A COMPLEX OPTION that grants the

buyer a payoff equal to the difference between an average STRIKE PRICE and the terminal value of the UNDERLYING market reference.
- See also ASIAN OPTION, AVERAGE PRICE OPTION.

AVERAGE UP A strategy of buying additional securities at increasing prices, thereby raising the average cost of the entire position.
- See also AVERAGE DOWN.

AVERAGE WORST-CASE RISK EXPOSURE POTENTIAL EXPOSURE of an OVER-THE-COUNTER DERIVATIVE that is based on the average maturity of the transaction and the worst-case movement of the UNDERLYING market reference.
- See also AVERAGE EXPECTED RISK EXPOSURE, TERMINAL EXPECTED RISK EXPOSURE, TERMINAL WORST-CASE RISK EXPOSURE.

AWAY FROM THE MARKET A BID on a LIMIT ORDER that is lower than the current price, or an ASK that is higher than the current price. The order is held for later execution unless it is specifically identified as an ALL-OR-NONE ORDER (i.e., FILL OR KILL).

B

B2B EXCHANGE See BUSINESS-TO-BUSINESS EXCHANGE.

B2C EXCHANGE See BUSINESS-TO-CONSUMER EXCHANGE

BA See BANKER'S ACCEPTANCE.

B&C LOAN See SUBPRIME LOAN.

BABY BOND [COL] A BOND with a small FACE VALUE denomination (e.g., $1000) that is targeted specifically at retail investors.

BACK DOOR [COL] A process where the BANK OF ENGLAND attempts to influence UK money supply indirectly by dealing in TREASURY BILLS through its own account, at market rates.
- See also FRONT DOOR.

BACK DOOR LISTING [COL] A process where an unlisted or private company gains a stock EXCHANGE listing through a MERGER or ACQUISITION with a company that is already listed.

BACK MONTH See FURTHEST MONTH.

BACK-TO-BACK LOAN (1) A pair of local currency LOANS between two companies, documented under a single agreement providing for the right of OFFSET, which allows the companies to on-lend the local currency funds to their own subsidiaries and eliminates the need for the subsidiaries to source their own local financing. (2) A loan commitment from a BANK to a real estate developer that includes a construction loan for initial building and a permanent MORTGAGE loan for ongoing financing once the project has been developed.
- (1) See also PARALLEL LOAN.

BACKING AWAY A situation where a MARKET MAKER refuses to perform on a quoted BID, generally in contravention of formal or informal market-making rules conveyed through AFFIRMATIVE OBLIGATIONS.

BACKSPREAD An OPTION strategy designed to take advantage of VOLATILITY. A LONG backspread is created through the sale of a smaller quantity of closer-to-the-money PUT OPTIONS or CALL OPTIONS and the purchase of a larger quantity of farther-from-the-money puts or calls.

Backspread payoff profile

- See also RATIO VERTICAL SPREAD.

BACKTESTING The process of determining the validity of a VALUE-AT-RISK model by comparing actual profit and loss experience with results predicted by the model. The process is also applicable in investment management, where a current securities selection methodology is applied to prior periods to create a hypothetical performance history.
- See also PROFIT AND LOSS EXPLAIN.

BACKUP LINE See SWINGLINE.

BACKWARDATION See NORMAL BACKWARDATION.

BACS See BANKERS' AUTOMATED CLEARING SERVICE.

BAD BANK [COL] A special BANK created and chartered to hold a sponsoring bank's NON-PERFORMING LOANS. The sponsoring bank transfers the loans to the bad bank, thus improving its asset quality and becoming a "good bank." The bad bank, which is generally established as a self-liquidating TRUST, attempts to manage and liquidate the PORTFOLIO of loans in the most efficient manner possible.

BALANCE OF PAYMENTS An economic account reflecting a country's transactions and dealings with other nations through its CURRENT ACCOUNT, CAPITAL ACCOUNT, and FOREIGN EXCHANGE reserves.

BALANCE OF TRADE The difference between a country's VISIBLE and INVISIBLE exports and imports, and a primary component of the BALANCE OF PAYMENTS CURRENT ACCOUNT. A surplus balance of trade means exports are greater than imports, a deficit means imports are greater than exports.

BALANCE SHEET COLLATERALIZED DEBT OBLIGATION A COLLATERALIZED DEBT OBLIGATION (CDO) arranged by a BANK or SECURITIES FIRM in order to transfer the DEFAULT risk in its credit PORTFOLIO to investors.
- See also ARBITRAGE COLLATERALIZED DEBT OBLIGATION, CASH COLLATERALIZED DEBT OBLIGATION, SYNTHETIC COLLATERALIZED DEBT OBLIGATION.

BALLOON LOAN A LOAN structured with periodic PRINCIPAL repayments throughout the transaction and a large principal repayment at maturity.
- See also BULLET LOAN.

BANCASSURANCE [FR] In Europe, a financial conglomerate that engages in a broad range of financial services, including LOANS, DEPOSITS, INSURANCE, securities UNDERWRITING, investment management, and TRADING. Bancassurance groups often deal through separately incorporated and regulated entities but face no particular restriction on the scope of services they can offer.
- See also UNIVERSAL BANK.

BANK A financial institution that is permitted, through its CORPORATE CHARTER, to accept DEPOSITS and extend commercial and retail LOANS, and perform various INTERMEDIATION and FIDUCIARY functions. COMMERCIAL BANKS specialize primarily in traditional forms of commercial lending and deposit taking, while INVESTMENT BANKS and SECURITIES FIRMS are active in CORPORATE FINANCE, securities UNDERWRITING and TRADING. UNIVERSAL BANKS and BANCASSURANCE groups engage in a broader range of activities, including traditional banking, securities underwriting, investment management, INSURANCE, and trading. Regulatory authorities generally monitor the activities of banks to ensure that clients, particularly small depositors, are properly protected.

BANK DISCOUNT RATE See BANKER'S ACCEPTANCE RATE.

BANK FOR INTERNATIONAL SETTLEMENTS (BIS) A supranational organization, often termed the "bank of the central banks," that was created in 1930 to coordinate World War I reparation payments and provide basic international banking services (most of which were assumed by the INTERNATIONAL MONETARY FUND after World War II); the BANK also acted as TRUSTEE and CLEARING AGENT for various supranational organizations in the post-war period. Over the past few decades the BIS has focused primarily on promulgating RISK-BASED CAPITAL standards, and sponsoring a series of rules and directives related to capital adequacy standards for CREDIT RISK and MARKET RISK (i.e., the BASLE ACCORD).

BANK LINE A REVOLVING CREDIT FACILITY established as an ADVISED LINE (i.e., the client is made aware of the size and terms of the facility) or a GUIDANCE LINE (i.e., the client is not advised of the specific size of the line).
- See also COMMITTED FUNDING.

BANK OF ENGLAND The CENTRAL BANK of the United Kingdom, originally established as a private banking organization in 1694 to manage the country's national DEBT. It became the country's central bank through the passage of the Bank Charter Act of 1844, and was nationalized in 1946. The bank became independent once again in 1997, and is now responsible for managing the United Kingdom's debt and FOREIGN EXCHANGE reserves, conducting MONETARY POLICY, supervising the financial system, and acting as LENDER OF LAST RESORT.

BANKER'S ACCEPTANCE (BA) A short-term LIABILITY or time DRAFT representing an order to pay a specified amount of funds to the holder at a defined time, generally 30 to 180 days after contract date. The BA is a discount instrument drawn by a company on a BANK; once the bank accepts the draft it is obligated to pay the holder funds at maturity, and effectively substitutes the company's credit with its own. BA's are used for international and domestic trade transactions (including shipping, financing, and storage), and are generally backed by invoices or BILLS OF LADING.
- See also BANKER'S ACCEPTANCE (BA) RATE.

BANKER'S ACCEPTANCE (BA) RATE The INTEREST RATE representing the discount between the FACE VALUE of a BANKER'S ACCEPTANCE and the amount a BANK is willing to pay for the draft, generally a function of the drawer's creditworthiness.
- Also known as BANK DISCOUNT RATE.

BANKERS' AUTOMATED CLEARING SERVICE (BACS) In the United Kingdom, a CLEARING system designed for check and credit clearing, retail payments, standing orders, and direct debits.
- See also CLEARINGHOUSE AUTOMATED PAYMENT SYSTEM (CHAPS).

BANKERS' BLANKET BOND An INSURANCE contract that protects a BANK from losses caused by employee FRAUD.

BANKING ACT OF 1933 See GLASS–STEAGALL ACT.

BANKMAIL [COL] An agreement between a BANK and a company attempting to acquire a target company through a HOSTILE TAKEOVER that bars the bank from financing another company's competing bid in exchange for a fee.

BANKRUPTCY A state where a company is unable to meet its obligations and seeks the protection of the courts. The procedure may be based on VOLUNTARY BANKRUPTCY or INVOLUNTARY BANKRUPTCY and typically involves the filing of a bankruptcy petition. An AUTOMATIC STAY is invoked once the petition is filed, prohibiting lawsuits from being filed and creditors from liquidating COLLATERAL or attempting to recover sums owed; the stay remains in place until the debt is discharged or a repayment plan is accepted. In the United States bankruptcy may occur under Chapter 7 of the US Bankruptcy Code (LIQUIDATION), Chapter 11 (corporate REORGANIZATION), or Chapter 9 (municipal reorganization).

- See also DEBTOR-IN-POSSESSION, RECEIVER, TRUSTEE.

BANQUE D'AFFAIRE [FR] In France, a MERCHANT BANK that invests its own CAPITAL in support of CORPORATE FINANCE transactions and engages in securities UNDERWRITING and TRADING.

BARBELL PORTFOLIO An investment PORTFOLIO comprised of NOTES and BONDS with short- and long-term maturities but few, or no, securities with medium-term maturities. A barbell may be constructed to take advantage of a particular view on the YIELD CURVE or to meet specific CASH FLOW requirements.

BARRIER A price, YIELD, or index level where a BARRIER OPTION becomes effective, causing an underlying EUROPEAN OPTION to be created or extinguished.

BARRIER OPTION A COMPLEX DERIVATIVE contract that creates or extinguishes an underlying EUROPEAN OPTION as the price of the market reference moves through a specified BARRIER. Four versions of the barrier option are commonly used, including the DOWN AND IN OPTION, DOWN AND OUT OPTION, UP AND IN OPTION, and UP AND OUT OPTION. The fact that the underlying option may be extinguished, or may never be created, means that a barrier option is typically less expensive than an otherwise equivalent European option.

- Also known as KNOCK-IN OPTION, KNOCK-OUT OPTION.
- See also REVERSE BARRIER OPTION.

BASE CURRENCY The currency against which all others in the FOREIGN EXCHANGE market are quoted, generally selected as a result of one country's dominance in economic and trade matters. Since the mid-20th century the US dollar has assumed the role of base currency, succeeding the British pound sterling (which had been used as a base since the latter half of the 19th century). At various other times the French franc and Dutch florin (guilder) have also served as base currencies.

- See also RESERVE CURRENCY.

BASE RATE A BENCHMARK INTEREST RATE set by a CENTRAL BANK or monetary authority that is used as a reference for other commercial LOAN and DEPOSIT rates.

BASIS The price differential between an underlying ASSET reference and a DERIVATIVE contract used as a HEDGE. The basis arises as a result of differences in supply/demand, reference indexes or friction costs (including COST OF CARRY, storage, INSURANCE, transportation).
- See also BASIS RISK, NEGATIVE BASIS, POSITIVE BASIS.

BASIS POINT 1/100th of 1%, commonly used in the measurement of INTEREST RATES.

BASIS RISK A RISK that is generated by two ASSETS or indexes that track, but do not precisely replicate, one another. Basis risk is often assumed as a means of minimizing DIRECTIONAL RISK or VOLATILITY RISK, and can arise from hedging an asset with a DERIVATIVE contract on the same (or similar) asset, or hedging an asset with a second asset.
- See also BASIS, CROSS-ASSET HEDGE.

BASIS SWAP An INTEREST RATE SWAP involving the exchange of two floating INTEREST RATE indexes for periods ranging from one to 10 years; common reference indexes include LIBOR, EURIBOR, COMMERCIAL PAPER rates, BANKER'S ACCEPTANCE RATES, and GOVERNMENT BILL rates. A basis swap may also be constructed by using floating rate indexes in two different currencies.

BASIS TRADING An ARBITRAGE or TRADING strategy, using a cash instrument and a related FUTURES contract, that seeks to take advantage of perceived opportunities in the BASIS.
- See also BASIS RISK.

BASKET A small PORTFOLIO of ASSETS that can be bought or sold or used as a reference in a DERIVATIVE contract. Baskets can be created out of securities or contracts from similar or different sectors/countries, depending on the specific HEDGING or investing goals being sought.
- See also BASKET OPTION, BASKET SWAP.

BASKET OPTION An OVER-THE-COUNTER COMPLEX OPTION that grants the buyer a payoff based on the difference between the price of a BASKET of ASSETS and a predefined STRIKE PRICE. The basket can be comprised of assets from similar or different sectors/markets.
- See also MULTI-INDEX OPTION.

BASKET SWAP A CREDIT DERIVATIVE contract that involves the exchange of a fixed or floating PREMIUM for a compensatory payment if one or more reference credits in a pre-defined BASKET DEFAULTS. The swap provides the seller with a credit PORTFOLIO investment and the buyer with a credit HEDGE.
- See also FIRST-TO-DEFAULT SWAP.

BASLE ACCORD An agreement between participating industrialized countries to adopt RISK-based CAPITAL methods developed by the

BANK FOR INTERNATIONAL SETTLEMENTS. The Accord, which addresses in detail capital standards for CREDIT RISK and MARKET RISK, has been through various revisions since the initial version was put forth in 1988.

BBA RATE See BRITISH BANKERS ASSOCIATION RATE.

BEAR HUG [COL] A TAKEOVER bid received by a target company that DIRECTORS urge shareholders to accept due to its attractive price. Though directors might prefer to reject the bid, the price makes it nearly impossible for them to do so; failure to recommend approval could constitute a breach of DUTY OF LOYALTY and result in legal action being taken.

BEAR MARKET A market state that is characterized by declining prices and low volumes over an extended period of time, often resulting from weakened economic conditions (i.e., slow growth or contraction, poor corporate earnings). A bear market is generally believed to be in effect when broad index levels are at least 20 percent lower than the previous peak.
- See also BULL MARKET, CORRECTION.

BEAR RAID [COL] An attempt by a group of investors to drive down the price of a company's COMMON STOCK in a coordinated fashion in order to generate a profit. Bear raids conducted through circulation of negative news or unfounded rumors are illegal. UPTICK and ZERO PLUS TICK rules, which only allow SHORT SALES to be initiated on an upward move, are intended to help protect against this type of activity.

BEAR SPREAD [COL] An OPTION strategy that attempts to take advantage of a BEAR MARKET; spreads can be structured as bearish CALL SPREADS (purchase of a CALL OPTION and sale of a second call,

Bearish put spread payoff profile

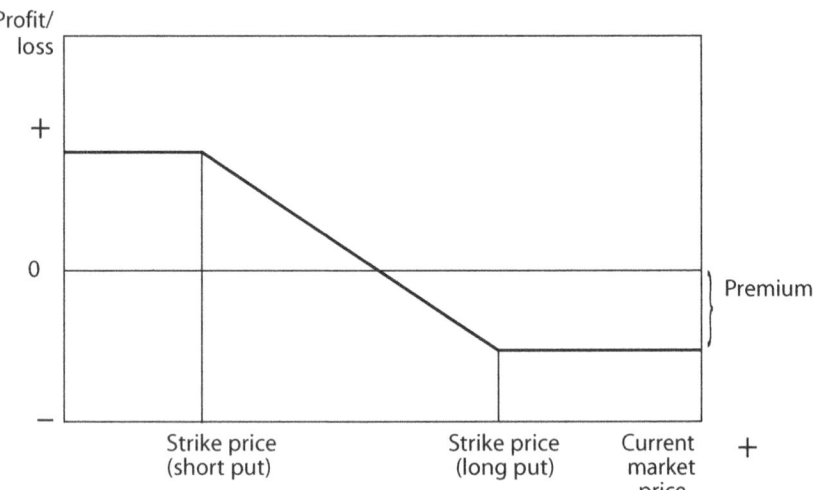

where the short call is struck closer-to-the-money) or bearish PUT SPREADS (purchase of a PUT OPTION and sale of a second put, where the long put is struck closer-to-the-money).
- Also known as MONEY SPREAD, PRICE SPREAD, VERTICAL SPREAD.
- See also BULL SPREAD.

BEAR TRAP [COL] A situation where a SHORT SELLER, anticipating further declines in the price of a security, fails to COVER its position in a rapidly rallying market, sustaining losses.
- See also SHORT SQUEEZE.

BEARER SECURITY A security that can be transferred or redeemed by the holder, who may or may not be the BENEFICIAL OWNER. Many securities are issued in bearer form, which eliminates the time and expense associated with re-registration.
- See also REGISTERED SECURITY.

BEAUTY CONTEST [COL] A process where UNDERWRITERS competing for an issuer's DEBT or EQUITY NEW ISSUE MANDATE submit proposals and are evaluated on the basis of structure, timing, pricing, distribution, and other relevant factors. The winner of the beauty contest becomes the LEAD MANAGER of the issue.

BED AND BREAKFASTING [COL] In the UK markets, the practice of selling COMMON STOCK of a company on one day and repurchasing it the following day in order to establish a gain or loss for tax purposes; bed and breakfasting was outlawed starting in 1997.
- See also WASH SALE.

BELLWETHER [COL] See BENCHMARK.

BELLY OF THE CURVE [COL] The intermediate maturities of the YIELD CURVE, generally considered to include the three to seven-year sector.
- See also LONG END, SHORT END.

BELLY UP [COL] A failed venture, or a company that has filed for VOLUNTARY BANKRUPTCY or INVOLUNTARY BANKRUPTCY.

BENCHMARK [COL] (1) A market-leading COMMON STOCK, BOND, or sector index that acts as a proxy for broader sentiment and movement in the market. Tradable benchmarks, which generally feature significant LIQUIDITY and narrow BID–OFFER spreads, are often used as an indexing, pricing, or hedging reference for other securities or DERIVATIVES. (2) An index that is used to gauge the relative performance of other ASSETS, securities, or PORTFOLIOS.
- (1) Also known as BELLWETHER.

BENEFICIAL OWNER The actual owner of securities and the rightful recipient of the benefits accorded; the beneficial owner is often different from the title holder (generally a financial institution holding the securities on behalf of clients).

BENEFICIARY The designated recipient of a contractual CASH FLOW or benefit from an INSURANCE contract, GUARANTEE, LETTER OF CREDIT, or other financial transaction. The beneficiary may be listed as primary (first recipient) or secondary (second recipient), and the selection may be revocable (changeable at any time) or irrevocable (changeable only with the express consent of the current beneficiary).

BERMUDA TRANSFORMER A Class 3 Bermuda-registered INSURER that is authorized to write and purchase INSURANCE and REINSURANCE and deal in DERIVATIVES. In order to comply with regulatory restrictions, banks often use transformers to convert derivatives into insurance or reinsurance and vice versa.

BERMUDAN OPTION An OPTION that can only be EXERCISED on specific dates prior to maturity (e.g., once every month, quarter, or year).
- Also known as a MID-ATLANTIC OPTION.
- See also AMERICAN OPTION, EUROPEAN OPTION.

BEST EFFORTS UNDERWRITING An agented NEW ISSUE of BONDS, COMMON STOCK, or PREFERRED STOCK, where the SYNDICATE attempts to place with investors as much of the issue as possible, but is not contractually obligated to fund any shortfall arising from securities that cannot be placed.
- See also ALL-OR-NONE UNDERWRITING, BOUGHT DEAL.

BETA A statistical measure of an ASSET's VOLATILITY in relation to the average volatility of a market PORTFOLIO or reference index, and a central component of ARBITRAGE PRICING THEORY and the CAPITAL ASSET PRICING MODEL. Beta is the slope of the line between the expected return on an asset and the return on the market portfolio; the intercept of the line, termed alpha, is simply the difference between the return on the asset and the beta-adjusted return on the market portfolio. A beta greater than 1.0 indicates that the asset is riskier than the market portfolio, but also has the possibility of generating higher returns; a beta less than 1.0 means that it is less risky than the portfolio. Investment managers often use beta to determine overall risk levels within their investment portfolios. The generic computation of beta is given as:

$$\beta_j = \frac{Cov(E(r_j), E(r_m))}{\sigma^2_{r_m}}$$

where $E(r_j)$ is the expected return on asset j, $E(r_m)$ is the expected return on the market portfolio, $Cov(E(r_j), E(r_m))$ is the COVARIANCE between asset j and the market portfolio, and $\sigma^2_{r_m}$ is the VARIANCE of the market portfolio.

The intercept, alpha, is simply:

$$\alpha = E(r_j) - \left((\beta_j \, (E(r_m))\right)$$

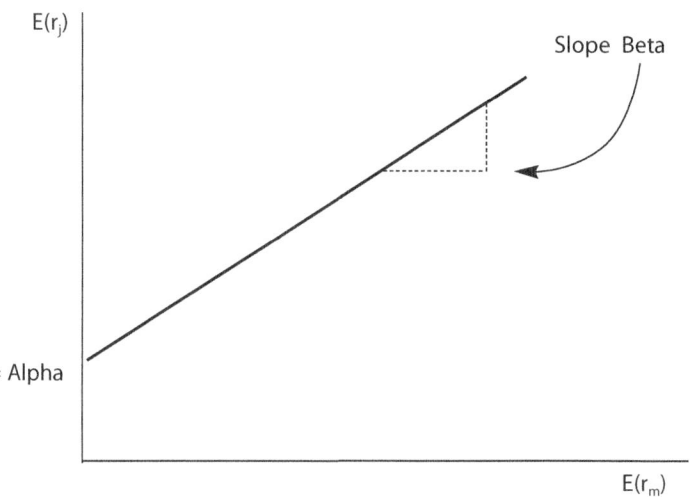

- See also CAPITAL MARKET LINE, SECURITY MARKET LINE.

BIAS The FEDERAL RESERVE BOARD's view on future INTEREST RATE movements and possible policy direction at future FEDERAL OPEN MARKET COMMITTEE meetings; the board may express a bias towards tightening or easing of rates, or maintaining a neutral stance.

BID A quoted purchase price for an ASSET from a DEALER or MARKET MAKER.
- See also OFFER.

BID-TO-COVER In the United States, the number of BIDS received in an auction of TREASURY BILLS, NOTES, or BONDS versus the number actually accepted. The higher the bid-to-cover ratio the greater the demand by investors, and the more successful the auction. A low bid-to-cover ratio reflects a weak auction, and may be characterized by a long TAIL (i.e., a wide differential between the average and high yields).

BIG BOARD [COL] See NEW YORK STOCK EXCHANGE.

BIG UGLIES [COL] COMMON STOCK issued by companies in industrial sectors that are not considered to be "leading edge" or "glamorous" and are thus often shunned by investors, such as steel, chemicals, heavy equipment, and coal.

BILATERAL COLLATERAL A COLLATERAL agreement between two COUNTERPARTIES that requires either party to post security,

depending on the value of the PORTFOLIO of contracts and the level of unsecured credit limits that have been established. This type of arrangement is often implemented when two counterparties have approximately equal CREDIT RATINGS.
- See also UNILATERAL COLLATERAL.

BILL FUTURE An INTEREST RATE FUTURES contract, bought or sold via an EXCHANGE, which references a short-term GOVERNMENT BILL rate.
- See also BOND FUTURE, DEPOSIT FUTURE.

BILL OF EXCHANGE A payment order written by one party (the drawer) to another party (drawee) with instructions to pay a third party (beneficiary) at some future date. The beneficiary may endorse the bill of exchange, creating a NEGOTIABLE INSTRUMENT.
- Also known as DRAFT.

BILL OF LADING A document used in the transportation of goods that evidences the receipt of goods by the shipper from the exporter. The bill must be presented under a BILL OF EXCHANGE, BANKER'S ACCEPTANCE, or DOCUMENTARY CREDIT, or if a CLAIM is being made under an INSURANCE contract.

BINARY-BARRIER OPTION A hybrid of the BARRIER OPTION and BINARY OPTION that grants the buyer a payoff equal to a fixed cash or ASSET amount if the price of the UNDERLYING market reference breaches the BARRIER. Payoff may be immediate or at expiry of the contract.
- Also known as an AMERICAN BINARY OPTION, ONE-TOUCH OPTION.
- See also ASSET-AT EXPIRY OPTION, ASSET-AT-HIT OPTION, AT-EXPIRY OPTION, AT-HIT OPTION, CASH-AT-HIT OPTION, CASH-AT-EXPIRY OPTION.

BINARY CREDIT OPTION See DEFAULT OPTION.

BINARY OPTION A COMPLEX OPTION that grants the buyer a payoff equal to a fixed cash or ASSET amount if the price of the UNDERLYING market reference breaches the STRIKE PRICE. Unlike a conventional option, the INTRINSIC VALUE of the binary contract does not depend on the degree of MONEYNESS. A binary may be structured as an AMERICAN OPTION or EUROPEAN OPTION.
- Also known as ALL-OR-NOTHING OPTION, DIGITAL OPTION.
- See also ASSET-OR-NOTHING OPTION, AT-EXPIRY OPTION, AT-HIT OPTION, BINARY-BARRIER OPTION, CASH-OR-NOTHING OPTION.

BINDER Temporary INSURANCE that provides an INSURED with coverage until the INSURER issues a permanent policy. Though insurers generally retain binding powers, certain AGENTS may have authority to bind.

BINOMIAL MODEL An OPTION pricing model developed by Cox, Ross and Rubinstein that traces price movements of an asset over discrete time intervals from trade date until maturity, making it possible to value AMERICAN OPTIONS. Under the parameters of the model the underlying asset can only move up or down by a specified amount in each period, meaning the process follows a binomial distribution. The general form of an American CALL OPTION under the binomial model is given as:

$$Call = S\, \Phi\left[a; n, p'\right] - X\, e^{-r_f t}\, \Phi\left[a; n, p\right]$$

where S is the stock price, X is the STRIKE PRICE, r_f is the RISK-FREE RATE, t is the time to expiry, n is the number of discrete periods until expiry, e is the exponential constant, p is equal to $(r' - d)/(u - d)$ (where r' is the risk-free rate for a single period, u is the possible upward move in S, and d is the possible downward move), a is the smallest non-negative integer greater than $ln(X/Sd^n)/ln(u/d)$, and Φ is the binomial function.

- Also known as COX, ROSS, and RUBINSTEIN MODEL.
- See also BLACK–SCHOLES MODEL, LATTICE MODEL.
- Additional references: Cox, Ross and Rubinstein (1979), Cox and Rubinstein (1985), Rendleman and Bartter (1979).

BIS See BANK FOR INTERNATIONAL SETTLEMENTS.

BLACK KNIGHT [COL] The party bidding for control of another company in a HOSTILE TAKEOVER.

- See also GRAY KNIGHT, WHITE KNIGHT, WHITE SQUIRE.

BLACK–SCHOLES MODEL A closed-form OPTION pricing model developed by Black and Scholes to value EUROPEAN OPTIONS on non-DIVIDEND paying COMMON STOCKS. The Black–Scholes framework generates option prices based on a series of assumptions including continuous movement of the UNDERLYING (i.e., a STOCHASTIC PROCESS), unlimited borrowing at a RISK-FREE RATE, and no friction costs. The equations for CALL OPTIONS and PUT OPTIONS are given as:

$$Call = S\, N(d_1) - X\, e^{-r_f t}\, N(d_2)$$

and

$$Put = X\, e^{-r_f t}\, N(-d_2) - S\, N(-d_1)$$

where S is the stock price, X is the STRIKE PRICE, t is the time to maturity, r_f is the risk-free rate,

$$d_1 = \frac{\ln\left(\frac{S}{X}\right) + \left(r_f + \frac{\sigma^2}{2}\right)t}{\sigma\sqrt{t}}, \text{ and } d_2 = d_1 - \sigma\sqrt{t}$$

σ^2 is the VARIANCE, and where the N values of $N(d_1)$ and $N(d_2)$ can be obtained from standard tables of probability functions.
- See also BINOMIAL MODEL.
- Additional reference: Black and Scholes (1973).

BLANK CHECK PREFERRED [COL] PREFERRED STOCK that can be issued at the sole discretion of a company's BOARD OF DIRECTORS in order to resist a HOSTILE TAKEOVER. The issuance of preferred stock dilutes earnings through payment of DIVIDENDS and provides additional cash to mount defensive measures, both of which may be sufficient to deter or combat a hostile action.

BLANKET LIMIT The maximum amount of INSURANCE an INSURER is willing or able to UNDERWRITE in a specific geographic location.
- See also BLOCK LIMIT.

BLIND BROKERING Brokered financial transactions where the BROKER does not give up the name of the underlying customer, even after the trade has been arranged and executed. Though the broker technically acts as AGENT, it *de facto* assumes the role of PRINCIPAL or DEALER.
- See also GIVE-UP.

BLOCK HOLDER A significant shareholder of a company's COMMON STOCK that has effective veto power over major company management decisions.

BLOCK LIMIT The maximum amount of INSURANCE an INSURER is willing or able to UNDERWRITE in a given metropolitan city block. Block limits are often used in areas that are deemed susceptible to CATASTROPHIC HAZARDS such as earthquakes or hurricanes.
- See also BLANKET LIMIT.

BLOCK TRADE (1) In general, a large trade in securities that is arranged through, and executed by, a BANK with sufficient CAPITAL to support the RISK exposure. In a typical block trade the bank purchases the securities with its own resources at a discount to the prevailing market price, and then attempts to distribute the block to end investors. (2) A trade on an EXCHANGE in excess of 10,000 shares.

BLOCK TRADING FACILITY (BTF) A facility offered by certain FUTURES EXCHANGES where two parties agree to cross (buy/sell) a large transaction away from the exchange in order not to skew prices. Once a transaction is concluded through the facility it is registered with the exchange and its CLEARINGHOUSE.

BLOWOUT [COL] The rapid sale of a new issue of securities, leaving the UNDERWRITERS with no residual RISK position after BREAKING SYNDICATE.

BLUE CHIP [COL] The COMMON STOCK of a high quality company, generally one with a large MARKET CAPITALIZATION, established reputation, and market share, and a strong record of growth and earnings.

BLUE SKY LAWS In the United States, state securities laws intended to protect investors against FRAUD by BANKS, BROKER/DEALERS, SECURITIES FIRMS, INVESTMENT ADVISORS, or other FIDUCIARIES.

BOARD OF DIRECTORS The governing body of a public CORPORATION that acts as AGENT of the COMMON STOCK shareholders. In many companies the board of directors is responsible for developing strategy, overseeing management, and protecting/representing the interests of shareholders through DUTY OF CARE and DUTY OF LOYALTY. The actual structure of the board depends on whether the national system adheres to the SINGLE BOARD SYSTEM or the DUAL BOARD SYSTEM.

BOGEY [COL] A price target on a security, index, or market that PORTFOLIO managers and other professional investors use to gauge performance.

BOILER ROOM [COL] A suspicious BROKER/DEALER operation, established with a minimum of CAPITAL, that employs high-pressure sales tactics to sell dubious or risky investments to unsophisticated investors; some boiler room operations attempt to defraud investors by using illegal sales practices, CHURNING accounts or embezzling funds.

- Also known as BUCKET SHOP.

BOILERPLATE [COL] Standard legal language that is contained in financial documents such as RED HERRINGS, PROSPECTUSES, INDENTURES, GUARANTEES, and CREDIT AGREEMENTS. Boilerplate may include standard terminology related to REPRESENTATIONS, WARRANTIES, terminations, and EVENTS OF DEFAULT.

BOLSA [SPN] Stock EXCHANGE.

BOND (1) In INSURANCE, a form of SURETY to cover or reimburse a third party in the event of loss. (2) In the CAPITAL MARKETS, a financial obligation representing the issuer's LIABILITY to repay DEBT CAPITAL provided by investors. Bonds are defined by form of INTEREST RATE (e.g., fixed rate, floating rate, structured), COUPON frequency, maturity, COLLATERAL, price, REDEMPTION, AMORTIZATION, transfer, and market of issue. Though local market conventions differ among countries, bonds are generally characterized by long-term maturities, ranging from 10 to 30 years. Bonds may be issued onshore or offshore, as REGISTERED SECURITIES or BEARER SECURITIES, in any one of several currencies; securities are often listed on an EXCHANGE, although most TRADING occurs OVER-THE-COUNTER. The most common bonds are those paying a periodic coupon during the life of issue, together with PAR VALUE redemption at maturity; the price of such bonds is given as:

$$P = + \sum_{n=1}^{t} \frac{C}{(1+r)^n} + \frac{M}{(1+r)^t}$$

where C is the coupon, r is the DISCOUNT RATE, n is the number of periods, t is the time to maturity, and M is the redemption value of the bond at maturity (generally par).
- (1) See also SURETY BOND, (2) see also BOND WITH WARRANTS, CONVERTIBLE BOND, EUROBOND, FIXED RATE BOND, FLOATING RATE NOTE, GLOBAL BOND NOTE, STRUCTURED NOTE, ZERO COUPON BOND.

BOND ANTICIPATION NOTE A short-term DEBT obligation of a municipality that provides interim funds for a capital improvement project; the NOTE is typically redeemed and replaced with long-term funding once the project is underway.

BOND CROWD [COL] A group of SPECIALISTS that trade in BONDS on the floor of the NEW YORK STOCK EXCHANGE.

BOND EQUIVALENT YIELD A measure that converts the YIELD of a FIXED INCOME discount instrument into terms of a standard COUPON instrument, permitting proper comparison of investment alternatives. It is generally computed via:

$$BEY = \frac{(Face - P)}{P} \left(\frac{n_I}{n_{MAT}} \right)$$

where $Face$ is FACE VALUE, P is purchase price, n_I is the number of days in the year following issuance, and n_{MAT} is the number of days until maturity.
- See also DISCOUNT YIELD, SIMPLE YIELD, TAXABLE EQUIVALENT YIELD, YIELD TO CALL, YIELD TO MATURITY.

BOND FLOOR See BOND VALUE.

BOND FUTURE An INTEREST RATE FUTURES contract, bought or sold via an EXCHANGE, which references a medium-term or long-term GOVERNMENT BOND rate.
- See also DEPOSIT FUTURE.

BOND ORDINANCE See BOND RESOLUTION.

BOND PREMIUM See INVESTMENT PREMIUM.

BOND RESOLUTION In the United States, a law that authorizes the issuance of BONDS or other FIXED INCOME securities, typically applicable to municipal or sovereign issuers.
- Also known as BOND ORDINANCE.

BOND SWAP The sale of a BOND prior to its final maturity or REDEMPTION and the purchase of another bond using the sale proceeds. A bond swap may involve an exchange of maturities, COUPONS, taxable status, price, or credit references, and is a common investment PORTFOLIO management technique.

BOND VALUE The lowest TRADING value of a CONVERTIBLE BOND, which occurs when the embedded equity OPTION is well OUT-OF-THE-MONEY and the bond is paying its normal COUPON. When a convertible is trading at bond value, its price is generally identical (or very similar) to a standard bond with the same coupon and maturity.
- Also known as BOND FLOOR.

BOND WITH WARRANT A standard BOND that is issued with attached WARRANTS (i.e., long-dated OPTIONS), which can often be detached and traded separately. By selling the package, the issuer lowers its effective COST OF CAPITAL. The bond, which can be denominated in one of various currencies and carry a maturity ranging from 1 to 10 years, is typically issued at PAR VALUE, but its ongoing value – with warrants retained – depends on the INTRINSIC VALUE and TIME VALUE of the warrants. While attached warrants can be issued on a range of references, they are often linked to the price of the issuer's COMMON STOCK or a broad equity index.
- See also COVERED WARRANT, EQUITY WARRANT.

BONUS ISSUE See STOCK DIVIDEND.

BONUS SHARE See STOCK DIVIDEND.

BOOK-BUILDING [COL] The process of gathering firm ORDERS or INDICATIONS OF INTEREST for a NEW ISSUE of securities. UNDERWRITERS involved in the new issue carry out book-building, and the results are used to determine final deal pricing and order allocations.

BOOK ENTRY SECURITY A DEBT or EQUITY security that is issued, traded, and transferred solely through electronic means, without SCRIP or physical certificates. Securities are increasingly issued in dematerialized form.
- See also DEFINITIVE SECURITY.

BOOK VALUE (1) The original purchase price of an ASSET. (2) The current accounting value of an asset, typically computed as MARKET VALUE or original purchase price less accumulated DEPRECIATION.

BOOKRUNNER [COL] See LEAD MANAGER.

BOOTSTRAPPING [COL] See STRIPPING THE YIELD CURVE.

BORDEREAU [FR] A report illustrating a history of losses and PREMIUMS on a specific RISK. The CEDING INSURER provides the report to the REINSURER so that an appropriate premium rate can be determined.

BORSA [ITL] Stock EXCHANGE.

BOSTON OPTION (1) Any OVER-THE-COUNTER OPTION where PREMIUM is paid at maturity rather than trade date. (2) See BREAK FORWARD.

BOTTOM FISHING [COL] An investment strategy focused on securities or markets that are perceived to be undervalued, out of favor, or CHEAP compared to other alternatives. CONTRARIAN investors are often bottom fishers.

BOUGHT DEAL [COL] A NEW ISSUE of DEBT or EQUITY securities where the LEAD MANAGER and participating UNDERWRITERS commit to purchasing the entire block and then distributing through their own investor bases. The issuer is guaranteed a set amount of funds, regardless of the UNDERWRITERS' success in ultimately placing the securities with other investors.
- Also known as COMMITTED UNDERWRITING, FIRM UNDERWRITING.
- See also ALL-OR-NONE UNDERWRITING, BEST EFFORTS UNDERWRITING.

BOURSE [FR] A Stock EXCHANGE, used generically for European exchanges.

BOUTIQUE [COL] An INVESTMENT BANK that specializes in a particular area of business, such as CORPORATE FINANCE, LEVERAGED BUYOUTS, or MERGERS and ACQUISITIONS. Boutiques do not offer the full range of investment banking services (e.g., TRADING, investment management, new issue UNDERWRITING), but may cooperate with full-service firms in order to offer clients appropriate access.

BRADY BOND [COL] An emerging market BOND resulting from an exchange of rescheduled sovereign DEBT, named after former US Treasury Secretary Brady. Brady bonds, which were developed for a number of LESSER DEVELOPED COUNTRIES in the late 1980s and early 1990s, liquefied NON-PERFORMING LOANS held by large BANKS, and have become actively traded in the SECONDARY MARKETS. Securities are collateralized by 30-year ZERO COUPON TREASURY BONDS (guaranteeing PRINCIPAL repayment) and a rolling GUARANTEE from the INTERNATIONAL MONETARY FUND (covering interest COUPONS).

BREAK FORWARD A FORWARD contract with a feature giving one party the ability to cancel the transaction at a future time in order to complete the underlying deal in the SPOT MARKET; if the party chooses to break the contract it pays the other party a cancellation fee.
▪ Also known as BOSTON OPTION.

BREAKING SYNDICATE [COL] The process of disbanding the group of UNDERWRITERS involved in pricing, marketing, and distributing a NEW ISSUE of securities. Once the SYNDICATE is broken the underwriters are free to trade securities in the SECONDARY MARKET without restriction. A typical syndicate is broken 30 days after initial launch, though it can be broken earlier by mutual agreement of the underwriters.

BREAKOUT A TECHNICAL ANALYSIS chart pattern reflecting movement in a security or index above a RESISTANCE LEVEL or below a SUPPORT LEVEL, which may portend future moves in the direction of the breakout.

BREAKPOINT An incremental order size for MUTUAL FUND shares that causes sales commissions to decline; the more breakpoints in an order, the lower the marginal rate of commissions.

BREAKUP VALUE The value of a company if operations are halted and the firm is decomposed and sold as separate units. In most instances breakup value is less than "going-concern" value, meaning a breakup strategy is not advisable; in some cases, however, breakup opportunities exist, particularly if ASSETS have been under-utilized. Estimating breakup value can be complex owing to the ILLIQUID nature of certain types of assets and the resulting uncertainty in cash values. Breakup value is distinct from LIQUIDATION VALUE, which ignores GOODWILL.
▪ Also known as TAKEOVER VALUE.
▪ See also ASSET STRIPPING.

BRETTON WOODS SYSTEM The system of fixed FOREIGN EXCHANGE rates that existed until 1971, which required participating nations to intervene when necessary in order to preserve the value of their currencies within particular bands. Following the collapse of the system in 1971, the financial markets turned towards a free market process of floating exchange rates.

BRICKS AND MORTAR [COL] The physical branches and infrastructure of a BANK or SECURITIES FIRM, distinct from the electronic banking platforms many institutions also operate.

BRIDGE LOAN A temporary LOAN granted by a BANK to a corporate or sovereign borrower, generally intended to be replaced by longer-term or permanent financing from the CAPITAL MARKETS. Bridge loans may be secured or unsecured and generally have maturities of less than one year.

- Also known as SWING LOAN.

BRITISH BANKERS ASSOCIATION (BBA) RATE The official INTEREST RATES quoted for FORWARD RATE AGREEMENTS traded in the London market. BBA rates are quoted for various forward starting periods in the world's major interest rates.

BROAD EVIDENCE RULE A rule allowing a wide scope of information to be used in determining the ACTUAL CASH VALUE of property that has been damaged or destroyed and which is subject to a CLAIM under an INSURANCE contract. Any evidence that is regarded as a relevant reflection of value is admissible.

BROKEN DATE [COL] An off-the-run COUPON payment date on a FIXED INCOME security, e.g., 28 or 58 days, rather than the conventional 30 or 60 days.

BROKER (1) In securities and investment, a professional that provides investment recommendations and execution services to an investing client, but acts as an AGENT of the financial firm providing services (e.g. BROKER/DEALER, SECURITIES FIRM, BANK). (2) In INSURANCE, a professional that represents an INSURED purchasing coverage from an INSURER; the insurance broker is thus an agent of the client. In most jurisdictions the appropriate regulatory authority must license financial and insurance brokers.

BROKER CALL LOAN See BROKER LOAN.

BROKER/DEALER A SECURITIES FIRM involved in investment advice, brokerage, and execution activities on behalf of clients, and TRADING activities for its own account. Some broker/dealers may also act as MARKET MAKERS or PRIMARY DEALERS.

BROKER LOAN A short-term secured demand LOAN granted by a BANK to a SECURITIES FIRM or BROKER/DEALER that is used to fund client securities positions. The loan is backed by the underlying securities and is usually callable by the lender with 24 hours' notice.

- Also know as BROKER CALL LOAN.

■ See also BROKER LOAN RATE.

BROKER LOAN RATE The INTEREST RATE charged by a BANK on a short-term BROKER LOAN.

BROKERED CERTIFICATE OF DEPOSIT (CD) A large-denomination CERTIFICATE OF DEPOSIT issued by a BANK to a BROKER/DEALER, which splits the certificate into smaller denominations suitable for distribution to retail investors. In some instances the bank may issue the certificate when the broker/dealer collects individual investments, amalgamates the funds, and deposits them with the bank as a lump sum.

■ Also known as BROKERED DEPOSIT.

BROKERED DEPOSIT See BROKERED CERTIFICATE OF DEPOSIT.

BTF See BLOCK TRADING FACILITY.

BUBBLE [COL] The speculative phase of a market cycle in which ASSET prices are BID up to unsustainably high levels through large amounts of LEVERAGED and unleveraged investor purchases. The bubble may be burst through regulatory intervention (e.g., a tightening of INTEREST RATES) or general investor discomfort leading to withdrawal.

BUCK [COL] Common reference for million.

■ See also TON, YARD.

BUCKET SHOP [COL] See BOILER ROOM.

BUILDING SOCIETY In the United Kingdom, a DEPOSITORY institution that is primarily involved in accepting retail DEPOSITS and granting residential MORTGAGES; deregulation during the 1980s broadened the scope of permissible activities to include commercial banking business and DERIVATIVES dealing, but many continue to focus on the core mortgage credit sector. While most building societies were originally formed as mutual organizations, many have gone through DEMUTUALIZATION and converted to public CORPORATIONS.

■ See also SAVINGS AND LOAN ASSOCIATION.

BULGE BRACKET [COL] The small group (i.e., less than half a dozen) of SECURITIES FIRMS, INVESTMENT BANKS, and BANKS that control the largest share of global CORPORATE FINANCE and securities UNDERWRITING business. Bulge bracket firms are often sought out by institutional clients as a result of their ability to arrange sophisticated transactions and distribute securities.

BULL MARKET A general market phase characterized by low INFLATION and INTEREST RATES, strong consumer confidence, growing corporate earnings, and rising COMMON STOCK prices and market indexes.

■ See also BEAR MARKET.

BULL SPREAD [COL] An option strategy that attempts to take advantage of BULL MARKETS. The SPREAD can be structured as a bullish CALL SPREAD (purchase of a CALL and sale of a second call, where the long call is struck closer-to-the-money) or a bullish PUT SPREAD (purchase of a PUT and sale of a second put, where the short put is struck closer-to-the-money).

Bullish call spread payoff profile

- Also known as MONEY SPREAD, PRICE SPREAD, VERTICAL SPREAD.
- See also BEAR SPREAD.

BULLET GUARANTEED INVESTMENT CONTRACT (GIC) A GUARANTEED INVESTMENT CONTRACT where the investor funds the entire GIC with a single payment rather than periodic payments that are characteristic of standard GICs. All other features of the bullet GIC are similar to the conventional GIC.
- See also NON-PARTICIPATING GUARANTEED INVESTMENT CONTRACT, PARTICIPATING GUARANTEED INVESTMENT CONTRACT, SYNTHETIC GUARANTEED INVESTMENT CONTRACT.

BULLET LOAN A LOAN with a PRINCIPAL balance that is repaid by the borrower in a single installment at maturity, rather than standard AMORTIZATION of payments over the life.
- See also BALLOON LOAN.

BUNCHING [COL] The process of grouping together many small retail trade ORDERS (i.e., ODD LOTS) and combining them into a single large order. Bunching often permits better execution levels and reduces the administrative expenses associated with processing each small trade individually.

BUND [GER] Abbreviated form of Bundasanleihem, the broad category of German federal GOVERNMENT BONDS. Bunds, denominated in EUROS, feature maturities of 6 to 30 years (with 10-year securities constituting the BENCHMARK) and pay interest COUPONS on an annual basis. They are issued through the federal bond SYNDICATE, via traditional UNDERWRITING, and through DUTCH AUCTION.

BUNDESBANK [GER] The German CENTRAL BANK, responsible for ensuring monetary stability within Germany and coordinating, as a member of the EUROPEAN MONETARY UNION (EMU), broader EMU MONETARY POLICY.

BURN RATE The speed at which a company, especially a new venture, utilizes its available cash to fund ongoing operations and expansion plans. The burn rate is an important measure for suppliers of VENTURE CAPITAL, as it indicates when (if) further rounds of financing will be required to expand the operation.

BURNING COST RATIO In INSURANCE, a measure indicating the degree to which losses exceed the PREMIUMS being charged; the burning cost ratio is generally computed as:

$$BC = \frac{Loss_{exc}}{Pr}$$

where $Loss_{exc}$ is excess loss and Pr is premium.

In general, the larger the ratio, the greater the shortfall between premiums and losses.

BUSINESS INTERRUPTION INSURANCE INSURANCE coverage designed to protect against financial losses arising from a disruption in normal business or commercial activities. Such coverage effectively compensates for CONSEQUENTIAL LOSSES that come from damage or destruction to production processes, and is generally arranged as a supplement to direct coverage obtained through PROPERTY AND CASUALTY INSURANCE.

BUSINESS JUDGMENT RULE A legal rule that permits DIRECTORS and executives of a company to make all relevant corporate business decisions, as long as they are made on an informed basis (i.e., with a DUTY OF CARE). The intent is to prevent the courts from adjudicating on whether or not a business decision is correct; they judge only whether it has been made on the basis of appropriate facts and information.

BUSINESS LIABILITY INSURANCE INSURANCE coverage for LIABILITIES arising from normal commercial activities, including direct and indirect liability, and medical payments.

BUSINESS RECOVERY RISK The RISK of loss arising from a temporary disruption in business activities due to lack of accessibility to physical infrastructure. Business recovery risk is typically firm-, business- or product-specific and generally not as damaging as DISASTER RECOVERY RISK. Business recovery losses can be protected through specific BUSINESS INTERRUPTION INSURANCE. A sub-category of PROCESS RISK.

BUSINESS-TO-BUSINESS (B2B) EXCHANGE An electronic commerce exchange where networks are used to connect institutional buyers and sellers of ASSETS, goods or services.
- See also ALTERNATIVE TRADING SYSTEM, BUSINESS-TO-CONSUMER (B2C) EXCHANGE, ELECTRONIC COMMUNICATIONS NETWORK.

BUSINESS-TO-CONSUMER (B2C) EXCHANGE An electronic commerce exchange where networks are used to connect consumers and retail buyers of ASSETS, goods or services with providers, manufacturers, or distributors.
- See also BUSINESS-TO-BUSINESS (B2B) EXCHANGE.

BUST-UP TAKEOVER A TAKEOVER or LEVERAGED BUYOUT where a portion of the target company's ASSETS are sold to third parties in order to repay a certain portion of the DEBT assumed in acquiring the company.

BUSTED CONVERTIBLE [COL] A CONVERTIBLE BOND that stands little or no chance of being converted into the issuer's COMMON STOCK because the stock price is well below the bond's CONVERSION PRICE. A busted convertible trades on BOND VALUE alone and remains a FIXED INCOME security until it is redeemed.

BUTTERFLY SPREAD A COMPOUND OPTION STRATEGY designed to take advantage of VOLATILITY within a market range. Butterflies are always created with the same ratio of PUT OPTIONS or CALL OPTIONS (i.e., one with a low STRIKE PRICE, two with middle strikes, one with a high strike) that expire at the same time. SHORT butterflies, which are similar to LONG STRADDLES without the extreme upside, consist of short low and high strike options and long middle strike options; long butterflies, which are similar to short straddles without the extreme downside, consist of long low and high strike options and short middle strike options. (See figures on opposite page.)
- See also CONDOR SPREAD.

BUY-BACK DEDUCTIBLE A DEDUCTIBLE on an INSURANCE contract that is eliminated through payment of an incremental PREMIUM, thus providing the INSURED with FIRST DOLLAR COVERAGE in the event of a loss.

BUY IN Covering of a SHORT POSITION by purchasing the UNDERLYING ASSET or taking delivery of securities. A SECURITIES FIRM expecting securities from another party that are not delivered buys

Long butterfly payoff profile

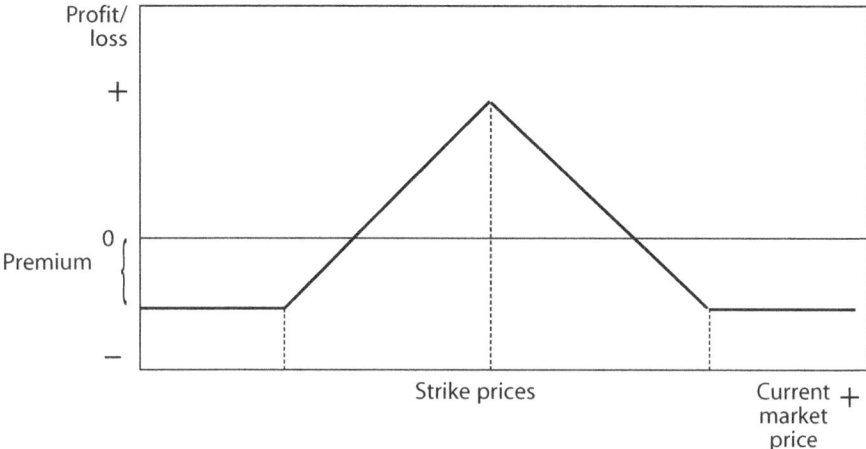

Short butterfly payoff profile

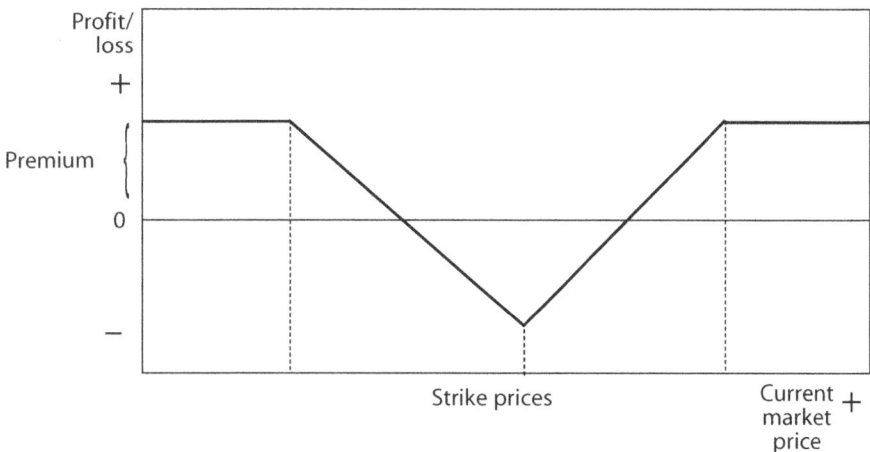

them in from another source and charges the original contracting firm any resulting price differential.

BUY MINUS [COL] An ORDER to purchase a block of securities at a price that is lower than the current market price.

BUY THE BOOK [COL] An ORDER given by a client to a BROKER to purchase all of a SPECIALIST's or MARKET MAKER's inventory of a security, as well as the inventory of other BROKER/DEALERS, at the current market price.

C

CABLE [COL] The sterling/US dollar FOREIGN EXCHANGE rate.

CALAMITY CALL A provision in a COLLATERALIZED MORTGAGE OBLIGATION requiring a portion of the issue to be retired if PREPAYMENTS rise to a level where insufficient CASH FLOW exists to meet scheduled payments of PRINCIPAL and COUPON interest.

CALENDAR See PIPELINE.

CALENDAR SPREAD See TIME SPREAD.

CALL See CALL OPTION.

CALL MONEY Funds placed in an interest-bearing DEPOSIT account that can be withdrawn by the depositor with one day's notice. In most instances call money refers to deposits placed by institutional investors, which tend to be withdrawn more rapidly than those placed by retail customers.

■ See also HOT MONEY.

CALL ON A CALL A COMPOUND OPTION that grants the buyer the right to purchase an underlying CALL OPTION from the seller of the compound. The option is generally purchased when the need for the underlying option is still uncertain.

■ See also CALL ON A PUT, PUT ON A CALL, PUT ON A PUT.

CALL ON A PUT A COMPOUND OPTION that grants the buyer the right to purchase an underlying PUT OPTION from the seller of the compound. The option is generally purchased when the need for the underlying option is still uncertain.

■ See also CALL ON A CALL, PUT ON A CALL, PUT ON A PUT.

CALL ON THE BEST OF N-ASSETS An OVER-THE-COUNTER COMPLEX OPTION that grants the buyer a payoff based on the difference between a predefined STRIKE PRICE and the best performing ASSET in a PORTFOLIO.

- See also CALL ON THE WORST OF N-ASSETS, MULTI-INDEX OPTION, OPTION ON THE BEST/WORST OF N-ASSETS, PUT ON THE BEST OF N-ASSETS, PUT ON THE WORST OF N-ASSETS.

CALL ON THE MAXIMUM An OVER-THE-COUNTER COMPLEX OPTION that grants the buyer a payoff based on the difference between a predefined STRIKE PRICE and the highest price achieved by the UNDERLYING reference ASSET over the life of the transaction.
- See also LOOKBACK OPTION, OPTION ON THE MAXIMUM/MINIMUM, PUT ON THE MINIMUM.

CALL ON THE WORST OF N-ASSETS An OVER-THE-COUNTER COMPLEX OPTION that grants the buyer a payoff based on the difference between a predefined STRIKE PRICE and the worst performing ASSET in a PORTFOLIO.
- See also CALL ON THE BEST OF N-ASSETS, MULTI-INDEX OPTION, OPTION ON THE BEST/WORST OF N-ASSETS, PUT ON THE BEST OF N-ASSETS, PUT ON THE WORST OF N-ASSETS.

CALL OPTION A DERIVATIVE contract that gives the buyer the right, but not the obligation, to purchase an UNDERLYING ASSET from the seller at a set STRIKE PRICE at, or before, expiry. In exchange, the buyer pays the seller a PREMIUM. Calls, which can be written on a broad range of financial and commodity references, are available as EXCHANGE-traded and OVER-THE-COUNTER contracts, and can be structured as AMERICAN OPTIONS, BERMUDAN OPTIONS, or EUROPEAN OPTIONS.

Long call payoff profile

Short call payoff profile

- See also PUT OPTION.

CALL PREMIUM The differential between the redemption price and the PAR VALUE of a CALLABLE BOND.

CALL PROTECTION A provision in a BOND INDENTURE that prevents the issuer from redeeming a BOND for a specific period of time (HARD CALL PROTECTION) or until certain price levels have been reached (SOFT CALL PROTECTION).
- See also CALL RISK, CALLABLE BOND, NON-CALLABLE BOND.

CALL RISK The RISK that the issuer will call and redeem a CALLABLE BOND when INTEREST RATES decline, exposing investors to reinvestment of CAPITAL at a lower rate.

CALL SPREAD An OPTION position created by buying and selling CALL OPTIONS with the same expiry date but different STRIKE PRICES (i.e., the purchaser of a call spread buys a closer-to-the-money call option and sells a farther out-of-the-money call option (a bullish strategy), the seller of a call spread does the reverse (a bearish strategy)). The spread limits the gain or LIABILITY to an area defined by the two strikes.
- See also BULL SPREAD, BEAR SPREAD, PUT SPREAD.

CALLABLE BOND A BOND with embedded CALL OPTIONS that allows the issuer to redeem the security, generally at a PREMIUM to PAR VALUE. An issuer may call a bond if it can refinance at a lower INTEREST RATE or no longer requires the capital proceeds; it is unlikely to call if prevailing rates are greater than the existing COUPON. From the investor's perspective, a callable bond can be

considered the equivalent of a NON-CALLABLE BOND and a SHORT POSITION in a call option(s) struck at the call price. In some cases investors are protected through CALL PROTECTION measures that limit an issuer's ability to redeem outstanding securities.
- See also CALL PREMIUM, CALL RISK, HYBRID BOND, PUTABLE BOND.

CALLABLE SWAP An OVER-THE-COUNTER SWAP structure that gives the institution paying fixed rates the OPTION to cancel the transaction at a future date.
- See also CANCELLABLE SWAP, PUTABLE SWAP.

CAMEL(S) [COL] Regulatory BANK ratings used in the US and UK financial systems based on a review of CAPITAL, ASSETS, management, MARKET RISK, earnings, and LIABILITIES/LIQUIDITY. CAMEL ratings are used to reflect the overall strength of a bank; those awarded the highest ratings (e.g., 5 on a 1–5 scale) need little, if any, improvement, while those receiving lower ratings are expected to implement recommendations set forth by the regulators.

CANCELLABLE SWAP An OVER-THE-COUNTER SWAP structure that gives either party involved in the swap the OPTION to terminate the transaction at a future date.
- See also CALLABLE SWAP, PUTABLE SWAP.

CANCELLATION PROVISION CLAUSE A provision in a PROPERTY AND CASUALTY INSURANCE contract that gives the INSURED the right to cancel the contract prior to the stated expiration date, as long as adequate written notice is provided.

CAP An OVER-THE-COUNTER INTEREST RATE OPTION contract that provides the buyer with a payoff when an underlying interest rate reference exceeds a predefined STRIKE PRICE.
- See also CAPTION, FLOOR, FLOORTION.

CAPACITY The maximum amount an INSURER is willing or able to underwrite in a specific LINE of RISK, generally a function of the level of its RETAINED EARNINGS and CAPITAL. Capacity can be increased through the use of REINSURANCE contracts, which allow the insurer to release UNEARNED PREMIUM RESERVES and increase the size of the retained earnings account.

CAPITAL The financial resources available to support a company's operations and absorb any unexpected losses. In a public company capital is typically comprised of COMMON STOCK, PAID-IN CAPITAL, CAPITAL SURPLUS, and RETAINED EARNINGS, though in some instances forms of SUBORDINATED PERPETUAL DEBT may also be included. From a basic accounting perspective

capital can be viewed as the difference between ASSETS and LIABILITIES.
- Also known as EQUITY, NET WORTH.
- See also ECONOMIC CAPITAL, REGULATORY CAPITAL.

CAPITAL ACCOUNT The national economic balance related to direct investment (inflows less outflows), purchases/sales of foreign securities by residents and domestic securities by non-residents, and FOREIGN EXCHANGE RESERVES.
- See also BALANCE OF PAYMENTS, CURRENT ACCOUNT.

CAPITAL ALLOCATION CAPITAL used to cover the RISKS inherent in a transaction or line of business; funds allocated act as a buffer against unexpected losses and help ensure SOLVENCY is maintained. Capital can be allocated through both internally-developed and regulatory mechanisms.
- See also ECONOMIC CAPITAL, REGULATORY CAPITAL, RESERVES, RISK-ADJUSTED CAPITAL, RISK-ADJUSTED RETURN ON CAPITAL.

CAPITAL ASSET PRICING MODEL (CAPM) A financial theory indicating that RISK is a combination of DIVERSIFIABLE RISK and NON-DIVERSIFIABLE RISK. Diversifiable risk can be reduced or eliminated by DIVERSIFICATION, meaning it is possible to create an optimal PORTFOLIO that maximizes return for a given level of risk. The non-diversifiable risk of an ASSET is fully measured by its sensitivity to the RISK PREMIUM of the market portfolio; in an efficient capital market the expected risk premium on an asset is proportional to BETA, a measure that indicates the riskiness, on a linear weighted basis, of the individual securities comprising the portfolio. Optimal portfolios are centered on the boundary of the EFFICIENT FRONTIER. Use of LEVERAGE (i.e., borrowing/lending at the RISK-FREE RATE) allows additional portfolios to be created, and is reflected in the CAPITAL MARKET LINE. CAPM assumes investors are risk averse and seek to maximize expected utility, asset return expectations are homogenous, assets are fixed, marketable, and divisible, a risk-free asset can be borrowed or lent without constraint, no friction costs exist, and all investors face the same investment horizon.

Under CAPM the expected return of security j is given as

$$E(r_j) = r_f + \beta [E(r_m) - r_f]$$

where r_f is the risk-free rate, β is beta, and $E(r_m)$ is the expected return on the market portfolio.
- See also ARBITRAGE PRICING THEORY.
- Additional references: Jensen (1972), Merton (1973), Roll (1977), Ross (1976), Sharpe (1964, 1971).

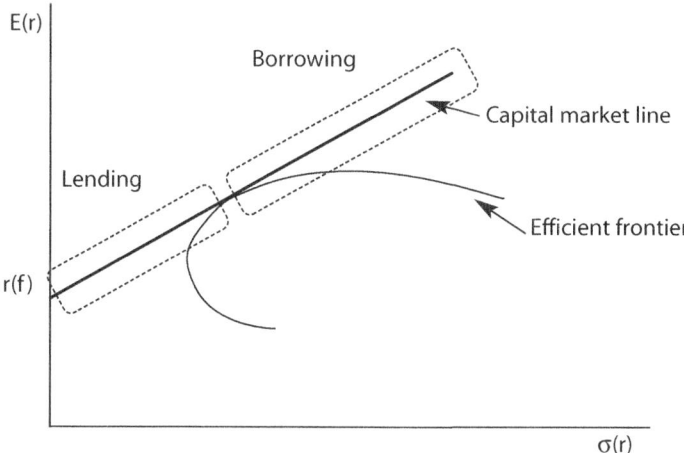

CAPITAL COMMITMENT A CAPITAL financing transaction, such as a NEW ISSUE or LOAN, where the arranging/lending institution uses its own resources to fund the transaction, with a view towards subsequent distribution/SYNDICATION to other investors or lenders.
- See also BOUGHT DEAL.

CAPITAL FLIGHT A sudden, and sometimes large, withdrawal of investment CAPITAL from a country, often as a result of SOVEREIGN RISK/COUNTRY RISK concerns or general political instability. A capital flight may involve non-resident (offshore) and resident investors; if the specter of loss appears real, investors will not be deterred by the potentially large transaction costs associated with shifting capital to a safe haven.
- See also FLIGHT TO QUALITY.

CAPITAL LEASE A long-term LEASE contract, structured in conventional or leveraged form, where the LESSEE accepts most/all of the RISKS and benefits of the leased property. Since the risks and economics are transferable, accounting rules generally require capital leases to be reflected on the corporate balance sheet. A capital lease is typically not cancellable, unless the lessee pays the LESSOR for any resulting losses.
- Also known as FINANCIAL LEASE.
- See also LEVERAGED LEASE, OPERATING LEASE.

CAPITAL MARKET The general marketplace for primary and secondary transactions in COMMON STOCK, PREFERRED STOCK, medium- to long-term BONDS, SECURITIZATIONS, and DERIVATIVES.
- See also MONEY MARKET.

CAPITAL MARKET LINE A relationship within the CAPITAL ASSET PRICING MODEL (CAPM) that relates the expected return of a PORTFOLIO to its expected RISK (as measured through STANDARD

DEVIATION). Under CAPM, all investors will choose a position on the capital market line by borrowing or lending at the RISK-FREE RATE, since this maximizes return for a given level of risk.
- See also SECURITY MARKET LINE.

CAPITAL MARKETS SUBSIDIARY A dedicated subsidiary owned by an INSURER, REINSURER, or COMMERCIAL BANK that is authorized to deal directly in a range of CAPITAL MARKET financing transactions and/or DERIVATIVES, including businesses normally associated with SECURITIES FIRMS and INVESTMENT BANKS.

CAPITAL NOTE A NOTE issued by a BANK or bank holding company that can qualify as TIER 2 CAPITAL. To be included in the Tier 2 computation, the security must be structured as a NON-CALLABLE BOND with an original maturity of at least 7 years, or a MANDATORY CONVERTIBLE BOND that results in conversion into the bank's COMMON STOCK at maturity.

CAPITAL SURPLUS A form of CAPITAL that can be created from issuance of COMMON STOCK at a PREMIUM over PAR VALUE, proceeds of stock repurchased and then resold (i.e., resale of TREASURY STOCK), a reduction in par value of common stock, or the purchase of another company with a surplus. The capital surplus does not include PAID-IN CAPITAL or RETAINED EARNINGS, which are treated separately for accounting purposes.

CAPM See CAPITAL ASSET PRICING MODEL.

CAPTION An OVER-THE-COUNTER OPTION on a CAP, granting the buyer the right to purchase a cap at a pre-determined STRIKE PRICE.
- See also FLOOR, FLOORTION.

CAPTIVE A vehicle established as an authorized INSURER or REINSURER that is used to facilitate a company's SELF-INSURANCE, RISK FINANCING, or RISK TRANSFER strategies. A captive, which can be controlled by a single owner or multiple owners (or sponsor(s)), can write INSURANCE/REINSURANCE business on behalf of one company/sponsor or many unrelated companies. Captives are often located in jurisdictions that have favorable insurance and tax laws, such as Bermuda, the Isle of Man, Guernsey, and Vermont.
- See also AGENCY CAPTIVE, GROUP CAPTIVE, PROTECTED CELL COMPANY, PURE CAPTIVE, RENT-A-CAPTIVE, SISTER CAPTIVE.

CAPTIVE AGENT An AGENT that represents a single INSURER and is required to submit business only to that insurer. In exchange for acting in an exclusive capacity, the insurer generally helps the captive agent defray marketing costs and provides additional financial benefits.

CARRIER An INSURER that is authorized to UNDERWRITE and ISSUE an INSURANCE contract.

CARROT EQUITY [COL] In the United Kingdom, a COMMON STOCK issue with a KICKER, or extra incentive, which allows investors to buy more stock if certain performance goals are met.

CARRYFORWARD LOSS See TAX CARRYFORWARD.

CARTEL A formal or informal agreement between firms in an industry or market to restrict competition by setting minimum price levels or maximum output quotas, and/or by segregating products or markets. Although establishment of a cartel can lead to profit growth in the short run, members may find it difficult to monitor each other's actions over the long term, leading in some instances to the gradual erosion of the arrangement.

CARVE-OUT [COL] A CORPORATE FINANCE transaction where a company segregates a portion of its business, places it in a separate corporate entity, and sells it to a third party or floats it through an INITIAL PUBLIC OFFERING. A carve-out may occur if the company seeks to permanently exit a business segment that is no longer deemed essential to strategic growth, or if it wishes to raise additional CAPITAL for other corporate operations.

▪ Also known as SPIN-OFF.

CASH-AND-CARRY ARBITRAGE An ARBITRAGE strategy where a profit can be secured by borrowing funds, using the proceeds to buy the ASSET, and selling a FORWARD or FUTURE on that asset. The arbitrage only exists when the FORWARD PRICE is greater than the SPOT PRICE plus the COST OF CARRY.

▪ See also REVERSE CASH-AND-CARRY ARBITRAGE.

CASH-AT-EXPIRY OPTION A BINARY OPTION that grants the buyer a payoff at expiry equal to a fixed cash amount if the price of the UNDERLYING market reference exceeds the STRIKE PRICE or BARRIER at any time during the transaction.

▪ See also BINARY-BARRIER OPTION.

CASH-AT-HIT OPTION A BINARY OPTION that grants the buyer an immediate payoff equal to a fixed cash amount once the price of the UNDERLYING market reference breaches the STRIKE PRICE or BARRIER.

▪ See also BINARY-BARRIER OPTION.

CASH BASIS A general accounting method that reports income when it is received and expenses when they are paid.

▪ See also ACCRUAL BASIS.

CASH COLLATERALIZED DEBT OBLIGATION (CDO) A COLLATERALIZED DEBT OBLIGATION that is created on a funded basis through the use of actual DEBT securities rather than CREDIT DERIVATIVE contracts. A cash CDO may be structured as a BALANCE SHEET CDO or an ARBITRAGE CDO, and may be managed statically or dynamically.

- See also SYNTHETIC COLLATERALIZED DEBT OBLIGATION.

CASH FLOW (1) A measure of a company's sources and uses of cash and the overall state of its LIQUIDITY. Cash flow is often divided into OPERATING CASH FLOW, INVESTING CASH FLOW and FINANCING CASH FLOW. (2) Any cash inflow or outflow associated with an investment or financing transaction.

CASH FLOW UNDERWRITING In INSURANCE, a pricing strategy where the PREMIUM charged is less than the EXPECTED LOSS LEVEL. The intent is to generate a large amount of premiums through the underpricing and use proceeds from reinvested premiums to cover expected losses and profit margin.

CASH MARKET See SPOT MARKET.

CASH ON DELIVERY (COD) See DELIVERY VERSUS PAYMENT.

CASH ON DELIVERY OPTION See CONTINGENT PREMIUM OPTION.

CASH-OR-NOTHING OPTION A BINARY OPTION that grants the buyer a payoff equal to a fixed cash amount if the price of the UNDERLYING market reference breaches the STRIKE PRICE at expiry.

- See also ALL-OR-NOTHING OPTION, BINARY OPTION.

CASH PRICE See SPOT PRICE.

CASH RATE See SPOT RATE.

CASH SURRENDER VALUE The amount an INSURER is required to return to the INSURED if an INSURANCE contract with savings features is cancelled prior to maturity.

CASUALTY LIABILITY or loss arising from an accident, negligence, or omissions, covered through INSURANCE contracts such as PROPERTY AND CASUALTY INSURANCE, COMMERCIAL GENERAL LIABILITY INSURANCE, or MULTIPLE PERIL INSURANCE.

CAT BOND See CATASTROPHE BOND.

CATASTROPHE BOND A SECURITIZATION of a CATASTROPHIC HAZARD, such as an earthquake, hurricane, or windstorm. Repayment of PRINCIPAL and/or COUPONS is contingent on the occurrence of a defined loss-making catastrophe; if a specified loss occurs, the issuer of the BOND (often an INSURER) may delay or cease making payments to investors, effectively transferring the RISK exposure to investors. The determination of whether payments are to be suspended under a catastrophe bond is generally based on one of three types of triggers: the INDEMNITY TRIGGER, INDEX TRIGGER, and PARAMETRIC TRIGGER.

- Also known as CAT BOND.
- See also INSURANCE-LINKED SECURITY, LIFE ACQUISITION COST SECURITIZATION, MORTGAGE DEFAULT

SECURITIZATION, RESIDUAL VALUE SECURITIZATION, WEATHER BOND.

CATASTROPHE PER OCCURRENCE EXCESS OF LOSS A REINSURANCE agreement providing the INSURER with cover for adverse loss experience from an accumulation of catastrophic events; such agreements often have an incremental DEDUCTIBLE and COINSURANCE.

CATASTROPHE REINSURANCE SWAP A synthetic financial SWAP that provides one of the contracting parties with a cash inflow in the event of loss from a defined catastrophic event. In exchange for the contingent CASH FLOW, the second party receives an upfront fee. Although the swap assumes the function of standard INSURANCE or REINSURANCE, the underlying documentation is often simpler and more flexible to negotiate.

- See also PURE CATASTROPHE SWAP.

CATASTROPHIC HAZARD A RISK event that is characterized by high severity and low frequency, leading to a large difference between expected and actual aggregate losses. Common catastrophic hazards include natural and human-made events such as earthquakes, hurricanes, windstorms, and terrorism. Although many catastrophic hazards can be protected via INSURANCE, REINSURANCE, or INSURANCE-LINKED SECURITIES some cannot, as the risk of loss may be too large or the required PREMIUM too high.

- See also CATASTROPHIC LOSS, CLASH LOSS, SHOCK LOSS.

CATASTROPHIC LOSS A high-severity, low-frequency loss event arising from a CATASTROPHIC HAZARD. A company often seeks to protect against catastrophic loss through INSURANCE, REINSURANCE, or CATASTROPHE BONDS. Catastrophic losses are often challenging to quantify and may, in some instances, be UNINSURABLE.

- See also CLASH LOSS, SHOCK LOSS.

CAVEAT EMPTOR [LAT] Literally "buyer beware." The term is often given as a warning to retail investors participating in risky or unproven investments.

CBO See COLLATERALIZED BOND OBLIGATION.

CD See CERTIFICATE OF DEPOSIT.

CDO See COLLATERALIZED DEBT OBLIGATION.

CEDANT See INSURED.

CEDE The process of transferring RISK from one party (the INSURED or CEDING INSURER) to another party (the INSURER or REINSURER) through an INSURANCE or REINSURANCE contract.

- See also RETROCEDE.

CEDING COMPANY A company that transfers, or CEDES, risk to an INSURER.

- See also INSURED.

CEDING INSURER An INSURER that transfers, or CEDES, risk to a REINSURER.

CENTRAL BANK A government owned or controlled BANK or monetary authority that is typically responsible for issuing local currency, managing the value of the currency, regulating money supply, setting RESERVE requirements, holding DEPOSITS of local banks, lending to the banking system, managing the local securities market, and acting as a LENDER OF LAST RESORT.
- See also BANK OF ENGLAND, BUNDESBANK, EUROPEAN CENTRAL BANK, FEDERAL RESERVE SYSTEM.

CENTRAL LIMIT THEOREM A statistical rule that indicates that the distribution of the average outcome approaches the NORMAL DISTRIBUTION as the number of observations becomes very large.

CERTIFICATE OF DEPOSIT (CD) A time DEPOSIT issued by a BANK to a depositor that pays a fixed or variable INTEREST RATE; in most instances the deposit represents a senior, unsecured LIABILITY of the issuing bank. A CD may be issued onshore or offshore in any one of several currencies, with a final maturity ranging from 1 week to 10 years. Certain CDs (i.e., NEGOTIABLE CDs) can be actively traded in the SECONDARY MARKET.
- See also FLOATING RATE CERTIFICATE OF DEPOSIT, LOCK-UP CERTIFICATE OF DEPOSIT.

CESSION A RISK exposure transferred from a CEDING COMPANY to an INSURER through an INSURANCE contract.

CFD See CONTRACT FOR DIFFERENCES.

CFTC See COMMODITY FUTURES TRADING COMMISSION.

CHAEBOL [KOR] The Korean form of CONGLOMERATE, generally comprised of a series of companies with cross-shareholdings and business relationships, but no central core company.

CHAPS See CLEARINGHOUSE AUTOMATED PAYMENT SYSTEM.

CHAPTER 11 [COL] A company in BANKRUPTCY that is in the process of REORGANIZATION proceedings, named in reference to Chapter 11 of the US Bankruptcy Code.
- See also LIQUIDATION.

CHASTITY BOND A BOND that can be redeemed by the issuing company at PAR VALUE in the event that it becomes the target of a TAKEOVER offer from another company.

CHEAP [COL] An ASSET that is perceived by market participants to be inexpensive compared to alternatives or proxies (i.e., the SPREAD is too wide in the case of a BOND or the price to low in the case of a COMMON STOCK, currency or commodity). Those believing the asset

is cheap will seek to profit by purchasing it, directly, synthetically, or through an ARBITRAGE trade.
- See also RICH.

CHEAPEST-TO-DELIVER (CTD) The cheapest of a series of ASSETS that are eligible for DELIVERY under an EXCHANGE-TRADED DERIVATIVE contract; the seller selects from the list of deliverables to determine the asset that will yield the greatest return (i.e., lowest cost, narrowest BASIS, or smallest loss).
- See also CONVERSION FACTOR.

CHECK KITING [COL] An illegal practice involving the writing of checks on two or more non-local BANKS, creating an unauthorized, interest-free LOAN or displaying a larger account balance until the checks are cleared.

CHERRY PICK [COL] A process where a RECEIVER or administrator in a BANKRUPTCY case attempts to have the court honor DERIVATIVE contracts (and/or REPURCHASE AGREEMENTS) that benefit the COUNTERPARTY in DEFAULT, while disallowing those that harm it. When a MASTER AGREEMENT is used to document the transactions and the legal jurisdiction recognizes the concept of NETTING, cherry picking cannot occur.

CHEWABLE PILL [COL] A POISON PILL defense clause that gives COMMON STOCK shareholders the right to revoke the pill in the face of a bona fide TAKEOVER offer, or which automatically nullifies the pill if the offer meets certain pre-defined criteria.

CHINESE WALL [COL] A process/structure within a BANK, INVESTMENT BANK, or SECURITIES FIRM that separates groups that call on clients and arrange deals (i.e., bankers) from those that are privy to non-public information related to those clients (i.e., research analysts). The intent is to minimize the exchange of sensitive information that might be used for competitive or personal gain.
- See also OVER THE WALL.

CHIPS See CLEARINGHOUSE INTERBANK PAYMENT SYSTEM.

CHOICE PRICE Identical BIDS and OFFERS provided by a MARKET MAKER or DEALER, meaning that a party can execute either side of the trade at the same price.
- See also LOCKED MARKET.

CHOOSER OPTION An OVER-THE-COUNTER COMPLEX OPTION that permits the buyer to choose between an underlying CALL OPTION and PUT OPTION with identical STRIKE PRICES and maturities from trade date until a defined "choice" date.
- Also known as a PREFERENCE OPTION, REGULAR CHOOSER OPTION.
- See also COMPLEX CHOOSER OPTION.

CHURNING [COL] An illegal practice where a BROKER urges clients to trade more actively than necessary in their investment accounts in order to generate more commissions. Accounts that reflect turnover of more than three to five times per year may indicate churning.
- Also known as OVERTRADING, TWISTING.

CIF See COST, INSURANCE, FREIGHT.

CIRCLE [COL] See INDICATION OF INTEREST.

CIRCUIT BREAKER [COL] Measures taken to halt TRADING on an EXCHANGE in the event predefined price levels are reached. Circuit breakers are intended to allow market participants to rebalance their positions in an orderly manner without contributing to further price pressures. Common breakers include temporary trading halts, curbs or bans on automated trading programs, and/or hourly/daily price limits.

CITY CODE [COL] Abbreviated form of the City Code on Takeovers and Mergers, a UK code of conduct established in 1968 under the direction of the BANK OF ENGLAND to ensure fair treatment for all parties involved in CORPORATE FINANCE transactions. The City Code defines the roles and responsibilities of BANKS (as advisors), acquiring companies, and target companies involved in a MERGER or ACQUISITION.

CLAIM (1) A request for loss indemnification made by an INSURED to an INSURER for a PERIL covered under an INSURANCE contract; the party submitting the claim is known as a claimant. In order for the claim to result in a SETTLEMENT, terms of the underlying contract must be met and proof of loss must generally be presented. (2) A general right, or title, to an ASSET or CASH FLOW.

CLAIMS MADE BASIS Determination of whether a CLAIM is covered by an INSURANCE contract. If the contract is written on a claims made basis and if a claim is made when the policy is in effect, the INSURER must pay the INSURED up to the stated amount.
- See also CLAIMS OCCURRENCE BASIS.

CLAIMS OCCURRENCE BASIS Determination of whether a CLAIM is covered by an INSURANCE contract. If the contract is written on a claims occurrence basis and a claim arises from an event when the policy is in force, the INSURER must pay the INSURED up to the stated amount, regardless of when the claim is actually filed (i.e., filing may occur after the policy has expired).
- See also CLAIMS MADE BASIS, OCCURRENCE LIMIT.

CLAIMS RESERVE Funds set aside by an INSURER for CLAIMS incurred or for claims outstanding that have not been settled. The claims reserve does not include accounting for losses INCURRED BUT NOT REPORTED.

CLASH LOSS A disaster scenario where various LINES of INSURANCE

are simultaneously impacted by losses. The resulting CLAIMS may be particularly large and can negatively impact the financial condition of INSURERS and REINSURERS.
- See also CATASTROPHIC HAZARD, SHOCK LOSS.

CLASH REINSURANCE An EXCESS OF LOSS REINSURANCE contract where the INSURER is covered against property and casualty losses when a single CASUALTY event causes losses for at least two CEDING INSURERS.

CLASSIFIED BOARD See STAGGERED BOARD.

CLASSIFIED STOCK Separate classes of COMMON STOCK issued by a company, with each class granting investors a distinct set of RENT RIGHTS and/or CONTROL RIGHTS. Classified stock is often used to increase or decrease the voting power of specific groups of shareholders.
- See also ALPHABET STOCK.

CLAWBACK [COL] The repayment, to RECEIVERS of a company in BANKRUPTCY, of any PREFERENCE payments, or monies deemed to have benefited one party at the expense of others during the period of FINANCIAL DISTRESS.
- See also PREFERENCE PERIOD.

CLEAN [COL] Matched buy and sell ORDERS on a BLOCK TRADE that leave the MARKET MAKER, DEALER, or intermediary without a RISK position.
- Also known as NATURAL.

CLEAN OPINION See UNQUALIFIED OPINION.

CLEAN PRICE [COL] The price of a BOND quoted without ACCRUED INTEREST.
- See also DIRTY PRICE.

CLEAN RISK See SETTLEMENT RISK.

CLEAN-UP REQUIREMENT A requirement that a borrower regularly repays all funds drawn under a REVOLVING CREDIT FACILITY as a way of demonstrating its ability to generate financing from other sources. Inability to meet the clean-up requirement may lead to a cancellation of the facility.

CLEARING A process where all EXCHANGE-TRADED DERIVATIVE contracts executed during a trading session are registered and reassigned to the CLEARINGHOUSE. Once reassigned, the clearinghouse becomes the official trade COUNTERPARTY on every transaction (which, along with a client's posting of MARGIN, helps to mitigate the effects of counterparty CREDIT RISK).
- See also CLEARING MARGIN, CLEARING MEMBER, HORIZONTAL CLEARING SERVICES.

CLEARING BANK In the United Kingdom, a large retail or wholesale commercial BANK.

- See also HIGH STREET BANK.

CLEARING MARGIN MARGIN posted by a CLEARING MEMBER with an EXCHANGE on behalf of clients or proprietary accounts.
- See also INITIAL MARGIN, VARIATION MARGIN.

CLEARING MEMBER An EXCHANGE member that is permitted to clear trades directly with the CLEARINGHOUSE, and which can accept trades for other clearing members and NON-CLEARING MEMBERS.

CLEARINGHOUSE (1) In the DERIVATIVES market, a subsidiary or division of an EXCHANGE or an independently owned entity that is responsible for CLEARING listed FUTURES and OPTIONS trades, computing and collecting daily MARGIN, and arranging for SETTLEMENT of financial or physical ASSETS related to trades. The CREDIT RISK normally associated with derivatives is neutralized as participants face the CLEARINGHOUSE, rather than each other, as their COUNTERPARTY. (2) In banking, a group of institutions that exchanges checks, drafts, and payment orders on a net basis, resulting in the creation of clearinghouse funds that are accessible within one to three business days.
- (2) See also CLEARINGHOUSE AUTOMATED PAYMENT SYSTEM, CLEARINGHOUSE INTERBANK PAYMENT SYSTEM.

CLEARINGHOUSE AUTOMATED PAYMENT SYSTEM (CHAPS) An automated CLEARINGHOUSE system in the United Kingdom that is used for large-value, same-day sterling transfers related to DRAFTS and payments.
- See also BANKERS' AUTOMATED CLEARING SERVICE (BACS).

CLEARINGHOUSE INTERBANK PAYMENT SYSTEM (CHIPS) A private sector, fully automated CLEARINGHOUSE system in the United States that is used for dollar-based checks and fund transfers, as well as payments associated with securities transactions and FOREIGN EXCHANGE trades.

CLIQUET OPTION An OVER-THE-COUNTER COMPLEX OPTION that allows the buyer to lock in gains at prespecified evaluation intervals if the option is IN-THE-MONEY at such points; gains are not relinquished if the market subsequently retraces. If the option is OUT-OF-THE-MONEY on an evaluation date the STRIKE PRICE resets AT-THE-MONEY based on the new market level.
- Also known as a RATCHET OPTION.
- See also LADDER OPTION, SHOUT OPTION.

CLO See COLLATERALIZED LOAN OBLIGATION.

CLONE FUND [COL] A MUTUAL FUND or UNIT TRUST that

attempts to replicate an existing fund through the use of DERIVATIVE contracts rather than actual securities.

CLOSE-OUT The process of establishing an equal and opposite DERIVATIVE position in order to neutralize or offset the RISK of an existing position. Although the close-out cancels the effects of risk, it grosses up the NOTIONAL amount of the contracts, which remain outstanding until final maturity.

CLOSE-OUT NETTING A contractual agreement where an institution and a COUNTERPARTY in DEFAULT agree to ACCELERATION, termination, and NETTING of all financial transactions.
- See also PAYMENT NETTING, SET-OFF.

CLOSED-END FUND An INVESTMENT COMPANY that raises CAPITAL by issuing a limited number of shares on an EXCHANGE, and invests proceeds in a range of ASSETS on behalf of investors. Once the initial PORTFOLIO of assets is assembled no new securities are added and few, if any, are sold prior to final maturity. The fund generally provides investors with a fixed return and typically allows no redemptions prior to the stated maturity. Closed-end funds often invest in BONDS or other assets that are ILLIQUID or difficult to price.
- See also MUTUAL FUND.
- Also known as INVESTMENT TRUST, UNIT INVESTMENT TRUST.

CMO See COLLATERALIZED MORTGAGE OBLIGATION.

COAT-TAILING [COL] The practice of replicating the investment strategies of institutional investors who are known, or believed, to have exhibited good performance.
- Also known as PIGGY-BACKING.
- See also TAILGATING.

COD See CASH ON DELIVERY.

COINSURANCE A feature of an INSURANCE contract that results in a sharing of losses between the INSURED and INSURER on a predetermined basis once any DEDUCTIBLE has been met. The insurer's total obligation under an insurance contract with a coinsurance feature is generally computed via:

$$Coins_{pmt} = L\left(\frac{Ins}{V(Co)}\right)$$

where L is the amount of the loss, Ins is the amount of insurance carried, V is the value of the insured property, and Co is the coinsurance clause percentage.

Indemnification can never exceed the amount dictated by the coinsurance relationship, the POLICY CAP, or the amount of the actual loss.

COLLAR A SPREAD consisting of a LONG CALL OPTION and a SHORT PUT OPTION, or long put and short call, with the same expiry date. The LONG POSITION (which requires payment of PREMIUM) is intended to provide RISK protection or speculative opportunity, while the SHORT POSITION (which results in receipt of premium) helps defray, and in some cases eliminate, the cost of the long option.
- See also ZERO COST COLLAR.

COLLATERAL ASSETS, such as cash, securities, ACCOUNTS RECEIVABLE, INVENTORY, LETTERS OF CREDIT, or physical property, taken to secure a CREDIT RISK exposure. By accepting collateral, the creditor has an additional source of repayment should its COUNTERPARTY be unable to perform on its obligations.

COLLATERAL RISK The RISK of loss arising from errors in the nature, quantity, pricing, or characteristics of COLLATERAL securing a transaction with CREDIT RISK. Institutions that actively accept and deliver collateral and are unable to manage the process accurately are susceptible to loss. A sub-category of PROCESS RISK.

COLLATERAL TRUST BOND A BOND secured by a PORTFOLIO of ASSETS owned by the issuer. Unlike a PASS-THROUGH SECURITY, the issuer retains sole ownership interest in the assets, which remain on the corporate balance sheet.
- See also MORTGAGE-BACKED BOND.

COLLATERALIZED BOND OBLIGATION (CBO) A SECURITIZATION structure that repackages credit-risky BONDS into TRANCHES with unique RISK and return (YIELD) profiles.
- See also COLLATERALIZED DEBT OBLIGATION.

COLLATERALIZED DEBT OBLIGATION (CDO) A SECURITIZATION structure that repackages credit-risky instruments (such as LOANS, BONDS, or CREDIT DERIVATIVES) into TRANCHES with unique RISK and return (YIELD) profiles. A CDO can be created by a sponsoring BANK or SECURITIES FIRM to transfer the DEFAULT risk in its credit portfolio to investors (BALANCE SHEET CDO) or to take advantage of profit opportunities in repackaging securities (ARBITRAGE CDO). A CDO can be structured as a COLLATERALIZED LOAN OBLIGATION (e.g., pools of loans) or COLLATERALIZED BOND OBLIGATION (e.g., pools of bonds) and can be created using physical instruments (CASH CDO) or credit derivatives (SYNTHETIC CDO). Portfolios may be managed statically (i.e., the portfolio is acquired and held until maturity) or dynamically (i.e., the portfolio changes during the life of the transaction, within certain parameters).

COLLATERALIZED LOAN OBLIGATION (CLO) A SECURITIZA-

TION structure that repackages credit-risky LOANS into TRANCHES with unique RISK and return (YIELD) profiles.
- See also COLLATERALIZED DEBT OBLIGATION.

COLLATERALIZED MORTGAGE OBLIGATION (CMO) A SECURITIZATION structure that repackages pools of MORTGAGE-BACKED SECURITIES, WHOLE LOANS, or mortgage-backed STRIPs into TRANCHES with specific RISK and return (YIELD) profiles. CMO structures are available in many different forms, some of them esoteric, risky, and ILLIQUID. However, the largest portion of the market is centered on standard instruments with reasonable RISK and LIQUIDITY parameters. The most common version of the CMO is based on sequential pay tranching, with COUPON payments, and then PRINCIPAL payments, allocated to investors in order of priority. Once all the tranches have been retired in sequence, the remaining ACCRUAL BOND (Z-BOND) is paid; since the accrual bond receives no CASH FLOWS until all others have been paid, it protects the cash flow payment stream for the entire structure.
- See also COMPANION BOND, INTEREST-ONLY STRIP, PLANNED AMORTIZATION CLASS BOND, PRINCIPAL-ONLY STRIP, TARGETED AMORTIZATION CLASS BOND.

COLLUSION A practice where parties act in concert, but without any formal agreement, to set or fix prices on a good, service, or ASSET. Collusion is considered illegal in many national systems, as it reflects anti-competitive behavior.

COMBINED RATIO A measure of an INSURER's profitability that compares earned PREMIUMS to losses from expenses and CLAIMS. The combined ratio is simply a combination of the LOSS RATIO and the EXPENSE RATIO, and is given as:

$$CR = \frac{L + LAE + IE}{Pr}$$

where L is the loss (from claims), LAE is LOSS ADJUSTMENT EXPENSE, IE is incurred expense (e.g., from UNDERWRITING activities), and Pr is premium.

If the ratio is greater than 100 the INSURANCE underwriting business is unprofitable, if it is less than 100 it is profitable.

COMMERCIAL BANK A financial institution that is permitted through regulatory approval and CORPORATE CHARTER to accept retail and INTERBANK DEPOSITS, extend commercial and retail LOANS, and perform various intermediation and FIDUCIARY duties. In some national systems commercial banks focus strictly on traditional banking services, while in others they have a broader scope, engaging in activities commonly associated with INVESTMENT BANKS or

SECURITIES FIRMS, such as securities UNDERWRITING and TRADING.
- See also BANCASSURANCE, BANK, UNIVERSAL BANK.

COMMERCIAL GENERAL LIABILITY POLICY An INSURANCE contract used by a firm seeking to cover RISK exposures to several LIABILITIES simultaneously, such as those arising from premises, products, contracts, contingencies, environmental damage, and FIDUCIARY breaches.
- See also COMMERCIAL UMBRELLA POLICY, MULTILINE POLICY, MULTIPLE PERIL PRODUCT.

COMMERCIAL LINES The general category of INSURANCE coverage for business organizations (rather than individuals), including institutionally focused policies such as the COMMERCIAL GENERAL LIABILITY POLICY, COMMERCIAL UMBRELLA POLICY, and MULTILINE POLICY.

COMMERCIAL PAPER (CP) Short-term, unsecured discount DEBT securities issued by highly rated financial companies (as FINANCIAL PAPER) and industrial companies (as INDUSTRIAL PAPER). Although most CP is unsecured, there is also a market for asset-backed CP and LETTER OF CREDIT-backed CP. In the US market CP maturities range from overnight to 270 days, while in the EUROMARKETS maximum maturity may extend to 360 days; the most common maturities in both markets are in the 14 to 30 day sector. Most CP is issued via DEALERS in the form of BEARER SECURITIES, although issues of REGISTERED SECURITIES are possible. In the US market it is common for CP programs to be partially backed by SWINGLINES so that issuers can access funds in the event they are unable to roll over their maturing notes.
- See also EURO COMMERCIAL PAPER.

COMMERCIAL UMBRELLA POLICY An INSURANCE contract that provides protection for very large exposure amounts (well in excess of those that might be obtained through a standard PROPERTY AND CASUALTY INSURANCE policy, a COMMERCIAL GENERAL LIABILITY POLICY or a MULTILINE POLICY). The umbrella policy covers a broad range of INSURABLE RISKS, but serves as an EXCESS LAYER facility rather than a FIRST LOSS cover.
- See also MULTIPLE PERIL PRODUCT.

COMMITMENT FEE An upfront or annual fee a BANK charges a customer for providing COMMITTED FUNDING or a REVOLVING CREDIT FACILITY. Payment of the commitment fee ensures the facility will not be withdrawn prior to its stated maturity and the borrower will have access to the funds when needed, presuming no COVENANTS have been breached.

- Also known as FACILITY FEE.

COMMITTED FUNDING A financing facility provided by a BANK to a borrower, which cannot be withdrawn unless the borrower breaches COVENANTS or other terms of the facility; this means the bank must provide funds when called on to do so, regardless of the market environment or borrower's financial condition. Funding facilities where the borrower has paid a COMMITMENT FEE and executed a credit agreement without a MATERIAL ADVERSE CHANGE clause or CONTINGENT TRIGGER may be regarded as committed.
- Also known as COMMITTED LINE.
- See also BANK LINE, REVOLVING CREDIT FACILITY.

COMMITTED LINE See COMMITTED FUNDING.

COMMITTED UNDERWRITING See BOUGHT DEAL.

COMMODITY DERIVATIVE An EXCHANGE-TRADED DERIVATIVE or OVER-THE-COUNTER DERIVATIVE with an UNDERLYING reference based on non-financial COMMODITIES including chemicals, energy, base and precious metals, livestock, GRAINS, and SOFTS. A commodity derivative can be structured as a COMMODITY FUTURE, commodity FORWARD, commodity OPTION, or COMMODITY SWAP.
- See also CREDIT DERIVATIVE, CURRENCY DERIVATIVE, EQUITY DERIVATIVE, INTEREST RATE DERIVATIVE.

COMMODITY FUTURE A FUTURES contract, bought or sold via an EXCHANGE, that references a non-financial physical commodity such as chemicals, energy, base and precious metals, livestock, GRAINS, and SOFTS.
- See also COMMODITY DERIVATIVE, CURRENCY FUTURE, INDEX FUTURE, INTEREST RATE FUTURE.

COMMODITY FUTURES TRADING COMMISSION (CFTC) A US regulatory agency, established in 1974, that is responsible for overseeing the EXCHANGE-TRADED DERIVATIVE marketplace. It assigns certain daily regulatory monitoring duties to SELF-REGULATORY ORGANIZATIONS, including the National Futures Association and individual EXCHANGES.

COMMODITY POOL A pool of investment CAPITAL, similar to a MUTUAL FUND or UNIT TRUST, that is invested by professional money managers solely in COMMODITY FUTURES and OPTIONS.

COMMODITY SWAP An OVER-THE-COUNTER SWAP transaction involving the exchange of fixed and floating commodity price references. Commodity swaps can be written on virtually any physical commodity (e.g. chemicals, energy, base and precious metals, livestock, GRAINS, and SOFTS) and can be structured to settle in cash or physical.

- See also COMMODITY DERIVATIVE.

COMMODITY TRADING ADVISOR (CTA) An INVESTMENT ADVISOR that develops and executes investment strategies for COMMODITY POOLS.

COMMON STOCK A CAPITAL instrument representing an ownership interest in a company. An investor in a company's common stock is granted RENT RIGHTS, including any DIVIDENDS that are declared and a share in any future capital appreciation, and CONTROL RIGHTS, including the ability to vote on specific issues at the ANNUAL GENERAL MEETING, file DIRECT and DERIVATIVE LAWSUITS, and receive regular financial information.
- Also known as EQUITY, ORDINARY SHARE, STOCK.
- See also PREFERRED STOCK.

COMPANION BOND A TRANCHE of a COLLATERALIZED MORTGAGE OBLIGATION that accompanies PLANNED AMORTIZATION CLASS (PAC) BONDS and TARGETED AMORTIZATION CLASS (TAC) BONDS. The companion serves to absorb PREPAYMENT RISK, giving PACs and TACs greater CASH FLOW, and thus price, stability.
- Also known as SUPPORT BOND.

COMPENSATING BALANCE A non-interest-bearing demand DEPOSIT placed by a customer with a BANK to compensate for LOANS or other services granted.

COMPETITION COMMISSION (CC) A UK body established in 1998 that ensures anti-MONOPOLY and free competition rules are upheld, particularly as related to MERGERS and ACQUISITIONS. The work of the Commission is non-binding and must be referred to the Office of Fair Trading for enforcement. The CC replaced the original Monopolies and Mergers Commission and Restrictive Practices Court.

COMPETITIVE BID A BID submitted in an AUCTION MARKET process that is placed in direct competition with other bids, meaning it will only be filled if it ranks at, or near, the highest price/lowest YIELD.
- See also NON-COMPETITIVE BID.

COMPETITIVE BID UNDERWRITING An UNDERWRITING of a NEW ISSUE of securities that is awarded by the issuing company to the UNDERWRITER that proposes the most favorable terms (generally a combination of lowest YIELD, lowest fees, broadest distribution, and strongest research and SECONDARY TRADING support).
- See also BEAUTY CONTEST, NEGOTIATED UNDERWRITING.

COMPETITIVE TENDER A general process where a company acquires goods or services by extending to suppliers an invitation to tender a proposal. In general, the tender with the lowest price wins the order, although factors related to quality, shipping, timeliness, and efficiency, may also be a consideration.

COMPLETION BOND A GUARANTEE provided by an INSURER to a BANK that is financing a project that ensures the bank will be repaid even if the project fails to be completed.
- See also PERFORMANCE BOND, SURETY BOND.

COMPLEX CHOOSER OPTION An OVER-THE-COUNTER COMPLEX OPTION that permits the buyer to choose between an underlying CALL OPTION (with a certain STRIKE PRICE and maturity) and an underlying PUT OPTION (with a different strike and maturity) between trade date and choice date.
- See also CHOOSER OPTION.

COMPLEX OPTION A conventional OPTION that is modified with respect to time, price, and/or payoff to produce unique RISK MANAGEMENT, investment, or speculative results. Certain complex options have risky payout profiles/LIABILITIES and demand considerable technical resources to ensure proper pricing and management.
- Also known as EXOTIC OPTION.
- See also PATH DEPENDENT OPTION, PATH INDEPENDENT OPTION.

COMPLEX STRUCTURED PRODUCT A CAPITAL MARKETS financing instrument, such as a BOND or NOTE, that contains embedded COMPLEX OPTIONS or COMPLEX SWAPS that alter RISK and return/YIELD characteristics in unique ways. Since complex structured products are highly customized they are often issued on a PRIVATE PLACEMENT basis and tend to feature very limited LIQUIDITY.
- See also STRUCTURED NOTE.

COMPLEX SWAP An OVER-THE-COUNTER SWAP that is modified with respect to time, price, NOTIONAL principal, and/or payoff to produce unique RISK MANAGEMENT, investment, or speculative results. Certain complex swaps have risky payout profiles/LIABILITIES and demand considerable technical resources to ensure proper pricing and management.
- Also known as EXOTIC SWAP.

COMPOUND OPTION An OVER-THE-COUNTER COMPLEX OPTION that allows the buyer to exercise into a second underlying option. Compound options are available in four forms, including a CALL ON A CALL (the right to buy an underlying CALL OPTION), a CALL ON A PUT (the right to buy an underlying PUT OPTION), a PUT ON A CALL (the right to sell an underlying call), and a PUT ON PUT (the right to sell an underlying put).

- Also known as NESTED OPTION.

COMPOUND OPTION STRATEGY A package of OPTIONS created to provide unique RISK MANAGEMENT, investment, or speculative results that cannot be achieved through simple positions. Common compound strategies include BULL SPREADS, BEAR SPREADS, STRADDLES, STRANGLES, and TIME SPREADS.
- See also DIRECTIONAL STRATEGY, SPREAD, VOLATILITY STRATEGY.

COMPOUNDING The process of adding periodic interest to an interest-bearing ASSET or LIABILITY, increasing the FUTURE VALUE to the investor and liability to the borrower. Compounding can be computed in simple or compound form via the following:

Simple compounding:

$$FV = PV(1 + (t\,r))$$

Annual compounding:

$$FV = PV(1 + r)^t$$

Annual compounding, n times per year:

$$FV = PV(1 + (r/n))^{tn}$$

Continuous compounding:

$$FV = PV\,e^{rt}$$

where PV is the PRESENT VALUE of the sum invested or borrowed, r is the DISCOUNT RATE, t is the time to maturity, n is the number of compounding periods per year, and e is the exponential constant.

COMPREHENSIVE GENERAL LIABILITY A COMMERCIAL LINE of INSURANCE providing the INSURED with protection against all exposures except those specifically excluded, generally those arising from products, premises, and actions of independent contractors.

CONCENTRATION RISK The RISK of loss arising from a large position in a single ASSET or market exposure. An excessive concentration can give rise to LIQUIDITY RISK or MARKET RISK losses.

CONCERT PARTY [COL] A group of speculators who band together to quietly acquire COMMON STOCK in a company, either to deflect attention prior to a public TAKEOVER offer (legal) or to avoid disclosure rules (which may be illegal).

CONDITIONAL PREPAYMENT RATE (CPR) A PREPAYMENT rate used to value MORTGAGE-BACKED SECURITIES and COLLATERALIZED MORTGAGE OBLIGATIONS, generally computed as an annualized rate of monthly prepayments to outstanding pooled MORTGAGES.

CONDITIONAL PUT CONVERTIBLE BOND A CONVERTIBLE BOND with a PUT OPTION feature that allows investors to sell the security back to the issuer under certain market conditions (i.e., the underlying stock price reaches a particular level).
■ See also PUTABLE CONVERTIBLE BOND.

CONDOR SPREAD A COMPOUND OPTION STRATEGY designed to take advantage of VOLATILITY. Condors are created with the same ratio of PUT OPTIONS or CALL OPTIONS (i.e., one low STRIKE PRICE, one middle low strike, one middle high strike, one high strike) that expire at the same time. SHORT condors, similar to LONG STRANGLES without the extreme upside, consist of short low and high strike options and

Long condor payoff profile

Short condor payoff profile

long middle low and high strike options. Long condors, similar to short strangles without the extreme downside, consist of long low and high strike options and short middle low and high strike options.
- See also BUTTERFLY SPREAD.

CONDUIT A SPECIAL PURPOSE ENTITY or TRUST that is used to acquire ASSETS forming part of a SECURITIZATION. The conduit may be owned and operated by a private firm (e.g., a BANK or SECURITIES FIRM as sponsor), or it may be associated with a governmental or sovereign agency. The sponsor sells or conveys earmarked assets to the conduit, which accumulates them until the full asset PORTFOLIO is created. Once complete, the conduit issues NOTES to investors under the terms of the securitization, or it sells the portfolio to a separate note issuing vehicle.

CONFIDENCE LEVEL A statistical interval that contains the actual parameter value of the population sampled to a stated probability (e.g., 90%, 95%, 99%). The width of the confidence level is an increasing function of the probability required, and a decreasing function of sample size. Confidence levels are widely used in certain financial applications, including ACTUARIAL PRICING, CREDIT RISK models, and VALUE-AT-RISK models.

CONFIRMATION A paper document or electronic slate that confirms all necessary details regarding a trade between two parties. The confirmation, which contains pertinent information related to trade size, price, reference ASSET/index, CASH FLOWS, PREMIUM, fees, and SETTLEMENT, can be created in a manner that makes it legally binding on both parties.

CONFIRMED LETTER OF CREDIT A transaction where a BANK guarantees ("confirms") an underlying LETTER OF CREDIT issued by another bank. If the original bank fails to perform under its contractual obligation, the confirming bank becomes liable to the BENEFICIARY. Confirmation often occurs when the original bank is small, less creditworthy, or located in a jurisdiction subject to a high degree of SOVEREIGN RISK.
- See also DIRECT PAY LETTER OF CREDIT, IRREVOCABLE LETTER OF CREDIT, STANDBY LETTER OF CREDIT, TRANSFERABLE LETTER OF CREDIT.

CONFIRMED LINE See ADVISED LINE.

CONGLOMERATE MERGER A MERGER between companies from unrelated sectors. Conglomerate mergers, which were popular during the 1960s and 1970s, have been relatively rare since many unsuccessful deals were dismantled in the 1980s. Academic and empirical evidence supports the idea that it is more efficient for an investor to hold a diversified PORTFOLIO of COMMON STOCKS,

than for a company to merge with, or acquire, a diversified group of companies.
- See also HORIZONTAL MERGER, VERTICAL MERGER.

CONSEIL D'ADMINISTRATION [FR] The EXECUTIVE BOARD of a French company that uses the DUAL BOARD SYSTEM.
- See also CONSEIL DU SURVEILLANCE.

CONSEIL DU SURVEILLANCE [FR] The SUPERVISORY BOARD of a French company that uses the DUAL BOARD SYSTEM.
- See also CONSEIL D'ADMINISTRATION.

CONSEQUENTIAL LOSS In INSURANCE, a loss arising from an inability to use property that has been damaged or destroyed by a covered PERIL. A consequential loss is generally not covered by a standard PROPERTY AND CASUALTY INSURANCE policy, and must therefore by insured separately through BUSINESS INTERRUPTION INSURANCE.
- Also known as INDIRECT LOSS.
- See also DIRECT LOSS.

CONSOL [COL] Abbreviated form of Consolidated Fund Annuities, representing PERPETUAL DEBT issued by the UK government as part of its GILT program. Consols, which form part of the government's tax revenue account at the BANK OF ENGLAND, are redeemable at PAR VALUE at the government's discretion, but in practice are never redeemed.

CONSOLIDATION (1) A form of MERGER where two companies combine to form an entirely new company. (2) An accounting process where the financial statements of group companies and subsidiaries are combined into a single set of accounts that reflects the entire financial standing of the group.
- (1) See also ACQUISITION.

CONSORTIUM BANK A form of MERCHANT BANK, popular in the EUROMARKETS during the 1970s and 1980s, jointly owned by several large international BANKS. Consortium banks were typically active in international LOAN origination and SYNDICATION, FOREIGN EXCHANGE and EUROBOND TRADING, and CORPORATE FINANCE transactions. With individual banks and INVESTMENT BANKS now operating similar businesses on their own, most consortium banks have scaled back their operations or ceased to exist.

CONSORTIUM UNDERWRITING An UNDERWRITING process in the INSURANCE market where a group of LLOYD'S OF LONDON underwriting SYNDICATES write business on behalf of other syndicates.

CONSTRUCTIVE TOTAL LOSS In INSURANCE, damage to property or ASSETS that is so significant that the cost of restoration is determined to be greater than the value of the restoration.

CONSUMER PRICE INDEX (CPI) An INFLATION measure used in the United States, Mexico, and other countries, based on the retail prices of a weighted index basket of market goods and services, including transportation, housing, health, and food. CPI is used as a reference in certain INFLATION-LINKED SECURITIES and INFLATION SWAPS.
- See also HARMONIZED INDEX OF CONSUMER PRICES, PRODUCER PRICE INDEX, RETAIL PRICE INDEX,

CONTAGION [COL] The spreading of economic disruption or financial VOLATILITY from one financial system or country to another. Contagion may occur or intensify as a result of excessive speculative forces, global economic interdependencies, and mobile investment CAPITAL. Government intervention is occasionally necessary when contagion spreads through the financial sector and threatens very broad systemic dislocation.

CONTANGO A market state where FUTURES prices are higher than expected SPOT prices and decline as contract maturity approaches.
- Also known as FORWARDATION.
- See also NORMAL BACKWARDATION.

CONTESTED TRANSACTION See HOSTILE TAKEOVER.

CONTINGENCY LOAN A LINE OF CREDIT that a company arranges in advance of a loss and invokes when one or more TRIGGER events occur; unlike a traditional BANK line of credit, the contingency loan can only be drawn to cover losses arising from a defined event.
- See also CONTINGENT CAPITAL.

CONTINGENCY RESERVE A RESERVE, established by INSURERS as a percentage of total retained surplus, which is used to cover unexpected losses and any shortfall in a previously declared DIVIDEND.

CONTINGENT CAPITAL A contractually agreed PRE-LOSS FINANCING facility that a company accesses in the aftermath of a loss event. Financing may take the form of CONTINGENT DEBT (i.e., COMMITTED CAPITAL FACILITIES, CONTINGENCY LOANS, CONTINGENT SURPLUS NOTES) or CONTINGENT EQUITY (e.g., PUT PROTECTED EQUITY, CATASTROPHE EQUITY PUT).

CONTINGENT CREDIT RISK The RISK of loss arising from a potential CREDIT RISK exposure that may appear in the future, such as draw down on a REVOLVING CREDIT FACILITY or payment under a GUARANTEE or LETTER OF CREDIT. A sub-category of CREDIT RISK.
- See also CONTINGENT LIABILITY, CORRELATED CREDIT

RISK, DIRECT CREDIT RISK, SETTLEMENT RISK, SOVEREIGN RISK, TRADING CREDIT RISK.

CONTINGENT DEBT A class of DEBT financing that becomes effective once a defined TRIGGER has been breached; the class includes COMMITTED CAPITAL FACILITIES, CONTINGENT SURPLUS NOTES, CONTINGENCY LOANS, and FINANCIAL GUARANTEES.
- See also CONTINGENT CAPITAL.

CONTINGENT EQUITY A class of EQUITY financing that becomes effective once a defined TRIGGER has been breached; the class includes LOSS EQUITY PUTS and PUT PROTECTED EQUITY.
- See also CONTINGENT CAPITAL.

CONTINGENT LIABILITY (1) The LIABILITY of an institution that assumes the role of a guarantor or endorser under a LETTER OF CREDIT, GUARANTEE, or SURETY BOND. (2) Accounting and RISK classification of an undrawn REVOLVING CREDIT FACILITY granted by a BANK to a borrower. (3) In INSURANCE, see VICARIOUS LIABILITY.
- (1) See also CONTINGENT CREDIT RISK.

CONTINGENT PREMIUM OPTION An OVER-THE-COUNTER COMPLEX OPTION where the buyer is only obliged to pay the seller PREMIUM if the contract ends IN-THE-MONEY. If the option ends in-the-money but the INTRINSIC VALUE is less than the premium due to the seller, the purchaser is still obligated to exercise the option and pay the premium.
- Also known as PAY LATER OPTION, WHEN-IN-THE-MONEY OPTION.

CONTINGENT SURPLUS NOTES A form of PRE-LOSS FINANCING where an INSURER or REINSURER issues NOTES to investors via a TRUST if a predefined loss-making TRIGGER event occurs. The issuance provides funding to compensate for losses sustained.
- See also CONTINGENT CAPITAL.

CONTINGENT TRIGGER A COVENANT in a credit agreement requiring a borrower to undertake certain actions (such as repaying DEBT, selling ASSETS, issuing COMMON STOCK) in the event a predefined TRIGGER event occurs. Common triggers include a CREDIT RATING downgrade or breach of a financial ratio, often those related to LIQUIDITY, LEVERAGE, or INTEREST COVERAGE.

CONTRA ACCOUNT An account in a dual entry accounting system that offsets or reverses the value of another account. Common contra accounts include ACCUMULATED DEPRECATION as a contra account to fixed, depreciable ASSETS, LOAN LOSS RESERVES as a contra account to LOANS, and TREASURY STOCK as a contra account to EQUITY.

CONTRACT A legal agreement between two parties that specifies actions, duties, and payments. A contract is only enforceable if it is based on legal activities and involves the exchange of consideration (i.e., each party to the contract provides some value).

CONTRACT FOR DIFFERENCES (CFD) See TOTAL RETURN SWAP.

CONTRACT MONTH The designated month(s) on which EXCHANGE-TRADED DERIVATIVES are offered for TRADING. Many contracts are offered on a quarterly cycle, while those that are extremely popular and feature a high degree of LIQUIDITY may be offered on a sequential monthly basis. Although monthly and quarterly cycles are most common, some derivatives are deliberately designed with very short maturity periods (e.g., overnight or intraday) to allow for instantaneous hedging or risk-taking.

CONTRARIAN [COL] An investor with a view that runs contrary to popular market sentiment or belief. Contrarians may be willing to take RISK or provide LIQUIDITY when other parties cannot, or will not.

CONTROL RIGHT The legal entitlements granted to an investor holding a share of COMMON STOCK, including the right to transfer shares, receive regular and accurate financial disclosure, vote on specific issues at the company's ANNUAL GENERAL MEETING, and file lawsuits (i.e., legal actions for abuses related to self-dealing, compensation, information disclosure, breaches of DUTY OF LOYALTY or DUTY OF CARE).

* See also RENT RIGHT.

CONVENIENCE YIELD The non-monetary return that is derived from holding an ASSET, such as not facing a shortfall in the event of excess demand. The existence of a convenience yield creates an incremental return that is included in FORWARD PRICE computations related to FUTURES or FORWARDS.

CONVERGENCE (1) In the EXCHANGE-TRADED DERIVATIVE

market, the gradual drawing together of SPOT PRICES and FUTURES PRICES as contract maturity approaches; the convergence means that the BASIS, or price difference, gradually narrows. (2) In the ALTERNATIVE RISK TRANSFER market a cross-sector fusion of business activities between INSURERS and BANKS; the two groups participate in each other's markets by creating mechanisms to assume and transfer various INSURABLE RISKS and FINANCIAL RISKS.

CONVERSION ARBITRAGE An ARBITRAGE strategy that takes advantage of mispricing of OPTIONS in relation to PUT–CALL PARITY. The strategy may involve the purchase of "undervalued" OPTIONS and the sale of SYNTHETIC OPTIONS, or the sale of "overvalued' options and the purchase of synthetics. A risk-free profit can be generated if the undervalued/overvalued options are truly mispriced.

	Conversion arbitrage strategy
Undervalued put	Purchase put and sell synthetic put (synthetic = purchase underlying, sell call)
Overvalued put	Sell put and purchase synthetic put (synthetic = sell underlying, purchase call)
Undervalued call	Purchase call and sell synthetic call (synthetic = sell underlying, sell put)
Overvalued call	Sell call and purchase synthetic call (synthetic = purchase underlying, purchase put)

CONVERSION FACTOR A multiplicative factor that is applied to a DELIVERABLE ASSET under an EXCHANGE-TRADED DERIVATIVE contract to determine the precise amount that needs to be delivered. Since different types and grades are often deliverable, the seller of the contract must use a conversion factor to make the appropriate adjustment.
- See also CHEAPEST TO DELIVER.

CONVERSION PARITY The market value of the shares of COMMON STOCK into which a CONVERTIBLE BOND can be exchanged, generally computed as:

$Conv_{pty} = Conv_{ratio}(S)$

where $Conv_{ratio}$ is the CONVERSION RATIO and S is the stock price.
- Also know as CONVERSION VALUE, PARITY.
- See also CONVERSION PREMIUM, CONVERSION PRICE, INVESTMENT VALUE.

CONVERSION PREMIUM The additional amount an investor in a CONVERTIBLE BOND pays above CONVERSION PARITY to acquire the bond, generally expressed as a percentage of parity:

$$Conv_{prem} = \left(\frac{P_{CB}}{Conv_{pty}} - 1\right)(100\%)$$

where P_{CB} is the price of the convertible bond and $Conv_{pty}$ is conversion parity.
- See also ADJUSTED BREAKEVEN, CONVERSION PRICE, CONVERSION RATIO, CONVERSION VALUE, EQUIVALENT BREAKEVEN, INVESTMENT PREMIUM, SIMPLE BREAKEVEN.

CONVERSION PRICE The price at which an investor holding a CONVERTIBLE BOND exchanges the bond for shares of COMMON STOCK, computed as:

$$Conv_{price} = \frac{Par_{CB}}{Conv_{ratio}}$$

where Par_{CB} is the PAR VALUE of the convertible bond and $Conv_{ratio}$ is the CONVERSION RATIO.
- See also CONVERSION PARITY, CONVERSION PREMIUM, CONVERSION VALUE.

CONVERSION RATIO The number of shares of stock an investor receives in converting the CONVERTIBLE BOND, computed via:

$$Conv_{ratio} = \frac{Par_{CB}}{Conv_{price}}$$

where Par_{CB} is the PAR VALUE of the convertible bond and $Conv_{price}$ is the initial CONVERSION PRICE.
- See also CONVERSION PARITY, CONVERSION PREMIUM, CONVERSION VALUE.

CONVERSION VALUE See CONVERSION PARITY.

CONVERTIBILITY The right to exchange one currency for another. Resident and non-resident holders can exchange a fully CONVERTIBLE CURRENCY at will, without seeking permission from government authorities; a NON-CONVERTIBLE CURRENCY requires permission prior to exchange. Some currencies have restricted convertibility, where non-residents may be able to exchange freely but residents may need to gain prior approval, or holders may be able to convert freely for CURRENT ACCOUNT purposes such as trade, but not for CAPITAL ACCOUNT purposes such as LOANS or ASSET acquisition.
- See also CONVERTIBILITY RISK, RESERVE CURRENCY.

CONVERTIBILITY RISK The RISK of loss arising from an inability to convert local currency into a fully CONVERTIBLE CURRENCY and/or to repatriate convertible currency back to a home country as a result of EXCHANGE CONTROLS. A sub-category of SOVEREIGN RISK.

CONVERTIBLE BOND A hybrid DEBT/EQUITY security that consists of a COUPON-bearing BOND and an embedded equity OPTION that allows the investor to convert into a specified number of shares of COMMON STOCK once the CONVERSION PRICE is reached. Convertible bonds are generally issued at par with CONVERSION PREMIUMS of 15–25 percent and final maturities of 10 to 15 years.
- See also CONDITIONAL PUT CONVERTIBLE BOND, EXCHANGEABLE BOND, LOW PREMIUM CONVERTIBLE BOND, MANDATORY CONVERTIBLE BOND, PUTABLE CONVERTIBLE BOND, REVERSE CONVERTIBLE BOND, ZERO COUPON CONVERTIBLE BOND.

CONVERTIBLE CURRENCY A currency that can be freely exchanged into another currency for any purpose, without regulatory restrictions. Convertible currencies are generally associated with open and stable economies, and their prices are typically determined through supply and demand forces in the FOREIGN EXCHANGE market.
- Also known as HARD CURRENCY.
- See also CONVERTIBILITY, EXOTIC CURRENCY, NON-CONVERTIBLE CURRENCY, RESERVE CURRENCY.

CONVERTIBLE PREFERRED STOCK A class of PREFERRED STOCK that allows the investor to convert it into a specified number of shares of COMMON STOCK once a conversion price is reached. Convertible preferreds pay DIVIDENDS rather than COUPON interest, often on a cumulative basis, and are generally perpetual. In certain cases issues are floated with mandatory conversion features, requiring conversion into new common stock by a specific date if a minimum price target is reached.

CONVEXITY A mathematical measure that quantifies the sensitivity of an ASSET to large changes in price or YIELD. In OPTION contracts convexity (commonly termed GAMMA) measures the change in DELTA for a change in the price of the UNDERLYING; in FIXED INCOME products it measures the change in DURATION for a change in YIELD or INTEREST RATES. Mathematically convexity is the first derivative of a change in value with respect to duration/delta, or the second derivative of a change in value with respect to yield/underlying.

Standard convexity calculations for a fixed income security with semi-annual coupons are given by:

$$Cvx = \sum_{t=1}^{n} \frac{t(t+1)C}{(1+y)^{t+2}} + \frac{n(n+1)M}{(1+y)^{n+2}}$$

or:

$$Cvx = \frac{2C}{y^3}\left[1 - \frac{1}{(1+y)^n}\right] - \frac{2Cn}{y^2(1+y)^{n+1}} + \frac{n(n+1)(100-C/y)}{(1+y)^{n+2}}$$

where C is COUPON, t is the time to maturity, y is the semi-annual yield, n is the number of semi-annual periods, and M is the redemption value of the bond (generally PAR VALUE).
- Also known as OPTIONALITY.
- See also NEGATIVE CONVEXITY, NON-LINEAR INSTRUMENT, POSITIVE CONVEXITY.

COOKIE JAR ACCOUNTING [COL] The practice of liberally interpreting, or manipulating, accounting rules in order to convey a stronger financial position. Smoothing income flows, reversing RESERVES, and capitalizing costs that should be expensed are forms of cookie jar accounting.
- Also known as COOKING THE BOOKS.

COOKING THE BOOKS [COL] See COOKIE JAR ACCOUNTING.

COOLING OFF PERIOD [COL] In the US markets, the period between the filing of a final PROSPECTUS and the offering of a NEW ISSUE of securities to public investors. The cooling off period is typically 20 days.

CORE INFLATION A measure of INFLATION at the consumer level, excluding certain items such as food and oil.
- See also CONSUMER PRICE INDEX, HARMONIZED INDEX OF CONSUMER PRICES, RETAIL PRICE INDEX.

CORNERING [COL] An attempt to gain sufficient market share in an ASSET or security in order to manipulate the price for gain. Cornering attempts, which are generally illegal, are usually unsuccessful unless the asset is very thinly traded.

CORPORATE CHARTER An authorizing document issued by a government or legal authority that delineates the activities a CORPORATION is permitted to undertake.
- See also ARTICLES OF INCORPORATION.

CORPORATE CONTROL MARKET The broad marketplace for transactions that are designed to change the ownership, structure, and/or control of a company. Common corporate control transactions include MERGERS, friendly or HOSTILE TAKEOVERS, LEVERAGED BUYOUTS, and RECAPITALIZATIONS. In some national systems the corporate control market also serves as a monitoring mechanism for GOVERNANCE purposes.

CORPORATE ETHICS The broad area dealing with the way in which a company behaves towards, and conducts business with, its internal and external STAKEHOLDERS, including employees, investors, creditors, customers, and regulators. In certain national systems minimum standards are required or recommended in order to eliminate potential conflicts of interest or client/employee mistreatment.

CORPORATE FINANCE (1) The general class of financial transactions that a company may consider to alter its structure, operations, or business focus, including MERGER, ACQUISITION, CARVE-OUT, DIVESTITURE, RECAPITALIZATION, LEVERAGED BUYOUT, or MANAGEMENT BUYOUT. (2) General financing activities carried out by a company through the CAPITAL MARKETS.

CORPORATE GOVERNANCE See GOVERNANCE.

CORPORATE SUSTAINABILITY The concept and action of ensuring that a corporate organization exists in perpetuity, providing returns and benefits for multiple generations of internal and external STAKEHOLDERS. Sustainability generally demands close ties and cooperation with a broad constituency of investors, customers, creditors, employees, and regulators, as well as the surrounding community.

CORPORATION Any company that issues COMMON STOCK to investors in order to raise capital; a corporation may be public or private, and is generally organized with LIMITED LIABILITY.
- See also JOINT STOCK COMPANY, LIMITED LIABILITY COMPANY, PUBLIC LIMITED COMPANY.

CORPUS [LAT] The PRINCIPAL component of a BOND.
- See also COUPON.

CORRECTION A temporary reversal of a securities price or broader market sector lasting several days to several months; though the retracement is not as severe as it is in a BEAR MARKET, prices may ultimately fall by 20 percent from the previous peak.
- See also BULL MARKET.

CORRELATED CREDIT RISK The RISK of loss arising from CREDIT EXPOSURE that increases precisely as a COUNTERPARTY's ability to perform declines, or when COLLATERAL taken as security deteriorates in tandem with a counterparty's ability to pay. A sub-category of CREDIT RISK.
- See also CONTINGENT CREDIT RISK, DIRECT CREDIT RISK, SETTLEMENT RISK, SOVEREIGN RISK, TRADING CREDIT RISK.

CORRELATION A statistical measure that indicates the extent to which two or more variables (such as financial ASSET prices) move in the same direction, or different directions. Correlation is often used to

price and manage certain COMPLEX DERIVATIVES (e.g., MULTI-INDEX OPTIONS), quantify PORTFOLIO RISK exposures, and determine appropriate HEDGE RATIOS.
- See also CORRELATION COEFFICIENT, CORRELATION RISK.

CORRELATION COEFFICIENT A measure of CORRELATION, typically computed as:

$$\rho_{A,B} = \frac{Cov(A, B)}{\sigma_A \, \sigma_B}$$

where $Cov(A,B)$ is the covariance between ASSETS A and B, σ_A is the STANDARD DEVIATION of asset A and σ_B is the standard deviation of asset B.

A perfect positive correlation coefficient (+1) means a unit change in the price of one reference leads to the same unit change in the price of the second; a perfect negative correlation coefficient (−1) means they move in equal but opposite directions; a correlation of 0 indicates prices are uncorrelated, or independent.
- See also CORRELATED CREDIT RISK, CORRELATION RISK.

CORRELATION RISK The RISK of loss arising from a change in the historical relationships, or CORRELATIONS, between ASSETS. Correlation risk can be found in certain COMPLEX OPTIONS and COMPLEX SWAPS and may also impact HEDGE RATIOS, CREDIT PORTFOLIO MODELS, and VALUE-AT-RISK models. A subcategory of MARKET RISK.

COST INFLATION INFLATION that results from increased costs of production, including raw materials and labor. Higher production costs are priced into goods and services, leading labor to demand higher wages to meet the higher prices; the resulting rise in labor costs is also priced into the final goods and services, raising the overall rate of inflation.
- See also DEMAND INFLATION.

COST, INSURANCE, FREIGHT (CIF) The declared value of imported goods, including the cost of purchase and associated INSURANCE and shipping charges from the point of export to the point of import. CIF does not include duties or the cost of freight within the country of import.
- See also FREE ON BOARD (FOB).

COST OF CAPITAL The total costs a firm bears in funding its operations through DEBT and EQUITY, equal to the rate of return needed to induce CAPITAL suppliers to invest or lend. The cost of capital is widely used for investment, reinvestment, financing, and capital budgeting decisions, and can be computed through:

$$r_{coc} = \left[r_D (1 - TR) \frac{D}{D+E} \right] + \left[r_E \frac{E}{D+E} \right]$$

where r_D is the average cost of debt, TR is the corporate tax rate (where $1 - TR$ provides benefits in the form of a TAX SHIELD), r_E is the average cost of equity (or expected return to COMMON STOCK shareholders), D is total amount of debt and E is total amount of equity.

COST OF CARRY The FUTURE VALUE of costs and benefits associated with holding an ASSET, which typically includes the cost of financing, INSURANCE, transportation and/or storage, less benefits derived from lending the asset and any CONVENIENCE YIELD. Cost of carry is used to determine theoretical FUTURES prices and ARBITRAGE opportunities.

COST OF RISK The implicit or explicit price a company must pay to manage its RISK exposures; it is typically comprised of the expected costs and direct and indirect losses arising from RISK RETENTION, LOSS CONTROL, LOSS FINANCING, and RISK REDUCTION activities.

COUNTERPARTY An institution that is a party to a financial transaction with CREDIT RISK, such as a LOAN, DERIVATIVE, or financing.

COUNTRY RISK The RISK of loss due to adverse economic events or political instability within a country; country risk is often considered to be larger in scope than SOVEREIGN RISK as it includes actions that affect private sector, as well as governmental, obligations. A subcategory of CREDIT RISK.

COUPON The periodic CASH FLOW payable by an issuer or borrower to an investor or lender for the use of DEBT-based CAPITAL. Coupon payments may be based on fixed or floating INTEREST RATES, and may be payable on a weekly, monthly, quarterly, semi-annual or annual basis, or accrued until final maturity of the LIABILITY.

■ See also CORPUS, PRINCIPAL.

COUPON STRIPPING See STRIPPING.

COVARIANCE A statistical measure of the relationship between two variables (e.g., financial ASSET prices), often used to determine the magnitude of CORRELATION. The covariance between two assets can be computed via:

$$Cov(A, B) = \sum_{j=1}^{n} \frac{\left[(x_{A,j} - \bar{x}_A)(x_{B,j} - \bar{x}_B) \right]}{n-1}$$

where $x_{A,j}$ is an observation of asset A, $\bar{x}_A$ is the MEAN of asset A, $x_{B,j}$ is an observation of asset B, $\bar{x}_B$ is the mean of asset B, and n is the number of observations.

■ See also CORRELATION COEFFICIENT.

COVENANT A clause in a LOAN agreement or BOND INDENTURE that requires the borrower to adhere to certain conditions. The conditions may be affirmative, such as paying PRINCIPAL and COUPONS on a timely basis or preserving an adequate amount of INSURANCE coverage, or negative (restrictive), such as not disposing of certain ASSETS, not breaching financial ratios, or not taking actions that might impair the value of any assets pledged as COLLATERAL. Violation of a covenant can result in the loan or bond being terminated and becoming immediately due and payable. Covenants are commonly based on RESTRICTED RETAINED EARNINGS (limiting the payment of DIVIDENDS if the borrower sustains operating losses), net tangible assets (limiting investment, dividends, and new debt if net tangible assets fall below a particular level), WORKING CAPITAL (limiting CORPORATE FINANCE transactions, dividends, and new debt if working capital declines), and LEVERAGE (limiting new debt if total debt to equity becomes too large).

COVER (1) The act of repurchasing or HEDGING a position previously SOLD SHORT or held naked. (2) Any form of INSURANCE or REINSURANCE.

COVERED CALL An OPTION position where the seller of a CALL OPTION owns the UNDERLYING ASSET that must be delivered if the buyer EXERCISES the option. Selling covered calls is a relatively low RISK way of generating PREMIUM income since the cost of the underlying is already known.
- See also COVERED OPTION, COVERED PUT, NAKED CALL.

COVERED INTEREST ARBITRAGE An ARBITRAGE transaction that takes advantage of any instance when the FORWARD PREMIUM or FORWARD DISCOUNT between two currencies does not equal the INTEREST RATE DIFFERENTIAL. When this occurs, ARBITRAGEURS can use covered interest arbitrage to generate profits until the relationships return to equilibrium. This may be done by buying one currency in the SPOT MARKET and simultaneously selling it in the FORWARD MARKET and using the spot proceeds to invest in an asset denominated in the spot currency; when the asset matures, the proceeds are used to fulfill the forward contract and the arbitrage transaction concludes with a risk-free profit.

COVERED OPTION An OPTION position where the seller of the option already holds the UNDERLYING ASSET or cash that must be delivered if the buyer EXERCISES the option. Selling covered options is a relatively low RISK way of generating PREMIUM income since the cost of the underlying is already known or sufficient cash exists to cover the purchase.

- See also COVERED CALL, COVERED PUT, COVERED WRITER, NAKED OPTION.

COVERED POSITION An outright LONG POSITION or SHORT POSITION that is protected by an offsetting HEDGE. Depending on the nature of the hedge, a covered position may have only negligible MARKET RISK and CREDIT RISK exposures.
- See also NAKED POSITION.

COVERED PUT An OPTION position where the seller of a PUT OPTION already has sufficient cash on hand to purchase the UNDERLYING ASSET if the buyer EXERCISES the option. Selling covered puts is a relatively low RISK way of generating PREMIUM income since the cash is available to cover the exercise.
- See also COVERED CALL, COVERED OPTION, NAKED PUT.

COVERED WARRANT A long-dated EQUITY OPTION (i.e., three to five years) issued by a financial intermediary on a company's COMMON STOCK, which can be EXERCISED by the holder into shares already outstanding in the market (making the transaction nondilutive). The covered warrant is not sponsored by the company and need not have the company's approval, since no new equity results.
- See also EQUITY WARRANT, WARRANT.

COVERED WRITER The seller of a COVERED OPTION that either owns the UNDERLYING ASSET (deliverable under a CALL OPTION) or has sufficient cash on hand to acquire the asset (under a PUT OPTION) should EXERCISE occur. A covered writer seeks to earn PREMIUM income on a relatively low RISK basis.
- See also NAKED WRITER.

COX, ROSS, and RUBINSTEIN MODEL See BINOMIAL MODEL.

CP See COMMERCIAL PAPER.

CPI See CONSUMER PRICE INDEX.

CPR See CONDITIONAL PREPAYMENT RATE.

CRACK SPREAD [COL] A SPREAD in the energy market reflecting the price differential between crude oil and a refined product, generally gasoline or heating oil; the spread can be traded through a single FUTURE or OPTION contract on certain EXCHANGES. A hedger or speculator can buy the crack spread (e.g., purchase crude and sell heating oil or gas) to take advantage of positive margins in refining, and sell the spread (e.g., sell crude and purchase heating oil or gas) to profit from negative margins.
- See also SPARK SPREAD.

CRAMDOWN A process where creditors with existing CREDIT RISK to a company that has filed a REORGANIZATION plan under BANKRUPTCY protection choose not to participate in the new plan and have their interests demoted or "crammed down."

A bankruptcy court can approve cramdown if at least one creditor agrees to the repayment plan and the plan does not discriminate among participating creditor claims.

CRAWLING PEG A FOREIGN EXCHANGE PEGGING process based on official CENTRAL BANK intervention activity that adjusts the value of the local currency through small pre-announced changes or average target rates over a period of time. The crawling feature avoids sudden jumps or VOLATILITY characteristic of DEPRECIATION or DEVALUATION, but may still be difficult and expensive to maintain over the long term.
- See also MANAGED FOREIGN EXCHANGE RATE.

CREDIT CONTROL A government policy of controlling aggregate economic demand by restricting access to credit, generally by influencing INTEREST RATES, limiting the total amount of speculative lending, and setting minimum RESERVE requirements for BANKS.

CREDIT DEFAULT MODEL An analytic model that is used to determine credit losses based on the probability a COUNTERPARTY will DEFAULT at a future time. A credit default model does not model losses attributable to credit deterioration (i.e., CREDIT SPREAD widening), it simply models default.
- See also CREDIT DEFAULT RISK, CREDIT MARK-TO-MARKET MODEL, INTENSITY MODEL, STRUCTURAL MODEL.

CREDIT DEFAULT RISK The RISK of loss arising from a COUNTERPARTY's failure to perform on its contractual obligations, including DERIVATIVES, LOANS, BONDS, and other credit-sensitive instruments.
- Also known as DEFAULT RISK.
- See also CREDIT INVENTORY RISK, CREDIT RISK, CREDIT SPREAD RISK.

CREDIT DEFAULT SWAP See DEFAULT SWAP.

CREDIT DERIVATIVE An OVER-THE-COUNTER DERIVATIVE with an UNDERLYING reference that is based on the credit performance of a reference COUNTERPARTY. Credit derivatives are available in various forms, including the BASKET SWAP, CREDIT FORWARD, CREDIT SPREAD OPTION, DEFAULT OPTION, DEFAULT SWAP, FIRST-TO-DEFAULT SWAP, and TOTAL RETURN SWAP.
- See also COMMODITY DERIVATIVE, CURRENCY DERIVATIVE, EQUITY DERIVATIVE, INTEREST RATE DERIVATIVE, SYNTHETIC COLLATERALIZED DEBT OBLIGATION.

CREDIT EXPOSURE See CREDIT RISK.

CREDIT FORWARD A single period OVER-THE-COUNTER

FORWARD contract that generates a payoff based on the difference between an agreed CREDIT SPREAD (or price) and the terminal credit spread (price) of a credit-risky DEBT reference.
- See also CREDIT DERIVATIVE.

CREDIT INVENTORY RISK The RISK of loss arising from a borrower's financial deterioration (reflected in a widening of its CREDIT SPREAD) and/or its failure to perform on an underlying LOAN or BOND obligation (reflected in DEFAULT).
- See also CREDIT DEFAULT RISK, CREDIT SPREAD RISK.

CREDIT MARK-TO-MARKET MODEL An analytic model that is used to determine credit losses based on the probability of a COUNTERPARTY's financial deterioration at various points in time. The MARK-TO-MARKET model considers losses due to both CREDIT SPREAD widening and DEFAULT (which is a single specific and unique state in the model).
- See also CREDIT DEFAULT MODEL, INTENSITY MODEL, STRUCTURAL MODEL.

CREDIT PORTFOLIO MODEL A general model that estimates credit losses arising from deterioration and DEFAULT in credit-risky PORTFOLIOS. Since the model examines portfolio losses, the analytics rely on default CORRELATION estimates between COUNTERPARTIES in the portfolio. A credit portfolio model can be used as a RISK MANAGEMENT, business management, portfolio optimization, and CAPITAL ALLOCATION tool.

CREDIT RATING A measure of an obligor's financial strength based on an assessment of financial standing, performance, and prospects. The rating analysis process focuses on the obligor's earnings, LEVERAGE, LIQUIDITY, capitalization, ASSET quality, funding access, management experience, strategy, competition, and operating environment. A credit rating may be established internally by a firm's own credit department, or through external rating agencies such as Moody's, Standard and Poor's and Fitch IBCA.

CREDIT RESERVE A contra account that is used to fund EXPECTED CREDIT LOSSES. Reserves are established by deducting required amounts from operating revenues or current income, and are used when a COUNTERPARTY ceases to perform on a contractual obligation, such as a LOAN, BOND, payable, or DERIVATIVE.
- See also LOAN LOSS RESERVE.

CREDIT RISK The RISK of loss arising from a COUNTERPARTY's failure to perform on a contractual obligation (CREDIT DEFAULT RISK) or from credit deterioration (CREDIT SPREAD RISK). Credit risk, which is a form of FINANCIAL RISK, can be sub-categorized into CORRELATED CREDIT RISK, CONTINGENT CREDIT RISK,

DIRECT CREDIT RISK, SETTLEMENT RISK, SOVEREIGN RISK (COUNTRY RISK), and TRADING CREDIT RISK.

CREDIT SPREAD (1) A measure of the RISK PREMIUM a credit-risky corporate or sovereign entity must pay to attract CAPITAL. The spread is generally quoted against a risk-free BENCHMARK, such as a GOVERNMENT BOND; the riskier the entity the wider the spread, and the worse the entity's financial condition/performance the larger the spread movements. Credit spreads are widely used in SECONDARY MARKET TRADING and as references for CREDIT DERIVATIVES. (2) Any OPTION SPREAD that results in a net inflow of PREMIUM.
- (1) See also CREDIT SPREAD RISK. (2) see also DEBIT SPREAD.

CREDIT SPREAD OPTION An OVER-THE-COUNTER OPTION that generates a payoff based on the difference between a CREDIT SPREAD (or price) and a predefined STRIKE PRICE. In standard form credit options generate a continuum of payoffs based on credit appreciation or depreciation; a credit option structured in binary form (as a DEFAULT OPTION) generates a payoff based solely on default by the reference credit.
- See also CREDIT DERIVATIVE.

CREDIT SPREAD RISK The RISK of loss arising from a deterioration in an entity's credit quality, generally reflected by a widening in the CREDIT SPREAD.
- See also CREDIT DEFAULT RISK, CREDIT INVENTORY RISK, CREDIT RISK.

CREDIT SUPPORT ANNEX (CSA) An attachment to the MASTER AGREEMENT framework set forth by the INTERNATIONAL SWAPS AND DERIVATIVES ASSOCIATION that defines credit terms between two COUNTERPARTIES, including credit thresholds, COLLATERAL requirements, and credit termination events.

CREDITOR COMMITTEE A group, formed by institutions that have a financial CLAIM on a company that has filed for BANKRUPTCY, which coordinates actions in order to maximize value in LIQUIDATION or approve the company's status as a new entity in REORGANIZATION.

CREEPING TENDER [COL] A CORPORATE FINANCE transaction where an investor group or acquiring company gradually purchases the COMMON STOCK of a target company. Once a specified block has been accumulated a formal TENDER OFFER is made for the balance of the company's shares.

CROSS-ASSET HEDGE A proxy or substitute HEDGE that is used when an exact replicating hedge is not available, generally by identifying a contract (e.g., a DERIVATIVE) that has a high degree of CORRELATION with the

underlying RISK exposure requiring protection. Although a highly correlated cross-asset hedge introduces elements of BASIS RISK, it reduces or eliminates first-order MARKET RISKS, including DIRECTIONAL RISK or VOLATILITY RISK.
- Also known as CROSS HEDGE.

CROSS COLLATERAL AGREEMENT A single COLLATERAL agreement that covers multiple LOANS or credit facilities.
- Also known as DRAGNET CLAUSE.
- See also POOLED PORTFOLIO COLLATERAL, TRANSACTION-SPECIFIC COLLATERAL.

CROSS CURRENCY SWAP See CURRENCY SWAP.

CROSS-DEFAULT CLAUSE A clause in a LOAN, BOND, or DERIVATIVE agreement indicating that a technical DEFAULT on one obligation triggers a technical default in all other obligations. Cross-default clauses are commonly used in credit agreements and MASTER AGREEMENTS.

CROSS GUARANTEE A GUARANTEE provided by one company to another company that is often related, such as a subsidiary or joint venture, and a reciprocal guarantee provided in the opposite direction. Cross guarantees may be highly correlated, meaning the financial performance of one guarantor can improve or deteriorate at the same time as that of the second guarantor; this can magnify any associated CREDIT RISK exposures.
- Also known as PIG ON PORK.
- See also FINANCIAL GUARANTEE.

CROSS HEDGE See CROSS-ASSET HEDGE.

CROSS-MARGIN AGREEMENT An agreement between two or more EXCHANGES that permits MARGIN requirements to be computed on a net, rather than gross, basis. Such an agreement avoids "double counting" of margins for LONG POSITIONS and SHORT POSITIONS, allowing clients to use their ASSETS more efficiently.

CROSS RATE A FOREIGN EXCHANGE rate between two currencies that does not involve the US dollar.

CROSS SHAREHOLDING Minority stakes held by two companies in each other; this is often done to help strengthen long-term business relationships, and is particularly prevalent in RELATIONSHIP MODEL countries such as Germany and Japan.

CROSSED TRADE A practice where ORDERS to buy and sell listed securities are matched ("crossed") without being channeled through an EXCHANGE; once crossed, the details may be reported to the exchange. Crossed trades are not permitted in certain market jurisdictions as they are thought to reduce transparency and leave open the possibility for unfair pricing practices.

CROWN JEWEL DEFENSE [COL] An ANTI-TAKEOVER DEFENSE used by a company seeking to avoid a future HOSTILE TAKEOVER by another company. In the event a hostile takeover is successful the CROWN JEWEL provision in the company's by-laws automatically triggers the sale of valuable corporate assets, leaving the acquiring company with less value than anticipated. By publicizing in advance the existence of a crown jewel provision, a company hopes to deter any potential takeover attempts.

CROWN JEWELS [COL] A company's most productive and/or profitable assets/operations.
- See also CROWN JEWEL DEFENSE.

CRUSH SPREAD [COL] A SPREAD in the GRAINS market reflecting the price differential between soybeans (as feedstock) and soybean oil or soybean meal (the two main by-products); the spread can be traded through a single FUTURE or OPTION contract on certain EXCHANGES. A hedger or speculator can buy the crush spread (e.g., purchase soybeans and sell oil or meal) to take advantage of positive margins, and sell the spread (e.g., sell soybeans and purchase oil or meal) to profit from negative margins.

CSA See CREDIT SUPPORT ANNEX.

CTA See COMMODITY TRADING ADVISOR.

CTD See CHEAPEST-TO-DELIVER.

CUMULATIVE PREFERRED STOCK PREFERRED STOCK that includes a feature allowing any foregone or suspended DIVIDEND payments to automatically accumulate. When the company restarts its program, cumulative preferred stock investors are entitled to receive all accumulated dividends before dividends can be paid to COMMON STOCK or NON-CUMULATIVE PREFERRED STOCK investors.

CUMULATIVE VOTING A form of proportional representation that permits investors to allocate all of their votes in support of a single director or issue; this type of voting can favor MINORITY INTERESTS as it gives them greater ability to concentrate their otherwise limited voting influence.

CURE PERIOD A time frame of 30 to 90 days during which a company that has gone into technical DEFAULT on a contractual payment is permitted to submit payment without further prejudice, and without being considered to have defaulted.
- Also known as GRACE PERIOD.

CURRENCY DERIVATIVE An EXCHANGE-TRADED DERIVATIVE or OVER-THE-COUNTER DERIVATIVE with an UNDERLYING reference based on FOREIGN EXCHANGE rates and flows. A currency derivative can be structured as a currency OPTION, currency forward, CURRENCY FUTURE, CURRENCY SWAP, or CURRENCY WARRANT.

- See also COMMODITY DERIVATIVE, CREDIT DERIVATIVE, EQUITY DERIVATIVE, INTEREST RATE DERIVATIVE.

CURRENCY FUTURE A FUTURES contract, bought or sold via an EXCHANGE, which references a specific FOREIGN EXCHANGE rate. Currency futures are available on both CONVERTIBLE CURRENCIES and select EXOTIC CURRENCIES.
- See also COMMODITY FUTURE, INDEX FUTURE, INTEREST RATE FUTURE.

CURRENCY SWAP An OVER-THE-COUNTER SWAP involving the exchange of two currencies. A typical currency swap involves the exchange of a fixed payment in one currency for a floating payment in a second currency, although the exchange of two fixed or two floating payments can also be arranged. Currency swaps involve the initial and final exchange of principal, which results in a high degree of CREDIT RISK.
- Also known as CROSS CURRENCY SWAP.
- See also CURRENCY DERIVATIVE.

CURRENCY TRANSACTION RISK See TRANSACTION RISK.

CURRENCY TRANSLATION RISK See TRANSLATION RISK.

CURRENCY WARRANT A long-dated currency OPTION (i.e., three to five years) that is typically attached to a BOND (as a BOND WITH WARRANTS). The warrant, which can be detached and traded separately, is generally denominated in a currency that is different from the currency of underlying bond issue and is included to give the issuer a lower overall cost of funding.

CURRENT ACCOUNT (1) The sum of a country's activity in net trade (exports less imports), INVISIBLES, receipts/remittances from abroad, international payment transfers, and gifts. (2) In the United Kingdom, an account with immediate funds access.
- (1) See also BALANCE OF PAYMENTS, CAPITAL ACCOUNT.

CURRENT ASSETS Any ASSET on the balance sheet with a final maturity of less than one year. Common current assets include cash, marketable securities (e.g., BONDS, COMMON STOCK, PREFERRED STOCK, and other investments), INVENTORY, and ACCOUNTS RECEIVABLE. Current assets generally exhibit a high degree of LIQUIDITY and can often be converted into cash very quickly, at a price near carrying value.
- See also CURRENT LIABILITIES, CURRENT RATIO.

CURRENT EXPOSURE METHOD A regulatory method of computing CREDIT RISK on a SWAP under the BANK FOR INTERNATIONAL SETTLEMENT's original 1988 Capital Accord based on the sum of FRACTIONAL EXPOSURE (i.e., POTENTIAL EXPOSURE arising in the future) and ACTUAL EXPOSURE (i.e., the current or MARK-TO-MARKET value of the transaction).

- See also INTERNAL RATINGS BASED APPROACH, ORIGINAL EXPOSURE METHOD.

CURRENT LIABILITIES Any LIABILITY contract on the corporate balance sheet with a final maturity of less than one year. Common current liabilities include COMMERCIAL PAPER, short-term NOTES, REPURCHASE AGREEMENTS, DEPOSITS, ACCOUNTS PAYABLE, and the current portion of medium- and long-term debt; certain deferred taxes and charges may also be included as current liabilities.
- See also CURRENT ASSETS, CURRENT RATIO.

CURRENT RATIO A measure of a company's LIQUIDITY and its ability to meet obligations that are coming due, typically computed as:

$$CR = \frac{CA}{CL}$$

where CA is CURRENT ASSETS and CL is CURRENT LIABILITIES. A current ratio above 1.0 indicates that the company has sufficient CASH FLOW from maturing assets to meet its short-term obligations. A ratio below 1.0 suggests the possibility of greater LIQUIDITY RISK pressures.
- See also QUICK RATIO.

CURRENT YIELD A current measure of the return on a COUPON-bearing FIXED INCOME security, generally computed as:

$$CY = \frac{C}{P}$$

where C is the coupon, and P is the purchase price of the security.
- See also BOND EQUIVALENT YIELD, DISCOUNT YIELD, SIMPLE YIELD, TAXABLE EQUIVALENT YIELD, YIELD TO CALL, YIELD TO MATURITY.

CURVE RISK The RISK of loss arising from a change in the shape of the YIELD CURVE (i.e., the TERM STRUCTURE of INTEREST RATES).

Curve positions	Short rates		Long rates	
	Rising	Falling	Rising	Falling
Long short end, Long long end	Loss	Profit	Loss	Profit
Long short end, Short long end	Loss	Profit	Profit	Loss
Short short end, Long long end	Profit	Loss	Loss	Profit
Short short end, Short long end	Profit	Loss	Profit	Loss

Although curve risk is generally associated with interest rates, it is also evident in other financial variables with a term structure, such as VOLATILITY of interest rates, FOREIGN EXCHANGE rates, and EQUITIES. A sub-category of MARKET RISK.

CUSHION BOND A CALLABLE BOND with a high COUPON that is selling for a PREMIUM. The cushion bond loses less value as rates rise and gains less value when rates fall when compared with a NON-CALLABLE BOND.

CUSTODIAN An AGENT that performs various duties on behalf of a client, including holding securities in safe CUSTODY, executing financial transactions under specific instructions, and collecting periodic CASH FLOWS from investments.

CUSTODY The act of holding securities or other ASSETS in safekeeping for another party. BANKS often provide custody services to their clients, reducing the inefficiency, inconvenience, and possible danger of conveying assets between locations/accounts.

CUSTOMER MARGIN MARGIN posted by a FUTURES COMMISSION MERCHANT or client with a CLEARING MEMBER to cover the requirements of trades that have been executed and temporarily covered by the member's own CLEARING MARGIN.

CUTTING THE MELON [COL] The process of granting current shareholders of a company's COMMON STOCK a SPECIAL DIVIDEND (in shares or cash). The process is periodically used as a means of returning excess capital to investors.

D

D&O COVER See DIRECTORS' AND OFFICERS' INSURANCE COVER.

DAC/RAP See DELIVER AGAINST CASH (DAC)/RECEIVE AGAINST PAYMENT (RAP).

DAIMYO [JPN, COL] A public BOND issued in Japanese yen by a non-Japanese company. Daimyos are generally listed on the Luxembourg Stock Exchange and cleared through Euroclear/Cedel.
- See also GEISHA, SAMURAI, SHIBOSAI, SHOGUN.

DAISY CHAIN [COL] An illegal TRADING scheme where a group of manipulators trade a company's COMMON STOCK among themselves in order to create the illusion of activity. Unsuspecting investors are lured into the scheme and bid prices up further, until a point where the manipulators sell their positions at a profit and leave remaining investors with losses as the market falls. Daisy chains are generally only possible in securities with relatively small float/volume that can be manipulated.
- Also known as PAINTING THE TAPE.
- See also PUMP AND DUMP.

DAWN RAID [COL] A CORPORATE FINANCE tactic where a potential acquirer purchases a substantial block of a target company's COMMON STOCK at the EXCHANGE open, but before the target's management is aware of what is occurring. If the initial raid is successful (i.e., enough shares are acquired at an appropriate price) a formal TAKEOVER is usually launched.
- See also PREMIUM RAID, SATURDAY NIGHT SPECIAL.

DAY COUNT CONVENTION A mechanism for computing COUPON payments/receipts on a FIXED INCOME security. Day count conventions, which vary by instrument, market, and country, are based on the period between coupon payments, the number of days in the month,

and number of the days in the year. The most common conventions include:
- Actual/360, which computes the actual number of days between two coupon dates and assumes the year has 360 days.
- Actual/365, which computes the actual number of days between two coupon dates and assumes the year has 365 days.
- Actual/actual, which computes the actual number of days between two coupon dates and assumes the year has 365 days or 366 days (depending on leap year).
- 30/360, which assumes that each month has 30 days and the year has 360 days (a European version of this modifies the end of month computation).

DAY COUNT NOTE See RANGE FLOATER NOTE.

DAY ORDER A LIMIT ORDER for the purchase or sale of securities that is automatically cancelled if it is not executed during the trading day.
- See also GOOD TILL CANCELLED.

DAY TRADING The process of actively buying and selling securities throughout the day but holding little or no open position at market close; the practice was initially popularized by the advent of ELECTRONIC COMMUNICATIONS NETWORKS and Internet-based TRADING platforms.
- See also SWING TRADING.

DAYLIGHT OVERDRAFT An intraday LOAN created when a BANK transfers funds in excess of its balance held in a reserve account with the CENTRAL BANK. Overdrafts may also occur in the accounts of interbank payment members and in correspondent banks.

DAYLIGHT RISK The RISK of loss arising from failure by a party to a contract to receive, within the same business day, cash or ASSETS after it has already delivered assets or cash to another party.
- See also DELIVERY RISK.

DCF See DISCOUNTED CASH FLOW.

DEAD CAT BOUNCE [COL] A temporary recovery in a market or security following a steady or sharp decline; the recovery is typically fleeting and the downward trajectory generally continues.

DEAD HAND CLAUSE [COL] A provision contained within some POISON PILL defenses preventing the acquisition of the company by another firm even if a majority of shareholders approve of the offer. Only incumbent DIRECTORS can remove the provision.
- Also known as DEAD HAND POISON PILL.

DEAD HAND POISON PILL See DEAD HAND CLAUSE.

DEADWEIGHT DEBT DEBT of a company that is used to fund operating losses or service other debt rather than support productive investment or ACQUISITIONS, or create incremental ENTERPRISE

VALUE. Although the debt is necessary to ensure survival, it can become burdensome unless the underlying ASSETS or operations being financed can be made productive or other borrowings can be reduced.

DEALER An institution acting as a PRINCIPAL, rather than as an AGENT of a customer, in a financial transaction. Dealers may be MARKET MAKERS, quoting two-way markets, or simply position-takers on one side of a market.

- See also BROKER, DEALER MARKET, PRIMARY DEALER.

DEALER MARKET A financial marketplace where activity is restricted to DEALERS acting as PRINCIPALS for their own accounts; BROKERS acting as agents for their clients are not permitted to participate.

- See also AUCTION MARKET.

DEALER MARKET ELECTRONIC COMMUNICATIONS NETWORK (ECN) An ELECTRONIC COMMUNICATIONS NETWORK where clients face a sponsor, rather than other clients, as price-maker and COUNTERPARTY. Dealer market ECNs can be regarded as an electronic mechanism of dealing with a single institution.

- See also HYBRID ELECTRONIC COMMUNICATIONS NETWORK, REGULATED ELECTRONIC COMMUNICATIONS NETWORK.

DEALING OVER TOMORROW See TOM NEXT.

DEATH SPIRAL [COL] A CONVERTIBLE BOND that allows investors to convert their bonds into the issuer's COMMON STOCK at below market prices. Investors can therefore establish SHORT POSITIONS to drive the price of the stock down, obtaining more shares at the time of conversion and using converted proceeds to cover their shorts. A death spiral is typically issued by a company in FINANCIAL DISTRESS that is increasingly desperate for any source of CAPITAL.

- Also known as FLOORLESS CONVERTIBLE.

DEBENTURE (1) In the United States, a medium- to long-term, unsecured BOND. (2) In the United Kingdom, a secured bond with a prior CLAIM on the issuing firm's ASSETS.

DEBIT SPREAD Any OPTION SPREAD that results in a net outflow of PREMIUM.

- See also CREDIT SPREAD.

DEBT Money owed by one party to another party. Debt can take many forms, including ACCOUNTS PAYABLE, BILLS OF EXCHANGE, BONDS, DEPOSITS, DRAFTS, LOANS, NOTES, and REPURCHASE AGREEMENTS, and is generally governed by a contractual agreement that reflects the borrowing party's LIABILITY and the specific obligations that must be met in order to discharge the liability.

DEBT–EQUITY SWAP An exchange of outstanding DEBT for EQUITY between a creditor and a corporate or sovereign debtor in order to ease the debtor's LEVERAGE burden and allow it to remain current on its remaining obligations; the swap is tantamount to a restructuring of the debtor's LIABILITIES. In a sovereign debt-equity swap, the equity allocated to the creditor may be from an unrelated sovereign-owned or controlled entity.

DEBT SERVICE Contractually required CASH FLOWS that a borrower must pay on a LOAN, BOND, LEASE, or other form of DEBT, generally comprised of COUPON interest, a fractional portion of PRINCIPAL (payable into a SINKING FUND), and/or a lease payment.
- See also DEBT SERVICE COVERAGE.

DEBT SERVICE COVERAGE A company's ability to manage its DEBT SERVICE requirement. A company with strong coverage possesses financial strength and flexibility, while one with weak cover is susceptible to FINANCIAL DISTRESS. Debt service coverage is often computed through the FIXED CHARGE COVERAGE ratio.
- See also INTEREST COVERAGE.

DEBTOR-IN-POSSESSION (DIP) A firm filing for BANKRUPTCY protection and REORGANIZATION that is permitted to act as its own TRUSTEE. The DIP typically attempts to secure DIP FINANCING in order to continue its operations while preparing a reorganization plan for court approval.

DEBTOR-IN-POSSESSION (DIP) FINANCING Funding arranged for a company in BANKRUPTCY that is filing a REORGANIZATION plan; the bank group providing DIP financing generally assumes some level of control and/or COLLATERAL in order to protect its new financing commitment.

DECLARATIONS Statements the INSURED makes to the INSURER regarding salient facts needed to arrange an INSURANCE contract. Since the insurer relies on the declarations to UNDERWRITE the RISK of the policy, the information must be accurate in order for the policy to be accepted and remain valid and enforceable.
- See also UBERRIMAE FIDEI.

DEDUCTIBLE The initial amount paid by the INSURED in the event losses are sustained from PERILS covered via an INSURANCE contract. The deductible, which creates a FIRST LOSS position for the insured, can be regarded as SELF-INSURANCE or a RISK RETENTION. The INSURER is only obligated to pay its share of any losses once the deductible has been met.
- Also known as FIRST LOSS RETENTION, SELF-INSURANCE RETENTION.

DEEMED RISK See FRACTIONAL EXPOSURE.

DEEP DISCOUNT BOND Any BOND that is originally issued at a price well below PAR VALUE, such as a ZERO COUPON BOND. DISTRESSED BONDS, which often trade at sharp discounts as a result of perceived or actual problems with the issuer's creditworthiness are not typically considered deep discount bonds as they are usually issued at par.
- See also ORIGINAL ISSUE DISCOUNT.

DEFAULT A state when a corporate, municipal, or sovereign entity fails to meet contractual obligations related to its outstanding LIABILITIES, such as non-payment of PRINCIPAL and/or interest COUPONS, or triggers some other defined EVENT OF DEFAULT. Default may be partial, such as a delay in payments or non-payment only on certain contracts, or total, such as a complete repudiation of all DEBT. Default can create credit losses for those who have extended unsecured funds to the defaulting party; upon default, creditors retain certain rights and may institute FORECLOSURE proceedings or ACCELERATION of contracts.
- See also CREDIT DEFAULT RISK.

DEFAULT OPTION An OVER-THE-COUNTER BINARY OPTION that grants the buyer a payoff if the reference credit DEFAULTS on a specific DEBT obligation; the payoff is equal to the difference between a predefined STRIKE PRICE and the trading level of the COUNTERPARTY's reference debt following default.
- Also known as BINARY CREDIT OPTION.
- See also CREDIT DERIVATIVE, CREDIT SPREAD OPTION.

DEFAULT RISK See CREDIT DEFAULT RISK.

DEFAULT SWAP An OVER-THE-COUNTER SWAP involving the exchange of deferred PREMIUM (often in the form of a floating rate CASH FLOW) for a lump-sum payment if an UNDERLYING reference credit DEFAULTS. The lump-sum payoff associated with the swap, which depends on the quoted price of the defaulted debt, is similar to that of a DEFAULT OPTION.
- See also CREDIT DERIVATIVE.

DEFEASANCE A process where an issuer of a BOND makes periodic COUPON interest payments into a TRUST and separately funds the trust with ASSETS (such as ZERO COUPON BONDS) that will yield sufficient proceeds to retire the bond at maturity. By defeasing the bond, the LIABILITY is carried off-balance sheet.

DEFENSIVE SECURITY Any security that exhibits less volatility than the market as a whole (i.e., its BETA is less than 1.0), providing lower, but more stable, returns. Investors often acquire defensive securities during periods of financial turmoil or uncertainty.

DEFERRED ANNUITY An ANNUITY funded with single or multiple payments that entitles the ANNUITANT to benefits at a future date.

DEFERRED PAYMENT AMERICAN OPTION An OVER-THE-COUNTER AMERICAN OPTION that permits the seller to utilize option proceeds from the time the buyer EXERCISES the contract, until the original maturity of the option. In exchange for relinquishing use of proceeds until maturity, the buyer pays the seller a lower PREMIUM.

DEFERRED STRIKE OPTION An OVER-THE-COUNTER COMPLEX OPTION with a STRIKE PRICE that is set at a future time period, often as a specific function of the SPOT value of the UNDERLYING market reference at that time. Once the strike is established, the contract assumes the form of a standard AMERICAN OPTION or EUROPEAN OPTION.

DEFICIENCY LETTER In the United States, a letter from the SECURITIES AND EXCHANGE COMMISSION to a company planning a NEW ISSUE of securities, indicating that its RED HERRING requires further revisions before REGISTRATION is considered complete and the issue can proceed.

DEFINITIVE SECURITY A DEBT or EQUITY security that is issued in the form of a physical certificate rather than as a dematerialized, electronic computer entry.

　▪ See also BOOK-ENTRY SECURITY, SCRIP.

DEFLATION A general reduction in the price level of goods and services, leading to a state where REAL INTEREST RATES are greater than NOMINAL INTEREST RATES.

　▪ See also INFLATION.

DELEVERAGING See RECAPITALIZATION.

DELIVER AGAINST CASH (DAC)/RECEIVE AGAINST PAYMENT (RAP) See DELIVERY VERSUS PAYMENT.

DELIVERABLE ASSET The specific type and quality of a financial or physical ASSET that can be delivered under the terms of an EXCHANGE-TRADED DERIVATIVE. Many contracts provide the selling party with the ability to select from a range of deliverable assets.

　▪ Also known as DELIVERABLE GRADE.
　▪ See also CHEAPEST TO DELIVER, CONVERSION FACTOR.

DELIVERABLE GRADE See DELIVERABLE ASSET.

DELIVERY The physical provision of an ASSET underlying a financial contract, generally associated with EXCHANGE-TRADED DERIVATIVES (though also applicable to certain OVER-THE-COUNTER DERIVATIVES, particularly those involving commodities). The selling party typically announces its intent to make delivery through a delivery note, which provides details regarding the asset and location.

DELIVERY DATE The specific date(s) during which DELIVERY of a physical ASSET can be made under an EXCHANGE-TRADED

DERIVATIVE. Each contract is governed by specific delivery dates and time periods, spanning from one day to more than a month.

DELIVERY OPTIONS A series of selections that the seller of a FUTURES contract on a US BOND can make that can increase the value of the contract. The delivery options include the quality option (ability to select a specific bond for DELIVERY), the wildcard option (ability to delay announcement of intent to deliver for a period of up to several hours), the ACCRUED INTEREST option (ability to deliver a security with a particular amount of accrued interest), and the end-of-month option (ability to use closing futures prices seven days before month end and deliver the bond at month end).

DELIVERY POINT The specific location where a physical asset referenced through an EXCHANGE-TRADED DERIVATIVE can be accepted for DELIVERY or storage. Each contract is governed by specific dealing locations, including warehouse storage facility, port, or pipeline.

DELIVERY RISK See SETTLEMENT RISK.

DELIVERY VERSUS PAYMENT (DVP) A SETTLEMENT practice in the financial markets where payment, generally in cash, is due to the seller of securities once the buyer has received the securities in its account. If payment is to be made before securities are received, the buyer faces SETTLEMENT RISK.

- Also known as CASH ON DELIVERY, DELIVER AGAINST CASH (DAC)/RECEIVE AGAINST PAYMENT (RAP).

DELTA The change in the value of an OPTION for a change in the value of the UNDERLYING market reference, all other variables held constant. Thus, the value of a purchased CALL OPTION increases as the price of the underlying asset increases, by an amount estimated through delta. Similar determinations can be made for long and SHORT POSITIONS in PUTS and calls. The value of delta is often used as a measure of DIRECTIONAL RISK and can be used to create an appropriate DELTA HEDGE. The deltas of the call and put under the BLACK–SCHOLES MODEL are given by:

$$\Delta_c = \frac{\delta c}{\delta S} = N(d_1)$$

$$\Delta_p = \frac{\delta p}{\delta S} = -N(-d_1)$$

where

$$d_1 = \frac{\ln\left(\frac{S}{X}\right) + \left(r_f \frac{\sigma^2}{2}\right)t}{\sigma\sqrt{t}}$$

and S is the stock price, X is the STRIKE PRICE, t is the time to maturity, r_f is the RISK-FREE RATE, σ^2 is the VARIANCE, and where the N value of $N(d_1)$ can be obtained from a standard table of probability functions.

The deltas of LONG and SHORT puts and calls are given as:

	Long call	Long put	Short call	Short put
Option delta	+	−	−	+

- See also DURATION, GAMMA, GREEKS, VEGA, THETA, RHO.

DELTA HEDGE The process of reducing or neutralizing the exposure of an OPTION to the direction of the market. Delta HEDGING is accomplished by establishing a DELTA-equivalent LONG POSITION or SHORT POSITION in the UNDERLYING reference against a long or short position in the option. Long CALL OPTIONS have a positive delta, i.e., the value of the option increases as the market increases, and can thus be hedged with a delta-equivalent short position in the underlying; short calls have a negative delta and are thus neutralized with a delta-equivalent long position in the underlying. Similar hedges can be constructed for long and short PUT OPTIONS. Delta hedging also works in reverse, where an underlying position can be protected through delta-equivalent positions in options. To remain effective, a delta hedge must be rebalanced as the market moves, which may mean several times per day.

Option position	Option delta	Delta hedge
Long call	+	Delta-equivalent short underlying
Long put	−	Delta-equivalent long underlying
Short call	−	Delta-equivalent long underlying
Short put	+	Delta-equivalent short underlying

DEMAND INFLATION INFLATION that results from an excess of demand, which causes the prices of goods and services to be bid up; the greater the demand, the more aggressive the price increases, and the larger the resulting inflation.
- Also known as DEMAND PULL INFLATION.
- See also COST INFLATION.

DEMAND PULL INFLATION See DEMAND INFLATION.

DEMUTUALIZATION The process of converting a member-owned mutual organization into a public company through the flotation of COMMON STOCK. Once demutualization occurs, members/customers are separate and distinct from owners/investors.

DEPOSIT Funds placed by an individual or institution with a BANK or authorized DEPOSITORY, which are then used to finance operations. Acceptance of the deposit creates a LIABILITY for the accepting bank and requires payment of periodic COUPON interest and return of funds at maturity or on presentation. Deposits can be issued in a variety of forms, including CERTIFICATES OF DEPOSIT, LOCK-UP CERTIFICATES OF DEPOSIT, INTERBANK DEPOSITS, NEGOTIABLE CERTIFICATES OF DEPOSIT, and TIME DEPOSITS, and can be floated in most major currencies with maturities ranging from overnight to 10 years.

DEPOSIT FUTURE An INTEREST RATE FUTURES contract, bought or sold via an EXCHANGE, that references a short-term INTERBANK DEPOSIT rate, such as LIBOR, EURIBOR, or TIBOR.
- See also BILL FUTURE, BOND FUTURE.

DEPOSITARY An AGENT authorized to place funds in a DEPOSITORY institution such as a BANK, SECURITIES FIRM, or SAVINGS AND LOAN.

DEPOSITORY An institution, such as a BANK, SECURITIES FIRM, or SAVINGS AND LOAN, that is authorized to hold funds or securities on behalf of third parties.

DEPOSITORY TRUST COMPANY (DTC) A US company owned by SECURITIES FIRMS that acts as a conduit in the SETTLEMENT of securities transactions. DTC holds ownership records in electronic form, allowing for electronic transfers among buyers and sellers, reducing settlement times and the RISK of operational errors.

DEPRECIATION A decline in the value of a physical corporate ASSET as a result of use, normal "wear and tear," and/or obsolescence. From an accounting perspective depreciation is generally treated as a non-cash expense and the net value of an asset is typically reflected as BOOK VALUE less accumulated depreciation. Depreciation can be computed through one of several different methods depending on the asset, its use and estimated useful life, and the accounting rules of the jurisdiction. Common methods include STRAIGHT LINE DEPRECIATION and ACCELERATED DEPRECIATION.

DERIVATIVE A financial contract that derives its value from a specific market reference, such as a COMMON STOCK, index, INTEREST RATE, commodity, or currency. Contracts are available as customized OVER-THE-COUNTER DERIVATIVES, including SWAPS, FORWARDS, OPTIONS, COMPLEX OPTIONS, COMPLEX SWAPS, and STRUCTURED NOTES with EMBEDDED OPTIONS, and standardized EXCHANGE-TRADED DERIVATIVES, including FUTURES, options, and FUTURES OPTIONS. Derivatives are commonly used to HEDGE, SPECULATE, and ARBITRAGE.
- See also COMMODITY DERIVATIVE, CREDIT DERIVATIVE,

CURRENCY DERIVATIVE, EQUITY DERIVATIVE, INTEREST RATE DERIVATIVE.

DERIVATIVE LAWSUIT A legal action where one or more shareholders sue the CORPORATION to bring suit against the corporation's BOARD OF DIRECTORS or executives for breach of duties.

■ See also DIRECT LAWSUIT.

DERIVATIVE PRODUCT COMPANY (DPC) A highly rated, BANKRUPTCY-remote SPECIAL PURPOSE ENTITY used by certain financial institutions to undertake DERIVATIVE transactions with COUNTERPARTIES demanding strong CREDIT RATINGS. Through design mechanics based on minimum CAPITAL, COLLATERAL, HEDGING, and DIVERSIFICATION, the DPC can often achieve AAA ratings, even if the sponsoring institution's ratings are below that level. DPCs are capital-intensive and generally only suitable for institutions with sufficiently low INVESTMENT GRADE CREDIT RATINGS that they cannot attract enough business without credit enhancement.

DESCENDING BOTTOM A TECHNICAL ANALYSIS charting figure depicting a declining securities price or index value over time, with ever-lower levels, generally considered to be a bearish signal.

■ See also ASCENDING TOP, FALLING TOP, RISING BOTTOM.

DESCENDING TOP See FALLING TOP.

DEVALUATION A sudden, and often large, decrease in the value of a national currency, arranged by a country's CENTRAL BANK or monetary authority in response to severe macroeconomic pressures, financial instability, speculative inflows/outflows, or capital imbalances. Once a currency has been devalued, its purchasing power in terms of other currencies declines, making exports cheaper abroad and imports more expensive domestically; this helps improve the country's

BALANCE OF TRADE. Currency devaluation, a manifestation of SOVEREIGN RISK, is distinct from more gradual currency depreciation, which generally arises from the interaction of free market forces over a period of time.

DIFFERENCE IN CONDITIONS INSURANCE INSURANCE coverage for physical structures, equipment, and inventory against CATASTROPHIC HAZARD (although certain EXCLUSIONS for fire and vandalism are common).
- Also known as PARASOL POLICY.

DIFFERENCE OPTION See SPREAD OPTION.

DIFFERENTIAL SWAP An OVER-THE-COUNTER COMPLEX SWAP involving a single currency exchange of floating INTEREST RATE references denominated in two different currencies (e.g., dollar LIBOR versus EURIBOR, payable in dollars). The swap permits an institution to express a view on foreign interest rate movements without assuming currency RISK.
- Also known as a QUANTO SWAP.

DIFFUSION AND AMORTIZATION EFFECT A concept indicating that the maximum CREDIT RISK of an INTEREST RATE SWAP occurs one-third to half-way through the life of a transaction. This occurs because simulated future INTEREST RATES used in the calculation of REPLACEMENT COST do not have a chance to move sufficiently in the early periods of a swap to pose the greatest economic loss (i.e., the 'diffusion' effect), and insufficient payments remain to be made toward the end of the swap to pose the greatest economic loss (i.e., the 'amortization' effect).

DIFFUSION PROCESS A continuous, STOCHASTIC PROCESS where the market variable (e.g., a COMMON STOCK price or FOREIGN EXCHANGE rate) exists in continuous time and its probability density function is continuous; the variable changes on a random and continuous basis, and as the time interval becomes larger, uncertainty in the returns increases in a predictable fashion. The diffusion process is widely used in modeling the value of certain financial contracts, such as DERIVATIVES.

DIGITAL OPTION See BINARY OPTION.

DILUTION The act of reducing the proportion of ownership held by current investors through issuance of new shares of COMMON STOCK (or through the exercise of outstanding stock OPTIONS or the conversion of CONVERTIBLE BONDS). In order to protect investors against dilution from new issuance, a company may choose to float a RIGHTS ISSUE, giving existing shareholders the right of first refusal in taking up new shares.
- See also FULLY DILUTED BASIS.

DIP FINANCING See DEBTOR-IN-POSSESSION FINANCING.

DIRECT CREDIT RISK The RISK of loss due to DEFAULT by a COUNTERPARTY on a direct extension of credit, such as a LOAN or DEPOSIT. Default on an unsecured direct credit risk transaction always results in a loss for the credit provider; this is in contrast to a situation involving TRADING CREDIT RISK, where the value of the contract may be in favor of the counterparty at the time of default. A sub-category of CREDIT RISK.
- See also CONTINGENT CREDIT RISK, CORRELATED CREDIT RISK, SETTLEMENT RISK, SOVEREIGN RISK.

DIRECT LAWSUIT A legal action where one or more shareholders sue DIRECTORS or executives directly, rather than through the CORPORATION, for breach of duties.
- See also DERIVATIVE LAWSUIT.

DIRECT LOSS In INSURANCE, a loss where the covered PERIL is the PROXIMATE CAUSE of damage. PROPERTY AND CASUALTY INSURANCE policies often limit protection to direct loss rather than direct loss and CONSEQUENTIAL LOSS.

DIRECT PAY LETTER OF CREDIT A LETTER OF CREDIT facility where a BANK automatically pays the BENEFICIARY an agreed amount and then seeks repayment from the underlying customer that has drawn the letter of credit; the beneficiary thus never faces the customer's CREDIT RISK.
- See also CONFIRMED LETTER OF CREDIT, IRREVOCABLE LETTER OF CREDIT, STANDBY LETTER OF CREDIT, TRANSFERABLE LETTER OF CREDIT.

DIRECT PLACEMENT The placement of a NEW ISSUE of securities by a company directly with an institutional investor, without the use of a financial intermediary. A direct placement, which can theoretically involve any type of security but in practice tends to involve DEBT issues, serves as an example of DISINTERMEDIATION. In general, only the largest companies directly place their securities, as the process requires name recognition and strong financial standing in order to attract a suitable base of investors.
- See also DIRECT PUBLIC OFFERING.

DIRECT PUBLIC OFFERING (DPO) A DIRECT PLACEMENT of COMMON STOCK that is offered by a company to investors, customers, and/or suppliers, without the use of an UNDERWRITER. Given the limited ability for companies to directly place their own shares and then encourage financial intermediaries to produce EQUITY research and quote SECONDARY MARKETS, DPOs are relatively uncommon.

DIRECT STAKEHOLDERS In GOVERNANCE, the parties most

immediately and directly impacted by a company's activities, prospects and actions, generally taken to include shareholders, creditors, employees, customers, suppliers, professional service providers, and communities.
- See also INDIRECT STAKEHOLDERS.

DIRECT WRITER An INSURER that writes INSURANCE policies through a direct selling process or an exclusive AGENCY arrangement, or a REINSURER that accepts ceded RISKS directly from other insurers rather than REINSURANCE BROKERS.

DIRECTIONAL RISK The RISK of loss arising from exposure to the direction of a reference ASSET or market. An investor holding a LONG POSITION experiences a loss if market prices fall and a gain if they rise; one holding a SHORT POSITION generates a gain when market prices fall and a loss as they rise. A sub-category of MARKET RISK.
- See also DELTA, GAMMA.

DIRECTIONAL STRATEGY An OPTION STRATEGY that seeks to take advantage of expected market direction rather than VOLATILITY to generate a profit. Common directional strategies include BULL SPREADS and BEAR SPREADS.
- See also VOLATILITY STRATEGY.

DIRECTOR An individual acting as AGENT of the shareholders of a company. A director is responsible, along with other members of the BOARD OF DIRECTORS, for overseeing the activities of the executive management team and exercising DUTY OF CARE and DUTY OF LOYALTY in protecting the interests of shareholders.
- See also EXECUTIVE DIRECTOR, INSIDE DIRECTOR, LEAD INDEPENDENT DIRECTOR, NON-EXECUTIVE DIRECTOR, OUTSIDE DIRECTOR.

DIRECTOR AND OFFICER (D&O) INSURANCE COVER INSURANCE coverage designed to protect the interests of DIRECTORS and executives from possible losses arising from shareholder lawsuits (except those related to FRAUD).

DIRTY FLOAT [COL] A situation where a CENTRAL BANK or monetary authority does not adjust the nation's money supply to offset any changes caused by active intervention in the FOREIGN EXCHANGE markets. The dirty float may ultimate result in INFLATION and an economic slowdown.
- See also STERILIZATION.

DIRTY PRICE [COL] The price of a BOND inclusive of ACCRUED INTEREST. Most SECONDARY MARKET bond transactions are based on dirty prices.
- See also CLEAN PRICE, INVOICE PRICE.

DIRTY STOCK [COL] Transferred COMMON STOCK that fails to convey good title to the new buyer as a result of errors or omissions in form or authorization.

DISAPPEARING DEDUCTIBLE A DEDUCTIBLE on an INSURANCE contract that the INSURED is not obligated to cover if losses exceed a particular threshold. If the threshold is breached the INSURER pays the insured a CLAIM that includes the original amount of the deductible, causing it to "disappear." If the threshold is not breached the policy functions as any normal insurance contract with a deducible.

DISASTER RECOVERY RISK The RISK of loss arising from damage to physical infrastructure – which prohibits use of real estate, plant and equipment, technology and communications – leading to a halt in operations; the disaster may be firm-specific, industry-based, regional, or system-wide. Disaster recovery risks can often be covered through specific BUSINESS INTERRUPTION INSURANCE. A sub-category of PROCESS RISK.
   See also BUSINESS RECOVERY RISK.

DISCOUNT RATE (1) A company's COST OF CAPITAL, often used to determine ENTERPRISE VALUE or the NET PRESENT VALUE of an investment opportunity. It is generally computed as the sum of a RISK-FREE RATE and an appropriate RISK PREMIUM. (2) The INTEREST RATE charged by the FEDERAL RESERVE BANKS for LOANS taken by member banks through the DISCOUNT WINDOW; the rate need not be the same across all 12 Federal Reserve Banks. (3) The interest rate charged by ACCEPTANCE HOUSES or BANKS when accepting a BILL OF EXCHANGE or BANKER'S ACCEPTANCE. (4) The SPOT RATE of interest.

DISCOUNT SWAP An OVER-THE-COUNTER NON-PAR SWAP where the receiver of fixed INTEREST RATES is granted an upfront payment by the floating rate payer in exchange for accepting a lower ongoing fixed rate inflow.
   See also PREMIUM SWAP.

DISCOUNT WINDOW In the United States, a facility made available by the FEDERAL RESERVE BANKS that permits authorized BANKS to borrow short-term funds on an emergency basis in order to balance cash outflows.

DISCOUNT YIELD The effective YIELD of any FIXED INCOME instrument issued on a discount, rather than COUPON-bearing, basis, generally computed as:

$$DY = \frac{(Face - P)}{Face}\left(\frac{360}{n_{MAT}}\right)$$

where *Face* is FACE VALUE, *P* is purchase price, and n_{MAT} is the number of days until maturity.
- See also BOND EQUIVALENT YIELD, SIMPLE YIELD, TAXABLE EQUIVALENT YIELD, YIELD TO CALL, YIELD TO MATURITY.

DISCOUNTED CASH FLOW A financial measurement technique used to evaluate the worth of capital investments, ACQUISITIONS, or other projects involving cash inflows and outflows over time. Net CASH FLOWS are discounted at a company's COST OF CAPITAL in order to crystallize the economic impact in current terms.
- See also INTERNAL RATE OF RETURN, NET PRESENT VALUE.

DISCRETE BARRIER OPTION See PARTIAL BARRIER OPTION.

DISCRETIONARY ACCOUNT A customer brokerage account where the client gives the BROKER authorization to act on his/her behalf in buying and selling securities. The client may limit the discretion granted through time and/or price constraints.

DISCRIMINATING MONOPOLY A state where a company with MONOPOLY power charges different prices in different markets, according to the characteristics of each market. This presumes the monopolist can clearly identify the source of demand in each market and can properly gauge PRICE ELASTICITY; if it can, it may be able to maximize its profitability.

DISENFRANCHISE The process of removing voting rights from a class of COMMON STOCK so that investors in that class are only entitled to RENT RIGHTS.
- See also DISENFRANCHISING TRANSACTION.

DISENFRANCHISING TRANSACTION A financial restructuring transaction, such as a DUAL CLASS RECAPITALIZATION, that removes voting rights from certain COMMON STOCK investors.

DISINTERMEDIATION The process of removing financial institutions, including BANKS, INVESTMENT BANKS, and SECURITIES FIRMS, from their traditional function in intermediating between suppliers and providers of CAPITAL and providing investment and CORPORATE FIANCE advice. If borrowers and investors/lenders can properly identify each other and disintermediate traditional providers, borrowers may be able to realize a cheaper COST OF CAPITAL and investors a greater return, as neither party will be required to pay implicit or explicit intermediation fees. Equally, if companies can arrange their own MEGERS or ACQUISITIONS, intermediaries can be excluded from the role and costs can be reduced. Disintermediation occurs in certain financing and corporate finance transactions, although the overall scope and volume are limited.

DISTRESSED ASSET An ASSET, generally a security or real property, that features a sharply reduced value as a result of actual or potential losses created by an excess of CREDIT RISK, MARKET RISK, or LIQUIDITY RISK. Securities, LOANS, or MORTGAGES of obligors that are at high risk of DEFAULT and those that contain significant amounts of LEVERAGE or ILLIQUIDITY may trade at deep discounts that are characteristic of distressed assets. VULTURE FUNDS and other sophisticated institutional investors periodically invest in such assets.
- See also FIRE SALE.

DISTRESSED FUND See VULTURE FUND.

DIVERSIFIABLE RISK A RISK that is unique to a company, ASSET, or market, meaning that it can be reduced or eliminated by holding a PORTFOLIO of assets that are uncorrelated.

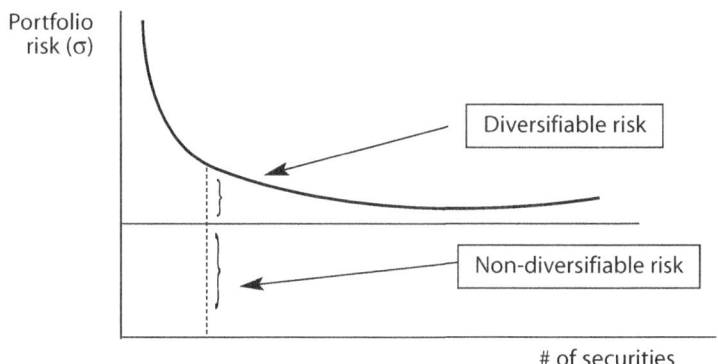

- Also known as IDIOSYNCRATIC RISK, UNSYSTEMATIC RISK.
- See also DIVERSIFICATION, NON-DIVERSIFIABLE RISK.

DIVERSIFICATION A spreading or dispersion of RISK, achievable by combining ASSETS or exposures that are not CORRELATED with one another; the process of diversification helps minimize concentrations of exposure and creates a more balanced set of risks. Ultimately, the risk of a diversified PORTFOLIO depends on the amount of risk that cannot be eliminated, i.e., NON-DIVERSIFIABLE RISK, which is often measured by BETA, or the sensitivity of an investment's return compared to the market. The variability of returns for a given security can thus be divided into diversifiable and non-diversifiable components:

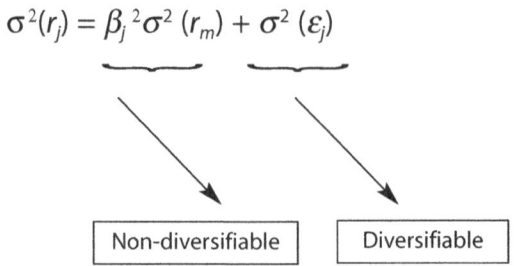

where β_j^2 is the square of the beta of security j, $\sigma^2(r_m)$ is the VARIANCE of the market portfolio, and $\sigma^2(\varepsilon_j)$ is the RESIDUAL VARIANCE of security j.
- See also DIVERSIFIABLE RISK, NON-DIVERSIFIABLE RISK, PORTFOLIO DIVERSIFICATION.
- Additional references: Markowitz (1952), Ross (1976), Sharpe (1971).

DIVESTITURE A CORPORATE FINANCE transaction where a company sells a subsidiary or a portion of its operations to a third party. A divestiture typically occurs when the company no longer views the ASSETS as essential to its business, prefers to refocus its operations more narrowly, or needs to raise funds for other purposes.
- See also CARVE-OUT.

DIVIDED COVER INSURANCE contracts on the same property and PERIL purchased by the INSURED from two or more INSURERS. The total SETTLEMENT will never exceed the amount of the loss, and will be divided on a PRO-RATA basis between insurers.
- See also APPORTIONMENT, OVERLAPPING INSURANCE, PRIMACY.

DIVIDEND A periodic amount a company pays from its net earnings to COMMON STOCK and/or PREFERRED STOCK investors; dividend payments are generally discretionary, meaning they can be suspended at will, though in certain instances they are made mandatory through terms of the securities issue. In most systems the BOARD OF DIRECTORS is responsible for setting dividend policy.
- See also DIVIDEND YIELD, PAYOUT RATIO.

DIVIDEND COVER See PAYOUT RATIO.

DIVIDEND DISCOUNT MODEL A quantitative measure used to estimate the fair value of a COMMON STOCK based on the discounted value of projected future DIVIDENDS. The price of a firm's stock can be estimated via:

$$S = \sum_{i=1}^{n} \frac{Div_i}{(1+r)^i}$$

where Div_i is the projected dividend payable in period i, r is the firm's DISCOUNT RATE, and n is the number of periods.

Value can also be estimated through growth and dividend assumptions: No growth and constant dividend:

$$S = \frac{Div_i}{r}$$

Growth and constant dividend:

$$S = \frac{Div_i}{r - g}$$

where g is the dividend growth rate and all other terms are as defined above.

- Additional references: J. Lintner (1956), M.Miller and F. Modigliani (1961).

DIVIDEND IN ARREARS A DIVIDEND that has accumulated for one or more payment periods and is payable to the current holders of CUMULATIVE PREFERRED STOCK. Dividends cannot be paid to COMMON STOCK or NON-CUMULATIVE PREFERRED STOCK investors until the arrears have been made current.

DIVIDEND YIELD The effective YIELD of a share of COMMON STOCK, typically calculated as:

$$y_{Div} = \frac{Div_i}{S_i}$$

where Div_i is the DIVIDEND paid in period i and S_i is the price of the stock in period i.

- See also PAYOUT RATIO.

DJIA See DOW JONES INDUSTRIAL AVERAGE.

DK [COL] Abbreviated form of "don't know," meaning one of the parties to a transaction disputes, refutes, or claims not to know, certain details of a trade. A trade that has been "DK'd" remains unreconciled until one of the parties concedes to a change in details or it is cancelled.

- Also known as OUT TRADE, QUESTIONED TRADE.

DOCUMENTARY CREDIT A commercial LETTER OF CREDIT committing the BANK to pay a named BENEFICIARY, such as a seller of goods, once a confirming document has been delivered to the buyer; the documentary credit is widely used in international trade transactions, where BILLS OF LADING often serve as the evidencing document.

- Also known as DOCUMENTARY DRAFT.

DOCUMENTARY DRAFT See DOCUMENTARY CREDIT.

DOG AND PONY SHOW [COL] See ROADSHOW.

DOLLAR ROLL A financial transaction involving the sale, and future repurchase, of MORTGAGE-BACKED SECURITIES for cash. Through the exchange the selling party effectively borrows money from the purchasing party on a collateralized basis for a period that normally covers several days to several weeks. The dollar roll is essentially a form of mortgage-backed REPURCHASE AGREEMENT.

DOUBLE AUCTION MARKET An AUCTION MARKET featuring multiple sellers and buyers, who have full transparency into dealings. In the double auction process the first BID or OFFER is given priority, the high bid and low offer take precedence, and a new auction begins when all bids and offers at a given price are successfully matched. Certain stock EXCHANGES use a form of the double auction to match buyers and sellers.

DOUBLE BOTTOM A TECHNICAL ANALYSIS charting formation that depicts two SUPPORT LEVELS followed by a BREAKOUT. The multiple rebounds are indicative of support and possible strength on the upside.

- Also known as a W FORMATION.
- See also DOUBLE TOP.

DOUBLE DIPPING [COL] An unethical (and sometimes illegal) practice where a BROKER sells commission-based products through a client's fee-based account, earning revenues from two sources and effectively overcharging the client.

DOUBLE LEVERAGE Borrowing at multiple levels within the corporate structure, such as the holding company and a primary operating subsidiary. Double leverage is generally considered to be a more accurate reflection of a group's true indebtedness as it incorporates LIABILITIES from multiple entities.

- See also STRUCTURAL SUBORDINATION.

DOUBLE RECOVERY An illegal attempt by an INSURED to file multiple CLAIMS on a single loss event with multiple INSURERS. Double recovery violates the principle of INDEMNITY, which states that an INSURANCE contract cannot result in a profit for the insured.

DOUBLE TOP A TECHNICAL ANALYSIS charting formation that depicts two RESISTANCE LEVELS followed by a BREAKOUT. The multiple declines suggest resistance on the upside and possible weakness on the downside.

- Also known as a REVERSE W FORMATION.
- See also DOUBLE BOTTOM.

DOUBLING OPTION A right granted by investors to an issuer of BONDS that allows the issuer to double the amount of the SINKING FUND provision in order to accelerate repayment and ultimate redemption.

DOW JONES INDUSTRIAL AVERAGE (DJIA) A BENCHMARK price-weighted index of the US stock market, comprised of 30 LARGE CAP STOCKS representing the industrial sector; the index is rebalanced periodically as industries and corporate leadership change. The DJIA, which is the oldest and most widely quoted US index, can be traded directly through EXCHANGE-TRADED FUNDS and DERIVATIVES.

DOWN AND IN OPTION A COMPLEX OPTION that creates a standard EUROPEAN OPTION if the price of the UNDERLYING market reference declines through a predefined BARRIER.
- See also BARRIER OPTION, DOWN AND OUT OPTION, KNOCK-IN OPTION, REVERSE KNOCK-IN OPTION, UP AND IN OPTION, UP AND OUT OPTION.

DOWN AND OUT OPTION A COMPLEX OPTION that extinguishes a standard EUROPEAN OPTION if the price of the UNDERLYING market reference declines through a predefined BARRIER. If the barrier is not breached the European option remains in effect.
- See also BARRIER OPTION, DOWN AND IN OPTION, KNOCK-OUT OPTION, REVERSE KNOCK-OUT OPTION, UP AND IN OPTION, UP AND OUT OPTION.

DOWN ROUND [COL] A second, third or fourth round of VENTURE CAPITAL financing that is done at lower valuation levels than early rounds, suggesting the company may be worth less than initially predicted.

DOWNTICK See MINUS TICK.

DPC See DERIVATIVE PRODUCT COMPANY.

DPO See DIRECT PUBLIC OFFERING.

DRAFT See BILL OF EXCHANGE.

DRAG ALONG RIGHTS Legal rights that allow majority shareholders of a company to force MINORITY INTERESTS to sell their shares in the event of a TAKEOVER bid; this is necessary in situations where the acquiring company requires 100 percent control. Drag along rights must be specifically negotiated in a CORPORATE FINANCE transaction.
- See also TAG ALONG RIGHTS.

DRAGON [COL] A public BOND issued simultaneously in various Asian centers by a non-Asian company, denominated in a local Asian currency or US dollars. The dragon is effectively a regional form of the GLOBAL BOND.

DRAGNET CLAUSE See CROSS COLLATERAL AGREEMENT.

DROP LOCK A mechanism where the INTEREST RATE on a FLOATING RATE NOTE or BOND is fixed once rates fall below a predefined level. The drop lock allows the issuer to lock in a lower rate of funding.
- See also DROP LOCK NOTE, SPREAD LOCK.

DROP LOCK NOTE A FLOATING RATE NOTE or BOND that converts into a fixed COUPON obligation when a reference INTEREST RATE is breached on the downside.
- See also DROP LOCK.

DROPDOWN A clause in a REINSURANCE contract that requires the REINSURER to provide coverage to an underlying INSURED if the INSURER cannot fulfill its obligations under the policy CEDED. A dropdown is most common in a FACULTATIVE REINSURANCE agreement where individual policies are analyzed and accepted.

DRY POWDER [COL] Cash RESERVES held on the corporate balance sheet for future investments, ACQUISITIONS, or LIQUIDITY needs.

DTC See DEPOSITORY TRUST COMPANY.

DUAL BOARD SYSTEM A corporate system where two separate BOARDS OF DIRECTORS are used to monitor and guide a company. Under a typical dual structure the SUPERVISORY BOARD is responsible for strategy and oversight/supervision of management, while the MANAGEMENT BOARD (or EXECUTIVE BOARD) is responsible for daily management and tactical issues. The supervisory board is generally staffed with OUTSIDE DIRECTORS, while the management board is comprised of senior executives.

■ See also SINGLE BOARD SYSTEM.

DUAL CLASS RECAPITALIZATION A restructuring of a company's existing COMMON STOCK into two classes with variable voting rights; creating a new class that conveys less than one vote per share is considered a DISENFRANCHISING TRANSACTION. A dual class recapitalization might be arranged to give a block of controlling shareholders even greater control over the firm.

DUAL CURRENCY BOND A BOND that pays interest COUPONS in one currency and PRINCIPAL redemption in a second currency. The exchange rates associated with the coupon and principal cash flows may be specified at the time of issuance, or they may be based on prevailing SPOT RATES at the time the coupons and principal are paid. A company may choose to issue a dual currency bond to HEDGE any FOREIGN EXCHANGE flows from its operations, or take a speculative view on currencies in order to obtain a lower COST OF CAPITAL.

DUAL PURPOSE FUND A MUTUAL FUND or UNIT TRUST that issues two separate types of securities, including income shares, which are entitled only to the DIVIDEND flows from the underlying securities, and capital shares, which are entitled only to any resulting capital gains.

DUAL TRIGGER An INSURANCE mechanism that provides the INSURED with a payout only if two separate TRIGGER events occur. One trigger is often related to a traditional insurable OPERATING RISK (e.g., damage or destruction in plant and equipment leading to business interruption), while the second may relate to a FINANCIAL RISK (e.g., a decline in operating revenues to a particular amount, or a fall in the stock price to a certain level). Since both events must occur in order for a SETTLEMENT to be paid, the PREMIUM is generally lower than on a conventional insurance contract.

■ See also MULTIPLE TRIGGER PRODUCTS, TRIPLE TRIGGER.

DUE DILIGENCE A process of detailed financial investigation into a company's operations and financial position, generally conducted by financial intermediaries, lawyers, and accountants. Due diligence is commonly performed in advance of NEW ISSUE UNDERWRITINGS and CORPORATE FINANCE transactions, and to develop FAIRNESS OPINIONS; results are intended to inform and protect investors and corporate DIRECTORS by verifying the financial condition of the subject company.

DUOPOLY A market that only features two sellers of goods or services, suggesting the sellers have a considerable degree of influence in setting prices.

■ See also DUOPSONY, MONOPOLY, OLIGOPOLY.

DUOPSONY A market that only features two buyers of goods or services, suggesting the buyers have an ability to influence the prices paid to suppliers.

- See also DUOPOLY, MONOPSONY, OLIGOPSONY.

DURATION The average CASH FLOWS of an INTEREST RATE sensitive ASSET or LIABILITY, takings account of YIELD, interest payments, maturity, and CALLABILITY. Duration quantifies the change in the price of a security for a small change in yield (e.g., the linear effects of market changes); the greater the duration, the more sensitive the price to changes in yield, the riskier the instrument. Securities with longer maturities or lower coupons have longer durations, which become even longer as yield declines. Duration is commonly used to estimate profit and loss on a bond, quantify INTEREST RATE RISK exposure, and create fixed income DELTA HEDGES. The standard dollar duration calculation for a semi-annual pay security is given as:

$$Dur = -\frac{1}{(1+y)}\left[\frac{1C}{(1+y)^1} + \frac{2C}{(1+y)^2} + \ldots + \frac{nC}{(1+y)^n} + \frac{nM}{(1+y)^n}\right]$$

where C is semi-annual coupon interest, y is the semi-annual yield, n is the number of semi-annual periods, and M is the maturity value of the bond (generally PAR VALUE).

The same calculation is often expressed as a percentage price change:

$$Dur\ (\%) = -\frac{1}{(1+y)}\left[\frac{1C}{(1+y)^1} + \frac{2C}{(1+y)^2} + \ldots + \frac{nC}{(1+y)^n} + \frac{nM}{(1+y)^n}\right]\frac{1}{P}$$

where P is the price of the bond.

Extensions of the duration formula include Macaulay's duration, computed as:

$$Dur\ (Mac) = \frac{\sum_{i=1}^{n}\frac{iC}{(1+y)^i} + \frac{nM}{(1+y)^n}}{P}$$

and MODIFIED DURATION, calculated as:

$$Dur\ (Mod) = \frac{Dur\ (Mac)}{(1+y)}$$

or:

$$Dur\ (Mod) = \frac{\frac{C}{y^2}\left[1 - \frac{1}{(1+y)^n}\right] + \frac{n\left(100 - \frac{C}{y}\right)}{(1+y)^{n+1}}}{P}$$

- See also DELTA, CONVEXITY.

DUTCH AUCTION An AUCTION MARKET technique used in certain marketplaces where the price of a security or ASSET being sold is lowered until a BID is obtained; the remaining orders are then filled at the same price.
- See also ENGLISH AUCTION.

DUTCH AUCTION PREFERRED STOCK ADJUSTABLE RATE PREFERRED STOCK with a floating DIVIDEND that is reset every 49 days through a DUTCH AUCTION process.
- Also known as AUCTION RATE PREFERRED STOCK.

DUTY OF CARE A legal requirement in certain systems where the BOARD OF DIRECTORS and executives must make informed decisions in discharging their FIDUCIARY responsibilities. An informed decision is generally based on gathering all relevant facts and material, giving such information due consideration, and then making a decision. A breach of duty of care can lead to legal action by shareholders.
- See also DUTY OF LOYALTY.

DUTY OF LOYALTY A legal requirement in certain systems where the BOARD OF DIRECTORS and executives must ensure that any action taken is done in good faith and with the best interests of shareholders in mind. A breach of duty of loyalty can lead to legal action by shareholders.
- See also DUTY OF CARE.

DVP See DELIVERY VERSUS PAYMENT.

DWARF [COL] A 15 year MORTGAGE-BACKED SECURITY issued by the FEDERAL NATIONAL MORTGAGE ASSOCIATION.
- See also GNOME, MIDGET.

E

E-TICKET See ELECTRONIC TICKET.

EARNED SURPLUS See RETAINED EARNINGS.

EARNINGS PER SHARE (EPS) The amount of net income earned by a company, after PREFERRED STOCK DIVIDENDS have been distributed, which is attributable to each outstanding share of COMMON STOCK. The EPS measure is used as a reflection of earnings power and corporate value; it is typically calculated on a FULLY DILUTED BASIS, which assumes that all outstanding stock OPTIONS are exercised, and any outstanding CONVERTIBLE BONDS are exchanged into new shares. The general computation is given as:

$$EPS = \frac{NI - Div_{pref}}{CS_{O/S}}$$

where NI is net after-tax income, Div_{pref} is preferred stock dividends, and $CS_{O/S}$ is the weighted average common stock shares outstanding (including those associated with options and convertible bonds for a fully-diluted calculation).

EARNINGS BEFORE INTEREST AND TAXES (EBIT) A commonly used measure of a company's core operating profitability. By removing interest and taxes, the analysis focuses on a company's ability to generate revenues and manage production costs and non-cash expenses associated with DEPRECIATION and AMORTIZATION.
- See also EARNINGS BEFORE INTEREST, TAXES, DEPRECIATION AND AMORTIZATION.

EARNINGS BEFORE INTEREST, TAXES, DEPRECIATION AND AMORTIZATION (EBITDA) A commonly used measure of a company's core operating profitability. By removing interest, taxes, DEPRECIATION, and AMORTIZATION, the analysis focuses on a company's ability to generate revenues and manage its production costs.

- See also EARNINGS BEFORE INTEREST AND TAXES.

EBIT See EARNINGS BEFORE INTEREST AND TAXES.

EBITDA See EARNINGS BEFORE INTEREST, TAXES, DEPRECIATION AND AMORTIZATION.

EBRD See EUROPEAN BANK FOR RECONSTRUCTION AND DEVELOPMENT.

ECB See EUROPEAN CENTRAL BANK.

ECN See ELECTRONIC COMMUNICATIONS NETWORK.

ECONOMIC CAPITAL CAPITAL resources that a company allocates internally to conduct its operations and support its RISKS (including FINANCIAL RISK and OPERATING RISK). Economic capital, which is a key measure of SOLVENCY, serves to absorb unexpected losses and allow a firm to continue its operations.
- Also known as MANAGEMENT CAPITAL.
- See also CAPITAL ALLOCATION, REGULATORY CAPITAL, RISK CAPITAL, TIER 1 CAPITAL, TIER 2 CAPITAL.

ECONOMIC VALUE See ENTERPRISE VALUE.

ECP See EURO COMMERCIAL PAPER.

ECU See EUROPEAN CURRENCY UNIT.

EDGE ACT BANK A US banking entity, owned by a state or nationally-chartered BANK, with an international business scope. Edge Act banks are authorized to operate interstate branches, accept DEPOSITS from offshore sources, invest in foreign securities and projects, and grant foreign LOANS.
- See also INTERNATIONAL BANKING FACILITY.

EFFECTIVE RATE The actual INTEREST RATE a BANK charges on a LOAN, after taking into account fees and COMPENSATING BALANCE requirements.
- See also EFFECTIVE YIELD.

EFFECTIVE SPREAD The actual difference between the BID and OFFER of a securities transaction, incorporating the direction of price movements.
- See also QUOTED SPREAD, REALIZED SPREAD.

EFFECTIVE YIELD The actual INTEREST RATE an investor earns on an investment after taking into account fees, actual price paid, and AMORTIZATION of PRINCIPAL or ACCRETION OF DISCOUNT.
- See also EFFECTIVE RATE.

EFFICIENT FRONTIER In the CAPITAL ASSET PRICING MODEL, a boundary defined by investment PORTFOLIOS that provide investors with the maximum possible return for a given level of RISK.
- See also CAPITAL MARKET LINE, SECURITIES MARKET LINE.

EFFICIENT MARKET HYPOTHESIS A theory stating that financial

markets reflect all publicly available information, suggesting that all investors have an equal opportunity to earn a given minimum return, and that it is not possible to predict whether one ASSET will generate a better risk-adjusted return than another one. The "weak form" of the hypothesis indicates that market prices reflect all information contained in past prices, the "semi-strong form" indicates that market prices reflect all information contained in past prices and published information, and the "strong form" indicates that market prices reflect all information contained in past prices, published information, and all other non-public information.
- See also RANDOM WALK.
- Additional reference: Fama (1970).

EFP See EXCHANGE FOR PHYSICAL.

EFT See ELECTRONIC FUNDS TRANSFER.

ELASTIC A state where a proportional change in one variable leads to the same or greater proportional change in another variable. Elastic demand is a strong demand response to a change in price, i.e., a proportional decline in the purchase price results in a larger proportional increase in demand. Elastic supply is a strong supply response to a change in price, i.e., a proportional increase in the selling price results in a larger proportional increase in the amount supplied.
- See also ELASTICITY, INELASTIC.

ELASTICITY The degree to which a proportional change in one variable impacts the proportional change in another variable, commonly used in reference to prices, supply, and demand. Price elasticity measures the proportional change in goods supplied or demanded for a proportional change in price; supply elasticity measures the proportional change in quantity supplied for a proportional change in price; and demand elasticity measures the proportional change in quantity demanded for a proportional change in price.
- See also ELASTIC, INELASTIC.

ELBOW [COL] An area of the YIELD CURVE that is deemed to be financially attractive (i.e., CHEAP) and where profits can be generated by simply ROLLING DOWN THE CURVE.

ELECTRICITY SWAP An OVER-THE-COUNTER SWAP involving the exchange of fixed and floating electricity prices based on the average level of a recognized electricity pool or pricing index; transactions are often settled monthly or quarterly (to coincide with billing cycles), on a physical or financial basis.
- Also known as POWER SWAP.
- See also POWER OPTION.

ELECTRONIC COMMUNICATIONS NETWORK (ECN) An electronic platform that allows electronic TRADING of financial or

physical ASSETS in cash or DERIVATIVE form. ECNs were popularized during the technology boom of the 1990s and have become a critical element in EXCHANGE and OVER-THE-COUNTER trading networks. Advanced ECNs provide for client connectivity, real-time pricing, execution, and reporting, and links into automated CLEARING and SETTLEMENT.
- Also known as ALTERNATIVE TRADING SYSTEM.
- See also DEALER MARKET ELECTRONIC COMMUNICATIONS NETWORK, HYBRID ELECTRONIC COMMUNICATIONS NETWORK, REGULATED ELECTRONIC COMMUNICATIONS NETWORK.

ELECTRONIC FUNDS TRANSFER (EFT) The transfer of cash through an electronic mechanism, such as an interbank wire system or a retail point-of-sale system, rather than a physical check or DRAFT.

ELECTRONIC PORTAL An integrated electronic interface where a sponsoring financial institution or EXCHANGE provides clients with access to a broad range of market information, research, quotes/pricing, analytics, and/or trade execution.

ELECTRONIC TICKET An electronically generated and communicated information "slate" used by certain EXCHANGES and ELECTRONIC COMMUNICATION NETWORKS to convey details of a trade. Relevant parties update the electronic ticket as new information becomes available during the TRADING and CLEARING processes. The resulting electronic ticket acts as a legally binding CONFIRMATION once accepted by both parties.
- Also known as E-TICKET.

ELEPHANT [COL] A large institutional client, such as a PENSION FUND, MUTUAL FUND, HEDGE FUND, CORPORATION, or sovereign entity, that financial institutions court in order to generate NEW ISSUE, CORPORATE FINANCE, or investment advisory business.
- See also ELEPHANT HUNTING.

ELEPHANT HUNTING [COL] A process where financial institutions attempt to win business or MANDATES from large institutional clients. Elephant hunting generally requires continuous communication with clients on deal-related ideas and a certain amount of pro-bono work in support of the ideas.
- See also ELEPHANT.

ELIGIBLE LIABILITY A BANK LIABILITY, such as an interbank or retail DEPOSIT, that attracts a regulatory RESERVE.

ELIGIBLE PAPER Short-term financial instruments (such as GOVERNMENT BILLS, CERTIFICATES OF DEPOSIT, BANKER'S ACCEPTANCES, or bank-endorsed corporate obligations) that can be used for collateralized borrowing in the REPURCHASE AGREEMENT market or through CENTRAL BANK mechanisms, such as the DISCOUNT WINDOW.

ELIGIBLE SECURITIES Securities that BANKS are allowed to purchase, hold, and trade on a direct basis, including GOVERNMENT BONDS and AGENCY SECURITIES. Those ruled ineligible under standing regulations must often be traded through a separately incorporated and regulated subsidiary.

EMBARGO Prohibition on trade with another country either generally (all goods and services) or specifically (targeted goods and services). An embargo, which is one manifestation of SOVEREIGN RISK, may arise as a result of a trade disputes, political constraints, regulations, or national safety issues.

EMBEDDED OPTION An OPTION that is incorporated into a STRUCTURED NOTE or OVER-THE-COUNTER SWAP to provide the investor or issuer with a lower funding cost, unique speculative payoff, or customized RISK MANAGEMENT solution.
- Also known as EMBEDDO.

EMBEDDO [COL] See EMBEDDED OPTION.

EMERGING CURRENCY See EXOTIC CURRENCY.

EMPLOYEE STOCK OWNERSHIP PLAN (ESOP) In the United States, a program where a company provides shares of its COMMON STOCK to employees through a TRUST. The program builds employee ownership and aligns employee/investor interests, and creates a tax deduction for the company.

EMTN See EURO MEDIUM TERM NOTE.

EMU See EUROPEAN MONETARY UNION.

ENCUMBRANCE A real property CLAIM that passes with title, often used in collateralized lending; the borrower encumbers the property by granting the lending BANK a LIEN. The encumbrance does not impact ownership transfer, but it can reduce the market value and marketability of the property.

ENDOGENOUS LIQUIDITY LIQUIDITY and LIQUIDITY RISK that are specific to a firm and the actions it takes in managing its ASSETS, LIABILITIES, and OFF BALANCE SHEET ACTIVITIES.
- See also ASSET LIQUIDITY RISK, ASSET-FUNDING LIQUIDITY RISK, EXOGENOUS LIQUIDITY RISK.

ENDORSEMENT (1) A signature appearing on a NEGOTIABLE INSTRUMENT that transfers legal ownership from one party (the ENDORSER) to another party (the BENEFICIARY). While endorsements may be unqualified, allowing for the free transfer of ownership, they may also be qualified, conditional, or restrictive, limiting transferability and thus marketability. (2) An agreement attached to an

INSURANCE contract that adds or removes particular coverages; the endorsement takes precedence over provisions incorporated in the original contract.

ENDORSER The party signing a NEGOTIABLE INSTRUMENT; once the endorser signs the instrument, ownership is transferred to the BENEFICIARY.
- See also ENDORSEMENT.

ENGLISH AUCTION An AUCTION MARKET technique applied in certain marketplaces where the price of a security being sold is publicly announced at each stage, allowing parties to submit higher BIDS. When no further bids are received, the orders are filled.
- See also DUTCH AUCTION.

ENTERPRISE RISK MANAGEMENT (ERM) A holistic RISK MANAGEMENT process that combines a company's current and anticipated RISKS into a single, multi-year program using various instruments and markets. ERM in its broadest sense allows a firm to use ALTERNATIVE RISK TRANSFER techniques/products, including INSURANCE, REINSURANCE, DERIVATIVES, CAPTIVES, CONTINGENT CAPITAL, and/or INSURANCE-LINKED SECURITIES to manage exposures.
- Also known as INTEGRATED RISK MANAGEMENT.

ENTERPRISE VALUE A measure of the value of a firm, typically computed as the sum of expected future net CASH FLOWS, discounted back to the present at a firm-specific DISCOUNT RATE. Enterprise value can be computed via:

$$EV = \sum_{t=1}^{n} \frac{NCF_t}{(1+r)^t}$$

where NCF_t is the expected net cash flow at time t, r is the discount rate, and n is the number of periods.
- Also known as ECONOMIC VALUE.
- See also ACCOUNTING VALUE.

ENTREPÔT [FR] A commercial trading center where goods are imported from several sources and then re-exported to various destinations. Although the entrepôt produces no goods of its own it may be able to operate successfully as a result of economies of scale and efficiencies and comparative advantages related to transportation, warehousing, INSURANCE, financing, and economic/political stability.

EONIA See EURO OVERNIGHT INDEX AVERAGE.

EPS See EARNINGS PER SHARE.

EPS BOOTSTRAPPING [COL] A CORPORATE FINANCE practice where an acquirer buys a company with a low PRICE/EARNINGS RATIO through a STOCK SWAP in order to boost the post-acquisition

EARNINGS PER SHARE (EPS) of the newly-formed group and create a rise in the stock price.

EQUITABLE CONTROL A theoretical concept where managers obtain or receive power from diffuse shareholders and act in the best interests of the firm.

EQUITY (1) In INSURANCE, the concept of pricing fairness across contracts. PREMIUMS must be set according to the loss expectations within RISK classifications; those with the same risk characteristics should face the same premium and should not be subject to any discriminatory pricing. (2) See CAPITAL, COMMON STOCK, STOCK.

EQUITY CALL SWAP An OVER-THE-COUNTER SWAP involving the exchange of a floating INTEREST RATE for potential gains from the appreciation an EQUITY reference index (which may take the form of a single COMMON STOCK, a BASKET, or a broad market index).
- See also EQUITY DERIVATIVE, EQUITY INDEX SWAP, EQUITY PUT SWAP.

EQUITY DERIVATIVE An EXCHANGE-TRADED DERIVATIVE or OVER-THE-COUNTER DERIVATIVE with an UNDERLYING reference based on COMMON STOCKS, BASKETS, and market indexes. An equity derivative can be structured as an equity OPTION, equity FUTURE, equity forward, EQUITY CALL SWAP, EQUITY INDEX SWAP, EQUITY PUT SWAP, or EQUITY WARRANT.
- See also COMMODITY DERIVATIVE, CREDIT DERIVATIVE, CURRENCY DERIVATIVE, INTEREST RATE DERIVATIVE.

EQUITY INDEX SWAP An OVER-THE-COUNTER SWAP involving the exchange of a floating INTEREST RATE for potential gains from the appreciation or depreciation of an EQUITY reference index (which may be a COMMON STOCK, a BASKET, or a broad market index).
- Also known as EQUITY SWAP.
- See also EQUITY CALL SWAP, EQUITY DERIVATIVE, EQUITY PUT SWAP.

EQUITY KICKER See KICKER.

EQUITY PUT SWAP An OVER-THE-COUNTER SWAP involving the exchange of a floating INTEREST RATE for potential gains from the depreciation of an EQUITY reference index (which may take the form of a single COMMON STOCK, a BASKET, or a broad market index).
- See also EQUITY CALL SWAP, EQUITY DERIVATIVE, EQUITY INDEX SWAP.

EQUITY SWAP See EQUITY INDEX SWAP.

EQUITY WARRANT A long-dated EQUITY OPTION (i.e., three to five years) issued by a financial intermediary on a company's COMMON STOCK, which can be EXERCISED by the holder into new shares (making the transaction dilutive). Since new equity results in the event

of exercise, an equity warrant must be sponsored and approved by the issuing company.
- See also BOND WITH WARRANT, COVERED WARRANT, WARRANT.

EQUIVALENT BREAKEVEN A measure of the number of years it takes for an investor to recover the initial CONVERSION PREMIUM paid in acquiring a CONVERTIBLE BOND, typically computed as:

$$EBE = \frac{Conv_{prem}}{C - (Conv_{ratio} \, DPS)}$$

where $Conv_{prem}$ is the conversion premium, C is the COUPON, $Conv_{ratio}$ is the CONVERSION RATIO, and DPS is DIVIDENDS per share.
- See also ADJUSTED BREAKEVEN, SIMPLE BREAKEVEN.

ERM See ENTERPRISE RISK MANAGEMENT.

ESCROW ACCOUNT A TRUST account that is used to collect from a debtor periodic payments related to a MORTGAGE, INSURANCE policy, or other contractual CASH FLOWS.

ESOP See EMPLOYEE STOCK OWNERSHIP PLAN.

ETF See EXCHANGE-TRADED FUND.

EURIBOR See EURO INTERBANK OFFERED RATE.

EURO A unit of currency adopted in 1999 by countries comprising the EUROPEAN MONETARY UNION; early commercial exchange transactions were ultimately supplemented by circulation of specie. The euro, which is comprised of a fixed percentage of the domestic currencies of participating nations, is considered a RESERVE CURRENCY.

EURO COMMERCIAL PAPER (ECP) Short-term, unsecured discount DEBT securities with maturities ranging from 1 to 360 days issued by companies in the EUROMARKETS. A SYNDICATE of DEALERS places ECP on a BEST-EFFORTS basis; unlike US COMMERCIAL PAPER, ECP issues may be unrated and need not be backed by SWINGLINES.
- See also EUROBOND, EURO MEDIUM TERM NOTE, EURONOTE.

EURO INTERBANK OFFERED RATE (EURIBOR) The OFFER side of the EURO-based interbank DEPOSIT market, or the rate at which prime BANKS are willing to lend funds. EURIBOR, which is set every business day at 11 am Brussels time by the European Banking Federation, is quoted for maturities of one week and monthly to one year, and serves as an important base reference for other financial instruments (e.g., DERIVATIVES, FLOATING RATE NOTES) with a floating rate component.
- See also EURO OVERNIGHT INDEX AVERAGE.

EURO MEDIUM-TERM NOTE (EMTN) A FIXED INCOME security issued by a company or sovereign entity in the EUROMARKETS from a standing program arranged by an UNDERWRITER; once the program is registered issuance can take place at will. Financing via an EMTN program gives an issuer considerable flexibility in accessing funds in the form, and at a time, deemed most beneficial. EMTNs can be issued in a range of currencies and maturities (up to 30 years), in fixed rate, floating rate, collateralized, amortizing, and credit-supported form. A single issue from an EMTN program can be likened to a EURONOTE or EUROBOND.
- See also EURO COMMERCIAL PAPER, MEDIUM-TERM NOTE.

EURO OVERNIGHT INDEX AVERAGE (EONIA) An overnight EURO-based INTEREST RATE, computed as a weighted average of all overnight unsecured lending transactions in the euro interbank market.
- See also EURO INTERBANK OFFERED RATE.

EUROBOND A BOND issued by a company or sovereign entity in the EUROMARKETS. Eurobonds are typically sold as BEARER SECURITIES through a SYNDICATE or TENDER PANEL, or via EURO MEDIUM-TERM NOTE programs, and are cleared and settled through Euroclear or Cedel. Bonds may be issued in fixed or floating rate form, with maturities ranging from 3 to 30+ years. Eurobonds are often listed on a national stock EXCHANGE, such as Luxembourg, Zurich, or London, although most secondary trading occurs OVER-THE-COUNTER.
- See also EURONOTE, EURO COMMERCIAL PAPER.

EUROCURRENCY An ASSET or LIABILITY created outside the country of origin, i.e., a US dollar LOAN outside the United States is a EURODOLLAR loan, a yen deposit outside of Japan is a Euroyen deposit. Eurocurrency transactions are typically free of home market regulations and may attract favorable tax and RESERVE treatment.

EURODOLLAR A US dollar asset or LIABILITY located outside the United States, and the single largest element of the EUROCURRENCY market. Eurodollar LOANS are created when a BANK lends dollars through an offshore branch, an EDGE ACT BANK, or an INTERNATIONAL BANKING FACILITY (IBF). Eurodollar DEPOSITS arise through the acceptance of funds from offshore branches or IBFs.

EUROMARKET The international CAPITAL MARKETS, or the marketplace for offshore, or non-domestic, securities offerings and DERIVATIVE activity in support of such financings. The Euromarket includes the PRIMARY MARKET and SECONDARY MARKET for INTER-

BANK DEPOSITS, EURO COMMERCIAL PAPER, EURONOTES, EURO MEDIUM TERM NOTES, EUROBONDS, and GLOBAL BONDS, as well as related derivatives. Although issuance and TRADING can theoretically occur in any non-domestic currency, in practice it is limited to major RESERVE CURRENCIES. The Euromarkets are subject to a degree of regulatory oversight, although requirements related to REGISTRATION, DUE DILIGENCE, and market-making tend to be more flexible than in other domestic markets.

EURONOTE A NOTE issued by a company or sovereign entity in the EUROMARKETS. Euronotes are typically sold as BEARER SECURITIES through a SYNDICATE or TENDER PANEL, or via EURO MEDIUM-TERM NOTE programs, and are cleared and settled through Euroclear or Cedel. Notes may be issued in fixed or floating rate form, in any one of several currencies, with maturities ranging from one to three years.

- See also EURO COMMERCIAL PAPER, EURO MEDIUM TERM NOTE, EUROBOND, NOTE ISSUANCE FACILITY, REVOLVING UNDERWRITING FACILITY.

EUROPEAN BANK FOR RECONSTRUCTION AND DEVELOPMENT (EBRD) An international development BANK created in 1990 to assist in the economic development of Central and Eastern European nations via infrastructure and project LOANS to private and public sector borrowers.

EUROPEAN BARRIER OPTION See POINT BARRIER OPTION.

EUROPEAN CENTRAL BANK (ECB) The CENTRAL BANK of the EUROPEAN MONETARY UNION (EMU), established in 1998 to manage INTEREST RATES and the value of the currency (i.e., the EURO) within the EMU. The ECB features an EXECUTIVE BOARD consisting of representatives from six member countries, and a SUPERVISORY BOARD comprised of the central bankers of 12 member countries.

EUROPEAN CURRENCY UNIT (ECU) A unit of account, created by the European Economic Community in 1979 as part of the European Monetary System, based on a weighted average of the currencies of the member countries. The ECU was superseded by the creation of the EUROPEAN MONETARY UNION and the introduction of the EURO in 1999.

EUROPEAN MONETARY UNION (EMU) The monetary system of member European nations that is based on coordinated management of INTEREST RATES, FOREIGN EXCHANGE rates, and INFLATION. The EMU created the EUROPEAN CENTRAL BANK to guide its policies, and developed and introduced the EURO as its core currency. The original 11 original participating countries – Austria, Belgium,

Finland, France, Germany, Italy, Ireland, Luxembourg, Portugal, and Spain – were joined by Greece in 2003.

EUROPEAN OPTION An OPTION contract that can only be exercised by the buyer at maturity.
- See also AMERICAN OPTION, BERMUDAN OPTION.

EVENT OF DEFAULT An instance of DEFAULT that is specific to a borrower or issuer of securities, caused by failure to make scheduled PRINCIPAL and/or interest payments, failure to comply with obligations in an INDENTURE, TRUST deed, or credit agreement, triggering of a CROSS-DEFAULT CLAUSE, initiation of BANKRUPTCY proceedings by outside creditors, or seizure of ASSETS by the courts.

EVENT RISK The RISK of loss from an unexpected credit or economic event/action, such as a CREDIT RATING downgrade, DEFAULT, MORATORIUM, or EXCHANGE CONTROLS. The onset of event risk can be difficult to predict and the potential financial impact can be hard to estimate, as losses do not follow traditional STOCHASTIC PROCESSES.

EVERGREEN [COL] (1) A REVOLVING CREDIT FACILITY without a specific maturity; the facility rolls over automatically every quarter or year until the BANK decides to convert it into a term LOAN with a defined maturity. (2) In the UK, a gradual infusion of CAPITAL into a new, or recapitalized, company.

EX-ALL A share of COMMON STOCK that lacks DIVIDEND rights and voting rights and is only entitled to possible capital appreciation.

EX-DIVIDEND (1) A share of COMMON STOCK without any rights to the current period DIVIDEND. (2) The time period between the announcement and payment of dividends.

EX-GRATIA [LAT] Literally, "from favor": a goodwill payment from an INSURER to an INSURED even though no SETTLEMENT is actually due or payable. Ex-gratias are generally arranged to strengthen business relationships.

EXCESS In the UK, a DEDUCTIBLE on an insurance policy.

EXCESS INSURANCE Any INSURANCE coverage that an INSURED arranges over and above the primary insurance contract, such as an UMBRELLA POLICY. Excess insurance is generally designed to protect against losses from LIABILITY or unexpected damage that are not adequately covered through the primary contract.
- Also known as EXCESS POLICY.

EXCESS LAYER Any INSURANCE coverage that becomes effective once the INSURED's DEDUCTIBLE has been exhausted. The excess layer also applies to INSURERS or REINSURERS who choose to set

their ATTACHMENT points at a particular distance above the EXPECTED LOSS level.
- See also HORIZONTAL LAYERING, VERTICAL LAYERING.

EXCESS OF LOSS (XOL) AGREEMENT A REINSURANCE arrangement where a REINSURER assumes RISKS and returns in specific horizontal or vertical layers; depending on the magnitude of losses and the sequence and level of ATTACHMENT, a reinsurer may or may not face some CESSION and allocation of losses on each loss event.
- See also PROPORTIONAL AGREEMENT, QUOTA SHARE, SURPLUS SHARE.

EXCESS POLICY See EXCESS INSURANCE.

EXCESS SURPLUS LINE INSURANCE See SURPLUS LINE INSURANCE.

EXCHANGE A central physical or electronic marketplace, generally approved or authorized by a regulatory authority, which provides the facilities needed to bring together buyers and sellers of ASSETS (such as BONDS, COMMON STOCK, and DERIVATIVES), and allow for appropriate price discovery. An exchange does not typically set prices or trade for its own account.

EXCHANGE CONTROLS Restrictions imposed by national monetary authorities on local currency flows that limit TRADING, prohibit exporters from drawing credit from a BANK, or forbid residents from owning foreign bank accounts or local bank accounts with foreign currency. Such controls, which are a manifestation of SOVEREIGN RISK, are generally imposed to discourage speculative inflows or outflows.

EXCHANGE FOR PHYSICAL (EFP) A facility offered by certain EXCHANGES where two parties can agree to swap, off exchange, a FUTURES contract for a physical ASSET at the price quoted on the exchange. Before an EFP transaction can be concluded through the facility it must be registered with the CLEARINGHOUSE.

EXCHANGE-TRADED DERIVATIVE A DERIVATIVE contract, traded through an authorized EXCHANGE and cleared through a CLEARINGHOUSE, that is characterized by standard terms and conditions, and is subject to standard MARGIN requirements and clearing rules. Trading in exchange derivatives may occur in physical OPEN OUTCRY form, or increasingly in electronic form. The three main classes of exchange-traded derivatives are FUTURES, OPTIONS, and FUTURES OPTIONS. Contracts are available on a broad range of national and international ASSET references, including INTEREST RATES, FOREIGN EXCHANGE, EQUITIES, and commodities.
- Also known as LISTED DERIVATIVE.

- See also OVER-THE-COUNTER DERIVATIVE.

EXCHANGE-TRADED FUND (ETF) A MUTUAL FUND on a security, BASKET, or index, that trades on an EXCHANGE with continuously quoted and constantly changing prices, and which provides investors with the ability to engage in SHORT SALES and borrow against a position. Unlike CLOSED-END FUNDS, which often trade at a substantial PREMIUM or DISCOUNT to NET ASSET VALUE (NAV), ARBITRAGE activity in the creation and redemption process ensures that ETFs trade very close to NAV. Authorized participants deposit PORTFOLIOS of securities with the TRUSTEE to create ETF shares and withdraw them to redeem shares; accordingly, they are aware of the value of the underlying PORTFOLIOS versus the price of the ETF and can take advantage of any perceived arbitrage opportunities, which keeps the quoted price near the NAV.

EXCLUDED PERIL See EXCLUSION.

EXCLUSION Specific RISK exposures that are not covered through an INSURANCE contract. The more exclusions an insurance contract contains, the smaller the amount of risk transferred from INSURED to INSURER or INSURER to REINSURER. Common exclusions include losses from uninsurable CATASTROPHIC HAZARDS, losses from normal use/depreciation, and duplicative (though not excess) covers. Exclusions may be contained within the policy, or in an EXCLUSION RIDER or ENDORSEMENT.
- Also know as EXCLUDED PERIL.
- See also RETENTION.

EXCLUSION RIDER An ENDORSEMENT attached to an INSURANCE contract eliminating coverage for previously included PERILS. The details of the rider supersede those contained in the original contract.

EXECUTION RISK The RISK of lowering ENTERPRISE VALUE by not being able to successfully gain entry into a new market, introduce a new product or service, or absorb a new acquisition.

EXECUTIVE BOARD See MANAGEMENT BOARD.

EXECUTIVE DIRECTOR A board DIRECTOR that is also a member of the company's management group. An executive director is not considered to be independent for GOVERNANCE and control purposes.
- See also LEAD INDEPENDENT DIRECTOR, NON-EXECUTIVE DIRECTOR.

EXEMPT SECURITY In the United States, a security that does not have to adhere to REGISTRATION requirements set forth by the SECURITIES AND EXCHANGE COMMISSION. Securities that are commonly exempted included TREASURY BILLS, TREASURY NOTES, TREASURY BONDS, AGENCY SECURITIES, MUNICIPAL BONDS, PRIVATE PLACEMENTS, and COMMERCIAL PAPER.

EXERCISE The process of utilizing the rights granted an OPTION buyer under the terms of a contract; for a CALL OPTION this means purchasing the reference ASSET at the STRIKE PRICE, and for a PUT OPTION it means selling the asset at the strike price. Exercise may occur at maturity of the contract (EUROPEAN OPTION), at any time until maturity (AMERICAN OPTION), or on specified dates (BERMUDAN OPTION).

EXERCISE PRICE See STRIKE PRICE.

EXHAUSTION POINT See POLICY CAP.

EXOGENOUS LIQUIDITY LIQUIDITY and LIQUIDITY RISK that relate to an entire industry or national system, and are not confined to, or significantly influenced by, a single firm and its actions.
- See also ASSET LIQUIDITY RISK, ASSET-FUNDING LIQUIDITY RISK, ENDOGENOUS LIQUIDITY, FUNDING LIQUIDITY RISK.

EXOTIC CURRENCY A currency that is not widely used in international trade and financial transactions and is thinly traded in the FOREIGN EXCHANGE markets; the general lack of LIQUIDITY can result in increased price VOLATILITY. Exotics, which are typically the currencies of LESSER DEVELOPED COUNTRIES or NEWLY INDUSTRIALIZED COUNTRIES, are often non-convertible and subject to partial or complete EXCHANGE CONTROLS.
- See also NON-CONVERTIBLE CURRENCY, RESERVE CURRENCY.

EXOTIC OPTION See COMPLEX OPTION.

EXOTIC SWAP See COMPLEX SWAP.

EXPECTATIONS THEORY A theory of INTEREST RATES indicating that the expectations of investors influence the TERM STRUCTURE of rates. Thus, if investors expect future rates will be higher than current rates, the YIELD CURVE will be upward sloping, and vice versa.
- Also known as MARKET EXPECTATIONS THEORY.
- See also LIQUIDITY PREFERENCE THEORY, MARKET SEGMENTATION THEORY.
- Additional references: Lutz and Lutz (1951), Meiselman (1962).

EXPECTED CREDIT LOSS An average, or mathematically expected, credit loss, generally determined through a combination of expected CREDIT RISK exposure, probability of DEFAULT, and anticipated RECOVERY IN DEFAULT. Financial institutions allocate CREDIT RESERVES in support of expected credit losses.
- See also UNEXPECTED CREDIT LOSS, WORST CASE CREDIT LOSS.

EXPECTED LOSS The EXPECTED VALUE, or MEAN, of a statistical loss distribution function. The loss distribution function may be created to compute credit losses, INSURANCE losses, or other financial losses.

EXPECTED LOSS RATIO See LOSS RATIO.

EXPECTED UTILITY The weighted average utility value – or satisfaction from income or wealth – that is derived from a particular activity. Utility is generally used in an economic or theoretical RISK MANAGEMENT framework; precise measurement of a company's utility is not generally considered feasible or practical.

EXPECTED VALUE (1) The MEAN of a distribution of values that a random variable can take. (2) The value that is obtained given certain possible outcomes and probabilities of occurrence. In financial RISK MANAGEMENT terms this is often summarized as frequency (probability) times severity (outcome), or:

$$ExpV = (\text{Prob}\,(O_1)) + ((1 - \text{Prob})\,(O_2))$$

where $Prob$ is the probability of occurrence, O_1 is outcome 1 and O_2 is outcome 2.

EXPENSE LOADING A margin an INSURER adds in the PREMIUM LOADING process to cover expenses such as AGENT commissions, premium taxes, marketing support costs, and contingencies.
- See also FAIR PREMIUM, PURE PREMIUM.

EXPENSE RATIO In INSURANCE, a measure of an INSURER's ability to cover its UNDERWRITING expenses with earned PREMIUM, computed as:

$$ER = \frac{IE}{Pr}$$

where IE is incurred expense and Pr is premium.

The lower the ratio, the more premium an insurer preserves as profit.
- See also COMBINED RATIO, LOSS RATIO.

EXPERIENCE ACCOUNT (1) An account established for future debits and credits related to a FINITE INSURANCE contract. (2) The specific history of loss experience an INSURER has with a given INSURED, which is often used to help formulate future PREMIUM rates for a broader class of insureds.
- (2) See also EXPERIENCE RATING.

EXPERIENCE RATED POLICY A LOSS-SENSITIVE INSURANCE CONTRACT where the INSURER charges a PREMIUM that is directly related to the INSURED's past loss experience: the greater the past losses, the higher the premium.

EXPERIENCE RATING A procedure to calculate PREMIUM on an INSURANCE contract through modifications based on past loss experience. The INSURER examines actual CLAIMS and associated

expenses for a group of INSUREDS in order to project possible future claims; based on its analysis it sets a premium that it believes will be sufficient to cover EXPECTED LOSS and PROFIT LOAD.
- See also EXPERIENCE ACCOUNT, SCHEDULE RATING.

EXPERIENCE REFUND The amount of PREMIUM an INSURER returns to an INSURED if the loss record is better than the amount indicated by the PURE PREMIUM incorporated in the basic premium rate.

EXPLODING OPTION A BULL SPREAD or BEAR SPREAD that generates a payoff once the two STRIKE PRICES defining the SPREAD are breached i.e., the spread "explodes," or terminates, resulting in an immediate payoff.

EXPORTS Goods and services produced domestically and sold to non-residents, including VISIBLES (such as goods) and INVISIBLES (services). Some invisibles are sent abroad, while non-resident visitors use others domestically; capital exports can involve LOANS to non-residents or the purchase of ASSETS or investments abroad.
- See also BALANCE OF TRADE, IMPORTS.

EXPRESS AUTHORITY See ACTUAL AUTHORITY.

EXTENDIBLE OPTION An OVER-THE-COUNTER COMPLEX OPTION that allows the buyer to EXERCISE the contract on a particular reset date or reset the STRIKE PRICE to the current market level and extend the option for another reset period. The extendible option is a variation of the PARTIAL LOOKBACK OPTION.

F

FACE VALUE The PRINCIPAL amount of a security; for standard securities transactions, face value, and PAR VALUE are often equivalent. Face value is distinguished from MARKET VALUE, although in many cases they converge to the same value at maturity.

FACILITY FEE See COMMITMENT FEE.

FACTOR A firm that specializes in FACTORING activities, generally a non-BANK financial institution with significant CREDIT RISK expertise.

FACTORING The process of obtaining short-term financing through the outright sale of ACCOUNTS RECEIVABLE to a third party FACTOR on a NON-RECOURSE basis.

- See also ACCOUNTS RECEIVABLE FINANCING, FORFAITING.

FACULTATIVE A process where a REINSURER can accept or reject coverage for individual RISKS presented for consideration by a CEDING INSURER.

- See also FACULTATIVE REINSURANCE.

FACULTATIVE OBLIGATORY TREATY A hybrid of FACULTATIVE REINSURANCE and TREATY REINSURANCE where the CEDING INSURER can choose to assign certain RISKS to the REINSURER, who is then required to accept them.

FACULTATIVE REINSURANCE A REINSURANCE agreement/process that involves a case-by-case submission of RISKS by a CEDING INSURER to a REINSURER, who can accept or reject them according to specific UNDERWRITING criteria. Unlike TREATY REINSURANCE, facultative reinsurance does not compel the ceding insurer to submit risks, nor does it require a reinsurer to accept them. The arrangement is often used for large or unique exposures that require special analysis. Risks that are ultimately CEDED/accepted may be done via QUOTA SHARE or SURPLUS SHARE.

- See also FACULTATIVE OBLIGATORY TREATY.

FAIL TO DELIVER A situation where a selling DEALER has not delivered securities to the buying dealer, and will thus not receive payment. Fails are commonly used as a measure of operations-based PROCESS RISK.
- See also FAIL TO RECEIVE, AGED FAIL.

FAIL TO RECEIVE A situation where a buying DEALER has not received securities from the selling dealer, and will thus not make its payment. Fails are commonly used as a measure of operations-based PROCESS RISK.
- See also AGED FAIL, FAIL TO DELIVER.

FAIR PREMIUM An INSURANCE pricing methodology where the PREMIUM charged an INSURED is intended to cover EXPECTED LOSSES and operating and administrative expenses, and provide an equitable return to providers of CAPITAL. Fair premium is comprised of PURE PREMIUM and PREMIUM LOADING (which also includes EXPENSE LOADING).
- Also known as GROSS RATE.

FAIR PRICE PROVISION A legal provision that protects a company from an ACQUISITION based on a TWO-TIER BID (i.e., a first tier comprised of an attractive front-loaded cash offer, and a second tier consisting of a lower price and/or lower percentage of cash). The provision requires that all of the target company's COMMON STOCK shareholders receive the same (or substantially similar) buyout price and terms.

FAIRNESS OPINION An analysis and opinion prepared by a BANK or INVESTMENT BANK for a client company's MERGER, ACQUISITION, or LEVERAGED BUYOUT, to determine whether the price being paid or received is fair. The opinion is intended to convey the relative financial worth of the transaction and demonstrate that DIRECTORS have performed their DUTY OF CARE; the results can be used to protect against potential shareholder lawsuits. The fairness opinion is typically developed from information generated via the DUE DILIGENCE process.

FALLEN ANGEL [COL] A BOND with an INVESTMENT GRADE CREDIT RATING at the time of issuance that has been downgraded to SUB-INVESTMENT GRADE status as a result of a deterioration in the issuer's financial position.
- See also HIGH-YIELD BOND.

FALLING TOP A TECHNICAL ANALYSIS charting figure depicting a declining securities price or index value over time, with ever-lower resistance levels, generally considered to be a bearish signal.
- Also known as DESCENDING TOP.

- See also ASCENDING TOP, DESCENDING BOTTOM, RISING BOTTOM.

FANNIE MAE [COL] See FEDERAL NATIONAL MORTGAGE ASSOCIATION.

FASB See FINANCIAL ACCOUNTING STANDARDS BOARD.

FAT TAIL A portion of a statistical distribution that is wider or larger than expected, increasing the probability that an extreme or unexpected value will result.

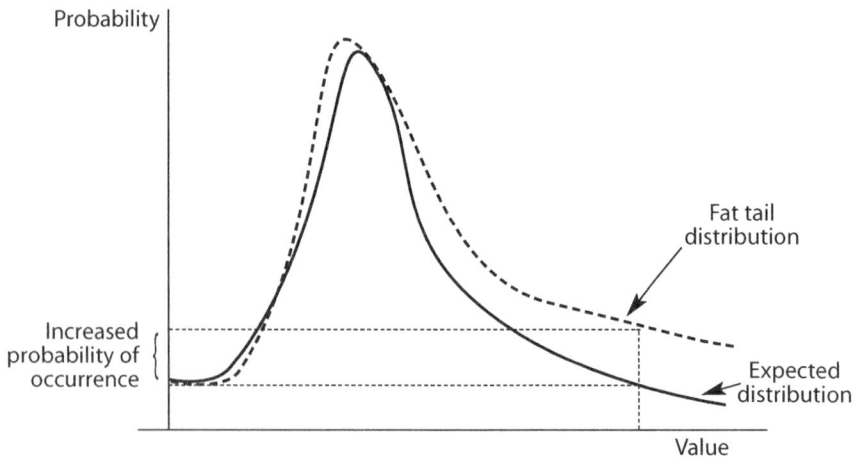

FCM See FUTURES COMMISSION MERCHANT.

FDIC See FEDERAL DEPOSIT INSURANCE CORPORATION.

FED WIRE An electronic network connecting the FEDERAL RESERVE BOARD, the 12 FEDERAL RESERVE BANKS, the US Treasury and US agencies, which is used for immediate payments, FEDERAL FUNDS transfers, and TREASURY NOTE, TREASURY BOND, and AGENCY SECURITY transfers.

FEDERAL DEPOSIT INSURANCE CORPORATION (FDIC) A US

federal agency that is responsible for managing the INSURANCE funds for BANKS and SAVINGS AND LOANS, providing depositors with protection of up to $100,000 per DEPOSIT account.

FEDERAL FUNDS In the United States, unsecured LOANS available to member BANKS from excess balances held at one of the 12 FEDERAL RESERVE BANKS. The process of borrowing Federal Funds is represented as a purchase of funds, while lending is the sale of funds. The majority of Federal Funds transactions mature the business day after they are contacted, though term transactions for from one week to six months can be arranged. Federal Funds are available immediately (i.e., they are considered GOOD MONEY), an advantage over interbank CLEARINGHOUSE funds, which are generally only accessible one to two days after contracting.

FEDERAL HOME LOAN MORTGAGE CORPORATION (FHLMC) A US agency established in 1970 that purchases MORTGAGES from mortgage originators and pools them into MORTGAGE-BACKED SECURITIES known as PARTICIPATION CERTIFICATES; the certificates, which convert ILLIQUID mortgage assets into marketable securities, carry the agency's guarantee of repayment on both PRINCIPAL and COUPON interest.
- Also known as FREDDIE MAC.
- See also FEDERAL NATIONAL MORTGAGE ASSOCIATION, GOVERNMENT NATIONAL MORTGAGE ASSOCIATION.

FEDERAL NATIONAL MORTGAGE ASSOCIATION (FNMA) A US federally chartered, publicly owned CORPORATION founded in 1938 that purchases government insured/guaranteed residential mortgages and pools them into MORTGAGE-BACKED SECURITIES (MBS); FNMA MBS, which essentially convert ILLIQUID mortgage ASSETS into marketable securities, carry the corporation's guarantee of repayment on both PRINCIPAL and COUPON interest.
- Also known as FANNIE MAE.
- See also FEDERAL HOME LOAN MORTGAGE CORPORATION, GOVERNMENT NATIONAL MORTGAGE ASSOCIATION.

FEDERAL OPEN MARKETS COMMITTEE (FOMC) The US FEDERAL RESERVE SYSTEM's policy committee, responsible for developing and implementing short-term MONETARY POLICY. The committee, which includes the seven FEDERAL RESERVE BOARD governors and five of the 12 FEDERAL RESERVE BANK presidents, conducts monetary policy via OPEN MARKET OPERATIONS and adjustments to both the DISCOUNT RATE and RESERVE REQUIREMENTS.

FEDERAL RESERVE BANKS The 12 BANKS in the US FEDERAL RESERVE SYSTEM that are responsible for providing CENTRAL

BANK services to member banks, lending via the DISCOUNT WINDOW, monitoring the activities of banks operating within their jurisdictions, and assisting in the formulation of MONETARY POLICY via the FEDERAL OPEN MARKETS COMMITTEE.

FEDERAL RESERVE BOARD The governing body of the US banking system, comprised of seven governors appointed by the US president. The board, which holds a voting majority on the FEDERAL OPEN MARKETS COMMITTEE, sets the DISCOUNT RATE and MARGIN requirements, establishes RESERVE REQUIREMENTS for national BANKS, and supervises the financial system at large through regulatory policies and declarations.

- See also FEDERAL RESERVE BANKS, FEDERAL RESERVE SYSTEM.

FEDERAL RESERVE SYSTEM The US CENTRAL BANK system, created in 1913 via the Federal Reserve Act, comprised of 12 FEDERAL RESERVE BANKS, the FEDERAL RESERVE BOARD, the FEDERAL OPEN MARKETS COMMITTEE, and member banks (which hold EQUITY in the 12 Federal Reserve banks). Operating responsibilities are divided between the board and the banks.

FEDERAL TRADE COMMISSION (FTC) A US federal agency responsible for promoting competitive behavior by preventing trade restraints, price discrimination, formation of MONOPOLY power, and illegal or predatory pricing policies. The FTC acts via voluntary enforcement and formal litigation.

FHLMC See FEDERAL HOME LOAN MORTGAGE CORPORATION.

FIAT MONEY Currency backed by an issuing nation's proclamation that it is legal tender rather than a specific reserve of gold or metal; fiat money is not specifically convertible into metal. Most currency in circulation throughout the world is fiat money.

FIDELITY BOND In INSURANCE, a BOND that guarantees an INSURER will pay the INSURED for losses caused by dishonesty or FRAUD of employees.

FIDUCIARY An individual or institution that is responsible for administering duties for the express benefit of other parties.

- See also FIDUCIARY DUTY.

FIDUCIARY DUTY (1) The legal duty that DIRECTORS and executives have in representing shareholder interests; this includes, but is not limited to, DUTY OF CARE and DUTY OF LOYALTY. (2) The legal duty that a FIDUCIARY has in administering assigned tasks or services.

FIFO See FIRST IN FIRST OUT.

FIGHTING THE TAPE [COL] The general practice of attempting to take a controlling position in a company's COMMON STOCK. Fighting the tape is generally unsuccessful in all but the most thinly traded stocks, and is illegal in certain jurisdictions unless accompanied by formal disclosure of holdings and/or a full TENDER OFFER.

FILL OR KILL [COL] A common form of designating an ALL-OR-NONE ORDER. Written trade tickets may be marked "FOK" as an abbreviation.
- See also GOOD TILL CANCELLED, MARKET ORDER, STOP LOSS ORDER.

FILZ [GER] Literally "interwoven" material or fabric; the term is commonly used in Switzerland to describe the close, and sometimes conflicted, relationships that exist between board DIRECTORS, including instances of nepotism and INTERLOCKING DIRECTORSHIPS.

FINANCIAL ACCOUNTING STANDARDS BOARD (FASB) A US self-regulatory advisory panel that is responsible for creating and promulgating accounting standards for certified public accountants via the Statements of Financial Accounting Standards, the core of US GENERALLY ACCEPTED ACCOUNTING PRINCIPLES (GAAP).
- See also INTERNATIONAL ACCOUNTING STANDARDS BOARD.

FINANCIAL DISTRESS A state of corporate financial weakness characterized by an increasing COST OF CAPITAL, deteriorating payment terms from creditors and suppliers, lower LIQUIDITY, higher LEVERAGE, and steady departure of key personnel. Distress may be induced by poor operations, weak market conditions, and/or financial mismanagement. Companies unable to cope with the effects of financial distress may ultimately be forced to file for BANKRUPTCY.

FINANCIAL GUARANTEE (1) A contract that provides for timely payment of PRINCIPAL and COUPON interest to providers of CAPITAL. (2) A RISK TRANSFER mechanism that functions as a form of CONTINGENT DEBT financing by giving the BENEFICIARY access to funds from the guarantor in the event a loss TRIGGER is breached.

FINANCIAL HOLDING COMPANY In the United States, a holding company authorized under the GRAMM–LEACH–BLILEY ACT that is permitted to own entities involved in securities TRADING and UNDERWRITING, CORPORATE FINANCE, INSURANCE, asset management, and commercial banking.

FINANCIAL INSURANCE See FINITE INSURANCE.

FINANCIAL LEASE See CAPITAL LEASE.

FINANCIAL LEVERAGE See LEVERAGE.

FINANCIAL PAPER COMMERCIAL PAPER issued by a BANK or SECURITIES FIRM.
- See also INDUSTRIAL PAPER.

FINANCIAL REINSURANCE See FINITE REINSURANCE.

FINANCIAL RISK The RISK of loss arising from the financial activities of a firm, broadly taken to include CREDIT RISK, MARKET RISK, and LIQUIDITY RISK.

FINANCIAL SERVICES AUTHORITY (FSA) The United Kingdom's independent consolidated financial regulator, formally created through the Financial Services and Markets Act of 2000. The FSA comprises bodies and functions that were previously divided among a number of separate regulatory entities, and is responsible for regulating institutions involved in DEPOSIT-taking, INSURANCE, and investments.

FINANCIAL SERVICES MODERNIZATION ACT OF 1999 See GRAMM–LEACH–BLILEY ACT.

FINANCIAL SETTLEMENT A DERIVATIVE contract that requires SETTLEMENT in financial or cash, rather than physical, terms.
- See also PHYSICAL SETTLEMENT.

FINANCIAL TIMES STOCK EXCHANGE (FTSE) 100 The BENCHMARK index of the London Stock Exchange, comprised of 100 LARGE CAP STOCKS representing a broad range of industries. The FTSE 100 can be traded directly through EXCHANGE-TRADED FUNDS and DERIVATIVES.
- Also known as FOOTSIE.

FINANCING CASH FLOW The portion of the corporate CASH FLOW statement depicting the cash inflows and cash outflows that impact a firm's LIABILITIES and CAPITAL, including issuance/repayment of short- and long-term DEBT, issuance of COMMON STOCK and PREFERRED STOCK, repurchase of TREASURY STOCK, and payment of DIVIDENDS.
- See also INVESTING CASH FLOW, OPERATING CASH FLOW.

FINITE INSURANCE An INSURANCE contract that is used primarily to finance, rather than transfer, an INSURED's RISK exposures. Finite contracts may be structured in the form of RETROSPECTIVE FINITE PROGRAMS (encompassing LOSS PORTFOLIO TRANSFER, ADVERSE DEVELOPMENT COVER, and RETROSPECTIVE AGGREGATE LOSS COVER) and PROSPECTIVE FINITE PROGRAMS.
- Also known as FINANCIAL INSURANCE, FINITE RISK CONTRACT.
- See also FINITE REINSURANCE.

FINITE QUOTA SHARE A FINITE REINSURANCE agreement where the REINSURER agrees to pay, on behalf of the CEDING INSURER, a fixed or variable proportion of CLAIMS and expenses as they occur; ceding commissions and investment income from reserves typically cover actual claims, but if they prove insufficient the reinsurer funds the shortfall and recovers the difference from the insurer over the life of the contract.

FINITE REINSURANCE A REINSURANCE agreement used primarily to finance, rather than transfer, a CEDING INSURER's RISK exposures. The insurer pays PREMIUMS into an EXPERIENCE ACCOUNT and the reinsurer covers losses under the policy once they exceed the funded amount (up to certain predetermined maximum limits). Finite reinsurance can be written in a variety of forms, including SPREAD LOSS, FINANCIAL QUOTA SHARE, LOSS PORTFOLIO TRANSFER, ADVERSE DEVELOPMENT COVER, FUNDED EXCESS OF LOSS. and AGGREGATE STOP LOSS.
- Also known as FINANCIAL REINSURANCE.
- See also FINITE INSURANCE.

FINITE RISK CONTRACT See FINITE INSURANCE.

FIRE SALE [COL] Liquidation of an ASSET at a distressed, or sharply discounted, price. A fire sale may be required if an investor or company is in urgent need of cash resources.
- See also DISTRESSED ASSET, VULTURE BID.

FIRM QUOTE A BID and/or OFFER supplied by a DEALER or MARKET MAKER to a BROKER or client that can be regarded as reliable and actionable.
- See also INDICATIVE QUOTE, QUOTED SPREAD.

FIRM UNDERWRITING See BOUGHT DEAL.

FIRST CALL DATE The first date on which an issuer can call back a CALLABLE BOND outstanding in the marketplace; a typical bond might have several sequential call opportunities appearing after the first date. The time period between the issuance of the security and the first call date is regarded as HARD CALL PROTECTION and protects the investor against REINVESTMENT RISK.
- See also YIELD TO CALL.

FIRST DOLLAR COVERAGE An INSURANCE contract that is not subject to a DEDUCTIBLE or which is made equivalent to a "no deductible" policy through an EXCESS INSURANCE clause. Under first dollar coverage the INSURER, rather than the INSURED, occupies the FIRST LOSS position.

FIRST IN FIRST OUT (FIFO) An INVENTORY management and accounting methodology where the first raw materials or work-in-progress inventory acquired for production of final goods are used first.
- See also LAST IN FIRST OUT (LIFO).

FIRST LOSS In an INSURANCE or REINSURANCE arrangement, the position that absorbs the initial losses arising from damage or destruction. The first loss position can be created through a DEDUCTIBLE where the INSURED bears the losses up to the ATTACHMENT point.

If no DEDUCTIBLE exists, the INSURER bears the first loss position up to the POLICY CAP, or the point at which REINSURANCE attaches.
- See also EXCESS LAYER.

FIRST LOSS RETENTION See DEDUCTIBLE.

FIRST-TO-DEFAULT SWAP An OVER-THE-COUNTER DEFAULT SWAP comprised of a BASKET of reference credits that entitles the purchaser to a payout on the first one that DEFAULTS; once a default occurs, the transaction terminates. Since swap pricing generally takes account of reference credit CORRELATIONS, the DERIVATIVE is cheaper than the purchase of individual contracts on the same reference credits.
- See also CREDIT DERIVATIVE.

FISCAL POLICY Taxation and spending activities undertaken by a government in order to influence growth in the economy. By altering national tax levels and the program of spending and investment, authorities attempt to shape aggregate DEMAND within the economy. Since fiscal actions may demand legislative change or lead-time in implementation, the effects often take longer to flow through the economy than those created through short-term MONETARY POLICY actions.

FIXED CHARGE COVERAGE A measure of a company's ability to repay its PRINCIPAL AMORTIZATION, COUPON interest, LEASE payments and other fixed charges with pre-tax earnings. Fixed charge coverage is computed via:

$$FCC = \frac{E_{BFC} + Tax}{FC}$$

where E_{BFC} equals earnings before fixed charges, Tax is income tax paid, and FC is fixed charges.

The larger the ratio, the greater the company's ability to cover its obligations.
- See also DEBT SERVICE COVERAGE, INTEREST COVERAGE, TIMES INTEREST EARNED.

FIXED INCOME The general class of marketable DEBT, or any security that pays an implicit or explicit INTEREST RATE return to investors on a discount or COUPON-bearing basis, including BILLS, NOTES, and BONDS.
- Also known as FIXED INTEREST.

FIXED INTEREST See FIXED INCOME.

FIXED PREMIUM PREMIUM payable by an INSURED for an INSURANCE contract that remains constant during the payment period.

- See also FLEXIBLE PREMIUM.

FIXED PRICE REOFFER An agreement among SYNDICATE members not to resell a NEW ISSUE of NOTES or BONDS at a price that is lower than the initial offer until issuance is complete and the syndicate has been broken.

FIXED-RATE BOND A DEBT obligation, such as a domestic BOND, EUROBOND, or GLOBAL BOND, which pays a fixed COUPON on a monthly, quarterly, semi-annual, or annual basis. Fixed-rate bonds, which carry maturities ranging from one to 30 years, can be issued directly or from MEDIUM-TERM NOTE or EURO MEDIUM-TERM NOTE programs, and may be sold as publicly-placed REGISTERED SECURITIES, BEARER SECURITIES, or PRIVATE PLACEMENTS.

- See also FLOATING RATE NOTE.

FIXED STRIKE LADDER OPTION An OVER-THE-COUNTER COMPLEX OPTION that allows the buyer to lock in any accumulated gains prior to expiry as the price of the UNDERLYING exceeds prespecified market levels (or 'rungs'); gains are not lost if the market subsequently retraces. This version of the option compares the terminal price and ladder rungs against a predefined STRIKE PRICE and allocates a gain to the larger of the two.

- See also CLIQUET OPTION, FLOATING STRIKE LADDER OPTION, LADDER OPTION, SHOUT OPTION.

FIXED STRIKE LOOKBACK OPTION See OPTION ON THE MAXIMUM/MINIMUM.

FIXED STRIKE SHOUT OPTION An OVER-THE-COUNTER COMPLEX OPTION that allows the buyer to lock in any accumulated gains when a 'shout' is declared (i.e., the buyer formally declares its intention to lock in); gains are not lost if the market subsequently retraces. This version of the option compares the terminal price and shout level against a predefined STRIKE PRICE and allocates a gain to the larger of the two.

- See also CLIQUET OPTION, FLOATING STRIKE SHOUT OPTION, LADDER OPTION, SHOUT OPTION.

FIXED TRIGGER A TRIGGER in an INSURANCE contract that indicates whether or not an event has occurred; a fixed trigger does not typically impact the payoff value of the contract, it simply indicates whether a SETTLEMENT will occur.

FLAG A TECHNICAL ANALYSIS pattern where a security or index price fluctuates in a narrow, and relatively stable, range (the body of the flag) preceded and/or followed by large upward or downward moves (the flagpole).

- See also PENNANT.

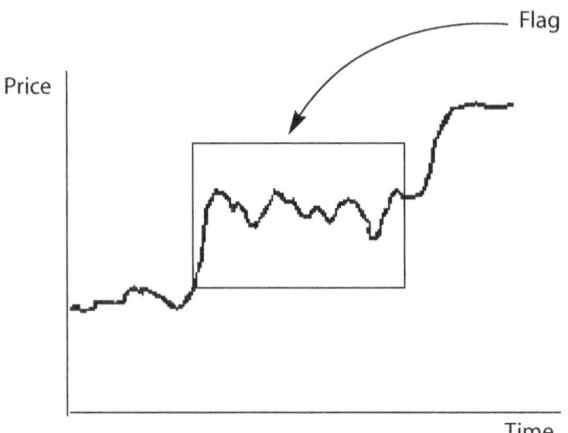

FLASH PRICE [COL] The current price of a security; during very heavy volume sessions on an EXCHANGE, quote tickers become delayed with "stale" price information, so flash prices periodically appear to signal the current value.

FLAT YIELD The current YIELD of a CONVERTIBLE BOND, typically computed via:

$$FY = \frac{C}{P_{CB}}$$

where C is the COUPON of the issue (in percentage terms) and P_{CB} is the current price of the convertible bond.
- Also known as RUNNING YIELD.
- See also EQUIVALENT BREAKEVEN, SIMPLE BREAKEVEN, YIELD ADVANTAGE.

FLEX OPTION See FLEXIBLE EXCHANGE OPTION.

FLEXIBLE EXCHANGE (FLEX) OPTION A standardized OPTION contract traded on an EXCHANGE that allows buyers and sellers to select key contract features such as STRIKE PRICE, EXERCISE style, and maturity date. Though not as bespoke as an OVER-THE-COUNTER (OTC) OPTION, the flex structure provides a degree of customization that allows it to compete with certain OTC contracts.

FLEXIBLE PREMIUM PREMIUM payable by an INSURED for an INSURANCE contract that may increase or decrease during the payment period.
- See also FIXED PREMIUM.

FLIGHT TO QUALITY [COL] A market action or event where investors liquidate risky or speculative securities holdings and deposit proceeds with BANKS or purchase GOVERNMENT BONDS or other "safe haven" ASSETS. Flight to quality may occur when financial markets

start becoming volatile and illiquid, economic conditions deteriorate, and/or systemic threats grow.
- See also CAPITAL FLIGHT.

FLIP IN PILL [COL] A POISON PILL that allows existing shareholders of a company that is the subject of a TAKEOVER to buy new shares at a discount; the pill increases DILUTION, and is thus intended to dissuade a potential acquirer from bidding for the company.
- See also FLIP OVER PILL.

FLIP OVER PILL [COL] A POISON PILL that allows existing shareholders of a company that is the subject of a TAKEOVER to buy the acquiring company's shares at a sharp discount if the transaction is completed; the pill is intended to dissuade an acquirer from bidding for the company.
- See also FLIP IN PILL.

FLIPPER [COL] An investor receiving an ALLOCATION in an INITIAL PUBLIC OFFERING, ADD-ON, or NEW ISSUE that sells the securities several hours or days after issuance to lock-in a short-term capital gain.
- Also known as STAG.

FLOAT (1) The value of all cash balances that result from delays in SETTLEMENT and processing of checks, DRAFTS, and other payments; collection float represents lost interest to depositors while payment float represents a gain to payers. (2) Funds established by an INSURER to pay for incurred losses under INSURANCE contracts. (3) The act of issuing new securities in the PRIMARY MARKET.

FLOATER (1) In INSURANCE, an ENDORSEMENT that allows coverage of moveable property to be transferred with the property between locations. (2) [COL] See FLOATING RATE NOTE.

FLOATING CHARGE See FLOATING LIEN.

FLOATING LIEN A general CLAIM against a group of ASSETS rather than a specific asset, i.e., a pool of current and future ACCOUNTS RECEIVABLE or INVENTORIES rather than designated receivables or inventories. A BANK granting a LOAN may choose to use the floating lien to secure its exposure, particularly if the tenor of the loan exceeds the average maturity of the assets being financed.
- Also known as FLOATING CHARGE.
- See also SECURITY INTEREST.

FLOATING RATE CERTIFICATE OF DEPOSIT (FRCD) A CERTIFICATE OF DEPOSIT issued by a BANK that pays a monthly, quarterly, semi-annual, or annual COUPON based on a floating INTEREST RATE, often LIBOR or EURIBOR. The most common FRCDs have a six-month maturity and a 30-day roll (e.g., ACCRUED INTEREST is paid every 30 days and the new coupon is set) and a 12-month maturity with a 90-day roll.

- Also known as VARIABLE RATE CERTIFICATE OF DEPOSIT (VRCD).
- See also LOCK-UP CERTIFICATE OF DEPOSIT, NEGOTIABLE CERTIFICATE OF DEPOSIT.

FLOATING RATE NOTE (FRN) A DEBT obligation with a final maturity of 1 to 15 years that pays a monthly, quarterly, semi-annual, or annual COUPON based on a floating INTEREST RATE reference, often LIBOR or EURIBOR. Floating rate notes can be issued directly or from MEDIUM-TERM NOTE or EURO MEDIUM-TERM NOTE programs, and may be sold as REGISTERED SECURITIES, BEARER SECURITIES, or PRIVATE PLACEMENTS in a range of currencies. FRNs are periodically issued as STRUCTURED NOTES such as RANGE FRNs, RANGE KNOCK-OUT FRNs, and INVERSE FRNs.
- Also known as FLOATER.
- See also FIXED RATE BOND, PERPETUAL FLOATING RATE NOTE.

FLOATING STRIKE LADDER OPTION An OVER-THE-COUNTER COMPLEX OPTION that allows the buyer to lock in any accumulated gains prior to expiry as the price of the UNDERLYING exceeds prespecified market levels (or 'rungs'); gains are not lost if the market subsequently retraces. This version of the option carries no preset STRIKE PRICE, it simply compares the terminal price and ladder rungs at maturity to determine the size of any gains.
- See also CLIQUET OPTION, FIXED STRIKE LADDER OPTION, LADDER OPTION SHOUT OPTION.

FLOATING STRIKE LOOKBACK OPTION An OVER-THE-COUNTER COMPLEX OPTION that provides the buyer with a maximum gain by 'looking back' over the price path of the UNDERLYING and determining the point that creates the greatest economic profit. This version of the option carries no preset STRIKE PRICE, it simply compares the terminal price against the lowest buying price (for CALL OPTIONS) or highest selling price (for PUT OPTIONS).
- See also LOOKBACK OPTION.

FLOATING STRIKE SHOUT OPTION An OVER-THE-COUNTER COMPLEX OPTION that allows the buyer to lock in any accumulated gains when a 'shout' is declared (i.e., the buyer formally declares its intention to lock in); gains are not lost if the market subsequently retraces. This version of the option carries no predefined STRIKE PRICE, it simply compares the terminal price and shout level at maturity to determine any profit.
- See also CLIQUET OPTION, FIXED STRIKE SHOUT OPTION, LADDER OPTION, SHOUT OPTION.

FLOOR An OVER-THE-COUNTER INTEREST RATE OPTION that

generates a payoff when an underlying interest rate reference falls below a STRIKE PRICE.
- See also CAP, CAPTION, FLOORTION.

FLOORLESS CONVERTIBLE See DEATH SPIRAL.

FLOORTION An OVER-THE-COUNTER OPTION on a FLOOR, granting the buyer the right to purchase a floor at a pre-determined STRIKE PRICE.
- See also CAP, CAPTION.

FLOTATION The act of UNDERWRITING a NEW ISSUE of securities in the PRIMARY MARKET.

FLOTATION COST The expense a company bears in issuing new securities, typically computed as the difference between the price received by the company on an issue and the amount charged to investors (the UNDERWRITING SPREAD) plus out of pocket expenses.
- See also ALL-IN COST.

FNMA See FEDERAL NATIONAL MORTGAGE ASSOCIATION.

FOB See FREE ON BOARD.

FOLLOWING THE FORTUNES [COL] A clause in a REINSURANCE contract that indicating that the REINSURER will be subject to the same financial fate as the CEDING INSURER. The clause is designed to align the interests of the two parties.

FOMC See FEDERAL OPEN MARKETS COMMITTEE.

FOOTSIE [COL] See FINANCIAL TIMES STOCK EXCHANGE (FTSE) 100 INDEX.

FORBEARANCE A decision by a BANK not to exercise its rights against a borrower in technical DEFAULT, in exchange for the borrower's promise to begin making regular payments of PRINCIPAL and/or interest.

FORCE MAJEURE [FR] Literally "irresistible force"; in the corporate sector it is a financial event of such gravity (e.g., systemic dislocation, severe CREDIT RATING downgrade, BANKRUPTCY) that a relationship/transaction (such as a LOAN, NEW ISSUE, or CORPORATE FINANCE deal) may be cancelled or accelerated.
- See also MATERIAL ADVERSE CHANGE CLAUSE, VIS MAJOR.

FORECLOSURE A legal process where creditors take possession of COLLATERAL securing a LOAN to a borrower in technical DEFAULT, generally through the filing of a foreclosure suit. In some systems the ability to seize ASSETS and foreclose may be limited or delayed by AUTOMATIC STAY provisions.

FOREIGN EXCHANGE (FX) A transaction that involves the exchange of two currencies. TRADING in foreign exchange is extremely active, with institutions regularly using SPOT and DERIVATIVE contracts to HEDGE, ARBITRAGE, or SPECULATE.

■ See also FOREIGN EXCHANGE (FX) RATE.

FOREIGN EXCHANGE (FX) RATE The price or value of a country's currency. Market forces may set a foreign exchange rate (i.e., a market exchange rate) or a country's CENTRAL BANK or monetary authority may control or influence the rate (i.e., a MANAGED FOREIGN EXCHANGE RATE, or a semi-floating rate determined through PEGGING or CRAWLING PEGS). Fixed foreign exchange rates may or may not reflect the perceived market value of the currency; where significant discrepancies arise a black, or parallel, market, based purely on market supply and demand forces, may develop.

FOREIGN EXCHANGE (FX) RESERVES ASSETS of a country, held with the CENTRAL BANK or monetary authority, which are used for currency management and intervention. Reserves are generally comprised of gold and major RESERVE CURRENCIES, along with SPECIAL DRAWING RIGHTS held with the INTERNATIONAL MONETARY FUND.

FORFAITING A process where an exporter sells to a BANK or specialized financial institution a PORTFOLIO of discounted long-term ACCOUNTS RECEIVABLE or PROMISSORY NOTES (generally backed by guarantees from the importer's own bank).
■ See also FACTORING.

FORTUITOUS EVENT An unforeseen, unexpected, or accidental occurrence; such an event is a general characteristic of an INSURABLE RISK and must be present in order for an INSURED to make a CLAIM under an INSURANCE contract.

FORWARD A bilateral OVER-THE-COUNTER DERIVATIVE that permits the purchaser to buy, and the seller to sell, a reference ASSET at a predetermined future price and future date. Unlike a SWAP, a forward contract features no intervening cash FLOWS, simply a final cash exchange at the conclusion of the contract. Forwards are highly customizable; the two parties can negotiate terms regarding amount, SETTLEMENT, maturity, and UNDERLYING reference. (See diagram on opposite page.)
■ See also FORWARD DISCOUNT, FORWARD FORWARD, FORWARD PREMIUM, FORWARD PRICE, FORWARD RATE, FORWARD RATE AGREEMENT, NON-DELIVERABLE FORWARD.

FORWARD BALANCE SHEET A future depiction of a firm's balance sheet and off balance sheet commitments and contingencies. Construction of a forward balance sheet is an important element in managing RISK, LIQUIDITY, and CAPITAL as it provides an estimate of how a firm's operations will change with the passage of time or the occurrence of contingent events.

Payoff profile of long forward

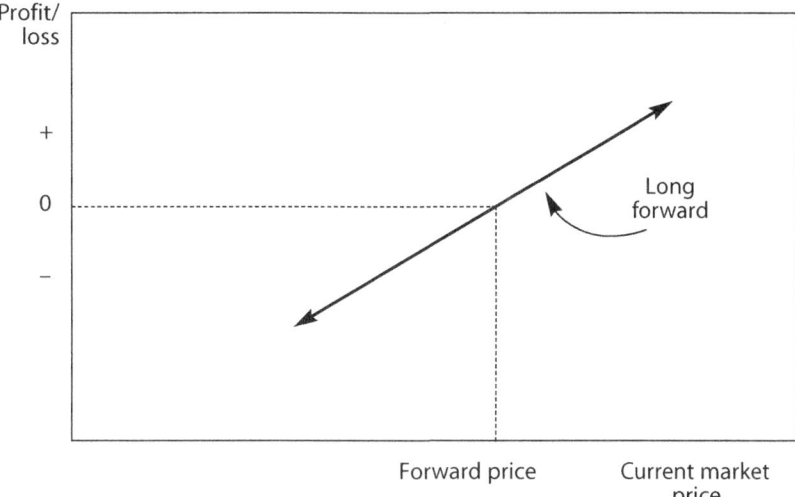

Payoff profile of short forward

FORWARD DISCOUNT A FORWARD PRICE (or rate) for future delivery of an ASSET that is lower than the SPOT PRICE (or rate) for immediate delivery.
- See also FORWARD PREMIUM.

FORWARD FOREIGN EXCHANGE (FX) CONVERSION An ARBITRAGE strategy in the FOREIGN EXCHANGE market to take advantage of mispricing in currency FORWARDS. The conversion occurs

when forwards appear CHEAP, and is created by buying a forward, selling a CALL OPTION, and buying a PUT OPTION (all with the same maturity date); if the forward is mispriced, the strategy yields an arbitrage profit.
- See also FORWARD FOREIGN EXCHANGE REVERSAL.

FORWARD FOREIGN EXCHANGE (FX) REVERSAL An ARBITRAGE strategy in the FOREIGN EXCHANGE market to take advantage of mispricing in currency FORWARDS. The conversion occurs when forwards appear RICH, and is created by selling a forward, buying a CALL OPTION, and selling a PUT OPTION (all with the same maturity date); if the forward is mispriced, the strategy yields an arbitrage profit.
- See also FORWARD FOREIGN EXCHANGE CONVERSION.

FORWARD FORWARD A FORWARD transaction that is contracted to start at a future date.
- See also FORWARD FORWARD RATE, FORWARD RATE AGREEMENT.

FORWARD FORWARD RATE The FORWARD RATE used as a reference in a FORWARD RATE AGREEMENT or an INTEREST RATE FORWARD contract; it can be considered the interest rate for a certain period of time applicable to a certain future starting point.

FORWARD MARKET The general marketplace for ASSETS or financial contracts that are settled and delivered at a future time.
- See also FORWARD, SPOT MARKET.

FORWARD PREMIUM A FORWARD PRICE (or rate) for future delivery of an ASSET that is higher than the SPOT PRICE (or rate) for immediate delivery.
- See also FORWARD DISCOUNT.

FORWARD POINTS The differential between a SPOT RATE and FORWARD RATE in the FOREIGN EXCHANGE markets. Forward points arise as a result of INTEREST RATE DIFFERENTIALS, market expectations related to currencies and INTEREST RATES, and/or currency supply and demand. While forward points can be computed as the difference between spot and forward currency rates, they can also be estimated via:

$$FP = \frac{FX_S \, (r_{diff}) \, (t)}{RB}$$

where FX_s is the spot currency rate, r_{diff} is the interest rate differential between the two currencies, t is the time to maturity (days), and RB is the rate basis (e.g., 360 or 365 days).

FORWARD PRICE The price quoted for future delivery of an ASSET under a FORWARD or FUTURE, comprised of the SPOT PRICE and a positive or negative COST OF CARRY; a quoted price may reflect a FORWARD PREMIUM or FORWARD DISCOUNT. The equilibrium, no-ARBITRAGE forward prices for various assets are given as follows:

- COMMON STOCK, no DIVIDENDS:

$$F = S\,e^{rt}$$

where S is the stock price, e is the exponential constant, r is a prevailing DISCOUNT RATE, and t is the time to maturity.

- Stock, continuous dividends:

$$F = S\,e^{(r-\delta)t}$$

where δ is the DIVIDEND YIELD and all other terms are as defined above.

- Currency:

$$F = Sp\,e^{(r_1 - r_2)t}$$

where Sp is the spot price, r_1 is the discount rate for currency 1, r_2 is the discount rate for currency 2, and all other terms are as defined above.

- Commodity with LEASE market:

$$F = Sp\,e^{(r-\varphi)t}$$

where φ is the lease payment rate and all other terms are as defined above.

- Commodity with carry market:

$$F = Sp\,e^{(r+\lambda)t}$$

where λ is the cost of storage and INSURANCE, and all other terms are as defined above.

- Commodity with carry market and CONVENIENCE YIELD:

$$F = Sp\,e^{(r+\lambda-cy)t}$$

where cy is the convenience yield, and all other terms are as defined above.

- See also FORWARD RATE.

FORWARD RATE (1) The rate quoted for future delivery of an ASSET, used in the calculation of FORWARDS and FUTURES. A quoted forward rate may reflect a FORWARD PREMIUM or FORWARD DISCOUNT. (2) See IMPLIED FORWARD RATE.

- (1) See also FORWARD PRICE.

FORWARD RATE AGREEMENT (FRA) A single period FORWARD contract on INTEREST RATES that does not involve an exchange of

PRINCIPAL; at maturity the parties simply exchange the differential prevailing between the interest rate and the rate agreed at the start of the transaction. FRAs are typically structured and quoted in the market with reference to a start date and an end date (e.g., a "3 x 9" FRA is a six-month forward starting in three months' time).
- Also known as INTEREST RATE FORWARD.
- See also FORWARD-FORWARD RATE

FORWARD START OPTION An OVER-THE-COUNTER COMPLEX OPTION that is contracted on trade date t to commence on forward date $t+1$, with the forward start date, STRIKE PRICE, and final maturity parameters established on trade date. Once the forward date is reached a conventional EUROPEAN OPTION comes into existence.

FORWARD SWAP An OVER-THE-COUNTER SWAP that is contracted on trade date t and commences on forward date $t+1$, with the INTEREST RATE and final maturity parameters established on trade date. Once the forward date is reached a conventional fixed/floating INTEREST RATE SWAP comes into existence.

FORWARDATION See CONTANGO.

FOUNDATION METHODOLOGY A credit-based CAPITAL ALLOCATION process promulgated by the BANK FOR INTERNATIONAL SETTLEMENTS (BIS) under the INTERNAL RATINGS BASED (IRB) APPROACH. BANKS use internal models to determine a COUNTERPARTY'S DEFAULT RISK, but use BIS-supplied RISK factors to estimate RISK EQUIVALENT EXPOSURE and LOSS GIVEN DEFAULT in order to obtain estimates of EXPECTED CREDIT LOSS and UNEXPECTED CREDIT LOSS. CAPITAL is then allocated to cover the resulting exposure.
- See also ADVANCED METHODOLOGY.

FRA See FORWARD RATE AGREEMENT.

FRACTIONAL EXPOSURE The amount of future CREDIT RISK inherent in an OVER-THE-COUNTER DERIVATIVE transaction, typically combined with ACTUAL EXPOSURE to determine total credit exposure. The amount of fractional exposure in a derivative is dependent on market movements in the UNDERLYING reference: the greater the potential future market moves, the greater the fractional exposure. Fractional exposure, which can be estimated through statistical or simulation methods, is positive at the inception of a transaction and declines as maturity approaches, since the opportunity for further market moves that can affect value becomes limited.
- Also known as DEEMED RISK, POTENTIAL MARKET RISK, PRE-SETTLEMENT RISK, TIME-TO-DECAY RISK.

FRAUD An act of intentional deception or dishonesty perpetrated by one or more individuals, generally for financial gain.

- See also FRAUDULENT MISREPRESENTATION.

FRAUDULENT MISREPRESENTATION A false CLAIM made by one party in order to gain economic advantage from a second party. Proof of misrepresentation can result in termination of contracts.
- See also FRAUD.

FRCD See FLOATING RATE CERTIFICATE OF DEPOSIT.

FREDDIE MAC [COL] See FEDERAL HOME LOAN MORTGAGE CORPORATION.

FREE CASH FLOW A CASH FLOW computation that is based on OPERATING CASH FLOW, less cash allocated to new and replacement ASSETS; alternatively, it is net operating income less the REPLACEMENT COST for depreciated assets, less new investments. The resulting figure is generally considered to be an accurate reflection of a company's true cash position.
- See also FINANCING CASH FLOW, INVESTING CASH FLOW.

FREE ON BOARD (FOB) The declared value of EXPORT goods, including the cost of production and transportation to the port of shipment. FOB does not include the cost of transportation from the port to the destination or the cost of INSURANCE, both of which are the responsibility of the importer.
- See also COST, INSURANCE, FREIGHT (CIF).

FREE RIDER [COL] An UNDERWRITER or SYNDICATE member that retains a portion of a PRIMARY MARKET offering in order to sell at what it hopes will be a higher SECONDARY MARKET price; the practice is illegal in many markets.

FREEZE-OUT [COL] The process of persuading MINORITY INTERESTS of a target company to sell their shares after a TENDER OFFER has been made. The intent behind the freeze-out is for the acquiring company to accumulate all shares so that the transfer is complete.
- See also DRAG ALONG RIGHTS, TAG ALONG RIGHTS.

FRIENDLY SOCIETY In the United Kingdom, a mutual institution for savings and life INSURANCE that is owned and operated by its members; the organizational structure of the friendly society conveys certain tax advantages to the mutual owners.

FRIENDLY TAKEOVER An acquisition that is agreed on amicable terms between the acquiring company and the target company. A friendly takeover may arise as a result of negotiations between the two companies, or it may be a WHITE KNIGHT response to a HOSTILE TAKEOVER offer from another party.

FRN See FLOATING RATE NOTE.

FRONT DOOR [COL] A process where the BANK OF ENGLAND attempts to influence UK money supply by lending directly to discount houses and other financial institutions.

- See also BACK DOOR.

FRONT MONTH See NEARBY CONTRACT.

FRONT RUNNING [COL] An illegal practice where a DEALER, MARKET-MAKER, or SPECIALIST executes a transaction in advance of a customer trade in order to capture favorable price movements.

FRONTING COMPANY See FRONTING INSURER.

FRONTING INSURER An INSURER that is interposed between a CEDING INSURER or CAPTIVE, and a REINSURER. Use of a fronting insurer allows the insurer or captive to access the professional reinsurance market directly and obtain coverage at more favorable PREMIUM rates.
- Also known as FRONTING COMPANY.

FSA see FINANCIAL SERVICES AUTHORITY.

FTC See FEDERAL TRADE COMMISSION.

FULL INSURANCE An INSURANCE contract where the INSURER provides the INSURED with complete coverage of a RISK exposure in exchange for a larger PREMIUM. It can be considered a contract of maximum RISK TRANSFER, and is characterized by a small (or no) DEDUCTIBLE, large POLICY CAP, limited (or no) COINSURANCE, and limited (or no) EXCLUSIONS. Such a policy is most suitable for extremely risk averse companies or individuals.
- See also PARTIAL INSURANCE.

FULL RECOURSE LOAN A LOAN with repayment that may come from the proceeds of the project/ASSET being financed or the sale of specific COLLATERAL, or from the resources of the borrower if project/collateral CASH FLOWS prove insufficient.
- See also RECOURSE, NON-RECOURSE, NON-RECOURSE LOAN, PARTIAL RECOURSE LOAN.

FULLY DILUTED BASIS A method of computing a company's EARNINGS PER SHARE by taking account of any potential new shares of COMMON STOCK that may be created through a planned NEW ISSUE of EQUITY, exercise of outstanding stock OPTIONS, or conversion of any existing CONVERTIBLE BONDS.
- See also DILUTION.

FUND OF FUNDS A MUTUAL FUND that invests in other mutual funds rather than individual securities. A fund of funds may be publicly registered and traded, or structured as a private, offshore, INVESTMENT COMPANY.

FUNDAMENTAL ANALYSIS An investment analysis approach that focuses on a company's financial and accounting value and its ability to generate core operating earnings in order to increase the stock price. Fundamental analysts advocate the purchase of stocks selling below

LIQUIDATION VALUE, which may be evidenced by a low PRICE/EARNINGS RATIO and CURRENT ASSETS that exceed CURRENT LIABILITIES and long-term DEBT.
- See also TECHNICAL ANALYSIS.
- Additional reference: Graham and Dodd (1962).

FUNDED PENSION PLAN A PENSION PLAN where all future LIABILITIES are fully covered by existing fund resources.
- See also UNFUNDED PENSION PLAN.

FUNDING AGREEMENT An unsecured financing facility for an INSURER, often arranged as a PRIVATE PLACEMENT and placed directly with large institutional investors (often MONEY MARKET FUNDS). Funding agreements generally have maturities extending from several months to several years, but may contain investor PUT OPTIONS that allow redemption with 7, 30, 90, or 180 days' notice.

FUNDING LIQUIDITY RISK The RISK of loss arising from an inability to roll over existing unsecured funding or obtain new unsecured funding without incurring a large cost. A sub-category of LIQUIDITY RISK.
- See also ASSET LIQUIDITY RISK, ASSET-FUNDING LIQUIDITY RISK, ENDOGENOUS LIQUIDITY RISK, EXOGENOUS LIQUIDITY RISK.

FUNGIBILITY The ability to exchange or substitute one ASSET with another. Fungibility is important in COLLATERAL management for OVER-THE-COUNTER DERIVATIVES and REPURCHASE AGREEMENTS, and in delivery decisions for EXCHANGE-TRADED DERIVATIVES.

FURTHEST MONTH An EXCHANGE-TRADED DERIVATIVE contract with the longest maturity date featuring trading volume; contracts with even longer maturity dates that are inactive or dormant are not considered to be the furthest month contract.
- See also NEARBY, NEXT NEARBY.

FUTURE An EXCHANGE-TRADED DERIVATIVE contract that permits the purchaser to buy, and the seller to sell, an ASSET at a predetermined future price and delivery date. Standardized futures contracts are available on assets/securities from the FIXED INCOME, EQUITY, FOREIGN EXCHANGE, and commodity markets, and can be settled in cash or physical (depending on contract specifications). Contracts are secured by INITIAL MARGIN and are MARKED-TO-MARKET on a daily basis by the CLEARINGHOUSE; VARIATION MARGINS are posted to cover daily market movement.
- See also FUTURES OPTION, FUTURES CALL, FUTURES PUT.

FUTURE VALUE A financial computation where the value of a current

CASH FLOW or lump sum is projected into the future through use of an appropriate investment return or YIELD. The general form of the equation is given as:

$FV = CF_0 (1 + r)^t$

where CF_0 is the current cash flow, t is the time to maturity, and r is the DISCOUNT RATE or yield.

The future value of a stream of cash flows, such as those characterizing an ANNUITY, can be computed through an extension of the same equation:

$FV_A = CF_P \left[\dfrac{(1 + r)^t - 1}{r} \right]$

where CF_P is the periodic future cash flow and other terms are as defined above.

- See also DISCOUNTED CASH FLOW, NET PRESENT VALUE, PRESENT VALUE.

FUTURES CALL An EXCHANGE-traded OPTION contract granting the buyer the right, but not the obligation, to buy a FUTURES contract at a pre-specified STRIKE PRICE.

- See also FUTURES PUT.

FUTURES COMMISSION MERCHANT (FCM) An intermediary that develops and executes FUTURES-based strategies and coordinates transactions with CLEARING MEMBERS on behalf of clients. FCMs are the only entities, apart from CLEARINGHOUSES, that can hold customer funds. In the United States, FCMs must meet certain minimum financial requirements and must be members of the National Futures Association, a SELF-REGULATORY ORGANIZATION; they may be structured as independent organizations or divisions of larger financial institutions

FUTURES OPTION An EXCHANGE-traded OPTION contract granting the buyer the right, but not the obligation, to buy or sell a FUTURES contract at a pre-specified STRIKE PRICE.

- See also FUTURES CALL, FUTURES PUT.

FUTURES PUT An EXCHANGE-traded OPTION granting the buyer the right, but not the obligation, to sell a FUTURES contract at a pre-specified STRIKE PRICE.

- See also FUTURES CALL.

FX See FOREIGN EXCHANGE.

G

G7 See GROUP OF 7.

G10 See GROUP OF 10.

GAAP See GENERALLY ACCEPTED ACCOUNTING PRINCIPLES.

GAMMA The change in the value of an OPTION's DELTA for a change in the value of the UNDERLYING market reference, all other variables held constant. Gamma, as a measure of the CONVEXITY of option prices, is often used to gauge sensitivity to large and sudden market moves. The gammas of the CALL OPTION and PUT OPTION under the BLACK–SCHOLES MODEL are identical and given by:

$$\Gamma_c = \frac{\partial \Delta_c}{\partial S} = \frac{\partial^2 c}{\partial S^2} = \frac{1}{S\sigma\sqrt{t}} N'(d_1)$$

$$\Gamma_p = \frac{\partial \Delta_p}{\partial S} = \frac{\partial^2 p}{\partial S^2} = \frac{1}{S\sigma\sqrt{t}} N'(d_1)$$

where

$$N'(d_1) = \frac{1}{\sqrt{2\pi}} e^{\frac{-d_1^2}{2}}$$

and S is the stock price, t is the time to maturity, σ is the STANDARD DEVIATION, and where the value of $N'(d_1)$ can be obtained from a standard table of probability functions. The gammas of long and short puts and calls are shown as:

	Long call	Long put	Short call	Short put
Gamma	+	+	−	−

- See also GAMMA HEDGE, NEGATIVE GAMMA, GREEKS, RHO, THETA, VEGA.

GAMMA HEDGE A HEDGE technique used primarily to manage or neutralize the effects of NEGATIVE GAMMA, which can create large losses if markets move sharply and quickly before DELTA HEDGES can be rebalanced. Creating a hedge for a negative gamma position generally requires the purchase or use of a position with positive gamma (e.g., an instrument with positive CONVEXITY, such as a LONG POSITION in a CALL OPTION or PUT OPTION).

GAP (1) The differential between interest RATE-SENSITIVE ASSETS and RATE-SENSITIVE LIABILITIES, often used as a measure of a BANK's exposure to LIQUIDITY RISK and MARKET RISK; the gap can be computed for individual maturity buckets and in total. A gap computation based on the final contractual maturity of each rate-sensitive asset and liability fails to take account of interim CASH FLOWS, PREPAYMENTS, AMORTIZATION or ACCRETION; accordingly, a preferred method calls for gaps computed through DURATION. A NEGATIVE GAP means the bank is borrowing short-term and lending long-term and is thus exposed to rising short-term rates or an inversion of the YIELD CURVE. A POSITIVE GAP means the bank is borrowing long-term and lending short-term, and is therefore exposed to falling short-term rates or a steepening of the yield curve. (2) In TECHNICAL ANALYSIS an intraday or overnight upward or downward break in a security price or index level. Gaps can be classified in different forms, including runaway gap (a gap in the same direction as recent large up/down moves), breakaway gap (a gap at the end of a consolidation period, signaling the beginning of a major market move), common gap (a one-day gap, often appearing in thinly traded markets), and exhaustion gap (a gap at the end of an extreme market move).
- (1) See also ASSET–LIABILITY MANAGEMENT, GAPPING.

GAPPING The process of deliberately mismatching ASSETS and LIABILITIES in order to take advantage of an anticipated change in INTEREST RATES. Although gapping has the potential of generating greater returns, it can also increase a firm's DIRECTIONAL RISK, CURVE RISK, and/or LIQUIDITY RISK.
- See also ASSET–LIABILITY MANAGEMENT, GAP, RATE-SENSITIVE ASSETS, RATE-SENSITIVE LIABILITIES,

GATHER IN THE STOPS [COL] Concentrated selling to drive a security price down to levels where STOP ORDERS are known to exist. This forces the stop orders to convert into buy or sell MARKET ORDERS, clearing the way for further upward or downward moves once executed.
- See also SNOWBALLING.

GATT See GENERAL AGREEMENT ON TARIFFS AND TRADE.

GC See GENERAL COLLATERAL.

GDP See GROSS DOMESTIC PRODUCT.

GDR See GLOBAL DEPOSITORY RECEIPT.

GDS See GLOBAL DEPOSITORY SHARE.

GEARING See LEVERAGE.

GEISHA [JPN, COL] A PRIVATE PLACEMENT, denominated in a currency other than Japanese yen, which is issued by a Japanese company.
- See also DAIMYO, SAMURAI, SHIBOSAI, SHOGUN.

GEMM See GILT-EDGED MARKET-MAKER.

GENERAL AGREEMENT ON TARIFFS AND TRADE (GATT) An agency of the United Nations established in 1948 to promote international free trade. GATT was actively involved in coordinating issues related to multilateral quotas and tariffs, export restraints, and intellectual property rights until it was replaced by its successor, the WORLD TRADE ORGANIZATION, in 1994.

GENERAL COLLATERAL (GC) COLLATERAL in the REPURCHASE AGREEMENT market that is in abundant supply and which does not therefore allow a repurchase agreement borrower to obtain a lower than normal borrowing rate.
- See also SPECIAL.

GENERAL OBLIGATION (GO) BOND In the United States, a MUNICIPAL BOND issued by a state or local authority that is typically used to finance non-revenue producing projects, such as schools and transportation systems. Bonds are generally repaid through the issuance of new DEBT or via tax revenues.
- See also REVENUE BOND.

GENERALLY ACCEPTED ACCOUNTING PRINCIPLES (GAAP) Accounting rules adopted by public companies that are intended to provide uniform treatment of activities impacting the balance sheet, income statement and statement of CASH FLOWS. Versions of GAAP are used in the United States, the United Kingdom and various other counties. In the United States, the FINANCIAL ACCOUNTING STANDARDS BOARD establishes GAAP rules.
- See also INTERNATIONAL ACCOUNTING STANDARDS.

GENSAKI [JPN] The broad Japanese MONEY MARKET, which includes trading in short-term GOVERNMENT BILLS, CERTIFICATES OF DEPOSIT, NOTES, REPURCHASE AGREEMENTS and REVERSE REPURCHASE AGREEMENTS.

GEOMETRIC BROWNIAN MOTION A lognormal, continuous-time STOCHASTIC PROCESS where the movement of a variable, such as a financial ASSET price, is random in continuous time; the instantaneous return (defined as the change in the price of the variable divided by the price of the variable) has a constant MEAN and VARIANCE.

Certain DERIVATIVE pricing methodologies are based on the Geometric Brownian motion process.

GHOSTING [COL] A practice where two or more MARKET MAKERS attempt to jointly influence the price of a security; ghosting is illegal in many jurisdictions as market makers are meant to compete against each other.

GILT Abbreviated term for gilt-edged stock, the broad category of UK GOVERNMENT BONDS used for general financing and MONETARY POLICY purposes. Gilts, denominated in sterling, are issued in four different versions with maturities ranging from one year to perpetuity: STRAIGHT BONDS (with a bullet repayment), convertible bonds (exchangeable into gilts with a longer maturity), index-linked bonds (tied to the RETAIL PRICE INDEX INFLATION measure), and IRREDEEMABLE BONDS (CONSOLS, or PERPETUAL BONDS). Gilts, which may be callable (e.g., double-dated gilts), are issued by a number of government departments (e.g., Exchequer, Treasury, Funding, Conversion, Consolidated Fund Annuities). Securities are sold in the PRIMARY MARKET via GILT-EDGED MARKET-MAKERS (GEMMs) or through special tap arrangements, and are traded in the SECONDARY MARKET by GEMMs, BANKS, and discount houses

GILT-EDGED MARKET-MAKER (GEMM) A PRIMARY DEALER in GILTS that commits to quoting two-way prices and bidding competitively at primary auctions. While GEMMs were once required to be separately capitalized legal entities, they may now form part of larger financial groups.

GINNIE MAE [COL] See GOVERNMENT NATIONAL MORTGAGE ASSOCIATION (GNMA).

GIRO A system of physical or electronic payment transfers for consumer purchases, used primarily in Europe and Japan. The giro results in a direct transfer of funds from the consumer, payer, or debtor to the seller or creditor without the need for using a BANK account. Giro payments, which are often conducted via local post offices, fulfill the role of the check in the US financial markets.

GIVE-UP A brokered trade executed on behalf on another party; once executed, the name of the party to the trade is "given up" by the BROKER to the trader so that the proper party of record can be recorded.

- See also BLIND BROKERING.

GLASS–STEAGALL ACT US Federal legislation enacted in 1933 to separate banking powers in the aftermath of the 1929 stock market crash. Glass–Steagall forced banking institutions to select between commercial banking (e.g., lending and DEPOSIT taking) and investment banking (e.g., securities UNDERWRITING and TRADING,

CORPORATE FINANCE). Restrictions under the act began eroding in 1987 when COMMERCIAL BANKS were permitted to underwrite and trade securities, and were largely eliminated in 1999 through passage of the GRAMM–LEACH–BLILEY ACT.
- Also known as BANKING ACT OF 1933.

GLOBAL BOND A BOND that is issued simultaneously in a domestic market and the EUROMARKETS. Global bonds, which may be fixed or floating rate and carry maturities ranging from 1 to 30 years, are generally issued by large, well-known CORPORATIONS or supranationals that have international operations and broad name recognition.
- See also DRAGON, EUROBOND.

GLOBAL DEPOSITORY RECEIPT (GDR) A negotiable certificate issued by a local BANK representing a non-local company's COMMON STOCK (shares of which are held in CUSTODY by the bank). GDRs, denominated in local currency (and occasionally dollars) are generally registered with local regulators and may be traded on an EXCHANGE or OVER-THE-COUNTER. GDRs may be sponsored (approved/backed by the company) or unsponsored (not backed/approved by the company).
- See also AMERICAN DEPOSITORY RECEIPT, AMERICAN DEPOSITORY SHARE, GLOBAL DEPOSITORY SHARE.

GLOBAL DEPOSITORY SHARE (GDS) COMMON STOCK issued by a non-local company in a local marketplace. GDSs, generally denominated in the local currency (and occasionally in US dollars), are typically registered with local regulators and may be traded on an EXCHANGE or OVER-THE-COUNTER.
- See also AMERICAN DEPOSITORY RECEIPT, AMERICAN DEPOSITORY SHARE, GLOBAL DEPOSITORY RECEIPT.

GNMA See GOVERNMENT NATIONAL MORTGAGE ASSOCIATION.

GNOME [COL] A 15-year PARTICIPATION CERTIFICATE issued by the FEDERAL HOME LOAN MORTGAGE CORPORATION.
- See also DWARF, MIDGET.

GO BOND See GENERAL OBLIGATION BOND.

GOING CONCERN VALUE The value of a firm as a complete operating business; going concern value is generally greater than LIQUIDATION VALUE as it includes the worth of GOODWILL and other INTANGIBLE ASSETS that may be sacrificed in a liquidation scenario, particularly if ASSETS are sold on a piecemeal basis.

GOLDBRICKS [COL] COMMON STOCKS that appear to be financially sound on the surface, but which feature little substance when examined more closely.

GOLDEN HANDCUFFS [COL] A compensation package intended to induce an executive to remain at a company; if the executive departs,

some or all of the benefits conveyed through the golden handcuffs may have to be returned.
- See also GOLDEN HANDSHAKE, GOLDEN HELLO, GOLDEN PARACHUTE.

GOLDEN HANDSHAKE [COL] A compensation clause that gives an executive a substantial guaranteed payout in the event of termination or dismissal (other than "for cause").
- See also GOLDEN HANDCUFFS, GOLDEN HELLO, GOLDEN PARACHUTE.

GOLDEN HELLO [COL] An upfront compensation package granted to an executive joining from another firm; depending on the structure of the package it may serve as a "buy out" of the package being left at the prior company, and thus limit the effectiveness of long-term, performance-driven financial rewards.
- See also GOLDEN HANDCUFFS, GOLDEN HANDSHAKE, GOLDEN PARACHUTE.

GOLDEN PARACHUTE [COL] A compensation clause that gives top executives guaranteed payouts in the event they lose their jobs through a FRIENDLY TAKEOVER or HOSTILE TAKEOVER.
- See also GOLDEN HANDCUFFS, GOLDEN HANDSHAKE, GOLDEN HELLO.

GOOD DELIVERY A security/certificate with all necessary details and ENDORSEMENTS that allows accurate and efficient transfer of title from one party to another.

GOOD FOR MONTH ORDER A LIMIT ORDER or STOP ORDER to buy or sell a security that remains in effect until the end of the current month.

GOOD MONEY [COL] Any source of funds that is available for immediate use, such as FEDERAL FUNDS.

GOOD TILL CANCELLED ORDER A LIMIT ORDER for the purchase or sale of a security at a specific price that remains in effect until the price target is met and the trade is executed, or is otherwise cancelled by the individual or institution placing the order.
- Also known as OPEN ORDER.
- See also DAY ORDER, MARKET ORDER, STOP ORDER.

GOODWILL The primary INTANGIBLE ASSET of a company, generally comprised of reputation, contact networks, intellectual property, and branding. Although the assets have value, they cannot be physically inspected and are extremely ILLIQUID. Goodwill may also include the PREMIUM a company pays in acquiring another company; although such additional value is generally reflected on the corporate balance sheet it must typically be amortized over a set period of time.

GOVERNANCE A formal process/structure intended to ensure a company's executives and DIRECTORS perform their assigned duties and responsibilities diligently, so that STAKEHOLDERS generally, and shareholders specifically, are properly protected. Governance may be enforced internally, through a BOARD OF DIRECTORS with independent oversight of the executive team, financial controls, policies, and executive compensation which is aligned with shareholder interests. It may also be enforced externally through regulatory requirements, controlling shareholder oversight, and CORPORATE CONTROL activities.

- Also known as CORPORATE GOVERNANCE.

GOVERNMENT BILL A MONEY MARKET instrument issued by a governmental authority as a funding mechanism and a tool for conducting MONETARY POLICY. Bills are often issued on a discount, rather than COUPON-BEARING, basis, and typically have maturities extending from one week to one year. Those issued by governments of industrialized nations are considered to be highly LIQUID and extremely creditworthy, with virtually no risk of DEFAULT.

- See also GOVERNMENT BOND.

GOVERNMENT BOND A DEBT instrument issued by a governmental authority as a funding mechanism. Government bonds are generally issued on a fixed or floating rate, COUPON-BEARING, basis, with maturities extending from 1 to 30 years; those within the 1 to 10-year sector may be referred to as government notes. Some countries also feature INFLATION-LINKED SECURITIES within their government issuance programs. Government bonds issued by industrialized nations are generally quite LIQUID (and may be very liquid in the BENCHMARK) and extremely creditworthy, with virtually no risk of DEFAULT.

- See also GOVERNMENT BILL.

GOVERNMENT NATIONAL MORTGAGE ASSOCIATION (GNMA) A US government-owned CORPORATION (and agency of the Department of Housing and Urban Development) that purchases residential MORTGAGES guaranteed by the Department of Veterans Affairs and the Federal Housing Administration and pools them into MORTGAGE-BACKED SECURITIES (MBS); GNMA MBS, which essentially convert ILLIQUID mortgage ASSETS into marketable securities, carry the agency's guarantee of repayment on both PRINCIPAL and COUPON interest.

- Also known as GINNIE MAE.
- See also FEDERAL HOME LOAN MORTGAGE CORPORATION, FEDERAL NATIONAL MORTGAGE ASSOCIATION.

GRACE PERIOD See CURE PERIOD.

GRAINS [COL] The general group of EXCHANGE-TRADED DERIVATIVES referencing wheat, corn, soybeans, maize, and sorghum.
- See also COMMODITY DERIVATIVE, SOFTS.

GRAMM–LEACH–BLILEY ACT US Federal legislation enacted in 1999 with various provisions related to financial deregulation, including the repeal of significant portions of the GLASS–STEAGALL ACT which had previously separated the powers of COMMERCIAL BANKS and INVESTMENT BANKS and prohibited all banks from engaging in INSURANCE business. The legislation also eliminated bank restrictions on securities UNDERWRITING contained in the Bank Holding Company Act of 1956, and named the FEDERAL RESERVE BOARD as the primary regulator of financial holding companies engaged in banking, securities, and insurance businesses.
- Also known as FINANCIAL SERVICES MODERNIZATION ACT OF 1999.

GRANNY BOND [COL] In the United Kingdom, an issue of GILTS with an enhanced COUPON or tax benefits that is only available to investors that have reached a pensionable age.

GRAVEYARD MARKET [COL] A phase appearing at the end of a prolonged BEAR MARKET where investors have sustained large losses and new investors are unwilling to commit CAPITAL; volumes are extremely light and direction may be uncertain.

GRAY KNIGHT [COL] A second unsolicited bidder in a HOSTILE TAKEOVER transaction that attempts to take advantage of the target company's reluctance to accept the BLACK KNIGHT's original bid by offering slightly more "attractive" terms.
- See also WHITE KNIGHT, WHITE SQUIRE.

GRAY MARKET [COL] The market for TRADING in new securities that have been priced but not yet allocated, or allocated but not yet settled. The gray market acts as an intersection between the PRIMARY MARKET and the SECONDARY MARKET, and trades are considered binding and enforceable (though members of a SYNDICATE involved in UNDERWRITING a NEW ISSUE may be expelled if they trade between pricing and allocation; any such trades would be considered null and void).

GREEKS [COL] RISK measures for DERIVATIVES that are used to determine the price sensitivity of contracts to changes in the UNDERLYING ASSET (DELTA, GAMMA), VOLATILITY (VEGA), passage of time (THETA), and INTEREST RATES (RHO). The greeks of individual contracts can be added to determine the sensitivities of an entire PORTFOLIO, allowing for efficient pricing and RISK MANAGEMENT. The general impact on the value of an option for a unit increase in the relevant variable is given as:

	Long call	Short call	Long put	Short put
Delta	+	−	−	+
Gamma	+	−	+	−
Vega	+	−	+	−
Theta	−	+	−	+
Rho	+	+	−	−

■ Also known as OPTION SENSITIVITIES.

GREENMAIL [COL] A targeted repurchase by a company of a block of its own COMMON STOCK from a corporate RAIDER or hostile acquirer, generally at a PREMIUM to the current market price. Greenmail payments, which were prevalent during the TAKEOVER cycle of the 1980s, are not common in the marketplace of the millennium as certain legal/regulatory regimes have deemed such payments illegal.

GREENSHOE [COL] An OPTION granted by an issuing company to the SYNDICATE UNDERWRITING a NEW ISSUE of EQUITY, which permits the syndicate to sell additional shares as part of the PRIMARY MARKET offering in the face of excessive demand, up to a maximum amount defined in advance.

■ Also know as OVERALLOTMENT OPTION, SHOE.

GROSS DOMESTIC PRODUCT (GDP) A measure of a the goods and services produced within a country's geographic boundaries. GDP is used as a primary indicator of a country's economic strength and progress; positive GDP indicates the country's economic base is expanding, while negative GDP reflects a contraction and possible recession. GDP is slightly narrower in scope than the associated gross national product measure, which also includes goods and services produced by a country's residents, regardless of location.

GROSS LINE The total amount of INSURANCE cover an INSURER will UNDERWRITE on a particular RISK, including the amount to be ceded via REINSURANCE.

GROSS PREMIUM A measure of an INSURER's total profitability from INSURANCE UNDERWRITING activities (before expenses), computed as:

$GP = Pr + OpE + AC$

where Pr is PREMIUM (net), OpE is operating expense, and AC is AGENT commissions.

The greater the gross premium, the larger the amount of business being underwritten.

■ See also FAIR PREMIUM.

GROSS RATE See FAIR PREMIUM.

GROSS SPREAD See UNDERWRITING SPREAD.

GROSS WORKING CAPITAL The sum of a company's CURRENT ASSETS and CURRENT LIABILITIES.
- See also NET WORKING CAPITAL, WORKING CAPITAL.

GROUP CAPTIVE A CAPTIVE formed as a licensed INSURER or REINSURER that is owned by a number of companies, and which writes INSURANCE cover for all of them. Since a group captive engages in a significant amount of third party business, it generally receives more favorable tax treatment than a PURE CAPTIVE.
- Also known as an ASSOCIATION CAPTIVE or MULTI-PARENT CAPTIVE.
- See also AGENCY CAPTIVE, CAPTIVE, PROTECTED CELL COMPANY, RENT-A-CAPTIVE, SISTER CAPTIVE.

GROUP OF 7 (G7) International finance ministers from eight industrialized nations who attempt to influence economic and monetary policies through coordinated actions. The original seven member nations were Japan, Germany, France, the United Kingdom, Italy, Canada, and the United States; Russia joined the original group as an associate member before the turn of the millennium, forming a group that is now widely known as G8.

GROUP OF 10 (G10) CENTRAL BANKS of 11 countries that attempt to coordinate supervision of financial markets and banking institutions. The original 10 member nations were Japan, Germany, France, the United Kingdom, Italy, Canada, Belgium, Sweden, the Netherlands and the United States; Switzerland joined as a member in the millennium.

GUARANTEE A contractual agreement where one party (the GUARANTOR) provides payment to a second party (the BENEFICIARY) should the contracting party DEFAULT on its obligations. Through the provision of the guarantee, the obligations of the contracting party assume the CREDIT RATING of the guarantor, often a highly-rated BANK or INSURER.
- See also CROSS GUARANTEE, FINANCIAL GUARANTEE.

GUARANTEED EXCHANGE RATE OPTION See QUANTO.

GUARANTEED INVESTMENT CONTRACT (GIC) A financial contract between an INSURER and an individual or PENSION PLAN (as BENEFICIARY) that provides the beneficiary with a specific return on CAPITAL invested over the life of the contract. The insurer bears the investment RISK associated with the securities in the GIC portfolio but is generally able to retain any excess it earns over the guaranteed return.
- See also NON-PARTICIPATING GUARANTEED INVESTMENT CONTRACT, PARTICIPATING GUARANTEED INVESTMENT CONTRACT, SYNTHETIC GUARANTEED INVESTMENT CONTRACT.

GUARANTOR The party providing a GUARANTEE on behalf of the contracting party.

GUIDANCE LINE A BANK LINE granted to a customer that is used by the lending institution for internal management purposes and is not specifically communicated to the customer. Since the client pays no COMMITMENT FEE, the guidance line can be cancelled or withdrawn by the lender at any time.

    ■ See also ADVISED LINE.

GUN JUMPING [COL] (1) The public solicitation of orders for a PRIMARY OFFERING before REGISTRATION is complete. (2) TRADING of securities on the basis of non-public information (as a form of INSIDER TRADING). Gun jumping in either form is illegal in most national jurisdictions.

GUNSLINGER [COL] A trader, investor, or PORTFOLIO manager that takes a considerable amount of speculative RISK in an attempt to generate high returns.

GYOSEI SHIDO [JPN] The Japanese practice of bureaucratic control (or "administrative guidance") of CORPORATIONS, exercised through regulation, KEIRETSU group pressure and access to BANK-supplied credit.

H

HAIRCUT [COL] (1) The upfront discount applied to the value of security taken as COLLATERAL on a LOAN, REVERSE REPURCHASE AGREEMENT, or DERIVATIVE in order to protect against price deterioration and the possibility of any CREDIT RISK exposure becoming unsecured. The same discounts are often applied to securities included in a firm's own LIQUIDITY WAREHOUSE to provide a more accurate reflection of LIQUIDATION value. In general, the greater the VOLATILITY of the reference security and the longer the time between valuation and MARGIN calls or liquidation, the larger the haircut. (2) In the United States, the formula used by BROKER-DEALERS to compute net CAPITAL requirements under rules established by the SECURITIES AND EXCHANGE COMMISSION.

HANDLE [COL] The figures appearing to the left of the decimal in a securities price quote, often ignored by DEALERS and MARKET MAKERS quoting BIDS or OFFERS as they are implicitly understood.

HARD CALL PROTECTION A CALL PROTECTION provision in a BOND INDENTURE that prevents the issuer from calling the security for a specific period of time.
- See also NON-CALLABLE BOND, SOFT CALL PROTECTION.

HARD CURRENCY See CONVERTIBLE CURRENCY.

HARD DOLLARS Direct payments made by clients to financial institutions for services rendered. In commercial banking a client may pay a fee for a credit facility; in securities a client may pay brokerage commissions for trade execution or a fee for a financial plan.
- See also SOFT DOLLARS.

HARD LANDING [COL] A state where fiscal or monetary restraint intended to curb excess demand and high INFLATION erodes confidence and activity, leading to economic slowdown and recession.
- See also SOFT LANDING.

HARD MARKET An INSURANCE market cycle where INSURERS reduce the amount of coverage they are willing to write, causing supply to contract and PREMIUMS to rise. A hard market can occur by the onset of very large and unexpected losses (i.e., CATASTROPHIC HAZARDS, CLASH LOSS, SHOCK LOSS) that causes a depletion of CAPITAL within the insurance and REINSURANCE sector; relative lack of capital creates a shortfall in RISK CAPACITY. A hard market may also arise from a gradual lowering of UNDERWRITING standards occurring during a SOFT MARKET cycle, leading to a greater loss experience over time.

HARMONIZED INDEX OF CONSUMER PRICES (HICP) An INFLATION index widely used throughout the European Union that measures changes in consumer prices. Unlike various other CONSUMER PRICE INDEX measures, HICP excludes owner-occupied rental costs.
　■　See also PRODUCER PRICE INDEX, RETAIL PRICE INDEX.

HAUSBANK [GER] In Germany, a BANK acting as the primary relationship banker to a company, providing or arranging a variety of credit-related services. Hausbanks often wield additional power by directly holding large shareholdings in client companies and by voting PROXIES on behalf of investors who leave their shares in bank CUSTODY.

HAZARD An event that creates or increases PERIL. While hazards are not specifically covered in most INSURANCE contracts, the perils they create or magnify form the core of INSURABLE RISKS.

HEAD AND SHOULDERS [COL] A TECHNICAL ANALYSIS charting figure of a security or index that features a supporting price plateau, followed by a spike, then a reversal to a second supporting price plateau; the formation of a head and shoulders might then lead to a BREAKOUT on the upside or downside.

- See also REVERSE HEAD AND SHOULDERS.

HEAVY MARKET [COL] A market or sector that suffers price declines through selling pressures generated by large ORDER IMBALANCES.

HEDGE A financial transaction that is intended to protect an underlying ASSET, LIABILITY, revenue, or expense from adverse movement in a particular reference; a correctly structured hedge transaction can offset losses by providing a gain when the UNDERLYING suffers a loss, and vice-versa. Hedges can be constructed using traditional financial instruments such as COMMON STOCKS, BONDS, FOREIGN EXCHANGE, and commodities, as well as OVER-THE-COUNTER DERIVATIVES and EXCHANGE-TRADED DERIVATIVES. The actual creation of a hedge may be quantified through a number of techniques, including HEDGE RATIOS. The process of hedging is often associated with RISKS that are uninsurable through a standard contractual INSURANCE framework and must therefore be transferred to a hedge COUNTERPARTY.

- See also ARBITRAGE, CROSS-ASSET HEDGE, HEDGER, HEDGING, SPECULATION.

HEDGE FUND A private partnership (for US investors) or INVESTMENT COMPANY (for non-US or tax-exempt investors) that establishes LONG POSITIONS or SHORT POSITIONS in a broad range of ASSETS and actively uses DERIVATIVES and LEVERAGE to enhance returns. Most hedge funds have minimum investment lock-up periods and are considered to be quite ILLIQUID. A general partner typically manages a hedge fund, earning increasing success fees as performance targets are reached. Since hedge funds are generally very risky, investors must be accredited (possessing minimum net worth and able to sustain potential loss of CAPITAL). Retail investors are often barred from investing directly in hedge funds.

HEDGE RATIO A measure that indicates the price relationship between a reference ASSET and a proxy HEDGE contract. The hedge ratio, which is generally based on a statistical process such as linear regression, reflects how much of an asset or DERIVATIVE contract is needed to protect or offset the RISK of the UNDERLYING reference. It can be computed via:

$$H = \frac{Cov(A, B)}{\sigma^2_B}$$

where $Cov(A, B)$ is the COVARIANCE between asset A and hedge instrument B, and σ^2_B is the VARIANCE of B.

- Also known as MINIMUM VARIANCE HEDGE RATIO.

HEDGER A party that employs HEDGING techniques in order to minimize, or neutralize, RISK, often through DERIVATIVE contracts.

- See also HEDGE, SPECULATOR.

HEDGING The process of creating a HEDGE in order to minimize, or neutralize, RISK.

- See also DELTA HEDGE, HEDGE RATIO, HEDGER.

HICP See HARMONIZED INDEX OF CONSUMER PRICES.

HIGH–LOW OPTION An OVER-THE-COUNTER COMPLEX OPTION that grants the buyer a payoff based on the difference between the high and low prices achieved by the UNDERLYING reference ASSET during the life of the transaction.

- See also CALL ON THE MAXIMUM, PUT ON THE MINIMUM.

HIGH STREET BANK [COL] In the United Kingdom, a COMMERCIAL BANK that caters primarily to retail customers, accepting DEPOSITS and granting consumer, personal, and MORTGAGE LOANS. Although such banks also engage in other institutional banking business, their marketing and focus is weighted heavily towards individuals.

HIGH-YIELD BOND A BOND issued by a firm with a SUB-INVESTMENT GRADE CREDIT RATING (i.e., below BBB– by Standard and Poor's, Baa3 by Moody's Investors Services). The increased likelihood of DEFAULT compared with INVESTMENT GRADE bonds results in a greater COST OF CAPITAL for the issuer and a higher YIELD for investors. High-yield bonds were popularized during the corporate expansion and TAKEOVER phase of the mid- to late 1980s and have become an integral part of the CAPITAL MARKETS, particularly in the United States and Europe.

- Also known as JUNK BOND.

- See also FALLEN ANGEL.

HIGHLY LEVERAGED TRANSACTION (HLT) LOAN A LOAN extended by a BANK to a company that already has a high degree of LEVERAGE. HLT loans may be secured or unsecured, and typically have stringent COVENANTS requiring the leveraged borrower to adhere to various financial operating ratios, including those related to minimum levels of LIQUIDITY and INTEREST COVERAGE.

HISTORICAL METHOD A CREDIT RISK exposure computation methodology for SWAPS using historical INTEREST RATES. Under the historical method past interest rate (or swap rate) data is used to create a statistical distribution of rates. Following an adjustment to a prespecified CONFIDENCE LEVEL, forward swap rates are determined, allowing the swap to be revalued at each forward point and discounted back to the present; the largest exposure obtained during the revaluation process becomes the swap's FRACTIONAL EXPOSURE.
- See also OPTION METHOD, SIMULATION METHOD.

HISTORICAL VOLATILITY A retrospective statistical measure of the price movement of an ASSET based on historical data, often conveyed in terms of VARIANCE or STANDARD DEVIATION. Historical volatility is applied to various financial and RISK valuation techniques, including FRACTIONAL EXPOSURE and VALUE-AT-RISK.
- See also IMPLIED VOLATILITY.

HIT THE BID [COL] A seller's willingness to accept a buyer's price on a transaction.
- See also TAKE THE OFFER.

HLT LOAN See HIGHLY LEVERAGED TRANSACTION LOAN.

HOLD HARMLESS AGREEMENT An agreement by one party to assume the LIABILITY of a second party, holding it harmless against any potential financial loss; such an agreement may exist implicitly or explicitly between PRINCIPAL and AGENT.

HOLDING PERIOD (1) The period of time that an investment manager holds an ASSET within a PORTFOLIO. (2) See LIQUIDATION PERIOD.

HOMOGENOUS EXPOSURE A group of RISKS that feature similar or identical characteristics, leading to the same EXPECTED LOSS levels. Homogenous exposures allow for more accurate and equitable ACTUARIAL PRICING of INSURANCE contracts and ultimately reduce the likelihood of ADVERSE SELECTION.

HORIZONTAL CLEARING SERVICES CLEARING services that are offered by the CLEARINGHOUSE of one EXCHANGE to other exchanges and ELECTRONIC COMMUNICATIONS NETWORKS as a means of generating additional revenues.

HORIZONTAL LAYERING A practice where different REINSURERS take percentage portions of the same loss layer under an EXCESS OF LOSS (XOL) REINSURANCE agreement. Each reinsurer becomes liable for its own fractional portion of coverage between the ATTACHMENT level and the POLICY CAP. Under this approach every reinsurer is exposed to losses and CLAIMS once the underlying DEDUCTIBLE is exceeded.

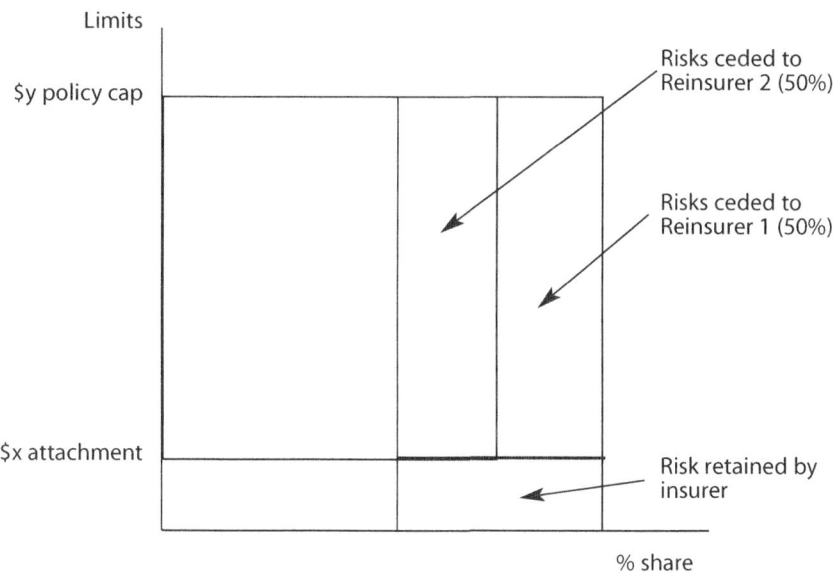

- See also EXCESS LAYER, VERTICAL LAYERING.

HORIZONTAL MERGER A MERGER between companies from the same industrial sector, sometimes direct competitors. A horizontal merger is often arranged in order to build market share or obtain better product or client coverage.
- See also CONGLOMERATE MERGER, VERTICAL MERGER.

HOSTILE TAKEOVER An unsolicited ACQUISITION offer from a RAIDER or BLACK KNIGHT that the target company's DIRECTORS and executives do not favor and attempt to thwart, through ANTI-TAKEOVER DEFENSES, ANTI-TAKEOVER LAWS, or SCORCHED EARTH DEFENSES, or by seeking a friendly partner in the form of a WHITE KNIGHT or WHITE SQUIRE.
- Also known as CONTESTED TRANSACTION.

HOT MONEY [COL] INTEREST RATE-sensitive DEPOSITS, overnight REVERSE REPURCHASE AGREEMENTS, and interbank funds that can be withdrawn rapidly based on market events or credit perceptions. BANKS funding their operations with a large amount of hot money, which is generally supplied by institutional investors, may encounter a

LIQUIDITY problem if they are unable to quickly replace funds that disappear within a span of hours or days. Banks with a stable base of core retail deposits are not as susceptible to problems generated by hot money.
- See also CALL MONEY.

HUNG DEAL [COL] A NEW ISSUE of securities that UNDERWRITERS fail to place at the primary launch SPREAD (or price). If the transaction is arranged as a BOUGHT DEAL the underwriters are obligated to take up the unsold securities and provide the issuer with funds as contracted; the group must then attempt to sell the securities on a secondary basis, often by widening the spread (lowering the price).
- Also known as STICKY DEAL, STUCK DEAL.

HYBRID BOND A FIXED INCOME security with embedded DERIVATIVES that alter RISK and return characteristics. The general class of hybrids includes CALLABLE BONDS, PUTABLE BONDS, BONDS WITH WARRANTS, CONVERTIBLE BONDS, and STRUCTURED NOTES.

HYBRID ELECTRONIC COMMUNICATIONS NETWORK An ELECTRONIC COMMUNICATIONS NETWORK (ECN) that incorporates the features of both DEALER MARKET ECNs and REGULATED ECNs.

HYBRID MODEL A general corporate system that is characterized by ILLIQUID CAPITAL MARKETS, an inactive or nonexistent CORPORATE CONTROL MARKET, and nascent regulatory and legal frameworks; family interests often hold large ownership stakes in companies, related company conglomeration is common, and ownership ties between companies and BANKS can be significant. Emerging nations often use the hybrid model.
- See also MARKET MODEL, RELATIONSHIP MODEL.

HYPOTHECATION A process where a borrower pledges ASSETS as COLLATERAL for a LOAN. No transfer of title occurs through hypothecation, but the lender accepting hypothecated assets is granted the right to dispose of the assets if the borrower DEFAULTS. The same process applies when an investor pledges securities to a BROKER to secure a PURPOSE (or MARGIN) LOAN or SHORT SALE. A broker, in turn, may use hypothecated securities to secure a BROKER LOAN through a process known as rehypothecation.

I

IAS See INTERNATIONAL ACCOUNTING STANDARDS.
IASB See INTERNATIONAL ACCOUNTING STANDARDS BOARD.
IBF See INTERNATIONAL BANKING FACILITY.
IBNR See INCURRED BUT NOT REPORTED.
IBRD See INTERNATIONAL BANK FOR RECONSTRUCTION AND DEVELOPMENT.
IDB See INTER-DEALER BROKER.
IDIOSYNCRATIC RISK See DIVERSIFIABLE RISK.
IFC See INTERNATIONAL FINANCE CORPORATION.
ILLIQUID (1) At a corporate level, the state of possessing insufficient cash to meet obligations. (2) At a market level, the state of having insufficient transaction volume to permit TRADING.
   ▪ See also LIQUID, LIQUID ASSETS, LIQUIDITY, ILLIQUIDITY.
ILLIQUIDITY (1) At a corporate level, lack of cash, NEAR CASH, unsecured funding access or unencumbered LIQUID ASSETS to meet expected or unexpected payments. (2) The state of being ILLIQUID or lacking LIQUID ASSETS. (3) At a market level, lack of TRADING volume in a security or ASSET; an illiquid market is characterized by large differences between BIDS and OFFERS.
   ▪ See also ENDOGENOUS LIQUIDITY, EXOGENOUS LIQUIDITY, LIQUIDITY, LIQUIDITY RISK.
ILS See INSURANCE-LINKED SECURITY.
IMF See INTERNATIONAL MONETARY FUND.
IMMEDIATE OR CANCEL ORDER An ORDER to purchase or sell securities where the BROKER is instructed to fill as much of the order as possible as soon as it is entered and cancel any portion that is not immediately filled.
IMMUNIZATION The process of protecting an INTEREST RATE-sensitive PORTFOLIO from future market movements so that a future

LIABILITY or cash outflow can be met. To protect against any changes in rates the portfolio must be invested in FIXED INCOME securities that have a DURATION equal to the investment horizon, and an initial PRESENT VALUE equal to the present value of a future liability. A portfolio is considered to be immunized when sufficient funds can be generated, or a target return can be obtained, regardless of the movement of rates.

IMPLIED FINANCING RATE See IMPLIED REPO RATE.

IMPLIED FORWARD CURVE A YIELD CURVE representing the TERM STRUCTURE of DISCOUNT RATES, starting in any designated future period. The implied forward curve, which is constructed from IMPLIED FORWARD RATES derived from the ZERO COUPON YIELD CURVE (itself a product of the observable PAR YIELD CURVE), is used to price instruments, such as DERIVATIVES, that require a forward estimate of rates. The shape and slope of the implied curve depends on the shape and slope of the par and zero coupon curves, as well as investor expectations regarding future interest rates.

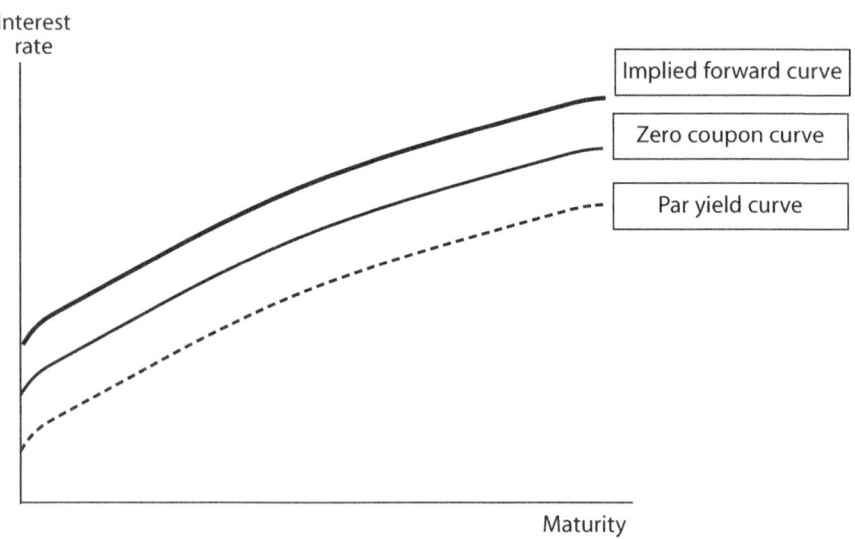

IMPLIED FORWARD RATE The INTEREST RATE that can be earned for a defined period of time, starting at some future point. The implied forward rate is the rate necessary to make funds invested at a short rate and reinvested at a forward rate (i.e., multiple period) precisely equal to the return invested at a long rate (i.e., single period).

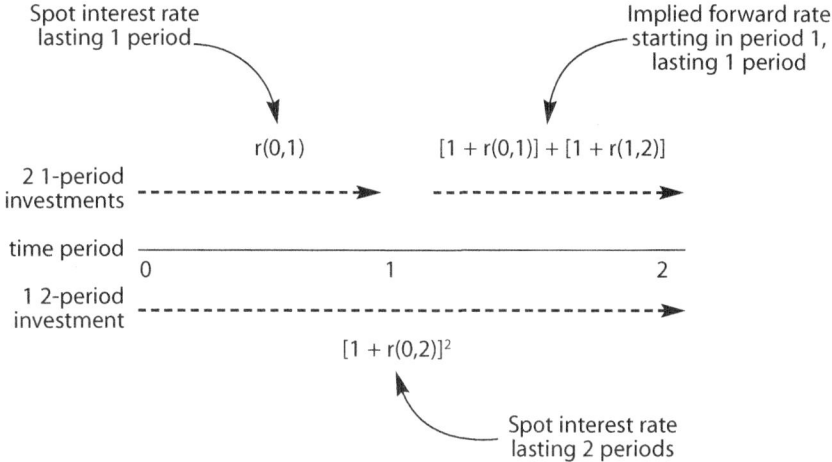

The t-year implied forward rate starting in n periods (semi-annual) is given by:

$$_nf_t = \left[\frac{(1 + r_{n+t})^{n+t}}{(1 + r_n)^n}\right]^{\frac{1}{t}} - 1$$

where r is the prevailing semi-annual SPOT RATE.
- Also known as FORWARD RATE.
- See also IMPLIED FORWARD CURVE, IMPLIED REPO RATE.

IMPLIED REPO RATE The return before financing costs implied by a CASH-AND-CARRY ARBITRAGE involving BONDS. The implied repo rate can be computed via:

$$IR = \left[\frac{(1 + r_{0,b})^b}{(1 + r^*_{a,b})^{b-a}}\right]^{1/a} - 1$$

where $r_{0,b}$ is the SPOT RATE to time period b and $r^*_{a,b}$ is the FUTURES rate covering periods a and b.
- Also known as IMPLIED FINANCING RATE.
- See also IMPLIED FORWARD RATE.

IMPLIED VOLATILITY A prospective measure of the price movement of an ASSET imputed from the market prices of traded OPTIONS. VOLATILITY is one of the central inputs of option pricing models but is not directly observable in the market; accordingly, traders use observed option prices to derive volatility.
- See also HISTORICAL VOLATILITY.

IMPORTS Goods and services produced offshore, transported or brought into the country, and sold to residents of the non-producing nation, including VISIBLES (goods) and INVISIBLES (services).

■ See also BALANCE OF TRADE, EXPORTS.

IMPREST ACCOUNT A fund established by a company as a SELF-INSURANCE mechanism to cover low-severity property losses.

IN-THE-MONEY A condition where the price of an UNDERLYING reference ASSET is higher than the STRIKE PRICE for a CALL OPTION or below the strike for a PUT OPTION, meaning the contract has immediate INTRINSIC VALUE if exercised.
■ See also AT-THE-MONEY, MONEYNESS, OUT-OF-THE-MONEY.

INCOME BOND A BOND that pays COUPON interest only if the issuer's operations can support the payments without impairing core operations. Such a security is generally issued by a weak credit, often in the context of a restructuring effort. Income bonds are generally priced without ACCRUED INTEREST given the uncertainty whether a coupon will be paid in any given period.

INCORPOREAL INTEREST The right to an INSURABLE INTEREST in a designated ASSET, conveyed when the assets are pledged as COLLATERAL.

INCUBATOR [COL] A firm that provides start-up ventures with seed CAPITAL, administrative services, and business plan support in exchange for a pre-INITIAL PUBLIC OFFERING EQUITY stake. Once the incubator has nurtured the start-up to a sufficient state of readiness the company is often referred to a VENTURE CAPITAL group for additional, and more formal, financing and management.
■ See also ACCELERATOR.

INCURRED BUT NOT REPORTED (IBNR) A loss covered by an INSURANCE contract that has already occurred but has not been reported by the INSURED to the INSURER. Insurers generally establish a minimum level of RESERVES to cover the lag in CLAIMS arising from an anticipated amount of IBNR items.

INCURRED LOSS In INSURANCE, a loss that has already occurred, whether or not the INSURER has paid a SETTLEMENT to the INSURED.
■ See also INCURRED LOSS RATIO.

INCURRED LOSS RATIO A measure of how much of an INSURER's PREMIUM is used to cover losses, computed as:

$$IL = \frac{Loss_{inc}}{Pr}$$

where $Loss_{inc}$ is the sum of INCURRED LOSSES and Pr is premium earned.

The larger the ratio, the greater the amount of premium that is used to cover losses.

INCURRED LOSS RETROSPECTIVE POLICY A LOSS-SENSITIVE INSURANCE CONTRACT requiring the INSURED to pay an incremental PREMIUM during the year based on the INSURER's best estimate of losses (i.e., actual losses plus an estimate of future losses).

INDEMNITY A fundamental principle of INSURANCE indicating that an INSURED cannot profit from an insurance contract, which exists only to cover a loss and not generate a speculative gain. The maximum amount payable under a contract of indemnity is the amount required to return the insured to the financial position that existed prior to the loss.
- See also INDEMNITY CONTRACT, INSURABLE INTEREST, VALUED CONTRACT.

INDEMNITY COMPANY An INSURER that specializes in UNDERWRITING a range of PROPERTY AND CASUALTY INSURANCE covers.

INDEMNITY CONTRACT An INSURANCE contract that provides the INSURED with restitution for actual losses sustained. The indemnity contract, which includes PROPERTY AND CASUALTY INSURANCE and LIABILITY INSURANCE, is designed to return the insured to the financial state it occupied prior to the loss.
- See also INDEMNITY, VALUED CONTRACT.

INDEMNITY TRIGGER A conditional event in an INSURANCE-LINKED SECURITY that causes suspension of COUPON interest and/or PRINCIPAL when actual losses sustained by the issuer reach a pre-defined amount.
- See also INDEX TRIGGER, PARAMETRIC TRIGGER.

INDENTURE The written terms and conditions of a BOND or NOTE issue, which generally includes details regarding form of security, COUPON interest, CALL/PUT provisions, COVENANTS, EVENTS OF DEFAULT, and PRINCIPAL repayment. The indenture also defines the rights, privileges, and obligations of the issuer, investor, and TRUSTEE related to the initial provision of CAPITAL and the timely payment of interest and repayment of principal.

INDEX AMORTIZING RATE SWAP See INDEX PRINCIPAL SWAP.

INDEX ARBITRAGE An ARBITRAGE strategy that attempts to capitalize on price discrepancies between index FUTURES and the individual COMMON STOCKS comprising the index. When index futures appear RICH to fair value, ARBITRAGEURS sell futures and purchase the underlying stocks; when they appear CHEAP, they buy futures and sell the stocks. The arbitrage can be preserved until the maturity of the underlying futures contracts, or rolled into the new contract cycle as trading becomes active.
- Also known as PROGRAM TRADING.

INDEX FUND A MUTUAL FUND that guarantees investors returns based on a defined market index or sub-index. Index funds generally feature lower costs than actively managed funds and are favored by investors who do not believe that a market index can be outperformed over the long-term.
- See also INDEXING, PASSIVE INVESTMENT STRATEGY.

INDEX FUTURE A FUTURES contract, bought or sold via an EXCHANGE, which references a specific BENCHMARK EQUITY index, index sector, or equity BASKET.
- See also COMMODITY FUTURE, CURRENCY FUTURE, INTEREST RATE FUTURE.

INDEX PRINCIPAL SWAP An OVER-THE-COUNTER SWAP with a NOTIONAL PRINCIPAL that amortizes as a floating INTEREST RATE reference declines through pre-specified BARRIER levels. As the notional declines, fixed and floating rate payments associated with the swap become smaller. The swap is often used as a HEDGE against ASSETS or LIABILITIES with CASH FLOWS that amortize with rate movements.
- Also known as INDEX AMORTIZING RATE SWAP.
- See also ACCRETING SWAP, AMORTIZING SWAP, REVERSE INDEX PRINCIPAL SWAP, VARIABLE PRINCIPAL SWAP.

INDEX TRIGGER A conditional event in an INSURANCE-LINKED SECURITY that causes suspension of COUPON interest and/or PRINCIPAL when the value of a recognized third-party index used to track RISK exposure or loss experience reaches a certain threshold.
- See also INDEMNITY TRIGGER, PARAMETRIC TRIGGER.

INDEXING A PASSIVE INVESTMENT STRATEGY based on replicating the performance of a specific ASSET index with a minimum of TRACKING ERROR.
- See also ACTIVE INVESTMENT STRATEGY, INDEX FUND.

INDICATED MARKET An estimated TRADING range for a security that has been halted on an EXCHANGE as a result of pending news or an ORDER IMBALANCE. The indicated market is a gauge of where the security may trade once it reopens, although supply and demand forces ultimately determine the actual starting level.

INDICATION OF INTEREST (IOI) Preliminary indication by an investor of possible interest in purchasing a NEW ISSUE of securities. Since IOIs are gathered informally while securities are still in the REGISTRATION process, the interest is considered non-binding; indeed, IOIs cannot be regarded as solicitation (by the UNDERWRITER) or commitment (by the investor). IOIs are an essential part of the BOOK-BUILDING process and provide UNDERWRITERS with valuable input on pricing and demand.

- Also known as CIRCLE.

INDICATIVE QUOTE A BID and/or OFFER supplied by a DEALER or MARKET MAKER to a BROKER or client that cannot be regarded as certain, but as a guide or estimate for informational purposes. Only when execution appears more likely to occur will the dealer provide an actionable FIRM QUOTE.
- See also QUOTED SPREAD.

INDIRECT LOSS See CONSEQUENTIAL LOSS.

INDIRECT STAKEHOLDERS In GOVERNANCE, the parties impacted by a company's activities and actions in a less obvious, immediate, or direct manner than DIRECT STAKEHOLDERS; this group generally includes regulators, taxpayers, and competitors.

INDUSTRIAL PAPER COMMERCIAL PAPER issued by a non-financial company.
- See also FINANCIAL PAPER.

INELASTIC A state where a proportional change in one variable leads to a smaller proportional change in a second variable. Inelastic demand is a weak demand response to a change in price, i.e., a proportional decline in the purchase price results in a smaller proportional increase in demand. Inelastic supply is a weak supply response to a change in price, i.e., a proportional increase in the selling price results in a smaller proportional increase in the amount supplied.
- See also ELASTIC, ELASTICITY.

INFLATION The rate of increase in prices of goods and services. Inflation can be measured at the wholesale level through indexes such as the PRODUCER PRICE INDEX, or at the retail level through the CONSUMER PRICE INDEX, RETAIL PRICE INDEX, or HARMONIZED INDEX OF CONSUMER PRICES.
- See also COST INFLATION, DEFLATION, DEMAND INFLATION, NOMINAL INTEREST RATE, REAL INTEREST RATE.

INFLATION-LINKED SECURITY A NOTE or BOND that pays a guaranteed return based on realized INFLATION for investors holding the security until maturity. In most inflation securities the COUPON provides a fixed rate of return while the PRINCIPAL is adjusted to take account of annual inflation recorded over the life of the security. Inflation-linked securities are issued by government authorities in the United States, the UK, the European Union, Mexico, and Canada.
- See also AJUSTABONOS, TREASURY INFLATION PROTECTED SECURITY.

INFLATION SWAP An OVER-THE-COUNTER SWAP involving the exchange of fixed and actual INFLATION rates, sometimes referred to as a CONSUMER PRICE INDEX (CPI) swap (US), RETAIL PRICE INDEX (RPI) swap (UK), or HARMONIZED INDEX OF

CONSUMER PRICES (HICP) swap (Eurozone). Inflation swaps, which are generally structured as ANNUAL INFLATION SWAPS or ZERO COUPON INFLATION SWAPS, often have final maturities of 10+ years.

INITIAL MARGIN (1) Security (generally cash, a LETTER OF CREDIT, or high-quality BONDS) posted by the buyer and seller of EXCHANGE-TRADED DERIVATIVE contracts at the inception of each transaction to protect the CLEARINGHOUSE against DEFAULT by a COUNTERPARTY. Initial margin is typically based on the price VOLATILITY of a contract's reference ASSET. (2) Security used to support PURPOSE LOANS or NON-PURPOSE LOANS under the FEDERAL RESERVE BOARD's Regulation T margin requirements.
- (1) Also known as ORIGINAL MARGIN.
- (1), (2) See also CLEARING MARGIN, MAINTENANCE MARGIN, VARIATION MARGIN.

INITIAL PUBLIC OFFERING (IPO) An inaugural issue of a company's COMMON STOCK in the public EQUITY markets. A SYNDICATE of INVESTMENT BANKS or SECURITIES FIRMS typically UNDERWRITES an IPO, pricing the transaction within a range suggested by comparables (i.e., common stock of competing firms), supply/demand forces, and INDICATIONS OF INTEREST. IPO shares are allocated by the syndicate to institutional and/or retail clients and are then traded through the SECONDARY MARKET. If demand is significant, the syndicate may exercise a GREENSHOE and float more shares.
- See also ADD-ON, RIGHTS ISSUE.

INSIDE DIRECTOR A board DIRECTOR who is related to the company and/or its executives in some manner, such as previous employment, business or consulting relationship, or personal relationships. Inside directors are generally not considered to be independent for GOVERNANCE purposes.
- See also OUTSIDE DIRECTOR.

INSIDE MARKET BIDS and OFFERS between DEALERS expressly for dealer accounts, rather than those intended for BROKERS or their clients.

INSIDER SYSTEM A corporate ownership system where controlling interests (e.g., family stakes, large corporate or BANK shareholdings) limit the ability of outside investors to influence the GOVERNANCE or management processes. Insiders systems are most commonly found in Continental Europe, Southeast Asia, and parts of Latin America.
- See also OUTSIDER SYSTEM.

INSIDER TRADING Any instance where non-public information is used to purchase or sell securities in order to generate a profit. In some systems insider trading is a criminal activity and is monitored and

regulated; violators may be punished through fines, disgorgement of profits, and/or incarceration. In other systems it is not considered a crime and/or rules against insider trading are widely ignored.
- See also GUN JUMPING.

INSOLVENCY A state where a company's LIABILITIES exceed the MARKET VALUE of its ASSETS (giving rise to negative EQUITY) or when it cannot pay DEBTS falling due in the normal course of business. Insolvency generally leads to filing of VOLUNTARY BANKRUPTCY or INVOLUNTARY BANKRUPTCY.
- See also DEFAULT, EVENT OF DEFAULT, SOLVENCY.

INSOLVENCY CLAUSE A clause in a REINSURANCE contract indicating that the REINSURER is still liable for its share of any CLAIM submitted by an INSURED, even if the insured's primary INSURER (i.e., the CEDING INSURER) is in a state of INSOLVENCY.

INSTALLMENT OPTION An OVER-THE-COUNTER COMPLEX OPTION allowing the buyer to pay the seller PREMIUM in installments, rather than upfront, and to cancel the contract at any time by suspending remaining payments. If the buyer completes all required payments, the seller grants a conventional EUROPEAN OPTION with contract details as specified on the trade date.

INSURABLE INTEREST The possibility that an individual or institution will sustain a monetary loss from an event that can be covered by INSURANCE. An insurable interest can be created through direct ownership or indirect CLAIM (e.g., vendor/vendee, mortgagor/mortgagee). In order for an insurance contract to be valid, insurable interest must exist at the time a contract starts and when a loss occurs.
- See also INDEMNITY.

INSURABLE RISK A RISK event that produces a loss that is definable, fortuitous, non-catastrophic, and homogenous, and that can be transferred through payment of a reasonably priced PREMIUM. Risk events that do not feature such characteristics may not be insurable as the cost of RISK TRANSFER may be prohibitively expensive.
- See also UNINSURABLE RISK.

INSURANCE A legally binding ALEATORY CONTRACT between two parties (the INSURER as protection provider and the INSURED as protection purchaser) that exchanges an ex-ante PREMIUM for an ex-post financial SETTLEMENT in the event of loss from a specified PERIL. In general, an insurance contract must represent INSURABLE RISKS, the insured must have an INSURABLE INTEREST and demonstrate an actual economic loss when making a CLAIM, and the risk of loss must be specifically transferred under a contract providing INDEMNITY. The insurance contract is one of UBERRIMAE FIDEI, executed in 'utmost good faith' through the conveyance of material

REPRESENTATIONS, and defines the insured's rights, the insurer's obligations, terms of coverage, rights of SUBROGATION, exceptions, EXCLUSIONS, limitations, conditions, and expiry. Common contracts include health insurance, life insurance, LIABILITY INSURANCE, PROPERTY AND CASUALTY INSURANCE, PROPERTY AND LIABILITY INSURANCE, and BUSINESS INTERRUPTION INSURANCE.

- Also known as ASSURANCE.
- See also INDEMNITY CONTRACT, VALUED CONTRACT.

INSURANCE-LINKED SECURITY (ILS) A NOTE or BOND that securitizes INSURABLE RISK by transferring exposures to the CAPITAL MARKETS; most issuers are INSURERS seeking to reduce risk within their PORTFOLIOS. An ILS is created when an insurer issues securities through a special-purpose reinsurer (SPR), who places them with investors and channels proceeds to a TRUSTEE for further reinvestment in the BOND market. Simultaneously, the SPR grants the insurer a REINSURANCE contract covering the specified risk. Payment of investor PRINCIPAL and/or COUPONS is dependent on losses arising from defined INSURANCE events; if losses exceed a predetermined threshold, the insurer may suspend payments, which has the net effect of creating a HEDGE against the underlying insurable risks. Suspension of payments is generally based on breach of a threshold defined via an INDEX TRIGGER, INDEMNITY TRIGGER, or PARAMETRIC TRIGGER. Most ILSs are based on catastrophic PERILS such as hurricanes, earthquakes, and windstorms.

- See also CATASTROPHE BOND, LIFE ACQUISITION COST SECURITIZATION, MORTGAGE DEFAULT SECURITIZATION, RESIDUAL VALUE SECURITIZATION, WEATHER BOND.

INSURED A party in an INSURANCE contract that transfers, or CEDES, RISK to an INSURER by paying a PREMIUM. The amount of risk the insured cedes is typically a function of its own financial profile and its desire to retain or transfer specific types of risks.
- See also CEDING COMPANY.
- Also known as CEDANT (CEDENT).

INSURED PERIL A PERIL that is specifically covered by an INSURANCE contract.

INSURER A regulated institution that accepts the RISKS of INSUREDS or CEDANTS through the INSURANCE mechanism. In order to meet potential future LIABILITIES and cover EXPECTED LOSSES, an insurer manages the risk in its own operations through RISK POOLING, DIVERSIFICATION, and the purchase of REINSURANCE. To supplement earnings from insurance UNDERWRITING activities, an insurer invests its ASSET PORTFOLIO in FIXED INCOME and EQUITY securities that generate investment income and/or capital gains. An insurer may be organized as a public JOINT STOCK COMPANY or a mutual organization.
- Also known as ASSURER, PRIMARY INSURER.
- See also ADMITTED INSURER, NON-ADMITTER INSURER, REINSURER.

INTANGIBLE See INTANGIBLE ASSET.

INTANGIBLE ASSET An ASSET with value but without physical characteristics, such as GOODWILL, trademarks, copyrights, or intellectual property. Intangibles are generally heterogeneous across firms, and are typically very ILLIQUID.
- Also known as INTANGIBLE.

INTENSITY MODEL A form of CREDIT DEFAULT MODEL that estimates the time of a COUNTERPARTY'S failure with a particular intensity over an uncertain time horizon. Such models have no direct reference to a firm's value but derive the probability of the event as an instantaneous likelihood of DEFAULT.
- See also STRUCTURAL MODEL, CREDIT MARK-TO-MARKET MODEL.

INTER-DEALER BROKER (IDB) A BROKER that deals exclusively with DEALERS and market professionals, rather than external clients. IDBs often execute their brokerage business on a "blind" basis in order to preserve confidentiality about trades and positions in the competitive institutional marketplace.

INTERBANK DEPOSIT A DEPOSIT obligation issued by one BANK (the debtor or obligor) to a second bank (the creditor). The deposit is generally short-term in nature, extending from overnight to several weeks, with a floating INTEREST RATE often pegged to LIBOR,

EONIA, EURIBOR, or TIBOR. Funds from interbank deposits are generally held in a "due to" (VOSTRO/NOSTRO) account. Wholesale banks that lack a broad base of retail branches are often significant users of interbank deposits.

- See also HOT MONEY.

INTEREST COVERAGE A financial indicator that measures a company's ability to manage its DEBT SERVICE, including payments of COUPON interest, PRINCIPAL, and/or LEASE obligations. A company with good interest coverage demonstrates financial strength and flexibility, while one with weak cover may be susceptible to FINANCIAL DISTRESS. Interest cover is often computed through the TIMES INTEREST EARNED measure.

- See also DEBT SERVICE COVERAGE.

INTEREST-ONLY (IO) STRIP A component of a stripped MORTGAGE-BACKED SECURITY or COLLATERALIZED MORTGAGE OBLIGATION that is entitled only to interest COUPONS from the underlying securities; PRINCIPAL flows are redirected to the PRINCIPAL-ONLY (PO) STRIP investors. Unlike other FIXED INCOME securities, the price of an IO declines when interest rates decline since PREPAYMENTS increase and lead to a smaller amount of coupon payments.

INTEREST RATE The price of DEBT CAPITAL. For a borrower, it represents the cost of funds or the cost of borrowing; for investors or lenders it is the earning rate on capital invested or lent.

INTEREST RATE DERIVATIVE An EXCHANGE-TRADED DERIVATIVE or OVER-THE-COUNTER DERIVATIVE with an UNDERLYING reference based on short-, medium- or long-term INTEREST RATES. An interest rate derivative may be structured as an INTEREST RATE FUTURE, interest rate OPTION, FORWARD RATE AGREEMENT, INTEREST RATE SWAP, or SWAPTION.

- See also CAP, COMMODITY DERIVATIVE, CREDIT DERIVATIVE, CURRENCY DERIVATIVE, FLOOR, PAYER SWAPTION, RECEIVER SWAPTION.

INTEREST RATE DIFFERENTIAL The difference between the FORWARD RATES of two currencies. The interest rate differential can be determined via:

$$r_{diff} = \frac{FP\,(RB)\,(100)}{FX_s\,(t)}$$

where FP is the FORWARD POINTS, FX_s is the SPOT FOREIGN EXCHANGE rate, t is the time to maturity (days), and RB is the rate basis (e.g., 360, 365 days).

INTEREST RATE FORWARD See FORWARD RATE AGREEMENT.

INTEREST RATE FUTURE A FUTURES contract, bought or sold via an EXCHANGE, which references a short-term INTEREST RATE (such as a GOVERNMENT BILL rate or INTERBANK DEPOSIT rate) or a medium-term or long-term rate (generally a GOVERNMENT BOND rate).
- See also BILL FUTURE, BOND FUTURE, CURRENCY FUTURE, DEPOSIT FUTURE, INDEX FUTURE, INTEREST RATE FUTURE.

INTEREST RATE PARITY A theory indicating that the INTEREST RATE DIFFERENTIAL between two currencies approximates the difference between the FORWARD DISCOUNT or FORWARD PREMIUM implied in FOREIGN EXCHANGE RATES.

INTEREST RATE SWAP An OVER-THE-COUNTER SWAP involving the exchange of two INTEREST RATE references for periods ranging from one to 10+ years. A typical interest rate swap involves the exchange of fixed rates and floating rates, though two floating rates can also be exchanged (in the form of a BASIS SWAP). Interest rate swaps do not involve the initial and final exchange of NOTIONAL PRINCIPAL and thus feature less CREDIT RISK than CURRENCY SWAPS. Swaps are commonly used to HEDGE exposure to rates or take a specific view on the direction of rates and/or the shape of the YIELD CURVE.

INTERLOCKING DIRECTORATE See INTERLOCKING DIRECTORSHIP.

INTERLOCKING DIRECTORSHIP A practice where executives or DIRECTORS from one firm serve as DIRECTORS on another firm's board, and vice-versa. From a GOVERNANCE perspective this may create conflicts of interest and lack of independence.
- Also known as INTERLOCKING DIRECTORATE.
- See also FILZ.

INTERMARKET SPREAD A DERIVATIVE position that seeks to take advantage of price differences between two unique, though often related, markets or ASSETS; the SPREAD attempts to capitalize on movements in the spread, or BASIS, rather than the absolute direction or VOLATILITY, of the references.

INTERMEDIATION (1) A process or structure where a financial institution stands between the suppliers and users of CAPITAL (or other financial instruments, transactions, or ASSETS) helping arrange both sides in exchange for a fee. (2) A process where an originating BANK executes a financial transaction through another party rather than directly with the end-user; the intermediary, rather than the bank, is thus exposed to the CREDIT RISK of the end-user.
- (1) See also DISINTERMEDIATION.

INTERNAL RATE OF RETURN (IRR) The rate of interest, compounded over each relevant period, which equates all net CASH FLOWS to the required outlay. IRR effectively measures the average YIELD or value of a project or financial investment, and can be computed by setting the NET PRESENT VALUE to zero (breakeven) and solving for the rate that forces cash outflows and inflows to the breakeven NPV. It is equivalent to the DISCOUNT RATE in a DISCOUNTED CASH FLOW computation, and YIELD TO MATURITY in a FIXED INCOME computation.

INTERNAL RATINGS-BASED (IRB) APPROACH A CAPITAL quantification methodology for CREDIT RISK introduced under the 2004 BASLE ACCORD that replaces computation methodologies promulgated under the original 1988 Capital Accord. The IRB approach can be implemented via the FOUNDATION METHODOLOGY or ADVANCED METHODOLOGY, both of which permit the use of an institution's own internally-developed models.
- See also CURRENT EXPOSURE METHOD, ORIGINAL EXPOSURE METHOD.

INTERNATIONAL ACCOUNTING STANDARDS (IAS) A body of accounting rules, adopted by public companies in many countries, intended to provide uniform treatment of activities impacting the balance sheet, income statement, and statement of CASH FLOWS. IAS rules are widely followed by public companies located outside the United States.
- See also GENERALLY ACCEPTED ACCOUNTING PRINCIPLES.

INTERNATIONAL ACCOUNTING STANDARDS BOARD (IASB) The international advisory panel that is responsible for creating and promulgating accounting rules collectively known as INTERNATIONAL ACCOUNTING STANDARDS.
- See also FINANCIAL ACCOUNTING STANDARDS BOARD.

INTERNATIONAL BANK FOR RECONSTRUCTION AND DEVELOPMENT (IBRD) A supranational banking institution established in 1946 to help reconstruct post-war economies and promote economic development and stability. The IBRD actively makes LOANS to public sector borrowers and state-guaranteed projects, and is funded by member countries through currencies, gold, and open call CAPITAL.
- Also known as WORLD BANK.
- See also INTERNATIONAL FINANCE CORPORATION (IFC).

INTERNATIONAL BANKING FACILITY (IBF) An international banking center within a US BANK that is permitted by the FEDERAL RESERVE BOARD to participate in EUROCURRENCY lending and accept RESERVE-free offshore DEPOSITS. The IBF is competitive with other offshore transactions as business is not subject to FEDERAL DEPOSIT INSURANCE CORPORATION PREMIUM payments and interest on deposits payable to foreign depositors is exempt from withholding taxes.

INTERNATIONAL FINANCE CORPORATION (IFC) An international INVESTMENT BANK, created in 1956 as an affiliate of the INTERNATIONAL BANK FOR RECONSTRUCTION AND DEVELOPMENT (IBRD), which is responsible for making development LOANS to private sector borrowers, primarily in LESSER DEVELOPED COUNTRIES and NEWLY INDUSTRIALIZED COUNTRIES.

INTERNATIONAL MONETARY FUND (IMF) A supranational organization created in 1946 to assist in maintaining financial stability and administer the fixed FOREIGN EXCHANGE rate regime that existed until 1971. The IMF now focuses on granting LOANS, managing external DEBT programs (via the Supplemental Reserve Facility and Country Credit Line program), and creating stability plans for debtor nations. The organization is financed via subscriptions from member countries.

INTERNATIONAL SECURITIES MARKETS ASSOCIATION (ISMA) An industry trade group representing the SECONDARY TRADING marketplace for international BONDS. The ISMA is responsible for establishing and promulgating the bond-dealing practices, and pricing and SETTLEMENT conventions, which are widely used in the international bond markets.

INTERNATIONAL SWAPS AND DERIVATIVES ASSOCIATION (ISDA) An industry trade group representing the OVER-THE-COUNTER DERIVATIVES marketplace. ISDA has been instrumental in developing and advancing key product and RISK MANAGEMENT mechanisms, including NETTING and MASTER AGREEMENTS.

INTERPOSITIONING The act of placing a BROKER or SPECIALIST between two PRINCIPALS to facilitate a trade. Interpositioning is illegal when a broker intercedes simply to generate additional commissions, or when a specialist intercedes to take one side of the trade for proprietary purposes.
- See also AFFIRMATIVE OBLIGATION, NEGATIVE OBLIGATION.

INTRINSIC VALUE One of two components, along with TIME VALUE, comprising the value of an OPTION. Intrinsic value measures the current MONEYNESS of an option, or the difference between the STRIKE PRICE and the UNDERLYING reference price. A contract that is IN-THE-MONEY has intrinsic value and can be EXERCISED for an immediate gain; those that are OUT-OF-THE-MONEY or AT-THE-MONEY have no intrinsic value.

INTRODUCING BROKER An intermediary standing between a client and a FUTURES COMMISSION MERCHANT (FCM) that develops and executes client strategies. Since the introducing broker cannot hold customer funds, it must deal through an FCM, which has proper authority.

INVENTORY ASSETS on the corporate balance sheet, including raw materials, work in progress, and finished goods, that are ultimately used to meet customer demand. In general, companies attempt to minimize their inventories so that they can deploy their assets in other productive endeavors; however, they must balance this against the need to provide customers with finished goods as needed. The cost of holding inventory is a combination of the cost of financing and storage, cost of obsolescence, and the opportunity COST OF CAPITAL.

- See also INVENTORY FINANCING, INVENTORY TURNOVER.

INVENTORY FINANCING A WORKING CAPITAL LOAN used to finance the acquisition of INVENTORY that a company ultimately uses for production and sales to customers. The proceeds of the inventory sale are typically used to repay the loan, making the transaction self-liquidating. Inventory financing may be secured or unsecured; if secured, the loan may include a charge over specific inventory or a FLOATING LIEN applicable to inventories in general.

INVENTORY TURNOVER A measure of a company's ability to sell INVENTORIES of finished goods, typically calculated as:

$$INV_{TO} = \frac{CGS}{INV_{AVG}}$$

where CGS is the cost of goods sold, and INV_{AVG} is average inventory on hand during the period.

A high turnover ratio is generally an indication of efficiency in managing the inventory process.

INVERSE FLOATER SWAP An OVER-THE-COUNTER COMPLEX SWAP involving the exchange of a fixed INTEREST RATE and an inverse rate defined by the general form [x% – floating rate]. The payment flows add a degree of LEVERAGE, making the transaction far more sensitive to rate changes than a standard INTEREST RATE SWAP.

- Also known as REVERSE FLOATER SWAP
- See also INVERSE FLOATER NOTE.

INVERSE FLOATING RATE NOTE (FRN) A STRUCTURED NOTE that provides the investor with a COUPON based on an inverse INTEREST RATE, generally defined by the form [x% – floating

rate]; rising rates create a lower interest coupon and falling rates a higher coupon. The inverse nature of the payment adds a degree of LEVERAGE to the structure, making it far more sensitive to changes in rates.
- Also known as REVERSE FLOATING RATE NOTE.
- See also CAPPED FLOATING RATE NOTE, INVERSE FLOATER SWAP, PERPETUAL FLOATING RATE NOTE, RANGE FLOATING RATE NOTE.

INVERTED YIELD CURVE See NEGATIVE YIELD CURVE.

INVESTING CASH FLOW The portion of the CASH FLOW statement depicting the flows impacting a firm's ASSET and investment accounts, including additions to, or disposals of, property, plant and equipment, marketable securities, and other corporate or subsidiary interests.
- See also FINANCING CASH FLOW, OPERATING CASH FLOW.

INVESTMENT ADVISOR A FIDUCIARY that acts as an AGENT for an investing client, ensuring all business is transacted in the best interests of that client. In most jurisdictions investment advisors must be registered with regulatory authorities and disclose any conflicts of interest they may have in providing particular investment recommendations.
- See also BROKER.

INVESTMENT BANK In the United States, a BANK that provides clients with CORPORATE FINANCE, RISK MANAGEMENT, and investment management advice, and deals actively in securities UNDERWRITING and TRADING. Unlike a COMMERCIAL BANK, an investment bank does not actively accept DEPOSITS or grant LOANS as a main line of business (although certain investment banks hold commercial bank licenses and perform the functions as an additional business line).
- See also BOUTIQUE, MERCHANT BANK, UNIVERSAL BANK.

INVESTMENT COMPANY A registered company that raises CAPITAL from investors by selling shares or units, and invests in a range of ASSETS on a LEVERAGED of unleveraged basis. In the United States, MUTUAL FUNDS (OPEN-END FUNDS) and UNIT INVESTMENT TRUSTS (CLOSED-END FUNDS) are the most popular forms of investment companies; in the UK, UNIT TRUSTS and INVESTMENT TRUSTS perform a similar function.

INVESTMENT CREDIT PROGRAM A tax-advantaged LOSS-SENSITIVE INSURANCE CONTRACT that contains elements of RISK FINANCING and RISK TRANSFER. Under the program the INSURED pays the INSURER an amount intended to cover

EXPECTED LOSSES up to a desired DEDUCTIBLE. Funds are placed in a TRUST account and used to finance losses as they occur. If the trust account moves into deficit, the insured pays an additional PREMIUM, and if it builds to a surplus, it receives the excess. Since funds are held in trust (and cannot be withdrawn by the insured) investment earnings are not taxed.

INVESTMENT GRADE A CREDIT RATING designation applied to any issuer of securities that is rated between AAA and BBB– by Standard and Poor's, or Aaa and Baa3 by Moody's Investors Services. Investment grade credits have the strongest financial profiles and the lowest likelihood of encountering FINANCIAL DISTRESS leading to DEFAULT.
- See also SUB-INVESTMENT GRADE.

INVESTMENT LETTER In the United States, a document between the buyer and seller of a PRIVATE PLACEMENT indicating that securities will not be offered for resale to the general public for a specific period of time; once the time period passes, they may be sold to a limited population under Rule 144 of the SECURITIES AND EXCHANGE COMMISSION.

INVESTMENT PREMIUM The additional amount an investor pays over the INVESTMENT VALUE of a CONVERTIBLE BOND to reflect the equity OPTION features of the convertible; the premium is typically expressed as a percentage of investment value:

$$I\,Prem = \left(\frac{P_{CB}}{IV} - 1\right)(100\%)$$

where P_{CB} is the price of the convertible bond and IV is investment value.
- Also known as BOND PREMIUM.
- See also CONVERSION PREMIUM.

INVESTMENT RATIO In INSURANCE, a measure of the extent to which an INSURER's gains come from investment, rather than UNDERWRITING activities, typically computed as:

$$IR = \frac{Inv}{Pr}$$

where Inv is gain on portfolio investments and Pr is PREMIUM earned.

The higher the ratio, the greater the insurer's reliance on investment income rather than core insurance underwriting.

INVESTMENT TRUST (1) In the UK, a PUBLIC LIMITED COMPANY traded on an EXCHANGE that raises CAPITAL through the placement of COMMON STOCK and DEBENTURES and invests the funds in a

range of financial ASSETS. Since investment trusts are permitted to issue debentures they can invest on a LEVERAGED basis, magnifying potential gains and losses. (2) In the United States, see CLOSED-END FUND.
- See also INVESTMENT COMPANY, MUTUAL FUND.

INVESTMENT VALUE The value of a CONVERTIBLE BOND if no EQUITY conversion rights existed, i.e., the equivalent straight BOND with identical maturity and coupon. Knowledge of investment value allows investors to determine the theoretical price of the equity OPTION embedded in the convertible bond.
- Also known as PURE BOND VALUE.
- See also CONVERSION PARITY, INVESTMENT PREMIUM.

INVISIBLES International trade involving services rather than goods; invisible exports include sales of services to non-residents, while invisible imports are based on the purchase of services from non-residents. Key items within the invisibles account include transportation, banking, INSURANCE, accounting, legal services, medical practices, and hotel/leisure services. Invisibles are a key element of a country's BALANCE OF TRADE and BALANCE OF PAYMENTS accounts.
- See also VISIBLES.

INVOICE PRICE The total amount the buyer of a BOND pays the seller; in most markets this is the bond's current market value plus ACCRUED INTEREST (i.e., the DIRTY PRICE).

INVOLUNTARY BANKRUPTCY A process where creditors file a petition to force a debtor into BANKRUPTCY after the debtor commits an "act of bankruptcy," generally a DEFAULT on a payment due. If the court accepts the petition the proceedings follow those established for LIQUIDATION or REORGANIZATION under VOLUNTARY BANKRUPTCY.

IO See INTEREST-ONLY STRIP.

IOI See INDICATION OF INTEREST.

IPO See INITIAL PUBLIC OFFERING.

IRR See INTERNAL RATE OF RETURN

IRREDEEMABLE SECURITY A security without a final maturity date, such as a PERPETUAL BOND or a CONSOL. This includes undated securities that are redeemable at the option of the borrower/issuer, but in practice are allowed to remain outstanding.

IRREVOCABLE LETTER OF CREDIT A LETTER OF CREDIT that can only be cancelled by agreement of both parties (i.e., the drawer and the BANK). The facility remains in place until mutual cancellation or final maturity.
- See also CONFIRMED LETTER OF CREDIT, DIRECT PAY

LETTER OF CREDIT, STANDBY LETTER OF CREDIT, TRANSFERABLE LETTER OF CREDIT.

ISDA See INTERNATIONAL SWAPS AND DERIVATIVES ASSOCIATION.

ISMA See INTERNATIONAL SECURITIES MARKETS ASSOCIATION.

ISSUED AND OUTSTANDING Shares of a company's COMMON STOCK authorized for issuance via the CORPORATE CHARTER that have been issued and are held by investors. Issued and outstanding shares are distinguished from those that have been issued and repurchased (i.e., TREASURY STOCK) and those that are unissued (e.g., authorized but not yet floated).

J

JAPANESE GOVERNMENT BOND (JGB) The general category of securities issued by the Japanese government for general financing and MONETARY POLICY purposes. JGBs, denominated in Japanese yen, are issued as discount bills with maturities of less than one year, and COUPON-bearing instruments with medium-term maturities (i.e., 5 and 10 years, the latter constituting the BENCHMARK) and long-term maturities (i.e., the 20 year "super-long" bond). Securities are issued through a SYNDICATE of DEALERS and through an AUCTION MARKET process; SECONDARY MARKET trading is heavily concentrated in the 10-year benchmark and a small number of associated issues.

JENSEN INDEX A common measure of the RISK-adjusted performance of an investment PORTFOLIO that compares the average return on the portfolio with the risk of the portfolio, as measured through BETA. The Jensen index, which uses the SECURITY MARKET LINE as a BENCHMARK, can be computed via:

$$JI = E(r_P) - \lfloor E(r_f) + (E(r_m) - E(r_f)) \beta_P \rfloor$$

where $E(r_P)$ is an estimate of the expected return of the target portfolio, $E(r_f)$ is the RISK-FREE RATE, $E(r_m)$ is the expected average return of the market portfolio, and β_P is the beta of the target portfolio.

- See also TREYNOR INDEX, SHARPE INDEX.
- Additional reference: Jensen (1969).

JGB See JAPANESE GOVERNMENT BOND.

JOBBER [COL] An individual or institution that takes positions in securities, generally on a very short-term basis, in expectation of generating profits. A jobber may or may not also be an authorized MARKET MAKER.

- See also JOBBING.

JOBBING [COL] The practice of continuously buying and selling securities or other ASSETS in an attempt to make small profits.
- See also JOBBER.

JOINT AND SEVERAL A legal condition where multiple GUARANTORS, borrowers, or obligors are liable for the entire amount of an agreed LIABILITY should the other party (or parties) fail to perform. Any party to a joint and several transaction can be sued for non-payment.
- See also SEVERAL BUT NOT JOINT.

JOINT STOCK COMPANY A company that issues COMMON STOCK to investors in order to raise CAPITAL; a joint stock company is generally organized with LIMITED LIABILITY.
- See also CORPORATION, PUBLIC LIMITED COMPANY.

JUMP PROCESS A mathematical process used to describe the movement of ASSET prices that are impacted by sudden, discontinuous moves, such as those generated by EVENT RISKS. Certain OPTION pricing models utilize a jump process, rather than a continuous STOCHASTIC PROCESS, to estimate values.

JUNIOR DEBT See SUBORDINATED DEBT.

JUNK BOND [COL] See HIGH-YIELD BOND.

K

KAFFIRS [COL] The COMMON STOCK of South African gold mining companies listed and traded in the UK stock market on a direct basis, and in the US market via AMERICAN DEPOSITORY RECEIPTS and AMERICAN DEPOSITORY SHARES.

KAPPA See VEGA.

KEIRETSU [JPN] A Japanese business CONGLOMERATE, generally comprised of a series of companies with cross-shareholdings and business relationships but no central core company. A main BANK generally serves as a provider of funding and *de facto* corporate monitor. The keiretsu replaced the centralized ZAIBATSU conglomerate that existed until the mid-1940s.
- See also CHAEBOL.

KEY MAN RISK The RISK arising from the departure of a person or team that is critically responsible for a vital management or business function within a company. Excessive reliance on such an individual(s) can lead to loss of revenues and/or an increase in PROCESS RISK.

KICK-IN OPTION See REVERSE KNOCK-IN OPTION.

KICK-OUT OPTION See REVERSE KNOCK-OUT OPTION.

KICKER [COL] A stake offered by a company to a BANK providing LOAN financing or an investor supplying CAPITAL through a NOTE or BOND. Although the compensation can take different forms, in practice it is often provided in the form of a WARRANT, generating gains if the company's stock price rises.
- Also known as EQUITY KICKER, SWEETENER.
- See also CARROT EQUITY.

KILLER BEES [COL] Investment bankers hired by a company to help defend against a HOSTILE TAKEOVER.

KINKED YIELD CURVE A TERM STRUCTURE where medium-term

INTEREST RATES are higher than long-term and short-term interest rates.
- See also NEGATIVE YIELD CURVE, POSITIVE YIELD CURVE, YIELD CURVE.

KIWI [COL] (1) A BOND, NOTE or CERTIFICATE OF DEPOSIT issued in New Zealand dollars in the New Zealand markets by a foreign company or BANK. (2) The New Zealand dollar.

KNOCK-IN OPTION A COMPLEX OPTION that leads to the creation of a EUROPEAN OPTION if the price of the UNDERLYING market reference moves above or below a pre-defined BARRIER level.
- See also BARRIER OPTION, DOWN AND IN OPTION, UP AND IN OPTION.

KNOCK-OUT OPTION A COMPLEX OPTION that extinguishes a EUROPEAN OPTION if the price of the UNDERLYING market reference moves above or below a pre-defined BARRIER level.
- See also BARRIER OPTION, DOWN AND OUT OPTION, UP AND OUT OPTION.

L

L A broad measure of liquid money supply, generally defined as M3 plus GOVERNMENT BILLS, COMMERCIAL PAPER, BANKER'S ACCEPTANCES, and EUROCURRENCY DEPOSITS of residents.

LABOR CODETERMINATION A legal rule, found primarily in Continental European nations, requiring a certain number of labor representatives to be elected to a company's BOARD OF DIRECTORS in order to give employees proper input into corporate affairs.

LADDER OPTION An OVER-THE-COUNTER COMPLEX OPTION that allows the buyer to lock in any accumulated gains prior to expiry as the price of the UNDERLYING market reference exceeds prespecified market levels (or "rungs"); gains are not surrendered if the market subsequently retraces.
- Also known as a RATCHET OPTION.
- See also CLIQUET OPTION, FIXED STRIKE LADDER OPTION, FLOATING STRIKE LADDER OPTION, SHOUT OPTION.

LADDERING [COL] An illegal practice where the UNDERWRITER of a NEW ISSUE of COMMON STOCK allocates shares to an investor if the investor agrees to purchase additional shares in the SECONDARY MARKET (which will help support the price and generate additional commissions).
- See also SPINNING.

LAG The time period between the occurrence of a loss, or filing of a CLAIM by the INSURED, and the receipt of a SETTLEMENT from the INSURER.

LAISSEZ-FAIRE [FR] An economic and business philosophy indicating that government intervention in commercial affairs should be limited so that market forces can play the leading role in resource allocation. Though free market economies adhere to basic tenets of *laissez-faire,* in practice some government involvement via regulation and monitoring is necessary in order to reduce inequalities and promote competition.

LAMBDA See VEGA.

LAPSE RATIO In INSURANCE, a measure indicating the degree to which new policies are written and existing policies are renewed, generally computed by comparing the percentage of policies in force at the start of the year versus those outstanding at the end of the year. A rising lapse ratio means policies are rolling off faster than new policies are being written and existing policies are being renewed.

LARGE CAP STOCK The COMMON STOCK of a company with a large MARKET CAPITALIZATION, generally in excess of $5 billion.
- See also MICRO STOCK, MID-CAP STOCK.

LARGE-DEDUCTIBLE POLICY A LOSS-SENSITIVE INSURANCE CONTRACT that features a DEDUCTIBLE that is much larger than one found on a standard fixed PREMIUM, full INSURANCE contract. The INSURED retains a much larger amount of RISK and pays the INSURER a smaller PREMIUM.

LARGE LINE CAPACITY The ability for an INSURER or REINSURER to UNDERWRITE a large RISK exposure under a single policy. Insurers and reinsurers with strong financial standing and significant CAPITAL resources are generally able to offer a greater amount of large line capacity without seeking REINSURANCE and RETROCESSION.

LARGE LOSS PRINCIPLE In INSURANCE, the concept of transferring high severity/low frequency losses to an INSURER. Assuming fair PREMIUM pricing, the principle is often considered to be a prudent and cost-effective form of corporate RISK MANAGEMENT, as catastrophic loss events are very difficult to predict and quantify and can create significant FINANCIAL DISTRESS in the absence of proper LOSS FINANCING.

LAST IN FIRST OUT (LIFO) An INVENTORY management and accounting approach where the last raw materials or work-in-progress inventory acquired for production of final goods are used first.
- See also FIRST IN FIRST OUT (FIFO).

LAST TRADING DAY The final day on which TRADING in a specific EXCHANGE-TRADED DERIVATIVE contract can occur.

LATE TRADING An illegal practice where clients enter MUTUAL FUND purchase ORDERS after the official market close in order to take advantage of late market-moving events.

LATTICE MODEL A general class of OPTION pricing models (e.g., BINOMIAL MODEL) that is based on the construction of a framework of upward and downward movements with specific probabilities of occurrence. The model examines possible terminal values of the UNDERLYING ASSET and works backwards through the lattice (via a process known as recombination) to generate a price of the option at each interval (or node). By valuing the option at each interval, the lattice model can be used to compute early EXERCISE of the contract, and is thus useful for pricing AMERICAN OPTIONS and BERMUDAN OPTIONS.

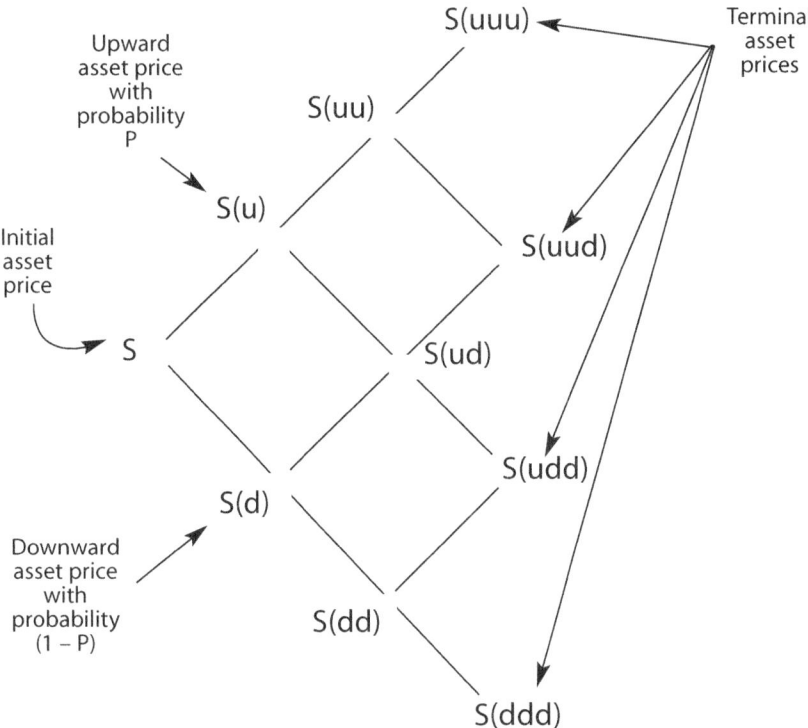

- Also known as RECOMBINING TREE.
- See also NON-RECOMBINING TREE.

LAUNDERING [COL] A process of converting illegal gains/CASH FLOWS into those that have the appearance of legality so that they can be absorbed into the mainstream of commercial activity.

LAW OF LARGE NUMBERS A statistical rule indicating that the average outcome approaches the EXPECTED VALUE or MEAN of the distribution as the number of observations or random samples becomes very large. The Law of Large Numbers is commonly used by INSURERS in developing ACTUARIAL PRICING methodologies, and is also incorporated in certain DERIVATIVE pricing models.

LBO See LEVERAGED BUYOUT.

LDC See LESSER DEVELOPED COUNTRY.

LEAD INDEPENDENT DIRECTOR A DIRECTOR that serves as leader of the other independent members of the BOARD OF DIRECTORS. The role can be found in a SINGLE BOARD SYSTEM when the roles of the chairman and chief executive officer are combined, and is intended to reinforce external scrutiny of management affairs.
- Also known as PRESIDING DIRECTOR.
- See also EXECUTIVE DIRECTOR, NON-EXECUTIVE DIRECTOR.

LEAD MANAGER An institution leading a SYNDICATE in the UNDERWRITING of a NEW ISSUE of securities on behalf of a corporate or sovereign issuer. The lead manager is responsible for assembling the syndicate, filing for REGISTRATION, organizing DUE DILIGENCE and ROADSHOWS, acting as AGENT for other syndicate members, finalizing terms, conditions, and pricing, allocating securities, and stabilizing the price of securities upon launch. In exchange for performing these functions the lead manager receives a greater share of deal fees and receives LEAGUE TABLE credit for managing the process.
- Also known as BOOKRUNNER, SYNDICATE MANAGER.

LEAPS See LONG-TERM EQUITY APPRECIATION SECURITY.

LEASE A transaction that gives one party (the LESSEE) possession and use of an ASSET for a period of time in exchange for periodic lease payments to another party (the LESSOR). A lease, which may be carried on or off the corporate balance sheet and feature full tax deductibility, generally has a maturity of several years, but can often be cancelled by the lessee. Although most lease transactions involve a single asset, master lease agreements covering multiple assets can also be arranged.
- See also CAPITAL LEASE, LEVERAGED LEASE, OPERATING LEASE.

LEGAL LENDING LIMIT The maximum amount that a BANK can lend to a single borrower on a consolidated basis, generally set as a percentage of a bank's EQUITY and/or ASSETS. The limit exists in order to avoid concentrated CREDIT RISK exposures to a single borrower and possible FINANCIAL DISTRESS that might arise should that borrower DEFAULT. In the United States, the legal lending limit for national banks is 15 percent of equity on an unsecured basis and 25 percent on a secured basis.

LEGAL MECHANISM CONTROL A structure or process where effective control of a company is obtained through legal or structural mechanisms (e.g., a pyramid holding company) rather than the purchase of a majority share of COMMON STOCK.
- See also MAJORITY CONTROL, MANAGEMENT CONTROL,

MINORITY CONTROL, TOTAL CONTROL, VOTING TRUST CONTROL.

LEGAL RESERVES (1) RESERVES held by BANKS in support of demand and time DEPOSIT balances, generally necessary in order to comply with RESERVE REQUIREMENTS imposed by a governing CENTRAL BANK or monetary authority. (2) Reserves established by a company to cover possible legal contingencies or lawsuits.

LEGAL RISK The RISK of loss arising from failures in the legal process, including unenforceability of contacts or lack of appropriate documentation related to business arrangements such as GUARANTEES, MASTER AGREEMENTS, or LOAN agreements.

LEGGING [COL] (1) Establishing or unwinding one of two segments of a STRADDLE, STRANGLE, or INDEX ARBITRAGE program, thus creating an exposure to the direction of the security or market until the accompanying position is added or the second leg is unwound. (2) The process of slowly accumulating a position in a security.

LENDER OF LAST RESORT A government institution, generally a CENTRAL BANK or monetary authority, that supplies emergency credit to BANKS or the broader banking system in order to avoid systemic dislocation arising from a bank DEFAULT or payment disruption. Existence of lender of last resort facilities is often implicit rather than explicit in order to avoid instances of MORAL HAZARD, and actual support is typically reserved for those institutions that are considered to be "TOO BIG TO FAIL."

LEPO See LOW EXERCISE PRICE OPTION.

LESSEE A party in a LEASE transaction that leases an ASSET from another party, paying periodic payments in exchange for use of the asset during the contract period.
  ▪ See also LESSOR.

LESSER DEVELOPED COUNTRY (LDC) A country that features an economy that is gradually developing and strengthening, but lacks a sufficiently robust industrial production base to contribute in a meaningful way to national income and EXPORTS. LDCs may impose certain trade barriers and/or EXCHANGE CONTROLS in order to protect their economies from excessive imports or speculative inflows. As a result of nascent market conduits and often weak financial standing, LDCs are typically characterized by a high degree of SOVEREIGN RISK.

LESSOR A party in a LEASE transaction that leases an ASSET to another party, receiving periodic payments in exchange for providing use of the asset during the contract period.
  ▪ See also LESSEE.

LETTER OF CREDIT A credit-based instrument issued by a BANK

guaranteeing the payments of its customer (the drawer) to a third-party BENEFICIARY. The letter of credit, which effectively substitutes the customer's credit standing with the bank's, is widely used in banking and international trade transactions.
- See also CONFIRMED LETTER OF CREDIT, IRREVOCABLE LETTER OF CREDIT, STANDBY LETTER OF CREDIT, TRANSFERABLE LETTER OF CREDIT.

LEVEL PREMIUM In INSURANCE, a PREMIUM that remains unchanged over time, even if the amount of RISK the INSURER assumes from the INSURED increases.

LEVERAGE The degree to which a company uses on and off balance sheet DEBT to fund its operations. Use of leverage magnifies the potential returns and RISKS of an investment or corporate strategy. In general, the greater the amount of leverage, the riskier the financial standing of the company and the greater the expectation of higher returns by suppliers of CAPITAL. A company's leverage can be measured through ratios such as debt to equity, debt to assets, and contingencies to assets:

$$DE = \frac{D}{E}$$

$$DTA = \frac{D}{TA}$$

$$CTA = \frac{Cont}{TA}$$

where D is total debt, E is EQUITY, TA is total ASSETS, and $Cont$ is off-balance sheet contingencies.

In general, the higher the resulting ratios, the greater the degree of leverage.
- Also known as FINANCIAL LEVERAGE, GEARING.
- See also DEBT SERVICE, INTEREST COVERAGE, MODIGLIANI–MILLER THEORY, OPM, OPERATING LEVERAGE.
- Additional reference: Miller and Modigliani (1958).

LEVERAGE ARBITRAGE An ARBITRAGE scheme intended to take advantage of a misperception that creates a gap between a company's CREDIT RATING and its actual financial activities/condition. This generally occurs when a highly rated company uses its strong rating to borrow a significant amount of DEBT at favorable rates and then invest in a range of speculative assets – leading to an "overstatement" of the company's actual rating.

LEVERAGED BUYOUT (LBO) The acquisition of a public company by

a specialist or management group that results in retirement of the public EQUITY through the assumption of a large amount of DEBT (i.e., the company is taken private through LEVERAGE). The ultimate goal of the control group is to refocus operations, reduce expenses, spin off unwanted operations, then refloat or sell the company over the medium-term.
- See also MANAGEMENT BUYOUT, REVERSE LEVERAGED BUYOUT.

LEVERAGED LEASE A CAPITAL LEASE where the underlying ASSET is acquired with borrowed funds. The LESSOR establishes a TRUST and contributes 20 to 40 percent of the purchase price of the asset; the trust then borrows the balance from a BANK on a NON-RECOURSE basis and buys the asset. The LOAN to the trust is secured by a first LIEN and an assignment of the lease and lease payments. Through the leveraged lease structure the lessor obtains the depreciation benefits from the asset and interest deduction from the loan.

LEVERAGED NOTE A STRUCTURED NOTE that provides an investor with the opportunity of earning an enhanced return through a COUPON that is leveraged to a particular financial reference, such as INTEREST RATES or FOREIGN EXCHANGE rates. Since the leverage magnifies the movement of the underlying reference, the note can be very risky; in some instances, PRINCIPAL may be at RISK.
- See also INVERSE FLOATING RATE NOTE.

LEVERAGED OPTION See POWER OPTION.

LEVERAGED RECAPITALIZATION A defensive strategy where a company borrows a large amount of funds from a BANK to make a SPECIAL DIVIDEND payment to existing shareholders. Through this type of recapitalization the company effectively leverages its balance sheet, making it appear less attractive to a potential acquirer.

LEVERAGED SWAP See POWER SWAP.

LIABILITY A legal obligation to make a payment or repay DEBT; a liability is often used to fund a productive ASSET. From an accounting perspective liabilities are debits to the corporate balance sheet, and may include ACCOUNTS PAYABLE, COMMERCIAL PAPER, DEPOSITS, LOANS, NOTES, BONDS, and certain deferred taxes and charges.

LIABILITY INSURANCE An INSURANCE contract providing an INSURED with coverage for losses sustained from payments it makes related to bodily injury or property damage. Coverage can be created for both personal and business exposures, including comprehensive personal liability, COMMERCIAL GENERAL LIABILITY, employers liability and workers compensation.

LIABILITY MANAGEMENT The general practice of using a mix of funding instruments and markets, and INTEREST RATE and FOREIGN

EXCHANGE HEDGES, in order to manage the LIQUIDITY RISK and MARKET RISK inherent in the corporate balance sheet.

LIBID See LONDON INTERBANK BID.

LIBOR See LONDON INTERBANK OFFERED RATE.

LIBOR IN ARREARS SWAP See ARREARS SWAP.

LICENSED CARRIER See ADMITTED INSURER.

LIEN See SECURED INTEREST.

LIFE ACQUISITION COST SECURITIZATION An INSURANCE-LINKED SECURITY that transfers the upfront costs associated with writing life insurance policies to CAPITAL MARKETS investors.
- See also CATASTROPHE BOND, MORTGAGE DEFAULT SECURITIZATION, RESIDUAL VALUE SECURITIZATION, WEATHER BOND.

LIFE INSURANCE An INSURANCE contract providing for a payment to a named BENEFICIARY in the event the INSURED dies; life insurance is available in many forms, including term life, whole life, ordinary life, and group life, each with different characteristics related to coverage, costs, and savings.
- See also LIFE REINSURANCE.

LIFE REINSURANCE A REINSURANCE agreement where an INSURER CEDES LIFE INSURANCE policies to a REINSURER individually (through FACULTATIVE REINSURANCE) or as a PORTFOLIO (TREATY REINSURANCE).

LIFO See LAST IN FIRST OUT.

LIMEAN See LONDON INTERBANK MEAN.

LIMIT BUY ORDER An ORDER to buy securities if a target level is reached, with an understanding between client and BROKER that there is no guarantee the order can be filled at the limit price.

LIMIT ON CLOSE ORDER An ORDER to buy or sell securities at the market close, but only if the closing price is better than the limit specified.

LIMIT ORDER An ORDER for the purchase or sale of a security at a specific price limit. If the price is not attained the order expires unfilled or it remains open until the client instructs otherwise.
- See also MARKET ORDER, STOP ORDER, TIME ORDER.

LIMITED LIABILITY A structural and legal concept where investors in a LIMITED LIABILITY COMPANY are only financially responsible up to the value of the CAPITAL they have invested in the company's COMMON STOCK; personal ASSETS are not at RISK in the event the company suffers losses that deplete capital. Limited liability is common in entities structured as public or private CORPORATIONS.
- See also PIERCING THE CORPORATE VEIL, UNLIMITED LIABILITY.

LIMITED LIABILITY COMPANY (LLC) Any company issuing

COMMON STOCK that is specifically organized with LIMITED LIABILITY.
- See also CORPORATION, JOINT STOCK COMPANY, PUBLIC LIMITED COMPANY.

LIMITED PARTNERSHIP An unregistered private partnership open to a certain number of ACCREDITED INVESTORS, or a registered public partnership that is open to a larger population of investors, which invests in a broad range of ASSETS. Limited partnerships, managed by one or more general partners, often acquire real estate, oil and gas properties, or equipment LEASES and provide investors with any returns generated; they may also focus on investment opportunities that provide current income (e.g., COUPON or DIVIDENDS), capital gains, or tax benefits.

LIMITED RECOURSE LOAN See PARTIAL RECOURSE LOAN.

LINE [COL] A general class of INSURANCE offered by INSURERS, typically grouped into one of five types: LIFE INSURANCE, health insurance, ANNUITY, PROPERTY AND CASUALTY INSURANCE, and LIABILITY INSURANCE.
- See also LINE LIMIT.

LINE LIMIT The maximum LINE of INSURANCE an INSURER will UNDERWRITE without seeking excess protection via REINSURANCE. The size of the line limit depends on an insurer's financial resources and expertise, its ability to diversify and reinsure, and its willingness to assume RISK of a particular type and magnitude.

LINE OF CREDIT See REVOLVING CREDIT FACILITY.

LINEAR INSTRUMENT A financial ASSET or transaction, such as a COMMON STOCK, FORWARD, or FUTURE that provides a unit payoff for a unit move in the underlying asset. Linear instruments feature no CONVEXITY.

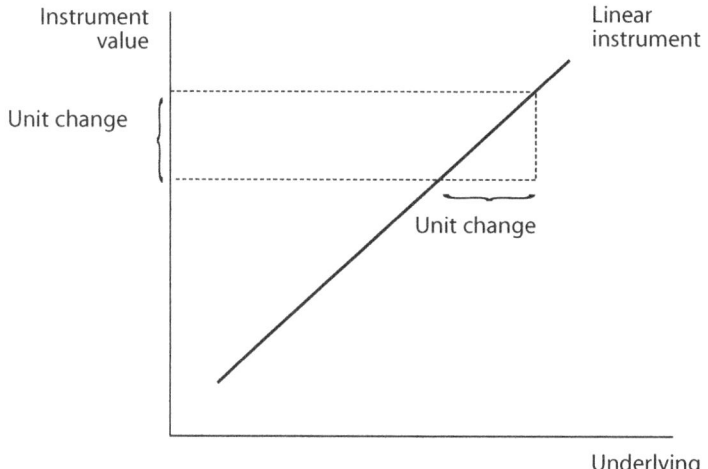

■ See also NON-LINEAR INSTRUMENT.

LIQUID (1) At a corporate level, the state of possessing sufficient cash to meet obligations. (2) At a market level, the state of having sufficient transaction volume to permit TRADING.

■ See also ILLIQUID, LIQUID ASSETS, LIQUIDITY.

LIQUID ASSETS ASSETS that can be converted into cash when needed at, or near, carrying value. Apart from cash, this generally includes very high-quality, short-dated securities, such as GOVERNMENT BILLS, highly rated MONEY MARKET instruments (i.e., COMMERCIAL PAPER, CERTIFICATES OF DEPOSIT, REPURCHASE AGREEMENTS, BANKER'S ACCEPTANCES); it may also include short-term, high-quality ACCOUNTS RECEIVABLE and certain classes of fungible INVENTORY.

■ See also LIQUIDITY, NEAR CASH.

LIQUIDATING DIVIDEND A DIVIDEND, payable by a company to shareholders, that represents a final return of CAPITAL. The dividend is paid when a company is halting its operations and no longer requires capital to support the operation.

LIQUIDATION (1) A state of corporate BANKRUPTCY that culminates in the disposal of ASSETS and payment of any residual value to creditors; liquidation generally occurs when efforts at REORGANIZATION have failed. (2) The sale of assets by a company to cover an expected or unexpected payment, or the sale of COLLATERAL held by a creditor to cover funds due from the borrower/debtor.

■ (1) Also known as WINDING-UP.
■ (1) See also VOLUNTARY LIQUIDATION.

LIQUIDATION PERIOD (1) In a VALUE-AT-RISK model, the assumed horizon over which a PORTFOLIO of risky ASSETS can be sold in order to neutralize RISK and recognize gains or losses. In most models a single liquidation period is applied to all asset classes, regardless of the inherent level of risk or LIQUIDITY. (2) In the INSURANCE sector, the period during which a previously funded ANNUITY provides CASH FLOWS to the ANNUITANT.

■ (1) Also known as HOLDING PERIOD.

LIQUIDATION VALUE The value of an ASSET, business, or company that is to be sold to a third party. If the sale of an entire business or company occurs on a piecemeal basis the value obtained may be less than if it is sold as a going concern, which reflects the financial worth of GOODWILL. If the sale must occur rapidly, the resulting liquidation value may also be lower as the seller will be recognized as a price taker.

■ See also ASSET STRIPPING, BREAKUP VALUE.

LIQUIDITY (1) At a corporate level, access to cash, NEAR CASH, unsecured funding and unencumbered ASSETS that can be used to cover

expected or unexpected payments. (2) The state of being LIQUID or having LIQUID ASSETS. (3) At a market level, activity or turnover in a security or ASSET; a liquid market is characterized by small differences between BIDS and OFFERS.
- See also CURRENT RATIO, ILLIQUIDITY, LIQUIDITY RISK, QUICK RATIO.

LIQUIDITY PREFERENCE THEORY A theory of INTEREST RATES indicating that investors will expect a higher return for ASSETS they prefer not to hold, leading to the creation of a LIQUIDITY PREMIUM (which is often expressed as the difference between FORWARD RATES and expected future SPOT RATES). The theory also allows for the fact that investor expectations help determine the shape of the YIELD CURVE, as set forth via the EXPECTATIONS THEORY.
- See also MARKET SEGMENTATION THEORY.
- Additional references: Hicks (1946), Lutz and Lutz (1951), Meiselman (1962).

LIQUIDITY PREMIUM The additional SPREAD that investors demand for holding ASSETS they prefer not to hold (including those that may be risky or ILLIQUID). Under the LIQUIDITY PREFERENCE THEORY the liquidity premium is also an increasing function of expectations regarding rising INTEREST RATES.

LIQUIDITY RISK The RISK of being unable to raise funding or sell or pledge ASSETS when needed without incurring a significant cost. Liquidity risk, which is a form of FINANCIAL RISK, is commonly segregated into three components: ASSET LIQUIDITY RISK, FUNDING LIQUIDITY RISK, and ASSET-FUNDING LIQUIDITY RISK.
- See also ENDOGENOUS LIQUIDITY RISK, EXOGENOUS LIQUIDITY RISK, LIQUIDITY, LIQUIDITY SPIRAL.

LIQUIDITY SPIRAL A self-fulfilling cycle where concerns about a company's LIQUIDITY cause creditors to cancel credit facilities, which leads to a repeated cycle of ASSET sales, CREDIT RATING downgrades, and further credit facility cancellations. The cycle continues until the company is able to secure sufficient funding or enters a stage of FINANCIAL DISTRESS.
- See also LIQUIDITY RISK.

LIQUIDITY TRAP (1) A situation during a recession or depression where individuals hold an excessive amount of money relative to actual needs and are insensitive to the return offered via savings or investment vehicles. In practice INTEREST RATES cannot be lowered without risking further damage to the economy. (2) A phenomenon where a one-way market (i.e., offered-only) temporarily exhibits signs of two-way business, causing new buyers to enter and creating the illusion of strong LIQUIDITY. Once new buyers stop entering, liquidity quickly erodes and the market returns to its normal one-way state, "trapping" those that still hold positions.

LIQUIDITY WAREHOUSE A PORTFOLIO of unencumbered high-grade securities that a company maintains in order to manage LIQUIDITY requirements that cannot be adequately met via existing unsecured funding. When additional cash is required a company can pledge or sell the unencumbered assets from the warehouse at, or near, carrying value. The liquidity warehouse is generally comprised of short- and medium-term securities with stable prices and strong CREDIT RATINGS.

LISTED DERIVATIVE See EXCHANGE-TRADED DERIVATIVE.

LLC See LIMITED LIABILITY COMPANY.

LLOYD'S BROKER A BROKER that specializes in placing INSURANCE with LLOYD'S SYNDICATES operating in the LLOYD'S OF LONDON marketplace.

LLOYD'S OF LONDON A London-based INSURANCE marketplace comprised of LLOYD's SYNDICATES (i.e., a group of NAMES) that UNDERWRITE a broad range of insurance, REINSURANCE, and RETROCESSION covers. Lloyd's itself does not write any insurance, though it maintains a backup RESERVE fund to cover any possible crisis situation.

▪ See also LLOYD'S BROKER.

LLOYD'S SYNDICATE A group of NAMES within LLOYD'S OF LONDON that specializes in UNDERWRITING specific types of RISKS.

LOAD (1) In investment management, the sales commission applied to investors buying certain MUTUAL FUNDS. (2) In INSURANCE, see EXPENSE LOADING, PREMIUM LOADING.

▪ (1) See also LOAD FUND.

LOAD FUND A MUTUAL FUND that levies an upfront sales charge on investors; sales commissions are generally added to the NET ASSET VALUE to generate the total purchase price. Despite the sales charge, load funds are not always more expensive than NO-LOAD FUNDS, which may have higher management and/or exit fees.

LOAN A DEBT financing extended by a BANK to a personal, corporate, or sovereign borrower. A loan may be granted with a fixed or floating INTEREST RATE, and PRINCIPAL that amortizes on a regular basis (although certain loans, including BALLOON LOANS and BULLET LOANS, are structured with back-end principal repayments). A loan may have a fixed maturity (i.e., TERM LOAN) or it may be rolled over prior to each contractual maturity date (i.e., EVERGREEN); it may also allow for instant draw-down, or be available as needed (i.e., a BANK LINE or REVOLVING CREDIT FACILITY). A loan may be unsecured,

or secured on physical assets; unsecured loans may be ranked as SENIOR DEBT or SUBORDINATED DEBT. Loans are typically documented through formal credit agreements that specify precise terms and conditions, including interest and principal repayment schedule, COVENANTS, and EVENTS OF DEFAULT.
- Also known as ADVANCE.
- See also LOAN COMMITMENT.

LOAN COMMITMENT A DEBT commitment extended by a BANK to a corporate or sovereign borrower. The commitment permits the borrower to draw on the facility at any time it chooses, up to a stated amount; if the borrower has not breached any COVENANTS, the bank is obligated to provide funds. In exchange for the commitment, the borrower pays the bank a fee (regardless of whether it ever uses the facility).
- See also LOAN, REVOLVING CREDIT FACILITY.

LOAN LOSS PROVISION A non-cash expense reflected through a BANK's income statement that is used to increase the LOAN LOSS RESERVE established for NON-PERFORMING LOANS.

LOAN LOSS RESERVE A CREDIT RESERVE established by a BANK to cover the potential charge-off of NON-PERFORMING LOANS (i.e., those that are classed as past-due or non-accrual). The reserve is typically shown as a CONTRA ACCOUNT on the ASSET portion of the balance sheet, and is increased through LOAN LOSS PROVISIONS taken via the income statement.

LOAN PARTICIPATION See PARTICIPATION LOAN.

LOAN-TO-VALUE (LTV) The percentage amount a BANK is willing to lend a borrower against the appraised value of the ASSET being financed, often real estate or plant and equipment. The higher the LTV the greater the LEVERAGE granted to the borrower, and the lower the protection afforded the bank in the event the borrower DEFAULTS. LTVs in the residential and commercial real estate sector typically range from 70 to 100 percent; those in the plant and equipment sector can range from 50 to 100 percent.

LOBSTER TRAP [COL] An ANTI-TAKEOVER DEFENSE provision that prevents an investor (or RAIDER) holding more than 10 percent of a company's COMMON STOCK from exchanging any CONVERTIBLE BONDS into voting class stock.
- See also SCORCHED EARTH DEFENSE.

LOCAL [COL] An individual TRADING on an EXCHANGE using personal CAPITAL.

LOCK-IN PROVISION See RATE LOCK.

LOCK-UP CERTIFICATE OF DEPOSIT (CD) A CERTIFICATE OF DEPOSIT that functions as a TIME DEPOSIT. Although a lock-up CD

is technically negotiable, it is held in CUSTODY by the issuing BANK on behalf of the depositor and generally held until maturity.
- See also FLOATING RATE CERTIFICATE OF DEPOSIT, NEGOTIABLE CERTIFICATE OF DEPOSIT.

LOCK-UP OPTION An OPTION, granted to a friendly WHITE KNIGHT by a company that is a potential TAKEOVER target, which allows the friendly party to purchase the company's most valuable ASSETS (i.e., the CROWN JEWELS) in the event of a HOSTILE TAKEOVER.

LOCKED MARKET [COL] A temporary market phenomenon where the BID and OFFER for an ASSET are precisely equal. A locked market, which generally lasts only for short periods of time, can appear when there is little news driving the market and participants lack strong directional views, or when extremely competitive forces on both sides of the market draw the bid offer SPREAD in.

LOCKOUT PERIOD A time period during which the NOTIONAL PRINCIPAL of an AMORTIZING SWAP or ACCRETING SWAP cannot be decreased or increased, regardless of the movement of reference INTEREST RATES. The lockout provision protects the party that has sold the embedded OPTIONS in the swap from a sudden movement in rates soon after the transaction commences.

LOGNORMAL DISTRIBUTION A statistical distribution, often used to characterize the distribution of ASSET prices, where the log of a random variable is normally distributed. A lognormal distribution, which is skewed to the right (i.e., asymmetrical around the MEAN), faces a lower bound of zero and an upper bound of infinity.

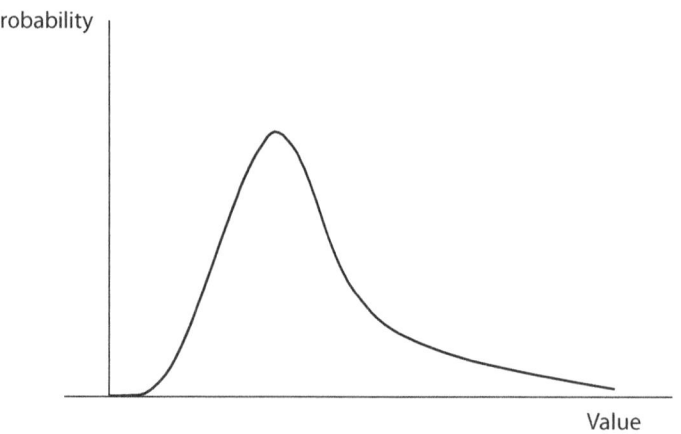

- See also NORMAL DISTRIBUTION.

LOMBARD RATE A short-term INTEREST RATE used in the German market, generally applied to LOANS collateralized by securities.

LONDON INTERBANK BID (LIBID) The BID side of the London Interbank DEPOSIT market, or the INTEREST RATE that a prime BANK must pay for interbank funds.
- See also LONDON INTERBANK MEAN, LONDON INTERBANK OFFERED RATE.

LONDON INTERBANK MEAN (LIMEAN) The MEAN of the LONDON INTERBANK BID and LONDON INTERBANK OFFERED RATES, or the average INTEREST RATE at which a BANK will DEPOSIT or accept interbank funds.
- See also LONDON INTERBANK BID, LONDON INTERBANK OFFERED RATE.

LONDON INTERBANK OFFERED RATE (LIBOR) The OFFER side of the London interbank DEPOSIT market, or the rate at which a prime BANK is willing to lend funds. LIBOR, which is set every business day at 11 a.m. London time by the BRITISH BANKERS ASSOCIATION, is quoted for deposits in a range of maturities and RESERVE CURRENCIES, and serves as an important base reference for other financial instruments with a floating rate component (e.g., DERIVATIVES, FLOATING RATE NOTES).
- See also LONDON INTERBANK BID, LONDON INTERBANK MEAN.

LONG See LONG POSITION.

LONG AND WRONG [COL] A LONG POSITION (purchased or owned) that loses money as a result of sudden or steady price declines.

LONG ARBITRAGE An ARBITRAGE strategy employed in the FUTURES market when the FORWARD RATE is lower than the futures rate, indicating that the cash market is overpriced when compared with the futures market; the strategy calls for selling the UNDERLYING ASSET and buying futures.
- See also SHORT ARBITRAGE.

LONG BOND [COL] In the United States, the 30-year TREASURY BOND (issuance of which was halted in the early part of the millennium, although existing issues will remain outstanding for a number of years).

LONG END [COL] The long maturities of the YIELD CURVE, generally taken to mean those in excess of seven years.
- See also BELLY OF THE CURVE, SHORT END.

LONG HEDGE A LONG POSITION in a DERIVATIVE contract or financial instrument that is used to protect a natural SHORT POSITION. As rising prices cause a loss on the natural short position, the long hedge produces an offsetting gain; the reverse occurs with falling prices.
- See also SHORT HEDGE.

LONG POSITION A purchased or owned position in a financial ASSET that benefits from price appreciation. In order to realize a gain generated by rising prices, the long position must be sold or offset.
- Also known as LONG.
- See also SHORT POSITION.

LONG-TERM EQUITY APPRECIATION SECURITY (LEAPS) Long-dated EQUITY CALL OPTIONS and PUT OPTIONS traded on various US EXCHANGES and OVER-THE-COUNTER. LEAPS, which are available as EUROPEAN OPTIONS and AMERICAN OPTIONS, feature maturities ranging from two to five years, and can be purchased or sold on a range of indexes and LARGE CAP STOCKS.

LOOKBACK OPTION An OVER-THE-COUNTER COMPLEX OPTION that grants the buyer a maximum gain by "looking back" over the price path of the ASSET and determining the point that creates the greatest economic profit.
- See also FIXED STRIKE LOOKBACK OPTION, FLOATING STRIKE LOOKBACK OPTION, OPTIONS ON THE MAXIMUM/MINIMUM.

LOSS ADJUSTMENT EXPENSE The cost an INSURER must bear in adjusting a CLAIM under an INSURANCE contract; some portion of the expense is generally passed back to INSUREDS through LOAD charges. Insurers that are efficient in their claims procedures have greater ability to lower their loss adjustment expenses and either improve their margins or reduce their load charges.

LOSS-BASED MODEL See CREDIT DEFAULT MODEL.

LOSS CONTROL A RISK MANAGEMENT TECHNIQUE where a firm employs safety precautions to reduce the likelihood that a particular RISK will impact its operations and create a loss. Loss controls may be physical, such as fire or security safety equipment, or intangible, such as training and education.
- Also known as LOSS PREVENTION.
- See also LOSS FINANCING, RISK REDUCTION.

LOSS EQUITY PUT A CONTINGENT EQUITY structure that results in the issuance of new EQUITY in the event a predefined TRIGGER event, such as a large loss from a CATASTROPHIC HAZARD, is breached. Although COMMON STOCK and PREFERRED STOCK can be issued under the put, preferred stock is often used in order to prevent DILUTION. If the trigger event occurs and the put is EXERCISED the put seller, generally a BANK, provides the put purchaser with funds in exchange for shares.
- See also PUT-PROTECTED EQUITY.

LOSS FINANCING A broad class of RISK MANAGEMENT TECH-

NIQUES, including RISK TRANSFER, RISK RETENTION, and HEDGING, that is primarily concerned with ensuring the availability of funds in the event of a loss. Loss financing may be funded from internal sources (e.g., through self-retention RESERVES) or external sources (e.g., through compensatory payments from INSURANCE or DERIVATIVE contracts).
- See also LOSS CONTROL, POST-LOSS FINANCING, PRE-LOSS FINANCING, RISK REDUCTION.

LOSS FREQUENCY METHOD In INSURANCE, a mechanism used to establish a core PREMIUM level by projecting the expected number of future losses in a given RISK class over a particular time frame.
- Also known as LOSS RATE.
- See also LOSS RATIO METHOD.

LOSS-GIVEN DEFAULT A value or percentage estimate of the amount, net of RECOVERY, which a BANK expects to lose if a COUNTERPARTY DEFAULTS (i.e., 1 − RECOVERY RATE). Loss-given default is an essential input into internal and regulatory CREDIT DEFAULT MODELS as it provides a financial estimate of the net amount that may ultimately be lost.

LOSS PORTFOLIO TRANSFER A FINITE RISK CONTRACT where the INSURED transfers a PORTFOLIO of unclaimed losses from previous LIABILITIES. The insured pays the INSURER a fee, PREMIUM, and the PRESENT VALUE of net RESERVES needed to cover existing portfolio liabilities, and the insurer assumes responsibility for the losses. Through this mechanism uncertain "lump sum" liabilities are transformed into certain liabilities, with a present value that is equal to the net present value of unrealized losses.
- See also RETROSPECTIVE AGGREGATE LOSS COVER, RETROSPECTIVE FINITE POLICY.

LOSS PREVENTION See LOSS CONTROL.

LOSS RATE See LOSS FREQUENCY METHOD.

LOSS RATIO In INSURANCE, a measure of an INSURER's ability to cover losses and LOSS ADJUSTMENT EXPENSE with PREMIUMS, generally computed as:

$$LR = \frac{L + LAE}{Pr}$$

where L is loss (from CLAIMS), LAE is loss adjustment expense, and Pr is premium.

The lower the ratio, the more premium the insurer preserves as profit.
- Also known as EXPECTED LOSS RATIO, PERMISSIBLE LOSS RATIO.
- See also COMBINED RATIO, EXPENSE RATIO.

LOSS RATIO METHOD In INSURANCE, a mechanism used to modify a core PREMIUM level by uniform percentages for related types of RISKS in order to align actual and expected LOSS RATIOS.
- See also LOSS FREQUENCY METHOD.

LOSS RESERVES A RESERVE account established by an INSURER or REINSURER that includes an estimate of CLAIMS reported and adjusted but not yet paid, claims reported and filed but not yet adjusted, and claims INCURRED BUT NOT REPORTED; the latter is often difficult to estimate on an ex-ante basis and actual results only appear over time.

LOSS-SENSITIVE INSURANCE CONTRACTS The general class of partial INSURANCE contracts with PREMIUMS that depend on loss experience. Common loss-sensitive contracts include EXPERIENCE-RATED POLICIES, INVESTMENT CREDIT PROGRAMS, LARGE DEDUCTIBLE POLICIES, and RETROSPECTIVELY RATED POLICIES.

LOSSES INCURRED In INSURANCE, a measure of the amount of PREMIUMS earned by the INSURER that must be allocated to cover losses; losses incurred can serve as a basis for establishing LOSS RESERVES.
- See also LOSSES OUTSTANDING.

LOSSES OUTSTANDING In INSURANCE, the amount of losses representing CLAIMS received but not yet paid by the INSURER to INSUREDS.
- See also LOSSES INCURRED.

LOW EXERCISE PRICE OPTION (LEPO) An EXCHANGE-traded or OVER-THE-COUNTER OPTION with a STRIKE PRICE that is set very close to zero. The creation of a low strike price allows the option's value to track closely the price of the UNDERLYING reference ASSET.

LOW-PREMIUM CONVERTIBLE BOND A CONVERTIBLE BOND, generally issued with a 10 to 15-year final maturity, which has a CONVERSION PRICE set at a small (i.e., < 5%) PREMIUM to the market price of the issuer's COMMON STOCK; the probability of rapid conversion into shares is thus very high. Since a low-premium convertible is essentially an EQUITY substitute, the coupon on the bond is usually only slightly higher than the existing DIVIDEND YIELD on the underlying common stock.

LTV See LOAN-TO-VALUE.

M

M1 Currency in circulation, COMMERCIAL BANK demand DEPOSITS, and demand savings accounts.
M2 M1 plus OVERNIGHT REPURCHASE AGREEMENTS, overnight EUROCURRENCY DEPOSITS, traditional savings accounts, small time deposits, and MONEY MARKET MUTUAL FUND shares.
M3 M2 plus large time DEPOSITS and term REPURCHASE AGREEMENTS.
  ▪ See also L.
MAC See MATERIAL ADVERSE CHANGE CLAUSE.
MACARONI DEFENSE [COL] An ANTI-TAKEOVER DEFENSE where a potential target company issues BONDS with a redemption clause forcing the securities to be redeemed at a very substantial PREMIUM to PAR VALUE in the event of a TAKEOVER; the provision makes the company unattractive to any potential acquirer.
  ▪ See also SCORCHED EARTH DEFENSE.
MAIN STREET [COL] In the United States, the broad class of individual investors.
MAINTENANCE MARGIN (1) The minimum MARGIN each party to an EXCHANGE-TRADED DERIVATIVE transaction must preserve, generally an amount that is somewhat less than the INITIAL MARGIN. Once the maintenance margin level has been breached, VARIATION MARGIN must be posted to return the position to initial margin levels or the transaction will be closed out. (2) The minimum margin an investor must retain in a securities account in support of a collateralized PURPOSE LOAN or NON-PURPOSE LOAN. If the maintenance level is not preserved, the BROKER is authorized to sell COLLATERAL in the account to repay the loan.
MAJORITY CONTROL A process or structure where effective corporate

control is gained by taking a majority, though not absolute, stake in the company's COMMON STOCK.
- See also LEGAL MECHANISM CONTROL, MANAGEMENT CONTROL, MINORITY CONTROL, TOTAL CONTROL, VOTING TRUST CONTROL.

MANAGED FOREIGN EXCHANGE RATE A FOREIGN EXCHANGE RATE whose value is set by a CENTRAL BANK or monetary authority via small/regular purchases and sales of currency and through macro-economic policies. Managed rates are not strictly fixed or pegged by government authorities, nor are they freely determined through pure market supply and demand forces.
- See also CRAWLING PEG, PEGGING.

MANAGEMENT BOARD The second BOARD OF DIRECTORS in a DUAL BOARD SYSTEM, approximately equivalent to the executive management team in companies operating under the SINGLE BOARD SYSTEM. This board, which typically includes 5 to 15 senior executives appointed by the SUPERVISORY BOARD, is headed by a chairman and is responsible for daily management of individual businesses/divisions or control functions.
- Also known as EXECUTIVE BOARD.

MANAGEMENT BUYOUT (MBO) The acquisition of a public company by a management group that results in retirement of the public EQUITY through the assumption of a large amount of DEBT (i.e., the company is taken private through the use of LEVERAGE); such transactions have the advantage of placing in direct control those who are most familiar with the company and its operations. The ultimate goal of the management team is to refocus operations, reduce expenses, spin off unwanted operations, and then refloat or sell the company over the medium-term.
- See also LEVERAGED BUYOUT, REVERSE LEVERAGED BUYOUT.

MANAGEMENT CAPITAL See ECONOMIC CAPITAL.

MANAGEMENT CONTROL A process or structure where management gains effective corporate control by accumulating a sufficiently large block of a company's COMMON STOCK to direct activities; as with MINORITY CONTROL, this process only works when ownership is so diffuse that even an organized MINORITY INTEREST fails to dominate the company and its actions.
- See also LEGAL MECHANISM CONTROL, MAJORITY CONTROL, TOTAL CONTROL, VOTING TRUST CONTROL.

MANDATE An authorization or approval to arrange a NEW ISSUE of securities or CORPORATE FINANCE transaction, awarded by a company or sovereign entity to a financial institution acting as intermediary. COMMERCIAL BANKS, INVESTMENT BANKS, and SECURITIES FIRMS that are hoping to generate fee income and gain LEAGUE TABLE credit compete aggressively for mandates.

MANDATORY CONVERTIBLE BOND A CONVERTIBLE BOND that must be exercised into the issuer's COMMON STOCK prior to final maturity. The convertible can be issued as an EQUITY contract note, where the issuer exchanges the bond for common stock at maturity; if the investor chooses not to accept the stock, the issuer sells the newly issued securities in the market and delivers cash proceeds to the investor. It can also be structured as an equity commitment note, where the investor does not have to exchange notes for new common stock, but the issuer commits to floating new stock and using the proceeds to redeem the outstanding bonds.

- See also REVERSE CONVERTIBLE BOND.

MANUSCRIPT INSURANCE A customized INSURANCE contract with terms that are tailored to an INSURED's specific requirements. A manuscript contract, which is used when coverage cannot be accommodated via a standard insurance form, reflects special needs, conditions, and PERIL coverages.

- Also know as MANUSCRIPT POLICY.

MANUSCRIPT POLICY See MANUSCRIPT INSURANCE.

MARGIN (1) Security, such as cash, a LETTER OF CREDIT, or certain high-quality BONDS, posted by the buyer and seller of an EXCHANGE-TRADE DERIVATIVE at the start of the trade (in the form of INITIAL MARGIN) and periodically thereafter (as VARIATION MARGIN). Use of margin helps mitigate the effects of CREDIT RISK. (2) Security posted by an investor buying or selling securities on a LEVERAGED basis through a BROKER-DEALER. (3) See PREMIUM.

- (1), (2) See also CLIENT MARGIN, MAINTENANCE MARGIN.
- (2) See also NON-PURPOSE LOAN, PURPOSE LOAN.

MARGIN LOAN See PURPOSE LOAN.

MARINE INSURANCE A general form of PROPERTY AND CASUALTY INSURANCE used to cover goods in transit (i.e., via air, land, or waterway) and the vehicles used for transportation.

MARK-TO-MARKET The process of revaluing a financial transaction based on closing market prices or rates. In the United States, Financial Accounting Standards Rule 115 states that financial institutions are required to mark-to-market their trading ASSETS every business day (although assets held in an investment account until maturity need not be). Marking-to-market is used to estimate daily profits and losses and quantify actual CREDIT RISK and MARKET RISK exposures. It is also an essential process for transactions that are based on MARGIN

or COLLATERAL, such as EXCHANGE-TRADED DERIVATIVES and MARGIN LOANS, since daily fluctuations in value can result in the call for, or return of, security.
- See also MARK-TO-MODEL, PROFIT AND LOSS (P&L) EXPLAIN.

MARK-TO-MARKET VALUE See ACTUAL EXPOSURE.

MARK-TO-MODEL The process of valuing a financial transaction based on mathematical models rather than market prices. This type of valuation occurs when a transaction is very unique (e.g., long-dated or complex), and transparent market prices are not available. Certain COMPLEX DERIVATIVES, esoteric STRUCTURED NOTES, and COLLATERALIZED MORTGAGE OBLIGATIONS are valued using models. Although marking-to-model provides an estimate of value where none would otherwise exist, it also introduces an element of MODEL RISK.
- See also MARK-TO-MARKET.

MARKET CAPITALIZATION A measure of a public company's current MARKET VALUE, computed as:

$$MC = S \, (Shs)$$

where S is the current price of the COMMON STOCK and Shs is the number of shares ISSUED AND OUTSTANDING.

Since the stock price changes on a daily basis, the market capitalization of the firm changes in tandem.

MARKET EXPECTATIONS THEORY See EXPECTATIONS THEORY.

MARKET IF TOUCHED ORDER An ORDER to purchase or sell a security if a particular price is reached; once attained, the order converts into a MARKET ORDER and is filled at the best available market price.

MARKET MAKER An institution that is obliged to quote BIDS and OFFERS at all times and fill either side of any ORDER received; for standard-sized transactions, the market maker must generally provide FIRM QUOTES rather than INDICATIVE QUOTES. In exchange for providing two-way quotes and LIQUIDITY, the market maker is often given additional visibility into trading flows and pending orders.

MARKET MODEL A general corporate system that is characterized by very diffuse shareholdings, LIQUID and deep CAPITAL MARKETS, dynamic CAPITAL reallocation, advanced legal and regulatory frameworks, and an active CORPORATE CONTROL MARKET. The United States, the UK, and Canada are representative examples of the market model.
- See also HYBRID MODEL, RELATIONSHIP MODEL.

MARKET ON CLOSE ORDER An ORDER to purchase or sell a security at the price prevailing at market close. The market on close is effectively equivalent to a delayed MARKET ORDER.

MARKET ORDER An ORDER for the purchase or sale of a security at the current market level; as long as sufficient LIQUIDITY is available, the order will be filled at the market price.
- See also LIMIT ORDER, MARKET IF TOUCHED ORDER, MARKET ON CLOSE ORDER, STOP ORDER, TIME ORDER.

MARKET OUT CLAUSE See MATERIAL ADVERSE CHANGE CLAUSE.

MARKET RISK The RISK of loss due to an adverse move in the market value of an ASSET, such as a COMMON STOCK, BOND, LOAN, FOREIGN EXCHANGE, commodity, or DERIVATIVE contract. Market risk, which is a form of FINANCIAL RISK, can be sub-categorized into BASIS RISK, CURVE RISK, DIRECTIONAL RISK, SPREAD RISK, and VOLATILITY RISK.

MARKET SEGMENTATION THEORY A theory of INTEREST RATES indicating that each maturity sector of the YIELD CURVE is separate and distinct; investors commit CAPITAL to the sector of their choice, impeding the free flow of capital to other segments.
- See also EXPECTATIONS THEORY, LIQUIDITY PREFERENCE THEORY.
- Additional references: Lutz and Lutz (1951), Meiselman (1962).

MARKET SWEEP A second offer for the purchase of outstanding shares of COMMON STOCK, made by an acquiring company to investors in the target company. The market sweep, which comes after an initial TENDER OFFER has been made, is intended to build the acquirer's position to a controlling stake and may be executed at a price that is higher than the initial tender.

MARKET VALUE The current value of an ASSET or LIABILITY based on quoted BIDS or OFFERS or an estimate through a MARK-TO-MODEL process. In general, a market value reflects a realizable economic value in the marketplace.
- See also BOOK VALUE.

MARKETABLE SECURITY Any security that can be sold without limitation in a SECONDARY MARKET. While many securities can be freely traded and are thus marketable, some, such as PRIVATE PLACEMENTS, are designed primarily as "hold to maturity" ASSETS and are more accurately considered NON-MARKETABLE SECURITIES. Certain ILLIQUID assets, such as MORTGAGES, LOANS, and ACCOUNTS RECEIVABLE, can be converted into marketable securities via the SECURITIZATION process.

MARKOV PROCESS A STOCHASTIC PROCESS where only the

current price of an ASSET is relevant in determining what may happen in the future, i.e., previous prices and the number of periods preceding the current observation are irrelevant. The Markov process is used in numerous DERIVATIVE pricing models.

MARRIED PUT [COL] A PUT OPTION that is acquired by an investor as a HEDGE at the same time the UNDERLYING reference ASSET is purchased. As the price of the underlying asset declines the value of married put increases, and vice versa.

MASTER AGREEMENT A formal agreement between two COUNTERPARTIES that documents the legal and credit aspects of DERIVATIVE transactions. A properly executed master agreement allows subsequent trades to be evidenced by short-form CONFIRMATIONS (rather than extensive long-form confirmations) and permits CREDIT RISK exposures to be managed on a net, rather than gross, basis. Common master agreements include the INTERNATIONAL SWAPS AND DERIVATIVES ASSOCIATION Master Agreement, the French Association Francaise Banque agreement and the German rahmenverstrag agreement.

MASTER NOTE COMMERCIAL PAPER offered by a direct issuer to the investment management/trust department of a BANK or an institutional investor that has periodic amounts to invest in short-term FIXED INCOME instruments. The master note, which pays a particular SPREAD above a stated commercial paper rate, is a dependable source of funds for the issuer and eliminates the administrative burden that would otherwise arise through the issuance of smaller denomination notes.

MATCHED BOOK A PORTFOLIO of ASSETS and LIABILITIES (such as the LOANS and DEPOSITS of a BANK, or the REPURCHASE AGREEMENTS and REVERSE REPURCHASE AGREEMENTS of a SECURITIES FIRM), with equal (or nearly equal) maturities or DURATIONS. A matched book minimizes or eliminates an institution's exposure to MARKET RISK and/or LIQUIDITY RISK, but generates a smaller return on CAPITAL.
- See also GAP, GAPPING, MISMATCH, OPEN BOOK, UNMATCHED BOOK.

MATERIAL ADVERSE CHANGE (MAC) CLAUSE A COVENANT contained in certain LOAN agreements that permits a BANK to cancel undrawn credit facilities and/or demand repayment of existing facilities if the borrower experiences a materially adverse change in its financial condition, or is subject to an adverse operating environment; triggering of a MAC can lead to the cancellation of facilities that otherwise appear to be available and committed. A material adverse change may be defined objectively (e.g., a CREDIT RATING downgrade or a rise in LEVERAGE) or subjectively.

- Also known as MARKET OUT CLAUSE.
- See also FORCE MAJEURE, VIS MAJOR.

MATILDA [COL] A BOND, NOTE, or CERTIFICATE OF DEPOSIT issued in Australian dollars in the Australian markets by a foreign company.

MAXIMUM FORESEEABLE LOSS A worst-case loss scenario applied by an INSURER or REINSURER to a potential CATASTROPHIC HAZARD.
- See also MAXIMUM PROBABLE LOSS

MAXIMUM LOSS A loss measure indicating the amount a firm might lose across a PORTFOLIO of MARKET RISKS by ignoring any offsetting effects obtained from DIVERSIFICATION. Maximum loss can be regarded as an extreme form of the VALUE-AT-RISK computation.
- See also SCENARIO ANALYSIS.

MAXIMUM PROBABLE LOSS An EXPECTED LOSS computation applied by an INSURER or REINSURER to a catastrophic or non-catastrophic RISK event.
- See also AMOUNT AT RISK, MAXIMUM FORESEEABLE LOSS.

MBO See MANAGEMENT BUYOUT.

MBS See MORTGAGE-BACKED SECURITY.

MEAN The unweighted average of a set of observations, which can be computed in arithmetic or geometric form:

Arithmetic mean:

$$\mu = \frac{\sum_{i=1}^{N} x_i}{N}$$

Geometric mean:

$$\mu = \left(\prod_i x_i\right)^{\frac{1}{N}}$$

where x_i is an observation and N is the number of observations.

MEAN REVERSION The observable tendency for INTEREST RATES and the VOLATILITY of interest rates to return to a MEAN level over the long term. Mean reversion is incorporated into certain BOND OPTION pricing models.

MEDIUM-TERM NOTE (MTN) A FIXED INCOME security issued by a company or sovereign entity in the US markets from a standing program arranged by an UNDERWRITER; once the program is registered issuance can take place at will. Financing via an MTN program gives an issuer considerable flexibility in accessing funds in the form,

and at a time, deemed most opportune. MTNs can be issued in fixed rate, floating rate, collateralized, amortizing, and credit-supported form, with maturities extending up to 30 years. Standard fixed-rate notes generally pay semi-annual COUPONS; floating rate notes typically pay monthly or quarterly coupons referenced to LIBOR, COMMERCIAL PAPER, TREASURY BILLS, or the PRIME RATE.
- See also EURO MEDIUM-TERM NOTE (EMTN)

MERCHANT BANK In the UK, a BANK that provides clients with CORPORATE FINANCE, RISK MANAGEMENT, and investment management advice, and deals actively in securities UNDERWRITING and TRADING and PRIVATE EQUITY investments. A merchant bank does not actively accept DEPOSITS or grant LOANS as a main line of business.
- See also BOUTIQUE, INVESTMENT BANK.

MERGER A CORPORATE FINANCE transaction where two companies combine their operations into a single venture, through a POOLING OF INTERESTS, an outright purchase, or a CONSOLIDATION. In a standard merger, shareholders of the two companies agree to the deal on a friendly basis and share in a specific percentage of shares in the new company. In a strict legal sense only transactions where one of the two original companies survives is classified as a merger; in practice, however, non-taxable poolings of interests and statutory consolidations are considered mergers.
- See also ACQUISITION, HORIZONTAL MERGER, TAKEOVER, VERTICAL MERGER.

MEZZANINE FINANCING (1) A second or third round of financing in a VENTURE CAPITAL, LEVERAGED BUYOUT, or restructuring transaction, which is generally SUBORDINATE to BANK LOANS but senior to early rounds of venture capital funding. Mezzanine financing is often considered to be pre-INITIAL PUBLIC OFFERING funding. (2) See SUBORDINATED DEBT.

MFN See MOST FAVORED NATION.

MICRO-CAP STOCK See MICRO STOCK.

MICRO STOCK The COMMON STOCK of a very small company, typically one with a MARKET CAPITALIZATION in the tens, or hundreds, of thousands of dollars. Such stocks, which are generally speculative and unproven, trade infrequently in the informal OVER-THE-COUNTER bulletin board market.
- Also known as MICRO-CAP STOCK.
- See also LARGE CAP STOCK, MID-CAP STOCK, SMALL CAP STOCK.

MID-ATLANTIC OPTION See BERMUDAN OPTION.

MID-CAP STOCK The COMMON STOCK of a company with a

medium-sized MARKET CAPITALIZATION, generally in the range of $1 billion to $5 billion.
- See also LARGE CAP STOCK, MICRO-STOCK, SMALL CAP STOCK.

MID-MARKET The middle point between the BID and OFFER on a price quotation.

MIDGET [COL] A 15-year GOVERNMENT NATIONAL MORTGAGE ASSOCIATION PASS-THROUGH security.
- See also DWARF, GNOME.

MINI [COL] An EXCHANGE-TRADED DERIVATIVE contract designed primarily for use by retail customers. Minis are structurally identical to other exchange FUTURES and OPTIONS but are offered in small denominations that make them suitable for retail clients. Given their size, minis are usually only traded through electronic mechanisms (even when an EXCHANGE features a physical trading floor).

MINIMUM FLUCTUATION The smallest price movement on a security or DERIVATIVE, typically set in relation to the specific characteristics of an ASSET or market.
- See also TICK VALUE.

MINIMUM VARIANCE HEDGE RATIO See HEDGE RATIO.

MINORITY CONTROL A process or structure where a small group of investors cooperates to gain effective control of a company; this is generally accomplished by attracting enough PROXIES from diffuse owners and can only work if no other large block holder exists.
- See also LEGAL MECHANISM CONTROL, MAJORITY CONTROL, MANAGEMENT CONTROL, MINORITY INTEREST, TOTAL CONTROL, VOTING TRUST CONTROL.

MINORITY INTEREST The economic and legal interests of shareholders who collectively own less than 50 percent of a company's outstanding COMMON STOCK.
- See also MINORITY CONTROL.

MINUS TICK Sale of a security at a price that is lower than the prior transaction, generally indicated through the display of a "–" next to the screen or tape price. A SHORT SALE cannot be initiated on a minus tick.
- Also known as DOWNTICK.
- See also PLUS TICK, ZERO PLUS TICK, ZERO MINUS TICK.

MISMATCH A state where a BANK's RATE-SENSITIVE ASSETS and RATE-SENSITIVE LIABILITIES are not perfectly matched with regard to maturity or DURATION. A mismatch implies the existence of LIQUIDITY RISK, INTEREST RATE RISK, and/or CURVE RISK, but may generate a greater return on invested CAPITAL.

■ See also GAP, GAPPING, MATCHED BOOK, UNMATCHED BOOK.

MISMATCHED SWAP See BASIS SWAP.

MIXED PERIL CONTRACT See MULTILINE POLICY.

MOB SPREAD See MUNICIPALS OVER BONDS SPREAD.

MOCHIAI [JPN] The network of cross-shareholdings held by KEIRETSU companies.

MODEL RISK The RISK of loss arising from flaws in the assumptions underpinning mathematical models/analytics used to value financial contracts such as DERIVATIVES, or from problems in implementing the associated technical code.

■ See also MARK-TO-MODEL.

MODIFIED DURATION A common measure of DURATION, or the average CASH FLOWS of a FIXED INCOME instrument, which estimates the change in the value of the instrument for a small change in YIELD. The modified duration of a BOND can be calculated via:

$$Dur\,(Mod) = \frac{\frac{C}{y^2}\left[1 - \frac{1}{(1+y)^n}\right] + \frac{n\left(100 - \frac{C}{y}\right)}{(1+y)^{n+1}}}{P}$$

where C is semi-annual COUPON interest, y is the semi-annual yield, n is the number of semi-annual periods, P is the price of the bond, and M is the redemption value of the bond (generally PAR VALUE).

MODIFIED LADDER OPTION See FIXED STRIKE LADDER OPTION.

MODIFIED SHOUT OPTION See FIXED STRIKE SHOUT OPTION.

MODIGLIANI–MILLER THEORY A key financial theory indicating that in a perfect market a firm's COST OF CAPITAL is independent of the financing method chosen (i.e., DEBT, EQUITY, RETAINED EARNINGS) and that management should be indifferent to the actual mix of CAPITAL employed. In practice market imperfections and frictions such as taxes and RISK mean that management generally focuses closely on LEVERAGE, DIVIDEND policy, and the proper mix of capital in order to minimize its overall cost of capital.

■ Additional reference: Miller and Modigliani (1958).

MOF See MULTIPLE OPTION FACILITY.

MOMENTUM INDICATOR A TECHNICAL ANALYSIS measure used to gauge the speed of upward and downward movements in a security or market index. Common momentum measures include relative strength indicators, MOVING AVERAGES, and convergence/divergence metrics.

MOMENTUM TRADING A TRADING strategy that is based purely on the short-term movement and momentum of a security or index rather than on FUNDAMENTAL ANALYSIS or TECHNICAL ANALYSIS.
- See also MOMO, NEGATIVE MOMENTUM TRADING, POSITION TRADING, SWING TRADING.

MOMO [COL] A trader or investor engaged in MOMENTUM TRADING.

MONETARY POLICY An action taken by a country's CENTRAL BANK or monetary authority to influence the supply, demand and cost of credit in order to promote economic growth and full employment, while keeping INFLATION pressures under control. Although specific approaches vary by national system, common techniques include buying/selling GOVERNMENT BILLS and GOVERNMENT BONDS through OPEN MARKET OPERATIONS, establishing RESERVE REQUIREMENTS for BANKS, and adjusting the official DISCOUNT RATE.
- See also FISCAL POLICY.

MONETIZATION A process, transaction, or strategy that allows financial value embedded in an ASSET to be converted into cash. Through monetization ILLIQUID, yet valuable, contracts and properties (such as ACCOUNTS RECEIVABLE, EMBEDDED OPTIONS, fixed plant and equipment) can be transformed into cash form so that proceeds can be used for other purposes. DERIVATIVES are often used to monetize value.

MONEY MARKET The short-term financial marketplace for issuance and TRADING of ASSETS and LIABILITIES with maturities extending from one day to 24 months. Instruments of the money market include GOVERNMENT BILLS, REPURCHASE AGREEMENTS, REVERSE REPURCHASE AGREEMENTS, BANKER'S ACCEPTANCES, CERTIFICATES OF DEPOSIT, COMMERCIAL PAPER, EURO COMMERCIAL PAPER, and short-term notes. Money market instruments are very LIQUID and generally feature only modest amounts of MARKET RISK and CREDIT RISK.
- See also CAPITAL MARKET.

MONEY MARKET FUND A MUTUAL FUND that invests exclusively in MONEY MARKET instruments, including COMMERCIAL PAPER, GOVERNMENT BILLS, BANKER'S ACCEPTANCES, and CERTIFICATES OF DEPOSIT. Money market funds are generally highly LIQUID and relatively low RISK, although returns are not guaranteed.

MONEY MARKET PREFERRED STOCK See ADJUSTABLE RATE PREFERRED STOCK.

MONEY SPREAD See BEAR SPREAD, BULL SPREAD.

MONEYNESS [COL] The degree to which an OPTION possesses or lacks INTRINSIC VALUE. An option with moneyness is said to be

IN-THE-MONEY and has intrinsic value; an option without moneyness is OUT-OF-THE-MONEY and has no intrinsic value.

MONOLINE POLICY An INSURANCE contract that only covers one LINE or class of RISK. If a loss occurs in the referenced PERIL, the INSURED is covered to a net amount that reflects a DEDUCTIBLE and POLICY CAP.

- See also MULTILINE POLICY.

MONOPOLY A market that features only one seller of goods or services, suggesting the seller has a significant degree of influence in setting prices. A monopoly can take the form of a natural monopoly, owing to the exclusive ownership of an input or process that would be prohibitively expensive to replicate, or a statutory monopoly, arising from approval given by a government or regulatory authority. In some national systems monopolies are prohibited or severely restricted, as they may be anti-competitive and create unfair pricing and price INFLATION pressures.

- See also DUOPOLY, MONOPSONY, OLIGOPOLY.

MONOPSONY A market that features only one buyer of goods or services, suggesting the buyer has an ability to influence the prices paid to suppliers.

- See also DUOPSONY, MONOPOLY, OLIGOPSONY.

MONTE CARLO SIMULATION A computer-intensive statistical process that generates ASSET paths based on user-defined inputs and drawings from a random number generator. Monte Carlo simulation is widely used for pricing DERIVATIVES, computing CREDIT RISK exposures and scenarios, and measuring PORTFOLIO RISKS.

- See also SIMULATION.

MORAL HAZARD Altering behavior by becoming less conservative and more reckless, knowing that INSURANCE or risk protection exists to compensate for damage or loss. INSURERS attempt to protect against moral hazard by remaining diligent in the UNDERWRITING procedures and requiring prospective INSUREDS to bear a portion of the economic exposure through DEDUCTIBLES, COINSURANCE, and/or POLICY CAPS.

- See also ADVERSE SELECTION.

MORATORIUM A sovereign suspension of COUPON interest and/or PRINCIPAL payments on DEBT, and a direct manifestation of SOVEREIGN RISK. Declaration of a moratorium, which may apply to all or selected classes of debt, is generally considered an EVENT OF DEFAULT under credit agreements and may ultimately lead to a rescheduling of payment terms and a write-off of the debt by the lenders/investors.

MORNING NOTES [COL] Late-breaking research information conveyed to investors by research analysts of INVESTMENT BANKS and SECURITIES FIRMS during morning conference calls.

MORTGAGE A LOAN granted by a BANK for the purchase of residential or commercial property, generally secured by the property being acquired. The mortgage may carry a fixed or floating INTEREST RATE, maturity extending from 5 to 30 years, LOAN-TO-VALUE of 50–100 percent, and PRINCIPAL repayment in conventional form (straight-line repayment), graduated form (increasing repayment), or balloon/bullet form (larger or total back-end repayment).

MORTGAGE-BACKED BOND A BOND that is collateralized by a MORTGAGE pledge. Unlike MORTGAGE-BACKED SECURITIES, which convey an ownership interest in a pool of mortgages to investors, the issuer retains the ownership interest of the mortgage; the transaction is thus considered a DEBT financing rather than a sale of assets.
- Also known as MORTGAGE BOND.
- See also COLLATERAL TRUST BOND.

MORTGAGE-BACKED SECURITY (MBS) A SECURITIZATION of a pool of MORTGAGES that results in the creation of a PASS-THROUGH SECURITY; investors acquiring the securities acquire an ownership interest in the underlying pools. MBSs can be assembled with small-size (conforming) retail mortgages, jumbo (non-conforming) retail mortgages, and commercial real estate mortgages. Mortgage originators often sell their pools into a CONDUIT managed by a sponsor financial institution, which then packages them into MBSs and issues them in the PRIMARY MARKET; once issued they are actively traded in the SECONDARY MARKET. MBSs have maturities ranging from 1 to 30 years and are available in fixed and floating rate form.
- See also COLLATERALIZED MORTGAGE OBLIGATION, PARTICIPATION CERTIFICATE, FEDERAL NATIONAL MORTGAGE ASSOCIATION, FEDERAL HOME LOAN MORTGAGE CORPORATION, GOVERNMENT NATIONAL MORTGAGE ASSOCIATION.

MORTGAGE BOND See MORTGAGE-BACKED BOND.

MORTGAGE DEFAULT SECURITIZATION An INSURANCE-LINKED SECURITY that permits purchasers of MORTGAGES to obtain protection against borrower DEFAULT. Repayment of PRINCIPAL and/or COUPONS is contingent on the repayment history of the underlying mortgages; if a specified loss occurs, the issuer of the BOND may delay or cease making payments to investors, meaning that it has HEDGED its RISK to instances of mortgage default.
- See also CATASTROPHE BOND, LIFE ACQUISITION COST SECURITIZATION, RESIDUAL VALUE SECURITIZATION, WEATHER BOND.

MORTGAGE SWAP (1) An OVER-THE-COUNTER AMORTIZING SWAP that replicates the CASH FLOW characteristics of a physical MORTGAGE-BACKED SECURITY, meaning it can be used as a synthetic MORTGAGE or HEDGE for a PORTFOLIO of MORTGAGES. (2) An exchange of mortgages for PARTICIPATION CERTIFICATES or PASS THROUGH SECURITIES backed by the same mortgages. Mortgage originators in the US market commonly swap seasoned mortgages with the FEDERAL NATIONAL MORTGAGE ASSOCIATION, GOVERNMENT NATIONAL MORTGAGE ASSOCIATION and FEDERAL HOME LOAN MORTGAGE CORPORATION for tradable securities or certificates, thereby adding LIQUIDITY to their balance sheets.

MOS See MUTUAL OFFSET SYSTEM.

MOST FAVORED NATION (MFN) Favorable trade status granted to certain nations, where IMPORTS from trading partner countries are treated no less favorably than imports from other countries, and no other foreign goods face a lower tariff than the partner country. Countries seek MFN status in order to bolster their trade activities and ultimately expand their own GROSS DOMESTIC PRODUCT.

MOVING AVERAGE A TECHNICAL ANALYSIS charting technique that computes the average price of a security or index over a particular time period, depicting general upward or downward trends. The averaging period rolls with each new observation period, which is generally set to daily, weekly, or monthly intervals.

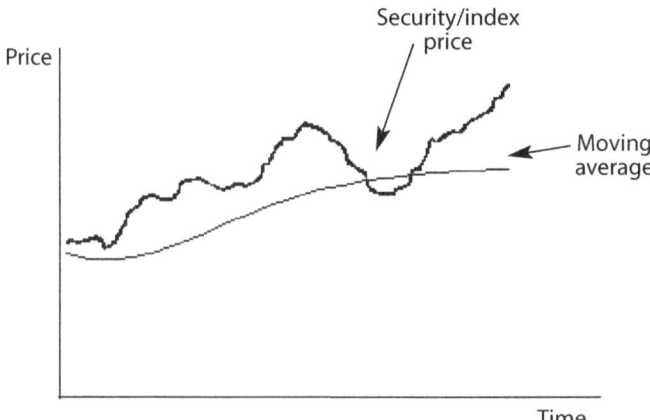

MTN See MEDIUM-TERM NOTE.

MULTI-CURRENCY NOTE FACILITY A short- or medium-term EURONOTE facility that permits an issuer to float notes in any one of several currencies. Although the borrower can select the borrowing currency, the lender can demand repayment in another currency at maturity.

MULTI-FACTOR OPTION See MULTI-INDEX OPTION.

MULTI-INDEX NOTE A STRUCTURED NOTE that pays investors an enhanced COUPON based on the performance of multiple indexes drawn from the same, or different, ASSET classes/markets. The most common multi-index notes are based on broad EQUITY indexes.

MULTI-INDEX OPTION An OVER-THE-COUNTER COMPLEX OPTION that grants the buyer a payoff based on the difference between two or more reference ASSETS and a predefined STRIKE PRICE; assets may be drawn from the same, or different, asset classes/markets.
- Also known as MULTI-FACTOR OPTION, RAINBOW OPTION.
- See also BASKET OPTION, MULTIPLE STRIKE OPTION, OPTION ON THE BEST/WORST OF N-ASSETS, OPTION ON THE BEST/WORST OF N-ASSETS AND CASH, SPREAD OPTION.

MULTI-RISK PRODUCT An INSURANCE contract that combines multiple RISKS in a single structure, allowing the client to obtain a consolidated, and often cheaper and more efficient, RISK MANAGEMENT solution.
- See also MULTIPLE PERIL PRODUCTS, MULTIPLE TRIGGER PRODUCTS.

MULTILINE POLICY An INSURANCE contract that covers multiple PERILS within the COMMERCIAL LINES areas. The standard multi-line policy contains common policy declarations and conditions and details on specific coverages, each with their own declarations and coverage forms. If a loss occurs in any of the mentioned perils, the INSURED is covered to a net amount that reflects a DEDUCTIBLE and POLICY CAP.
- Also known as MIXED PERIL CONTRACT, PACKAGE POLICY.
- See also MONOLINE POLICY, MULTIPLE PERIL PRODUCT.

MULTIPLE See PRICE/EARNINGS RATIO.

MULTIPLE BARRIER OPTION An OVER-THE-COUNTER COMPLEX OPTION package that contains at least two BARRIER OPTIONS that create or extinguish an underlying EUROPEAN OPTION. Sine the multiple barrier option has two barriers the probability of knock-in or knock-out increases.
- See also TWIN-IN OPTION, TWIN-OUT OPTION.

MULTIPLE OPTION FACILITY (MOF) A medium-term EURONOTE facility that allows an issuer to access funds in a range of currencies, reference INTEREST RATES, and maturities. The range of options available to the borrower are contained within the MOF agreement.

MULTIPLE PERIL POLICY An INSURANCE contract that provides coverage for multiple classes of related or unrelated PERILS. Within the PROPERTY AND CASUALTY INSURANCE sector coverage generally extends to property, LIABILITY, crime, and boiler and machinery.
- Also known as ALL LINES INSURANCE.
- See also COMMERCIAL GENERAL LIABILITY POLICY, MULTILINE POLICY.

MULTIPLE STRIKE OPTION An OVER-THE-COUNTER COMPLEX OPTION that grants the buyer a payoff based on the best or worst performing of a series of ASSETS, each with a specific STRIKE PRICE. Option references may be drawn from the same, or different, asset classes/markets.
- See also MULTI-INDEX OPTION.

MULTIPLE TRIGGER PRODUCT An INSURANCE contract that provides the INSURED with a compensatory payment only if multiple events occur (i.e., two or more TRIGGERS are breached). Since the probability of several events happening simultaneously is lower than the probability of single event occurrence, the protection provided through the multiple trigger product is generally cheaper than it is for a standard single trigger contract. Since multiple trigger products can be structured to protect against different dimensions of RISK, they are frequently applied in the management of VOLUMETRIC RISK, which is driven by both volume and price factors.
- See also DUAL TRIGGER, TRIPLE TRIGGER.

MUNICIPAL BOND A BOND issued by a state or municipal authority or agency in order to fund general obligations or specific projects. Bonds can be issued with fixed or floating COUPONS and maturities ranging from 1 to 30 years, and can be backed by the specific credit of the municipal issuer or the CASH FLOWS of a project (as a NON-RECOURSE obligation). Interest earned on municipal bonds is generally exempt from federal taxation, although it is taxable at the state or municipal level. Notes are available in various forms, including tax, revenue, and bond anticipation notes, project notes, short coupon notes, and seven-day demand notes.
- See also GENERAL OBLIGATION BOND, REVENUE BOND.

MUNICIPAL BOND INSURANCE An INSURANCE contract written by an INSURER to cover an event of DEFAULT by the issuer of a MUNICIPAL BOND. The insurance, which may assume the form of a FINANCIAL GUARANTEE, is designed to protect investors from loss of PRINCIPAL and/or COUPON interest.

MUNICIPALS OVER BONDS (MOB) SPREAD The YIELD differential between tax-free MUNICIPAL BONDS and TREASURY BONDS of the same maturity. The spread provides an indication of the relative credit perception of a municipal issuer, with a widening reflecting deterioration, and a tightening indicating an improvement.

MUTUAL ASSENT A condition that only permits a contract to become valid when both parties have agreed to the terms and conditions.

MUTUAL FUND (1) In the United States, an INVESTMENT COMPANY that raises CAPITAL from investors and uses the proceeds to purchase ASSETS; owners of mutual fund shares own a proportional share in the pool of invested assets. Mutual funds can issue an unlimited number of shares, which are redeemable on demand at the quoted NET ASSET VALUE (or the net asset value less a back-end LOAD, or commission charge). Mutual funds are an extremely popular form of investment, particularly among retail investors who often lack the expertise, time, and/or resources, to create and manage a PORTFOLIO of securities. (2) In the UK, see UNIT TRUST.
- (1) Also known as OPEN-END FUND, OPEN-END INVESTMENT COMPANY.
- (1) See also CLOSED-END FUND, LOAD FUND, NO-LOAD FUND, 12b-1 MUTUAL FUND.

MUTUAL OFFSET SYSTEM (MOS) A formal arrangement between two EXCHANGES where EXCHANGE-TRADED DERIVATIVE contracts initiated on one exchange can be transferred to, or closed out on, another exchange. The MOS extends trading hours significantly, and can increase the LIQUIDITY of a given contract. In order for the MOS mechanism to work the contracts on the participating exchanges must be fungible.

MUTUAL ORGANIZATION A corporate structure where members, rather than external investors, own the organization. Although the mutual has the advantage of limiting external influence on corporate affairs, it generally caps the amount of CAPITAL that is available for expansion.

N

NAKED CALL An OPTION position where the seller of a CALL OPTION does not own the UNDERLYING ASSET that must be delivered if the buyer EXERCISES the contract. Selling naked calls is generally a high RISK strategy since the seller must acquire the asset in the open market should exercise occur, at a prevailing price that will be higher than the STRIKE PRICE.
- See also COVERED CALL, NAKED OPTION, NAKED PUT.

NAKED OPTION An OPTION position where the seller of the option does not own the UNDERLYING ASSET or cash that must be delivered if the buyer EXERCISES the contract. Selling naked options is generally a high RISK strategy since the seller must acquire the underlying asset in the open market or source cash should exercise occur.
- Also known as UNCOVERED OPTION.
- See also COVERED OPTION, NAKED CALL, NAKED PUT, NAKED WRITER.

NAKED POSITION An outright LONG POSITION or SHORT POSITION that is not protected by an offsetting HEDGE. A naked position may be exposed to elements of MARKET RISK, CREDIT RISK, and/or LIQUIDITY RISK.
- See also COVERED POSITION.

NAKED PUT An OPTION strategy where the seller of a PUT OPTION does not have cash on hand to purchase the UNDERLYING ASSET if the buyer EXERCISES the contract. Selling naked puts can be a high RISK strategy since the seller must be able to source enough cash to cover the higher STRIKE PRICE. Simply selling the asset will not generate enough proceeds, meaning the put seller must be able to borrow funds from alternative sources.
- See also COVERED PUT, NAKED CALL, NAKED OPTION.

NAKED SHORTING An illegal SHORT SALE of securities that are not certain to exist. In certain jurisdictions parties contemplating a short sale must first confirm that sufficient securities exist and can be borrowed to fulfill the short.

NAKED WRITER The seller of a NAKED OPTION that does not have the UNDERLYING ASSET (deliverable under a CALL OPTION) or sufficient cash on hand to acquire the asset (under a PUT OPTION) should EXERCISE occur. A naked writer attempts to earn PREMIUM income through a relatively high RISK strategy.

- See also COVERED WRITER.

NAMED INSURED The party in an INSURANCE contract that is designated as an INSURED.

NAMED PERIL COVER See NAMED PERIL POLICY.

NAMED PERIL POLICY An INSURANCE contract that provides coverage only for PERILS that are specifically enumerated in the policy; coverage is thus much narrower than it is under an ALL RISKS POLICY, although the corresponding PREMIUM payable by the INSURED to the INSURER is smaller.

- Also known as NAMED PERIL COVER.

NAMES [COL] Individuals providing CAPITAL to SYNDICATES UNDERWRITING INSURANCE and REINSURANCE contracts through LLOYD'S OF LONDON. In the event CLAIMS exceed RESERVES, participating names must cover their share of the losses (as well as those that cannot be met by other participants, as most syndicates feature JOINT AND SEVERAL LIABILITY). Since names face UNLIMITED LIABILITY, their personal ASSETS are at risk. Although individuals have historically been the primary providers of capital, Lloyd's allowed CORPORATIONS to act as names in the provision of underwriting capital starting in the mid-1990s.

NASD See NATIONAL ASSOCIATION OF SECURITIES DEALERS.

NASDAQ See NATIONAL ASSOCIATION OF SECURITIES DEALERS AUTOMATED QUOTATION SYSTEM.

NASDAQ 100 A BENCHMARK technology index comprised of 100 LARGE CAP STOCKS in the technology sector. The index can be traded directly through EXCHANGE-TRADED FUNDS and DERIVATIVES.

NATIONAL ASSOCIATION OF SECURITIES DEALERS (NASD) A US SELF-REGULATORY ORGANIZATION, comprised of BROKER/DEALERS and SECURITIES FIRMS dealing in OVER-THE-COUNTER securities, which is responsible for enforcing investor protection rules promulgated by the SECURITIES AND EXCHANGE COMMISSION. The NASD also oversees TRADING of securities through the NATIONAL ASSOCIATION OF SECURITIES DEALERS AUTOMATED QUOTATION SYSTEM.

NATIONAL ASSOCIATION OF SECURITIES DEALERS AUTOMATED QUOTATION SYSTEM (NASDAQ) An electronic EXCHANGE that trades the COMMON STOCKS of over 5000 US companies, including many related to the technology sector, through a system of MARKET MAKERS. The NATIONAL ASSOCIATION OF SECURITIES DEALERS oversees the exchange. It features two separate markets, the NASDAQ National Market, which supports LARGE CAP STOCKS, and the NASDAQ SmallCap Market, which supports emerging companies. The exchange also owns the American Stock Exchange and the Philadelphia Stock Exchange.

NATURAL [COL] See CLEAN.

NAV See NET ASSET VALUE.

NCD See NEGOTIABLE CERTIFICATE OF DEPOSIT.

NEAR MONEY [COL] ASSETS that are nearly equivalent to cash, meaning they can be liquidated immediately at carrying value, but which still generate a small YIELD or return. Common examples of near money include short-term GOVERNMENT BILLS, COMMERCIAL PAPER, BANKER'S ACCEPTANCES, and sight DEPOSITS.
- See also L, M1, M2, M3.

NEARBY CONTRACT The current, or closest, EXCHANGE-TRADED DERIVATIVE contract on a reference ASSET, generally the most LIQUID until several days or weeks prior to expiry, when participants often begin rolling positions into the NEXT NEARBY CONTRACT.
- Also known as FRONT MONTH, PROMPT MONTH.

NEGATIVE BASIS A market state where the price of the cash or SPOT MARKET security is below the price of the underlying FUTURES contract.
- See also BASIS RISK, POSITIVE BASIS.

NEGATIVE CARRY A state where the return earned on an ASSET is lower than the cost of financing and storing the asset.
- See also POSITIVE CARRY.

NEGATIVE CONVEXITY A characteristic of certain financial ASSETS where losses are greater, and gains are smaller, than those of linear contracts or those with POSITIVE CONVEXITY. SHORT OPTIONS and certain types of MORTGAGE-BACKED SECURITIES (e.g., INTEREST-ONLY STRIPS) feature negative convexity.
- See also NEGATIVE GAMMA, NON-LINEAR INSTRUMENT.

NEGATIVE GAMMA MARKET RISK exposure to large price moves in the UNDERLYING generated through the sale of PUT OPTIONS or CALL OPTIONS. A seller of options can suffer a loss from negative gamma as it may not have an opportunity to properly rebalance a DELTA HEDGE. In common with other NEGATIVE CONVEXITY instruments, negative gamma positions feature losses that are

greater and gains that are smaller than instruments with POSITIVE CONVEXITY.
- See also GAMMA, POSITIVE GAMMA.

NEGATIVE GAP A general measure of a firm's exposure to INTEREST RATE REPRICING RISK. A negative gap arises when RATE SENSITIVE ASSETS are smaller than RATE-SENSITIVE LIABILITIES, and means the firm will experience a loss if rates rise and a gain if rates fall.
- See also GAP, GAPPING, POSITIVE GAP.

NEGATIVE MOMENTUM TRADING A short-term, speculative TRADING strategy based on purchasing COMMON STOCKS that have fallen quickly and dramatically as a result of bad or unexpected news. Negative momentum traders believe market moves may be an over-reaction, and attempt to profit by purchasing shares for the very short term, until the negative news has been absorbed and other investors re-enter the market.
- See also MOMO, MOMENTUM TRADING.

NEGATIVE OBLIGATION The duty for a SPECIALIST or MARKET MAKER dealing in a COMMON STOCK not to take one side of an ORDER on a proprietary basis when it can be matched directly with another order.
- See also AFFIRMATIVE OBLIGATION, INTERPOSITIONING.

NEGATIVE PLEDGE A COVENANT in a LOAN agreement or BOND INDENTURE that prohibits a borrower from pledging unencumbered ASSETS in support of new financing unless existing debt holders remain equally secured and/or their seniority rankings remain unchanged. If a borrower violates the negative pledge, existing debt holders can generally demand repayment of their funds.

NEGATIVE WORKING CAPITAL A financial state where a company's CURRENT LIABILITIES exceed its CURRENT ASSETS. Negative working capital generally indicates the presence of LIQUIDITY problems, since insufficient assets exist to cover obligations coming due.
- See also NET WORKING CAPITAL, POSITIVE WORKING CAPITAL.

NEGATIVE YIELD CURVE A TERM STRUCTURE where short-term INTEREST RATES are higher than long-term interest rates. A negative curve may be caused by strong demand for short-term credit, high INFLATION, and/or weak investor confidence.
- Also known as INVERTED YIELD CURVE.
- See also KINKED YIELD CURVE, POSITIVE YIELD CURVE, YIELD CURVE.

NEGOTIABLE CERTIFICATE OF DEPOSIT (NCD) A large denomination marketable CERTIFICATE OF DEPOSIT (i.e., $100,000+) with

a fixed or variable INTEREST RATE, issued by a BANK; the negotiability feature allows the NCD to be traded in the SECONDARY MARKET. NCDs have maturities ranging from one week to over 10 years and can be floated in a broad range of currencies.
- See also FLOATING RATE CERTIFICATE OF DEPOSIT, LOCK-UP CERTIFICATE OF DEPOSIT.

NEGOTIABLE INSTRUMENT A written order, such as a BILL OF EXCHANGE, PROMISSORY NOTE, or check, which is signed by the endorser as being payable to the holder/bearer without conditions.

NEGOTIATED SWAP A CORPORATE FINANCE transaction involving an exchange of ASSETS (e.g., a subsidiary, company, or block shares) between two parties. A negotiated swap is an efficient mechanism for a firm to substitute assets that it no longer requires for others that may represent a better strategic fit.

NEGOTIATED UNDERWRITING A non-competitive UNDERWRITING of a NEW ISSUE of securities where the issuer and UNDERWRITER agree in advance on an appropriate UNDERWRITING SPREAD, deal size, and distribution strategy.
- See also COMPETITIVE BID UNDERWRITING.

NESTED OPTION See COMPOUND OPTION.

NET ASSET VALUE (NAV) The per share market price of a MUTUAL FUND or CLOSED-END FUND, generally based on the previous day's closing prices for the underlying ASSETS held in the fund. NAV can be computed via:

$$NAV = Sec_{MV} + Cash + AI - Liab$$

where Sec_{MV} is the MARKET VALUE of quoted securities in the PORTFOLIO, $Cash$ is cash on hand, AI is ACCRUED INTEREST, and $Liab$ is LIABILITIES.

NET INTEREST MARGIN In banking, a measure of the income differential between interest-generating ASSETS (e.g., LOANS, FIXED INCOME investment securities) and interest-bearing LIABILITIES required to fund the assets (e.g., DEPOSITS, REPURCHASE AGREEMENTS, BONDS), generally computed as:

$$NIM = II - IE$$

where II is interest income and IE is interest expense.

The larger the NIM, the greater the profitability of core banking operations.

NET LINE LIMIT The maximum amount of INSURANCE an INSURER will write on a given LINE of RISK; a limit is used to control the insurer's exposure and cap potential losses.

NET LOSS In INSURANCE, the actual loss sustained by an INSURER in meeting an INSURED's CLAIMS, after taking account of REINSURANCE coverage and any amounts recovered via SUBROGATION or ABANDONMENT.

NET PREMIUMS WRITTEN In INSURANCE, the total PREMIUMS written by an INSURER, less the amount CEDED to a REINSURER.

NET PRESENT VALUE (NPV) A measure of the net value of an investment or capital project, measured by discounting future CASH FLOWS to the present using an appropriate DISCOUNT RATE or COST OF CAPITAL (which is also equal to the INTERNAL RATE OF RETURN); the original cost of the investment made at the inception of the project is deducted in order to provide a net figure. The general form of the equation is given as:

$$NPV = \sum_{t=1}^{n} \frac{CF_t}{(1+r)^t} - I_0$$

where CF_t is the expected cash flow at time t, r is the discount rate, n is the number of periods, and I_0 is the original cost of the investment.

■ See also PRESENT VALUE, FUTURE VALUE.

NET PROFIT MARGIN A measure of a company's ability to transform its revenues into net income, typically calculated as:

$$NP = \frac{EBITDA - Tax}{Rev}$$

where *EBITDA* is EARNINGS BEFORE INTEREST, TAXES, DEPRECIATION AND AMORTIZATION, *Tax* is taxes paid, and *Rev* is revenues.

The greater the net profit margin, the stronger the operating efficiencies and cost control.

NET RETAINED LINES The net amount of INSURANCE held by an INSURER after taking account of any REINSURANCE coverage.

NET SINGLE PREMIUM In INSURANCE, the core PREMIUM designed to cover the PRESENT VALUE of future CLAIMS, excluding any LOAD factor to account for costs or profit margin.

NET UNDERWRITING PROFIT In INSURANCE, a measure of profitability associated with core insurance UNDERWRITING business, generating computed as:

$$NUP = P_{C\&E} - Div$$

where $P_{C\&E}$ is profit after CLAIMS and expenses, and *Div* is policyholder DIVIDENDS

The greater the net underwriting profit, the stronger the INSURER's core business.

NET WORKING CAPITAL A general measure of corporate LIQUIDITY, typically calculated as CURRENT ASSETS less CURRENT LIABILITIES. Positive net working capital indicates that a company is likely to have sufficient resources to meet payments or obligations coming due, while a negative figure is a signal of potential LIQUIDITY problems.
- See also CURRENT RATIO, GROSS WORKING CAPITAL, NEGATIVE WORKING CAPITAL, POSITIVE WORKING CAPITAL, QUICK RATIO, WORKING CAPITAL.

NET WORTH See CAPITAL.

NETTING An arrangement that condenses payments between two COUNTERPARTIES into a single CASH FLOW, allowing CREDIT RISK exposures to be offset. In order to be effective, netting must be legally documented through an appropriate MASTER AGREEMENT and recognized by the relevant legal system where dealing occurs; if these prerequisites are not fulfilled, a non-defaulting counterparty may be CHERRY-PICKED in a BANKRUPTCY court by a defaulting counterparty's RECEIVERS.
- See also NOVATION, PAYMENT NETTING, SET-OFF.

NEW ISSUE An offering of COMMON STOCK, BONDS, or PREFERRED STOCK in the PRIMARY MARKET. A new issue is generally UNDERWRITTEN by a SYNDICATE comprised of BANKS, INVESTMENT BANKS, and/or SECURITIES FIRMS, who may agree to place securities on an agented basis (i.e., a BEST EFFORTS UNDERWRITING) or as principals (i.e., a BOUGHT DEAL). An issuer's inaugural issue of securities is known as a PRIMARY OFFERING, and any subsequent new issue is considered to be a SECONDARY OFFERING.

NEW YORK STOCK EXCHANGE (NYSE) The largest US stock EXCHANGE, founded in 1792, which trades over 3000 COMMON STOCKS (along with WARRANTS, OPTIONS, and RIGHTS ISSUES) through a network of DEALERS and SPECIALISTS. BOND trading is conducted on a separate floor through traders known as the BOND CROWD. The exchange continues to feature a physical trading floor where it conducts OPEN OUTCRY trades, although portions of the process are now managed electronically. The exchange is organized as an unincorporated association with voting membership held by more than 1300 members (or SEATS); a separate division is responsible for overseeing adherence to regulations through its powers as a SELF-REGULATORY ORGANIZATION.
- Also known as BIG BOARD.

NEWLY INDUSTRIALIZED COUNTRY (NIC) A country that features a strong, and rapidly growing, industrial production base that contributes substantially to both national income and EXPORTS. NICs generally possess greater industrial development and exports than LESSER DEVELOPED COUNTRIES.

NEXT NEARBY CONTRACT An EXCHANGE-TRADED DERIVATIVE contract on a particular reference ASSET with the second closest maturity. Though generally not as actively traded as the NEARBY CONTRACT, the next nearby is usually very LIQUID and becomes even more liquid as the nearby contract approaches maturity and participants start rolling their positions.

NIC See NEWLY INDUSTRIALIZED COUNTRY.

NIF See NOTE ISSUANCE FACILITY.

NIFTY FIFTY [COL] The top 50 COMMON STOCK holdings of large US institutional investors; the list changes periodically but generally includes a core of BLUE CHIP stocks that investors hold for the long term.

NIKKEI 225 One of two BENCHMARK indexes of the Japanese stock market (along with the TOKYO STOCK PRICE INDEX), comprised of 225 LARGE CAP STOCKS listed on the Tokyo Stock Exchange. The Nikkei 225, which is a price-weighted index, can be traded directly through EXCHANGE-TRADED FUNDS and DERIVATIVES.

NO-LOAD FUND A MUTUAL FUND that does not carry a sales commission charge (or LOAD). Despite the lack of a commission no-load funds are not always cheaper than LOAD FUNDS, as they may feature higher annual management fees or exit fees.

▪ See also NET ASSET VALUE.

NOMINAL INTEREST RATE A measure of the level of INTEREST RATES, computed as the REAL INTEREST RATE plus INFLATION.

NOMINEE A party acting as registered owner of securities (i.e., the holder of record) on behalf of a client, either for ease of execution/transfer or for reasons related to client anonymity. BROKERS commonly act as nominees by holding client securities in STREET NAME.

NOMING THE PIPES [COL] Abbreviated form of "nominating the pipes," a scheduling process in natural gas TRADING where physical delivery of gas is allocated through the network of interconnecting gas pipelines based on supply, demand, time, and price constraints.

NON-ACCRUAL LOAN See NON-PERFORMING LOAN.

NON-ADMITTED INSURANCE An INSURANCE contract written by an INSURER that is not licensed in the state or jurisdiction where the INSURED'S RISK exists.

▪ Also known as UNAUTHORIZED INSURANCE.

- See also ADMITTED INSURANCE, SURPLUS LINES INSURANCE.

NON-ADMITTED INSURER An INSURER that is not licensed to sell an INSURANCE policy in a given state or jurisdiction.
- Also known as UNAUTHORIZED INSURER.
- See also ADMITTED INSURER.

NON-CALLABLE BOND A BOND that cannot be called or redeemed by the issuer prior to final maturity under any circumstances. A non-callable bond provides the investor with protection against REINVESTMENT RISK until final maturity.
- Also known as STRAIGHT BOND.
- See also CALL RISK, CALLABLE BOND, HARD CALL PROTECTION, SOFT CALL PROTECTION.

NON-CLEARING MEMBER An EXCHANGE member that is not permitted to clear trades directly with the CLEARINGHOUSE, and must therefore direct all CLEARING activities through a CLEARING MEMBER.

NON-COMPETITIVE BID In an AUCTION MARKET, a BID that is not placed in competition with other bids. Noncompetitive bids are generally filled at the average price of the COMPETITIVE BIDS.

NON-COMPETITIVE TRADING An illegal practice where a DEALER or MARKET-MAKER executes a client order within a proprietary account, without first exposing it to the market. Non-competitive trading reduces transparency into order flows and allows dealers to profit at the expense of clients.

NON-CONCURRENCY A situation where an INSURED's multiple INSURANCE policies are not properly structured or synchronized, and fail to provide comprehensive cover in the event of a loss.

NON-CONFORMING LOAN A residential MORTGAGE that exceeds standard specifications related to size and LOAN-TO-VALUE established for inclusion in a pool of PASS-THROUGH SECURITIES (such as those created by FEDERAL NATIONAL MORTGAGE ASSOCIATION, GOVERNMENT NATIONAL MORTGAGE ASSOCIATION, or FEDERAL HOME LOAN MORTGAGE CORPORATION). If a mortgage originator wishes to securitize non-conforming loans, it must generally do so through a private label CONDUIT sponsored and managed by a financial institution.

NON-CONVERTIBLE CURRENCY A currency that cannot be freely exchanged into another currency without prior regulatory approval. Some currencies are non-convertible for all holders, and for any purpose. Others feature restricted convertibility: non-residents may be able to exchange holdings but residents may require approval, or holders may be permitted to convert freely for CURRENT ACCOUNT

purposes such as trade, but not for CAPITAL ACCOUNT purposes such as LOANS or ASSET acquisition. Non-convertible currencies are generally associated with planned or managed economies, and their prices are often set or influenced by the local CENTRAL BANK or monetary authority.
- See also CONVERTIBILITY, CONVERTIBLE CURRENCY, EXCHANGE CONTROL.

NON-CUMULATIVE PREFERRED STOCK PREFERRED STOCK that pays DIVIDENDS to investors when, and if, they are declared and paid, and provides for no right to, or CLAIM on, dividends that have been suspended for one or more periods. Since the dividends do not accumulate, they are permanently sacrificed.
- See also CUMULATIVE PREFERRED STOCK.

NON-DELIVERABLE FORWARD A bilateral OVER-THE-COUNTER DERIVATIVE that permits the purchaser to buy, and the seller to sell, an ASSET at a predetermined future price and future date with SETTLEMENT in financial/cash terms, rather than via delivery of the UNDERLYING reference asset. Non-deliverable forwards are commonly used in transactions where sourcing and/or delivery of an asset is restricted, such as NON-CONVERTIBLE CURRENCIES that are subject to EXCHANGE CONTROLS.

NON-DIVERSIFIABLE RISK A RISK that is common to all companies, ASSETS, or markets and cannot therefore be reduced or eliminated through DIVERSIFICATION.
- Also known as SYSTEMATIC RISK.
- See also DIVERSIFIABLE RISK

NON-EXECUTIVE DIRECTOR A DIRECTOR who is not a member of the executive management team and, presuming no conflicts of interest, may be considered to be independent from a GOVERNANCE perspective.
- See also EXECUTIVE DIRECTOR, LEAD INDEPENDENT DIRECTOR.

NON-INSURANCE TRANSFER A RISK TRANSFER technique that makes use of contractual relationships, such as HOLD HARMLESS agreements or PRINCIPAL/AGENT relations, rather than traditional INSURANCE arrangements.

NON-LINEAR INSTRUMENT A financial contract, such as an OPTION or WARRANT, with a payout that varies with changes in the movement of the UNDERLYING reference market or ASSET. A unit change in the value of the reference leads to a greater than unit change in the contract, which may be positive or negative depending on whether the instrument has POSITIVE CONVEXITY or NEGATIVE CONVEXITY.

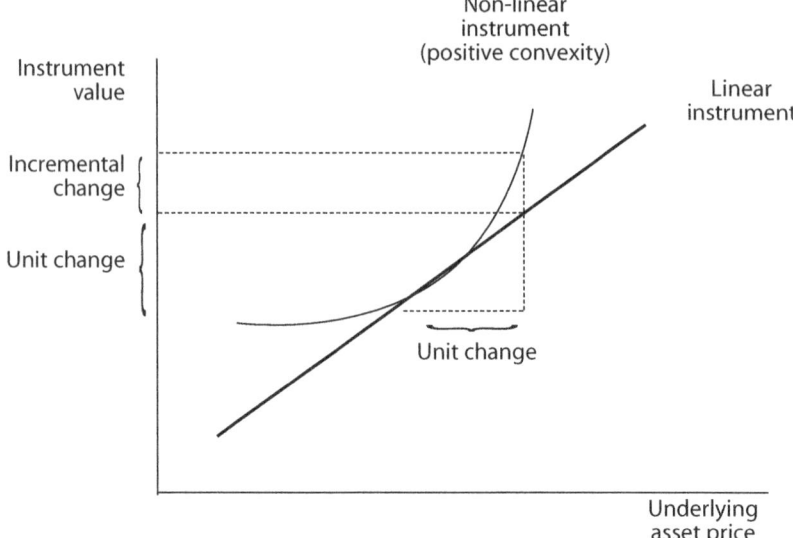

- See also CONVEXITY, GAMMA, LINEAR INSTRUMENT, NEGATIVE GAMMA, POSITIVE GAMMA.

NON-PAR SWAP An OVER-THE-COUNTER SWAP, such as a PREMIUM SWAP or DISCOUNT SWAP, which is transacted at off-market INTEREST RATES.
- Also known as OFF-MARKET SWAP.

NON-PARTICIPATING GUARANTEED INVESTMENT CONTRACT (GIC) A GUARANTEED INVESTMENT CONTRACT with a fixed return and a fixed term; the investor does not receive any excess benefit from surplus returns generated by the INSURER in managing the ASSET PORTFOLIO.
- See also PARTICIPATING GUARANTEED INVESTMENT CONTRACT, SYNTHETIC GUARANTEED INVESTMENT CONTRACT.

NON-PERFORMING LOAN A LOAN in which the borrower is no longer making regular payments of interest and/or PRINCIPAL. A non-performing loan is generally classified as a substandard asset and supported by appropriate LOAN LOSS RESERVES. If the loan is not made current by the borrower over a particular period it is generally written off against reserves; legal actions may then be taken against the borrower to recover amounts due.
- Also known as NON-ACCRUAL LOAN.

NON-PRIME LOAN See SUBPRIME LOAN.

NON-PURPOSE LOAN A LOAN, collateralized by securities and subject to MARGIN rules, where the proceeds are not used to acquire additional securities.

- See also PURPOSE LOAN.

NON-RECOMBINING TREE A LATTICE MODEL used to price OPTIONS where the assumed upward and downward movements are not equal. This yields an uneven or skewed lattice, and causes option value to be weighted more heavily in the direction of the larger market moves.
- See also BINOMIAL MODEL.

NON-RECOURSE The lack of a CLAIM on a contracting party. A non-recourse transaction is dependent solely on the ASSETS or CASH FLOWS associated with the transaction, indicating that the financial position/capabilities of the sponsor or contracting party are irrelevant and cannot be considered.
- See also NON-RECOURSE LOAN, RECOURSE.

NON-RECOURSE LOAN A LOAN with repayment that depends solely on the proceeds from the project or ASSET being financed, or the sale of specific COLLATERAL supporting the transaction. The lending BANK has no ability to seek repayment from the borrower in the event of a shortfall.
- See also FULL RECOURSE LOAN, NON-RECOURSE, PARTIAL RECOURSE LOAN, RECOURSE.

NON-REFUNDABLE DEBT A BOND or NOTE that cannot be redeemed and replaced by alternative DEBT. In some instances the INDENTURE of a non-refundable bond will allow limited refunding, but only if INTEREST RATES decline to a particular level.
- See also CALL PROTECTION, NON-CALLABLE BOND.

NON-VOTING STOCK COMMON STOCK that carries standard RENT RIGHTS, but only limited CONTROL RIGHTS – including the right to obtain financial disclosure and file lawsuits, but not to vote.
- See also DISENFRANCHISING TRANSACTION.

NORMAL BACKWARDATION A market state where the SPOT PRICE on a FUTURE or FORWARD is higher than the FORWARD PRICE, often as a result of temporary ASSET shortages or an excess supply for future delivery.
- Also known as BACKWARDATION.
- See also CONTANGO.

NORMAL DISTRIBUTION A statistical distribution, symmetrical around the MEAN, with no lower or upper bounds. Given the properties of the distribution, approximately 68 percent of observations lie within +/− one STANDARD DEVIATION of the mean, 95 percent within approximately +/− two standard deviations, and 99.7 percent within approximately +/− three standard deviations. The normal distribution is widely used in a variety of financial and ACTUARIAL PRICING techniques.

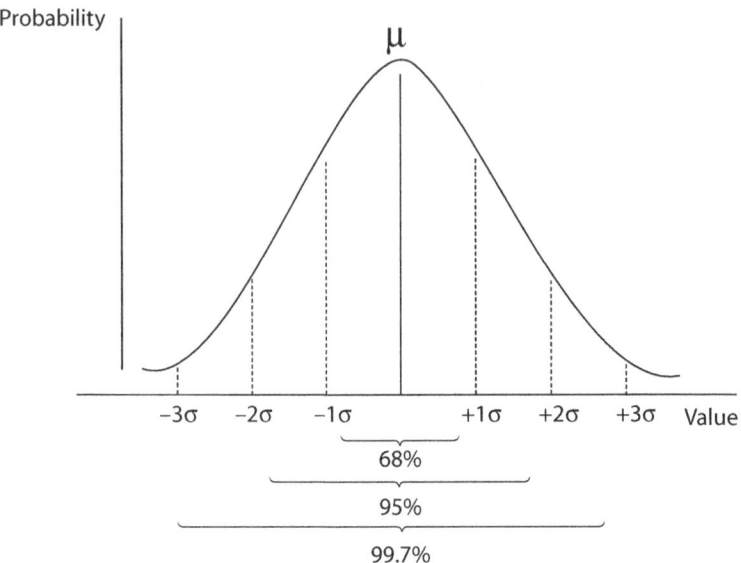

- See also CENTRAL LIMIT THEOREM, LAW OF LARGE NUMBERS, LOGNORMAL DISTRIBUTION.

NOSTRO [LAT] Literally "our account"; a local account a foreign BANK maintains with a local bank to accommodate local currency business, e.g., a US bank has a yen nostro with a Japanese bank to manage its yen inflows and outflows.
- See also VOSTRO.

NOTE In the CAPITAL MARKETS, a financial obligation representing the issuer's LIABILITY to repay CAPITAL provided by investors. Notes are defined by form of INTEREST RATE (e.g., fixed rate, floating rate, structured), COUPON frequency, currency, maturity, COLLATERAL, price, redemption, AMORTIZATION, transfer, and market of issue. Notes are generally floated with maturities ranging from 1 to 10 years. They may be issued onshore or offshore, as REGISTERED SECURITIES or BEARER SECURITIES, in any one of several currencies; securities are often listed on an EXCHANGE, although most TRADING occurs OVER-THE-COUNTER.
- See also BOND, EURONOTE, MEDIUM TERM NOTE, EURO MEDIUM TERM NOTE, FLOATING RATE NOTE, GOVERNMENT NOTE, LEVERAGED NOTE, NOTE ISSUANCE FACILITY, STRUCTURED NOTE.

NOTE ISSUANCE FACILITY (NIF) A EURONOTE program where a borrower issues unsecured NOTES to investors via a TENDER PANEL. If the notes cannot be successfully placed, the underwriting BANKS agree to purchase them through the extension of medium-term LOANS, thus guaranteeing the borrower funds.

- See also REVOLVING UNDERWRITING FACILITY.

NOTIONAL A common method of denominating the size, though not necessarily the RISK, of a DERIVATIVE transaction (generally SWAPS and FORWARDS). In most instances notional is used only as a reference to compute amounts payable and/or receivable, although for CURRENCY SWAPS the full notional is typically exchanged on trade date and at final maturity.

NOVATION A process where all contractual payments between two parties are amalgamated and settled during a particular interim period (monthly or quarterly). Remaining contracts are then rewritten at the current market value and the process is repeated during the next netting period. Novation creates greater efficiencies in the CASH FLOW settlement process.

- See also PAYMENT NETTING, RECOUPONING, SET-OFF.

NOYAU DUR [FR] The French concept of shareholder loyalty; stakes taken by certain institutional or corporate shareholders in other companies with which they have long-standing ties or business relationships are used to support management and DIRECTORS in their attempt to direct the company.

NPV See NET PRESENT VALUE.
NPV MODEL See CREDIT MARK-TO-MARKET MODEL.
NYSE See NEW YORK STOCK EXCHANGE.

O

OAS See OPTION-ADJUSTED SPREAD.

OBJECTIVE RISK A measure of the deviation between an INSURER's actual losses and its EXPECTED LOSSES (as predicted through ACTUARIAL PRICING techniques). The greater the objective risk, the larger the losses and the less accurate the pricing methodologies.

OCCURRENCE LIMIT The maximum amount an INSURER is required to pay the INSURED for a loss occurrence that leads to a CLAIM, even if the total loss is larger than the amount specified by the limit.

- See also CLAIMS OCCURRENCE BASIS.

ODD LOT An ORDER that is smaller than the standard institutional TRADING size in a particular security or market. Odd lots, which are most often associated with retail investors, are generally subject to higher commissions/fees than ROUND LOTS.

ODD LOT THEORY A theory indicating that as ORDERS executed on an ODD LOT basis rise, speculative forces may be at work in pushing individual securities or broader markets to new peaks as individual investors often drive the final stages of a BUBBLE.

OECD See ORGANIZATION FOR ECONOMIC COOPERATION AND DEVELOPMENT.

OFF BALANCE SHEET ACTIVITIES Contingent financial transactions that are not fully reflected through the balance sheet. For financial institutions this may include STANDBY LETTERS OF CREDIT, IRREVOCABLE LETTERS OF CREDIT, REVOLVING CREDIT FACILITIES, REVOLVING UNDERWRITING FACILITIES, NOTE ISSUANCE FACILITIES, written GUARANTEES, ASSET sales with RECOURSE, RISK participations in BANKER'S ACCEPTANCES, DERIVATIVES, and certain types of LEASES; for companies it is generally limited to leases and/or derivatives. Institutions active in these businesses face varying degrees of contingent risk exposure and must generally set aside sufficient CAPITAL to cover potential risks.

OFF-MARKET SWAP See NON-PAR SWAP.

OFFER A quoted selling price for an ASSET from a DEALER or MARKET MAKER.
- Also known as ASK.
- See also BID.

OFFERING CIRCULAR See PROSPECTUS.

OFFSET (1) The right of a creditor to take possession of financial ASSETS of a delinquent debtor through a process known as garnishment. (2) The right of a firm with amounts payable to a COUNTERPARTY in DEFAULT to deduct any amounts receivable from the counterparty.
- (2) See also NETTING.

OID See ORIGINAL ISSUE DISCOUNT.

OLIGOPOLY A marketplace with only a few sellers who can collectively influence selling prices. If each has enough of a market share, then the actions of other sellers must be considered when developing pricing and distribution strategies.
- See also DUOPOLY, MONOPOLY, OLIGOPSONY.

OLIGOPSONY A marketplace with only a few buyers who can collectively influence overall purchase prices. If each has enough of a market share, then the actions of other buyers must be considered when developing pricing and acquisition strategies.
- See also DUOPSONY, MONOPSONY, OLIGOPOLY.

OMEGA See THETA.

OMNIPRESENT SPECTER [COL] A legal rule requiring a BOARD OF DIRECTORS to demonstrate that it is not acting in its own self-interest when rejecting a corporate control transaction bid such as a TAKEOVER, i.e., that rejection of the bid and the creation of any ANTI-TAKEOVER DEFENSES are required in order to protect shareholders.

ONE-FACTOR INTEREST RATE MODELS OPTION pricing models that value BOND options by generating an entire YIELD CURVE through a single INTEREST RATE reference (generally a short-term rate). Although such models are generally considered to be less precise than TWO-FACTOR INTEREST RATE MODELS, they are simpler to implement.

ONE-MAN PICTURE [COL] A market situation where the only available BID and OFFER on a transaction come from the same source.

ONE-TOUCH OPTION See BINARY-BARRIER OPTION.

OPEC See ORGANIZATION OF PETROLEUM EXPORTING COUNTRIES.

OPEN BOOK A general financial strategy of borrowing on a short-term basis and lending on a long-term basis. BANKS routinely run an open book in a normal POSITIVE YIELD CURVE environment in order to maximize NET INTEREST MARGIN. In doing so, however, they are subject to CURVE RISK, and possible losses should the curve begin to flatten or invert. SECURITIES FIRMS and BROKER/DEALERS may follow a similar strategy with their REPURCHASE AGREEMENT/ REVERSE REPURCHASE AGREEMENT operations.
- See also MISMATCH.

OPEN-END FUND See MUTUAL FUND.

OPEN-END INVESTMENT COMPANY See MUTUAL FUND.

OPEN INTEREST A measure of EXCHANGE-TRADED DERIVATIVE contract LIQUIDITY, generally computed as the number of outstanding FUTURES or OPTION contracts that are not offset by opposing transactions or accommodated by DELIVERY.

OPEN MARKET OPERATIONS A technique of MONETARY POLICY involving the purchase or sale of GOVERNMENT BILLS or GOVERNMENT BONDS by a CENTRAL BANK or monetary authority, with the express intent of influencing the level of INTEREST RATES and money supply. A purchase of securities causes prices to rise, rates to fall, and money supply to expand; a sale causes prices to fall, rates to rise, and money supply to contract.

OPEN MARKET PURCHASE The purchase of a block of a company's COMMON STOCK in the open market by another firm, generally as a prelude to a formal TENDER OFFER.

OPEN ORDER See GOOD TILL CANCELLED ORDER.

OPEN OUTCRY A TRADING process/mechanism based on physical communication between floor traders working on an EXCHANGE. Floor traders agree on purchase and sale terms through verbal discussion and/or hand-signals.

OPEN REPURCHASE AGREEMENT A REPURCHASE AGREEMENT with no specific maturity, cancellable on 24 hours' notice by either party to the transaction. This is akin to an OVERNIGHT REPURCHASE AGREEMENT that is automatically rolled over every day as a continuing financing contract. The DEALER in an open repo retains the right to substitute COLLATERAL. The opposite transaction side of the transaction is referred to an open REVERSE REPURCHASE AGREEMENT.
- See also OVERNIGHT REPURCHASE AGREEMENT, TERM REPURCHASE AGREEMENT.

OPERATING CASH FLOW The portion of the CASH FLOW statement that reflects the flows impacting a firm's core operations, starting with net income, adding in DEPRECIATION, benefits, and provisions, and

adjusting through debits/credits any changes in ACCOUNTS RECEIVABLE, INVENTORIES, accrued LIABILITIES, and deferred income taxes.
- See also FINANCING CASH FLOW, INVESTING CASH FLOW.

OPERATING LEASE A LEASE with a contract period that is shorter than the expected economic life of the underlying ASSET; the contract is generally cancellable at the option of the LESSEE. Operating leases, which are generally classified as OFF BALANCE SHEET ACTIVITIES, are commonly written on equipment, with the lessee assuming responsibility for maintenance costs and taxes.
- See also CAPITAL LEASE.

OPERATING LEVERAGE The degree to which a company's costs are fixed; the greater the percentage of a company's costs that are fixed, rather than variable, the greater the resources it has flowing to the net income account once the break-even point has been reached.
- See also LEVERAGE.

OPERATING RISK The RISK of loss arising from temporary or permanent disruption in the daily physical operating and production activities of a firm and/or changes in non-financial inputs and outputs.

OPERATIONAL ERROR RISK The RISK of loss due to problems or errors involving internal operations, such as late or misdirected payments or mishandling/misdirecting securities. A sub-category of PROCESS RISK.

OPERATIONAL RISK See PROCESS RISK.

OPM [COL] Abbreviation for "other people's money," typically employed in describing a company's use of financial LEVERAGE in its operations or in the context of a potential ACQUISITION.

OPTION A DERIVATIVE contract granting the buyer the right, but not the obligation, to buy or sell a reference ASSET at a predefined STRIKE PRICE; in exchange for the right, the buyer pays the seller a PREMIUM. Options are available on many UNDERLYING asset references from the FIXED INCOME, EQUITY, FOREIGN EXCHANGE, commodity, and credit markets, and can be bought or sold as OVER-THE-COUNTER DERIVATIVES or EXCHANGE-TRADED DERIVATIVES.
- See also CALL OPTION, PUT OPTION, COMPLEX OPTION.

OPTION-ADJUSTED CONVEXITY The CONVEXITY of a CALLABLE BOND, PUTABLE BOND, or other FIXED INCOME security with OPTIONALITY, which reflects the actual convexity of the security after adjusting for the effects of the EMBEDDED OPTION(s). The option-adjusted convexity of a callable bond is given as:

$$Cvx_{OA} = \left[\frac{P_{noncall}}{P_{call}}\right]\left[Cvx\,(1-\Delta) - [\,P_{noncall}\,(\Gamma)\,(Dur)^2\,]\right]$$

where $P_{noncall}$ is the price of the equivalent NON-CALLABLE BOND, P_{call} is the price of the callable bond, Cvx is the convexity of a non-callable bond, Dur is the DURATION of a non-callable bond, and Γ is the GAMMA of the option.
- See also OPTION-ADJUSTED DURATION, OPTION-ADJUSTED SPREAD, OPTION-ADJUSTED YIELD.

OPTION-ADJUSTED DURATION The DURATION of a CALLABLE BOND, PUTABLE BOND, or other FIXED INCOME security with OPTIONALITY, which reflects the actual duration of the security after adjusting for the effects of the EMBEDDED OPTION(s). The option-adjusted duration of a callable bond is given as:

$$Dur_{OA} = \left[\frac{P_{noncall}}{P_{call}}\right]\left[Dur\,(1-\Delta)\right]$$

where $P_{noncall}$ is the price of the equivalent NON-CALLABLE BOND, P_{call} is the price of the callable bond, Dur is the duration of a non-callable bond, and Δ is the DELTA value of the option.
- See also OPTION-ADJUSTED CONVEXITY, OPTION-ADJUSTED SPREAD, OPTION-ADJUSTED YIELD.

OPTION-ADJUSTED SPREAD (OAS) A quantitative valuation technique applied to BONDS with EMBEDDED OPTIONS, such as MORTGAGE-BACKED SECURITIES, CALLABLE BONDS, PUTABLE BONDS, or STRUCTURED NOTES, where the OAS is equal to the SPREAD over the BENCHMARK RISK-FREE RATE after taking account of the fact that the option will cause the bond's CASH FLOWS to change as rates change.
- See also OPTION-ADJUSTED DURATION, OPTION-ADJUSTED YIELD, OPTION-ADJUSTED CONVEXITY.

OPTION-ADJUSTED YIELD The YIELD of a CALLABLE BOND, PUTABLE BOND, or other FIXED INCOME security with OPTIONALITY that results if the security is held until maturity, i.e. the yield that makes the PRESENT VALUE of the CASH FLOWS from the bond (held to maturity) equal to the implied price of a BOND with no CALL OPTION or PUT OPTION features.
- See also OPTION-ADJUSTED CONVEXITY, OPTION-ADJUSTED DURATION, OPTION-ADJUSTED SPREAD.

OPTION METHOD A methodology where the FRACTIONAL EXPOSURE of a SWAP is estimated through an OPTION pricing framework. The swap is viewed as a package of options giving the holder the right to buy a FIXED RATE BOND and sell a FLOATING RATE

NOTE (or vice versa); the options are exercised jointly in the event of DEFAULT by the COUNTERPARTY, but only if they are IN-THE-MONEY.
- See also HISTORICAL METHOD, SIMULATION METHOD.

OPTION ON THE BEST/WORST OF N-ASSETS An OVER-THE-COUNTER COMPLEX OPTION that grants the buyer a payoff based on the best or worst performing of a PORTFOLIO of ASSETS against a predefined STRIKE PRICE; assets in the portfolio may be from identical or different asset classes/markets.
- See also CALL ON THE BEST OF N-ASSETS, CALL ON THE WORST OF N-ASSETS, MULTI-INDEX OPTION, PUT ON THE BEST OF N-ASSETS, PUT ON THE WORST OF N-ASSETS.

OPTION ON THE BEST/WORST OF N-ASSETS AND CASH An OVER-THE-COUNTER COMPLEX OPTION that grants the buyer a payoff based on the best or worst performing of a PORTFOLIO of ASSETS and cash; assets may be from identical or different asset classes/markets. The option has no STRIKE PRICE and always produces a minimum payoff equal to the predefined cash amount.
- See also MULTI-INDEX OPTION.

OPTION ON THE MAXIMUM/MINIMUM An OVER-THE-COUNTER COMPLEX OPTION that grants the buyer a maximum gain by "looking back" over the price path of the ASSET and determining the point that creates the greatest economic value. This version of the LOOKBACK OPTION carries a preset STRIKE PRICE and produces a gain based on the difference between the strike and the maximum price (for a CALL ON THE MAXIMUM) or minimum price (for a PUT ON THE MINIMUM) achieved by the asset.
- Also known as FIXED STRIKE LOOKBACK OPTION.

OPTION REPRICING The practice of converting an OPTION that is OUT-OF-THE-MONEY into one with INTRINSIC VALUE by resetting the STRIKE so that the contract is IN-THE-MONEY.
- See also UNDERWATER.

OPTION SENSITIVITIES See GREEKS.

OPTIONALITY See CONVEXITY.

ORDER Instructions from one party (e.g., BROKER or client) to a second party (e.g., DEALER or MARKET-MAKER) to execute the purchase or sale of securities or other ASSETS. There are four broad classes of orders: MARKET ORDERS, LIMIT ORDERS, STOP ORDERS, and TIME ORDERS, each with their own variations related to time, price, and discretion.

ORDER-DRIVEN MARKET A marketplace where securities ORDERS are grouped in the books of intermediaries such as PRINCIPALS,

SPECIALISTS, or AGENTS, and are then matched according to certain auction-based rules; many public EQUITY markets are order-driven.
- See also AUCTION MARKET, QUOTE-DRIVEN MARKET.

ORDER IMBALANCE An excess of purchase or sale ORDERS waiting to be filled via an EXCHANGE or OVER-THE-COUNTER that can disrupt LIQUIDITY and cause divergences between BIDS and OFFERS; in more extreme cases an imbalance can lead to temporary suspension of TRADING. An imbalance can arise from positive or negative news or rumors about a company or marketplace.

ORDINARY SHARE See COMMON STOCK.

ORGANIZATION FOR ECONOMIC COOPERATION AND DEVELOPMENT (OECD) An international economic organization, comprised primarily of industrialized countries (and a small number of NEWLY INDUSTRIALIZED COUNTRIES) created to assist members in developing policies to promote economic growth and general financial stability.

ORGANIZATION OF PETROLEUM EXPORTING COUNTRIES (OPEC) An organization of countries that produce and export crude oil, established in 1973 to coordinate production levels and dealings with oil companies; OPEC essentially functions as an oil CARTEL and has some ability to influence global oil prices over the short term. Member countries have included Algeria, Iran, Iraq, Kuwait, Libya, Nigeria, Saudi Arabia, the United Arab Emirates, and Venezuela.

ORIGINAL EXPOSURE METHOD A regulatory method of computing SWAP CREDIT RISK, under the original 1988 BASLE ACCORD put forth by the BANK FOR INTERNATIONAL SETTLEMENTS, which focuses solely on future credit exposure (*de facto* ignoring ACTUAL EXPOSURE or MARK-TO-MARKET value). Since the methodology takes no account of ongoing mark-to-market value, it features higher future exposure risk factors.
- See also CURRENT EXPOSURE METHOD, INTERNAL RATINGS BASED METHOD.

ORIGINAL ISSUE DISCOUNT (OID) The size of the price discount to PAR VALUE at the time of a BOND's issuance. Accretion of the price from OID to par value is treated as interest income for tax purposes.

ORIGINAL MARGIN See INITIAL MARGIN.

OSCILLATOR In TECHNICAL ANALYSIS, a measure of market movements used to identify OVERBOUGHT or OVERSOLD conditions; different oscillators exist, including the relative strength of the market (average number of days ending up divided by number of days ending down).

OTC See OVER-THE-COUNTER.

OUT-OF-THE-MONEY A condition where the price of an UNDERLYING reference ASSET is lower than the STRIKE PRICE for a CALL OPTION, or higher than the strike for a PUT OPTION, meaning the contract has no immediate INTRINSIC VALUE if exercised or sold.

* See also AT-THE-MONEY, IN-THE-MONEY, MONEYNESS.

OUT TRADE See DK.

OUTPERFORMANCE OPTION An OVER-THE-COUNTER COMPLEX OPTION that grants the buyer a payoff based on the degree to which a market reference or SPREAD outperforms a predefined STRIKE PRICE.

* See also SPREAD OPTION, UNDERPERFORMANCE OPTION.

OUTSIDE BARRIER OPTION An OVER-THE-COUNTER COMPLEX OPTION with a BARRIER that is triggered by a market reference that is distinct from the one defining the UNDERLYING option, leading to the creation of a multivariate structure. The likelihood of a payout to the buyer is dependent, in part, on the relative CORRELATIONS between the barrier reference and the underlying reference.

* See also BARRIER OPTION.

OUTSIDE DIRECTOR A board DIRECTOR that is not related to the company or its executives in any fashion, i.e., the director has no former employment ties, or any existing business, consulting, or personal relationships with executives. Outside directors are often considered to be independent for GOVERNANCE purposes.

* See also INSIDE DIRECTOR.

OUTSIDER SYSTEM A corporate ownership system where no significant controlling interests exist and shareholder influence over the GOVERNANCE and management processes is theoretically strong. The outsider system is found in the United States, the United Kingdom, Canada, and Australia.

* See also INSIDER SYSTEM.

OVER-THE-COUNTER (OTC) Any financial transaction that is arranged or traded away from a formal EXCHANGE. Dealing may be done in telephonic form or in electronic form (via ELECTRONIC COMMUNICATIONS NETWORKS and other network-based platforms), and may feature varying degrees of price transparency. Most trading in FIXED INCOME, FOREIGN EXCHANGE, and customized DERIVATIVES occurs OTC rather than via exchange.

OVER-THE-COUNTER (OTC) DERIVATIVES Customized DERIVATIVE contracts that are traded directly between two parties rather than via a formal EXCHANGE. The flexibility regarding transaction size, trade and settlement dates, UNDERLYING market references, and payoff profiles makes OTC derivatives extremely popular with institutional hedgers and speculators. However, the lack of standardized dealing terms means many OTC contracts are not as LIQUID as EXCHANGE-TRADED DERIVATIVE contracts; in addition, the lack of MARGINS or CLEARINGHOUSES means that many OTC contracts feature some amount of COUNTERPARTY CREDIT RISK. Broad classes of OTC derivatives including SWAPS, FORWARDS, OPTIONS, COMPLEX OPTIONS, and COMPLEX SWAPS. Contracts are regularly purchased and sold on references from the FIXED INCOME, EQUITY, FOREIGN EXCHANGE, commodity, and credit markets.

- See also COMMODITY DERIVATIVE, CREDIT DERIVATIVE, CURRENCY DERIVATIVE, EQUITY DERIVATIVE, INTEREST RATE DERIVATIVE, WEATHER DERIVATIVE.

OVER THE WALL [COL] A process where bankers inform a research analyst within the BANK about an impending CORPORATE FINANCE or NEW ISSUE transaction for a company; once "over the CHINESE WALL," the analyst cannot produce research information as it is apt to be influenced by, or contain details of, non-public information.

OVERALLOTMENT OPTION See GREENSHOE.

OVERBOUGHT A situation where a security or market has been the focus of aggressive buying over a short period of time, and which may be due for a correction due to a relative lack of new buyers.

- See also OVERSOLD.

OVERCOLLATERALIZATION A credit enhancement technique where excess COLLATERAL is posted to secure the CREDIT RISK elements of a risky transaction. The pledge of incremental collateral creates a buffer to cover any unexpected RISKS, and generally results in a stronger credit profile and higher CREDIT RATING. Overcollateralization is commonly used to elevate the credit ratings of certain TRANCHES in a SECURITIZATION.

OVERHANG (1) A sizeable amount of securities known to be held by investors or intermediaries, which, if placed in the market, would cause significant price declines. An overhang can result from a large block of unsold NEW ISSUE securities. (2) A measure of COMMON STOCK and OPTIONS awarded or subject to conversion under executive compensation plans; a large overhang (10% + of outstanding shares) can depress a company's stock price since award and/or conversion results in DILUTION.

OVERHEDGING Excessive HEDGE protection that might not be required when broader PORTFOLIO exposures with "beneficial" CORRELATIONS that produce natural offsets are considered.

OVERINSURANCE Excessive INSURANCE protection that might not be required when broader portfolio exposures with "beneficial" correlations that produce natural offsets are considered.

▪ See also UNDERINSURANCE.

OVERISSUE Issuance of COMMON STOCK by a company in excess of its authorized share limit. The corporate registrar is typically responsible for ensuring that overissue does not occur.

OVERLAPPING INSURANCE A situation where an INSURED has two or more INSURANCE policies covering the same RISK. If a CLAIM is made, the insured will not be able to receive payment under all policies, since insurance cannot result in a net profit; the amount of the claim is generally divided on PRO-RATA basis between the policies.

▪ See also APPORTIONMENT, DIVIDED COVER, PRIMACY.

OVERLINED [COL] A temporary situation where a COMMERCIAL PAPER issuer has repaid all outstanding notes and has excess SWINGLINE availability.

OVERNIGHT REPURCHASE AGREEMENT A REPURCHASE AGREEMENT with a 24-hour maturity, which is generally renewed or rolled over on a daily basis. The opposite transaction side of the transaction is referred to as an overnight REVERSE REPURCHASE AGREEMENT.

▪ See also OPEN REPURCHASE AGREEMENT, TERM REPURCHASE AGREEMENT.

OVERSOLD A situation where a security or market has been the focus of aggressive selling over a short period of time, and which may be due for a price rebound due to a lack of additional sellers.

▪ See also OVERBOUGHT.

OVERSUBSCRIPTION A situation where the number of ORDERS for a NEW ISSUE of securities is greater than the available supply, suggesting the price of the security will rise sharply at launch. If an EQUITY issue is oversubscribed, the UNDERWRITERS may exercise the GREENSHOE and float more shares; if a DEBT issue is oversubscribed, the issuer may authorize the underwriters to increase the size of the deal.

OVERTRADING See CHURNING.

P

P/E RATIO See PRICE/EARNINGS RATIO.

PAC BOND See PLANNED AMORTIZATION CLASS BOND.

PAC MAN DEFENSE [COL] An ANTI-TAKEOVER DEFENSE where a target company initiates a counterbid for the company that is attempting a HOSTILE TAKEOVER of its operations. The counterbid may involve the use of a considerable amount of LEVERAGE, making the defense strategy financially risky.

PACKAGE INSURANCE See MULTILINE POLICY.

PAID-IN CAPITAL Investment CAPITAL received by a company from the flotation of COMMON STOCK through an INITIAL PUBLIC OFFERING, RIGHTS ISSUE, or ADD-ON.
- Also known as PAID-IN SURPLUS.
- See also RETAINED EARNINGS, CAPITAL SURPLUS.

PAID-IN SURPLUS (1) A measure of an INSURER's SOLVENCY, computed as the excess of an insurer's admitted ASSETS over the total value of its LIABILITIES and minimum required CAPITAL. (2) See PAID-IN-CAPITAL.

PAID LOSS RETROSPECTIVE POLICY A LOSS-SENSITIVE INSURANCE CONTRACT where the INSURED's incremental PREMIUM is due when the INSURER makes actual SETTLEMENT payments; since the payment period can span several years, the insured gains the benefit of a multi-year financing.

PAINTING THE TAPE [COL] See DAISY CHAIN.

PAIRED SHARES The COMMON STOCK of two companies, managed by the same executive team, that are traded together through a single certificate.
- Also known as STAPLED STOCK.

PAPER SWAP (1) An OVER-THE-COUNTER SWAP based on a physical commodity (often an energy product) that is transacted strictly on paper, with no attempt or intent to make or take delivery of the underlying physical goods; paper swaps are always settled on a cash, or financial, basis, or are OFFSET prior to expiry. (2) A COMMODITY DERIVATIVE involving the exchange of fixed and floating prices related to paper products, such as pulp, paperboard, and newsprint. The paper swap can serve as a HEDGE for firms exposed to the selling or buying price of paper products.

PAR VALUE The stated value, or FACE VALUE, of a security established at the time of issuance, and generally also its redemption value. For BONDS and NOTES it is the amount to be repaid to investors at maturity, for COMMON STOCK or PREFERRED STOCK it is simply an artificial value that has no bearing after the initial launch of shares.

PAR YIELD CURVE A YIELD CURVE representing observable INTEREST RATES across a spectrum of maturities, obtained from FIXED INCOME securities traded in the marketplace. The par yield curve is used for pricing, investment, HEDGING, and RISK MANAGEMENT, and is the foundation for developing the IMPLIED FORWARD CURVE used to price DERIVATIVES and other financial contracts that rely on a forward estimate of rates.

- See also TERM STRUCTURE, ZERO COUPON YIELD CURVE.

PARALLEL LOAN A pair of LOANS between two companies and their two offshore subsidiaries, which permits efficient funding of local currency requirements across borders; parallel loans are effectively balance sheet versions of CURRENCY SWAPS. One company lends the local subsidiary of a second company funds in the local currency, while the second company lends the subsidiary of the first company funds in its local currency. This arrangement eliminates the need for the two companies to convert proceeds before on-lending to their local operations. The loans are governed by separate agreements that do not normally include the right of OFFSET.

- See also BACK-TO-BACK LOAN.

PARALLEL SHIFT The process of moving the YIELD CURVE up or down by an equal number of BASIS POINTS throughout every maturity on the curve and recalculating the value of a FIXED INCOME transaction or PORTFOLIO. The parallel shift reveals the sensitivity of the fixed income position(s) to equal changes in the curve, and can be used to calculate hypothetical profits and losses and the effectiveness of possible HEDGES.

- See also TWIST.

PARAMETRIC TRIGGER A conditional event in an INSURANCE-LINKED SECURITY that results in suspension of COUPON interest and/or PRINCIPAL when a specific damage metric reaches a

certain value. The metric is generally based on location and severity parameters.
- See also INDEMNITY TRIGGER, INDEX TRIGGER.

PARASOL POLICY See DIFFERENCE IN CONDITIONS INSURANCE.

PARI PASSU [LAT] Literally "on equal standing." In finance it applies to granting a party the same rights/seniority that have been granted to others. A *pari passu* clause is often included in VENTURE CAPITAL, BOND, and LOAN agreements to ensure that seniority classes remain unaffected by future financial transactions.
- See also NEGATIVE PLEDGE, STRUCTURAL SUBORDINATION.

PARIS CLUB MEETING A meeting between a sovereign debtor and government creditors and BANKS (generally those from GROUP OF 10 countries), to consider bilateral reschedulings of the debtor country's DEBT in order to avoid MORATORIUM or DEFAULT. So named as the meetings are coordinated via the French finance ministry.

PARITY See CONVERSION PARITY.

PARKING [COL] The transfer of ASSETS, LIABILITIES, or CASH FLOWS to another party, without the transfer of associated RISKS, for the purpose of altering a financial statement. Parking is illegal in many jurisdictions as it conveys a false profile of financial standing.

PARTIAL BARRIER OPTION A BARRIER OPTION with a BARRIER that is only in effect during a portion of the option's life, often one week, month, or quarter of a multi-quarter/year deal.
- See also POINT BARRIER OPTION.

PARTIAL INSURANCE An INSURANCE contract providing fractional RISK TRANSFER in exchange for a smaller PREMIUM. For INSUREDS with the proper RISK TOLERANCE, the lower cost of protection achieved via partial insurance may be preferable under a cost/benefit framework. Fractional coverage is generally achieved through DEDUCTIBLES, EXCLUSIONS, and/or POLICY CAPS.
- See also FULL INSURANCE.

PARTIAL LOOKBACK OPTION An OVER-THE-COUNTER COMPLEX OPTION that allows the purchaser to reset the STRIKE PRICE on a particular evaluation date if the option is OUT-OF-THE-MONEY.
- Also known as RESET OPTION.
- See also LOOKBACK OPTION.

PARTIAL PLAN TERMINATION A CORPORATE FINANCE scheme designed to take advantage of an overfunded PENSION PLAN to free up cash for use in other endeavors. Under the termination transaction, the pension plan is split into two distinct components and the overfunded portion is terminated, releasing cash into the general corporate account. Partial plan termination only works when the total plan is overfunded with respect to both retirees and current employees.

PARTIAL RECOURSE LOAN A LOAN where the lending BANK must initially rely on CASH FLOWS from the ASSET or project being financed for repayment but may then turn to the borrower for repayment.
- Also known as LIMITED RECOURSE LOAN.
- See also FULL RECOURSE LOAN, NON-RECOURSE, NON-RECOURSE LOAN, RECOURSE.

PARTICIPATING FORWARD A FORWARD contract with a feature that allows the first party to share in any gains earned by the second party on a predetermined basis. In exchange, the second party receives a more favorable forward price.

PARTICIPATING GUARANTEED INVESTMENT CONTRACT (GIC) A form of a GUARANTEED INVESTMENT CONTRACT granting the investor a share of any investment earnings from the ASSET PORTFOLIO exceeding the guaranteed rate.
- See also NON-PARTICIPATING GUARANTEED INVESTMENT CONTRACT, SYNTHETIC GUARANTEED INVESTMENT CONTRACT.

PARTICIPATING POLICY An INSURANCE contract where the INSURED receives periodic DIVIDENDS from the INSURER, thus sharing in the insurer's overall profitability. The participating policy essentially grants the insured an increasing PREMIUM rebate as the insurer's UNDERWRITING and investment management performance improves.

PARTICIPATING PREFERRED STOCK A form of PREFERRED STOCK that pays investors a standard preferred DIVIDEND and a portion of a COMMON STOCK dividend if certain financial performance targets are met. Such issues are relatively rare.

PARTICIPATION CERTIFICATE A security that represents an investment interest in an underlying pool of ASSETS, generally MORTGAGES; the term is often used generically to refer to MORTGAGE-BACKED SECURITIES.
- See also PASS-THROUGH SECURITY.

PARTICIPATION FINANCING See PARTICIPATION LOAN.

PARTICIPATION LOAN A LOAN granted jointly by several BANKS to a single borrower; a participation loan is arranged when the financing is so large that it exceeds any single bank's LEGAL LENDING LIMIT.
- Also known as LOAN PARTICIPATION, PARTICIPATION FINANCING.

PASS-THROUGH SECURITY A generic SECURITIZATION structure that provides investors with the CASH FLOWS generated by an underlying ASSET or PORTFOLIO. A pass-through can be issued in modified form (guaranteeing payment of PRINCIPAL and COUPON interest, but only timely payment of interest) or fully modified form (guaranteeing timely payment of both principal and interest). Pass-through securities can be created from a range of assets, including MORTGAGES, ACCOUNTS RECEIVABLE, LOANS, and BONDS. Common examples include MORTGAGE-BACKED SECURITIES (MBS) issued by the GOVERNMENT NATIONAL MORTGAGE ASSOCIATION and FEDERAL NATIONAL MORTGAGE ASSOCIATION, PARTICIPATION CERTIFICATES issued by the FEDERAL HOME LOAN CORPORATION, MBS and COLLATERALIZED MORTGAGE OBLIGATIONS issued by private-label CONDUITS, and COLLATERALIZED BOND OBLIGATIONS and COLLATERALIZED LOAN OBLIGATIONS issued by BANKS and SECURITIES FIRMS.

PASSIVE INVESTMENT STRATEGY A process of managing a PORTFOLIO of securities by relying on a minimum amount of ASSET reallocation; passive strategies are often implemented through INDEXING.
- See also ACTIVE INVESTMENT STRATEGY, INDEX FUND.

PASSIVE LOSS RULES Rules that limit the amount of deductions or income that can be sheltered from taxes. Deductions on passive losses are generally limited to an amount equal to earnings from passive sources; in addition, losses and gains must generally come from similar businesses or investments.

PASSIVE RETENTION A state where a company unknowingly retains RISK and is therefore not actively managing exposure through RESERVES or SELF-INSURANCE. Passive retentions can lead to unexpected losses.
- See also RETENTION, RISK RETENTION.

PATH-DEPENDENT OPTION A VANILLA or COMPLEX OPTION whose payoff at expiry or EXERCISE is dependent on the price path of the UNDERLYING reference ASSET at previous points in time. Common path-dependent options include BARRIER OPTIONS, ASIAN OPTIONS, FLOATING STRIKE LOOKBACK OPTIONS, HIGH–LOW OPTIONS, LADDER OPTIONS, CLIQUET OPTIONS, SHOUT OPTIONS, and INSTALLMENT OPTIONS.
- See also PATH-INDEPENDENT OPTION.

PATH-INDEPENDENT OPTION A VANILLA or COMPLEX OPTION whose payoff at expiry or EXERCISE is dependent solely on the price of the UNDERLYING reference ASSET at expiry or exercise. Common path-independent options include BINARY OPTIONS, MULTI-INDEX OPTIONS, COMPOUND OPTIONS, CHOOSER OPTIONS, CONTINGENT PREMIUM OPTIONS, DEFERRED

PAYMENT AMERICAN OPTIONS, EXPLODING OPTIONS, and FORWARD START OPTIONS.
- See also PATH-DEPENDENT OPTION.

PAY LATER OPTION See CONTINGENT PREMIUM OPTION.

PAYBACK RULE A basic measure of the amount of time it takes for a company or investor to recover an initial investment. The rule is based strictly on CASH FLOWS occurring over a stated period of time, with no weight given to those generated after the stated cutoff period, which can skew the result. A refinement of the payback rule discounts the cash flows by a relevant DISCOUNT RATE.
- See also INTERNAL RATE OF RETURN, NET PRESENT VALUE.

PAYER SWAPTION A SWAPTION granting the buyer the right to enter into an OVER-THE-COUNTER INTEREST RATE SWAP to pay fixed rates and receive floating rates. The buyer is likely to exercise the swaption as floating rates rise above a particular STRIKE PRICE.
- See also RECEIVER SWAPTION.

PAYMENT IN KIND (PIK) SECURITY A security that pays COUPONS or DIVIDENDS in the form of additional securities rather than cash (e.g., PIK BONDS pay interest in the form of additional PIK bonds, PIK PREFERRED STOCK pays dividends with additional PIK preferreds). PIK securities are generally issued by companies that have difficulty raising cash or are attempting to preserve cash to fund corporate operations.
- See also RESET PAYMENT IN KIND BONDS.

PAYMENT NETTING A NETTING arrangement where an institution and its COUNTERPARTY agree to net all payments in the normal course of business.
- See also NOVATION, SET-OFF.

PAYOUT RATIO The amount of corporate earnings paid out to stockholders in the form of COMMON STOCK DIVIDENDS, calculated as:

$$Payout = \frac{DIV_n}{EPS_n}$$

where DIV_n is the dividend paid in period n and EPS_n is the EARNINGS PER SHARE achieved in period n.
- See also DIVIDEND YIELD, PLOWBACK RATIO.

PEGGING (1) In the FOREIGN EXCHANGE markets, the process of linking the value of a national currency to the value of a foreign currency (or a BASKET of currencies). This implies that the national currency is not free-floating, but dependent on the MONETARY POLICY and trade activities of reference countries. (2) In the securities markets, an illegal practice where manipulators attempt to keep the

price of a listed security trading close to its PAR VALUE. (3) In the NEW ISSUE market, the legal practice of stabilizing the price of a new offering, generally through buying efforts coordinated by the LEAD MANAGER.
- (1) See also CRAWLING PEG, MANAGED FOREIGN EXCHANGE RATE.

PENNANT A TECHNICAL ANALYSIS charting figure of a security or market that resembles the FLAG, but features a narrowing of the tip as the peaks and troughs draw closer together; once at the tip of the pennant, the price of the security or index is expected to rise or fall sharply.

PENNY JUMPING [COL] An illegal practice where a SPECIALIST or MARKET MAKER in a COMMON STOCK does not match offsetting LIMIT ORDERS and MARKET ORDERS, filling only one side and keeping the other for its proprietary book until it determines how the market moves. If the market moves favorably, the specialist retains the position and profits, if it moves unfavorably, it fills the order for the original client. Under this scenario the most the specialist risks is a penny per share.

PENNY STOCK [COL] The COMMON STOCK of a company that trades for less than $1 per share, generally associated with a firm that has a short history of financial performance or one that has entered a phase of FINANCIAL DISTRESS and has been delisted from a larger EXCHANGE. Penny stocks are traded OVER-THE-COUNTER and are quoted on the PINK SHEETS.

PENSION FUND See PENSION PLAN.

PENSION PLAN A retirement program for the employees of a company, based on employer- and/or employee-funded contributions, that

generates monthly payments for those that have retired. Funds are held in a TRUST and managed by trustees who may be nominated by the employer. In order to ensure sufficient funds to pay pension obligations, the plan may be invested in a range of FIXED INCOME and EQUITY securities. Plans may be fully funded (e.g., already actuarially solvent under a range of scenarios) or partially funded (e.g., the employer must cover any shortfall as it comes due). In the United States the pension plan can be one of defined contribution (e.g., a variable payment) or defined benefit (e.g., a fixed monthly payment).
- Also known as PENSION FUND.

PEOPLE PILL [COL] An ANTI-TAKEOVER DEFENSE where a well-regarded management team threatens to depart, en masse, in the event of a TAKEOVER.
- See also POISON PILL.

PERCENTAGE OF LOSS DEDUCTIBLE In INSURANCE, a contract with a percentage-based DEDUCTIBLE that increases as the INSURED's losses grow larger. Through this feature the insured preserves, or even increases, its RISK RETENTION.

PERFORMANCE BOND A FINANCIAL GUARANTEE providing payment to a third party BENEFICIARY if the purchaser of the guarantee fails to perform as contracted. Common performance bonds include SURETY BONDS and COMPLETION BONDS (purchased from INSURERS) and STANDBY LETTERS OF CREDIT (purchased from banks).

PERIL A cause of loss, and an exposure that individuals and institutions often seek to protect against through INSURANCE.
- See also HAZARD.

PERIODIC COLLATERAL A process where a financial institution extending credit to a COUNTERPARTY takes a smaller amount of initial COLLATERAL but revalues the credit exposure and collateral periodically and makes necessary adjustments (i.e., calling for additional collateral if in deficit, returning excess collateral if in surplus).
- See also UPFRONT COLLATERAL.

PERMISSIBLE LOSS RATIO See LOSS RATIO.

PERPETUAL DEBT A BOND that is issued without a stated final maturity. The DEBT acts as a PERPETUITY, paying investors regular COUPONS but never repaying the PRINCIPAL balance.
- Also known as UNDATED SECURITY.
- See also CONSOL, IRREDEEMABLE BOND, PERPETUAL FLOATING RATE NOTE.

PERPETUAL FLOATING RATE NOTE (FRN) A hybrid security comprised of a FLOATING RATE NOTE and PERPETUAL DEBT that is issued without a stated final maturity. The perpetual FRN pays

investors a regular floating rate COUPON, often based on LIBOR or EURIBOR, but does not repay PRINCIPAL.
- See also CAPPED FLOATING RATE NOTE, INVERSE FLOATING RATE NOTE, RANGE FLOATING RATE NOTE.

PERPETUITY An ASSET or financial contract that pays investors a stated CASH FLOW on a continuous basis but does not provide for PRINCIPAL repayment. The PRESENT VALUE of constant and growing perpetuities are given as:

Constant:

$$PV = \frac{CF}{r}$$

Growing:

$$PV = \frac{CF}{r - g}$$

where CF is the stated cash flow, r is the DISCOUNT RATE, and g is the growth rate.
- See also ANNUITY.

PETRODOLLARS Dollar CASH FLOWS paid for oil to oil-producing nations, which are often re-deposited (or recycled) through the Western banking system.

PFANDBRIEFE [GER] Abbreviated form of hypoteken pfandbriefe, or MORTGAGE-BACKED BOND. Pfandbriefe are secured BONDS that convert a credit CLAIM, MORTGAGE, or ASSET pool into a negotiable security. Unlike standard SECURITIZATIONS, the assets underlying the bonds remain on the issuer's balance sheet, but are reserved (or ring-fenced) for the benefit of investors, who receive a first priority claim in the event of DEFAULT. Pfandbriefe were originally issued in Germany, but have since been extended to other countries in Europe.

PHANTOM STOCK [COL] A corporate security that gives employees, executives, and DIRECTORS the RENT RIGHTS associated with the company's COMMON STOCK (e.g., price appreciation, DIVIDENDS) without granting physical shares or CONTROL RIGHTS (e.g., PROXY voting).
- Also known as SHADOW STOCK.

PHYSICAL SETTLEMENT A DERIVATIVE contract that requires settlement in physical ASSETS rather than cash terms.
- See also FINANCIAL SETTLEMENT.

PIERCING THE CORPORATE VEIL [COL] An exceptional legal circumstance where the tenet of LIMITED LIABILITY is suspended and shareholders are liable for paying for corporate losses from their

personal ASSETS. Actual instances of such "piercing" are rare, occurring primarily when the PRINCIPALS of very closely held companies have breached their duties and generated losses.
- See also UNLIMITED LIABILITY.

PIG ON PORK [COL] See CROSS GUARANTEE.

PIGGY-BACKING [COL] See COAT-TAILING.

PIK SECURITIES See PAYMENT IN KIND SECURITIES.

PIN RISK The RISK of loss that arises when a very large OPTION position (or many small ones) trades near the STRIKE PRICE as maturity or expiration approaches. A small move above/below the strike price can dramatically change the HEDGE requirement and potentially induce large losses (or gains).

PINK SHEETS [COL] A mechanism used to quote OVER-THE-COUNTER securities, including PENNY STOCKS. Pink sheets were previously printed and distributed on pink paper, but are now accessible electronically.

PINNING THE STRIKE [COL] A tendency for the price of a COMMON STOCK with heavily traded OPTIONS to close near the STRIKE PRICE of the most actively traded PUT OPTIONS or CALL OPTIONS.

PIP [COL] The fifth decimal point in a FOREIGN EXCHANGE quotation, e.g., 0.00001.
- See also POINT.

PIPELINE [COL] Future deal flow being arranged by BANKS, INVESTMENT BANKS, and SECURITIES FIRMS on behalf of clients. The pipeline includes future NEW ISSUES and CORPORATE FINANCE activity, and serves as a measure of strength/weakness in the financial and corporate sectors.
- Also known as CALENDAR, VISIBLE SUPPLY.
- See also SHADOW CALENDAR.

PLACED BUSINESS An INSURANCE contract that has been completed and delivered to the INSURED, and where the INSURER has received its PREMIUM.

PLANNED AMORTIZATION CLASS (PAC) BOND A TRANCHE of a COLLATERALIZED MORTGAGE OBLIGATION (CMO) that exhibits considerable price and return stability by deflecting PREPAYMENT RISK to a COMPANION BOND. The companion bond shields the PAC from accelerating PREPAYMENTS, providing investors with a constant YIELD for a band of PREPAYMENT SPEEDS (rather than a specific speed, as is characteristic of the TARGETED AMORTIZATION CLASS BOND). Unlike other CMO tranches, the PAC bond has a SINKING FUND that remains in effect while prepayments remain within the specified prepayment speed bands.

- Also known as SIMULTANEOUS PAY BOND.
- See also SEQUENTIAL PAY BOND.

PLC See PUBLIC LIMITED COMPANY.

PLOWBACK RATIO The amount of CAPITAL a firm reinvests in its operations, such as earnings that are retained and reinvested rather than paid to shareholders in the form of DIVIDENDS. The formula is given as:

$PBR = 1 - Payout$

where *Payout* is the PAYOUT RATIO.

PLUS TICK Sale of a security at a price that is higher than the prior transaction, generally indicated through the display of a "+" next to the screen or tape price. A SHORT SALE can be initiated on a plus tick.
- Also known as UPTICK
- See also MINUS TICK, ZERO PLUS TICK, ZERO MINUS TICK.

PO STRIP See PRINCIPAL ONLY STRIP.

POINT [COL] The fourth decimal point in a FOREIGN EXCHANGE quotation, e.g., 0.0001.
- See also PIP.

POINT AND FIGURE CHART A TECHNICAL ANALYSIS chart that depicts upward and downward moves in a security or market but ignores time dimensions. A typical chart is comprised of Xs to depict upward moves and Os for downward moves. Continuous up or down moves are reflected in the same column for each occurrence, but when the trend shifts (e.g., to a new down or up) a new column is started. The chart that results is intended to reveal directional momentum.

POINT BARRIER OPTION A BARRIER OPTION with a BARRIER that is only in effect at a single point in time, often maturity, rather than the entire life of the transaction.
- Also known as EUROPEAN BARRIER OPTION.
- See also PARTIAL BARRIER OPTION.

POISON PILL [COL] A general class of ANTI-TAKEOVER DEFENSES designed to make a target company's COMMON STOCK look less attractive to a potential acquirer planning a TAKEOVER, often through excessive DILUTION.
- See also CHEWABLE PILL, FLIP-IN PILL, FLIP-OVER PILL.

POISON PUT [COL] An OPTION contained within a company's BOND INDENTURE that allows investors to present bonds for redemption if certain defined events occur, such as a HOSTILE TAKEOVER, payment of excessively large DIVIDENDS to shareholders, or assumption of additional DEBT. While poison put provisions are intended to protect debt investors, they can also be used the issuing company as an ANTI-TAKEOVER DEFENSE, as any hostile approach leading to redemption will lead to a reduction in cash, making the company appear less attractive.

POLICY CAP The maximum amount payable by an INSURER to an INSURED, or a REINSURER to a CEDING INSURER, under an INSURANCE or REINSURANCE CONTRACT.
- Also known as AGGREGATE LIMIT, EXHAUSTION POINT.

POLITICAL RISK INSURANCE INSURANCE that provides an INSURED with coverage against financial losses from SOVEREIGN RISKS, including ASSET expropriation, confiscation, nationalization, or contract frustration/repudiation.
- See also WRAP-AROUND INSURANCE.

POOL (1) A SYNDICATE of INSURERS or REINSURERS organized to underwrite a LINE of RISK. Each pool member shares in PREMIUMS, losses, and LOSS ADJUSTMENT EXPENSES. (2) A group of ASSETS combined into a PORTFOLIO for SECURITIZATION or COLLATERAL management purposes.
- (1) See also REINSURANCE POOL.

POOLED PORTFOLIO COLLATERAL A COLLATERAL management technique where ASSETS securing a PORTFOLIO of DERIVATIVES or other credit-sensitive transactions are held in a general POOL that can be applied to incremental transactions as they arise; pooled collateral can generally be managed on a dynamic basis through the right of substitution.
- See also CROSS COLLATERAL AGREEMENT, TRANSACTION-SPECIFIC COLLATERAL.

POOLING See RISK POOLING.

POOLING OF INTERESTS An accounting methodology used for a MERGER that is arranged as a non-cash, tax free exchange of voting COMMON STOCK. The process involves a pure addition of ASSETS, LIABILITIES, and EQUITY, without any corresponding adjustment for fair MARKET VALUE.
- See also PURCHASE TRANSACTION.

POOP AND SCOOP [COL] An illegal practice where a pool of investors circulates false negative news about a company in order to drive down the price of its COMMON STOCK; once the price has been pushed down, the investors purchase shares and wait for a rebound. This type of scheme is typically targeted at small, thinly traded stocks.
- See also PUMP AND DUMP.

PORCUPINE PROVISION [COL] See ANTI-TAKEOVER DEFENSE.

PORTFOLIO A group of ASSETS that is managed jointly, often to provide proper DIVERSIFICATION, RISK MANAGEMENT, or investment opportunities that cannot be obtained by holding individual assets.

- See also PORTFOLIO DIVERSIFICATION, PORTFOLIO RISK, PORTFOLIO THEORY.

PORTFOLIO DIVERSIFICATION The practice of combining securities that are not CORRELATED with one another in order to diffuse RISK.
- See also DIVERSIFICATION, DIVERSIFIABLE RISK, NON-DIVERSIFIABLE RISK, PORTFOLIO THEORY.

PORTFOLIO INSURANCE A technique that allows participants to benefit from a rising market by increasing exposure to COMMON STOCKS and protecting against a declining market by decreasing exposure. The primary downside RISK MANAGEMENT application is centered on the sale of index FUTURES to protect an investment PORTFOLIO against a fall in prices.

PORTFOLIO PUMPING [COL] A quarter-end or year-end practice where investment managers purchase additional amounts of COMMON STOCK to supplement existing holdings in order to push up prices and improve end-of-period performance statistics.
- See also WINDOW DRESSING.

PORTFOLIO REINSURANCE A REINSURANCE contract granted over a CEDING INSURER'S entire portfolio of RISKS; the contract effectively provides the insurer with macro protection against all LINES of INSURANCE business written.

PORTFOLIO RISK The RISK of loss arising from adverse movements in a PORTFOLIO of ASSETS or businesses. Portfolio risks can often be managed or mitigated through DIVERSIFICATION techniques, including those that make use of uncorrelated exposures.
- See also CORRELATION, CORRELATION RISK.

PORTFOLIO THEORY The practice of analyzing and managing investments on a PORTFOLIO, rather than security-specific, basis. The process is based on measuring portfolio asset risks and returns (including those that are characterized as DIVERSIFIABLE and NON-DIVERSIFIABLE RISKS), creating investment allocation strategies, and optimizing portfolio components. The ultimate goal is to create a diversified portfolio of investments that maximizes return for a given level of risk.

POSITION TRADING A speculative TRADING strategy based on holding a LONG POSITION or SHORT POSITION for several weeks or months. Position trading, though relatively short-term in nature, has a longer horizon than MOMENTUM TRADING.

POSITIVE BASIS A market state where the price of the cash or SPOT MARKET security is greater than the price of the underlying FUTURES contract.
- See also BASIS RISK, NEGATIVE BASIS.

POSITIVE CARRY A state where the return earned on an ASSET is greater than the cost of financing and storing the asset.

- See also NEGATIVE CARRY.

POSITIVE CONVEXITY A characteristic of certain financial ASSETS where gains are greater, and losses are smaller, than those of linear contracts or those with NEGATIVE CONVEXITY. LONG OPTIONS and BONDS with no OPTIONALITY feature positive convexity.
- See also NEGATIVE CONVEXITY, NON-LINEAR INSTRUMENT, POSITIVE GAMMA.

POSITIVE GAMMA MARKET RISK exposure to large price moves in the UNDERLYING generated through the purchase of PUT OPTIONS or CALL OPTIONS. In common with other POSITIVE CONVEXITY instruments, positive gamma positions feature gains that are greater and losses that are smaller than instruments with NEGATIVE CONVEXITY.
- See also GAMMA, NEGATIVE GAMMA.

POSITIVE GAP A general measure of a firm's exposure to INTEREST RATE REPRICING RISK. A positive gap arises when RATE-SENSITIVE ASSETS are greater than RATE-SENSITIVE LIABILITIES, meaning the firm will experience a loss if rates fall and a gain if rates rise.
- See also GAP, GAPPING, NEGATIVE GAP.

POSITIVE OBLIGATION See AFFIRMATIVE OBLIGATION

POSITIVE WORKING CAPITAL A financial state where a company's CURRENT ASSETS exceed its CURRENT LIABILITIES. Positive working capital indicates the availability of sufficient LIQUIDITY to cover obligations coming due.
- See also NEGATIVE WORKING CAPITAL.

POSITIVE YIELD CURVE A TERM STRUCTURE where short-term INTEREST RATES are lower than long-term interest rates. The positive yield curve is the most common state of the term structure in financial systems operating under normal market conditions (i.e., low INFLATION, stable economic growth).
- Also known as UPWARD SLOPING YIELD CURVE.
- See also KINKED YIELD CURVE, NEGATIVE YIELD CURVE, YIELD CURVE.

POST-FUNDED POLICY See RETROSPECTIVE FINITE POLICY.

POST-LOSS FINANCING Funding that is arranged in response to, rather than in anticipation of, a loss event; financing may come from cash or RESERVES, RETAINED EARNINGS, LOANS or DEBT or EQUITY issuance. In some instances post-loss financing may prove more expensive and uncertain than PRE-LOSS FINANCING, as CAPITAL may not be available and/or the company have entered a period of FINANCIAL DISTRESS.
- See also LOSS FINANCING.

POT [COL] A portion of a NEW ISSUE that is retained by the LEAD MANAGER to facilitate large block sales to institutional investors.

POTENTIAL EXPOSURE A measure of the current and future CREDIT RISK exposure of a financial contract with uncertain or variable value, such as a DERIVATIVE, REPURCHASE AGREEMENT, or LOAN COMMITMENT. It is often calculated as the sum of ACTUAL EXPOSURE (MARK-TO-MARKET value) and FRACTIONAL EXPOSURE (an estimate of future value obtained through statistical or SIMULATION-based models).

- Also known as RISK EQUIVALENT EXPOSURE.

POTENTIAL MARKET RISK See FRACTIONAL EXPOSURE.

POWER BARRIER OPTION An OVER-THE-COUNTER COMPLEX OPTION with an exponential payoff that is either created (i.e., knocks in) or extinguished (i.e., knocks out) when a particular BARRIER is breached.

- See also POWER OPTION, BARRIER OPTION.

POWER-OF-ATTORNEY A legal authorization given by one party (the PRINCIPAL) to another party (the ATTORNEY-IN-FACT) to deal in specified, and binding, transactions on its behalf.

POWER OPTION (1) An OPTION that grants the buyer an exponential payoff if the contract moves/finishes IN-THE-MONEY. A power option raises the price of the UNDERLYING reference to a prespecified exponent (or power) and compares the result against a predefined STRIKE PRICE to determine any economic gain. (2) An option contract with an UNDERLYING that references electricity prices in a particular pool or grid. Power options can be traded OVER-THE-COUNTER and via certain EXCHANGES.

- (1) Also known as LEVERAGED OPTION, TURBO OPTION.
- (2) See also ELECTRICITY SWAP.

POWER SWAP (1) An OVER-THE-COUNTER COMPLEX SWAP that generates a payoff by multiplying the fixed or floating INTEREST RATE payments by a LEVERAGE factor; the use of leverage compounds the upward or downward movement of the market reference, magnifying potential RISK and return. Leverage can be applied to any swap and can be defined in any fashion. (2) See ELECTRICITY SWAP.

- (1) Also known as LEVERAGED SWAP, RATIO SWAP.

PRE-EMPTIVE RIGHT The right of existing shareholders to invest in a NEW ISSUE of COMMON STOCK before it is offered to the market at large; only when shareholders have waived or transferred this right can new shares be offered to new shareholders. Where pre-emptive rights do not specifically exist, shareholders may still be protected through SUBSCRIPTION WARRANTS.

- Also known as ANTI-DILUTION PROVISION, SUBSCRIPTION PRIVILEGE.
- See also RIGHTS ISSUE.

PRE-LOSS FINANCING Funding that is arranged in advance of a loss situation, typically through mechanisms such as INSURANCE contracts, DERIVATIVES, and CONTINGENT CAPITAL. Pre-loss financing may be less expensive than POST-LOSS FINANCING, as it can be arranged before any instance of FINANCIAL DISTRESS and can be developed on a committed basis so that funds are available when required.
- See also LOSS FINANCING.

PRE-PACK [COL] See PRE-PACKAGED BANKRUPTCY.

PRE-PACKAGED BANKRUPTCY In the United States, a filing under CHAPTER 11 of the US BANKRUPTCY Code where creditors agree in advance to REORGANIZATION terms in order to accelerate the process and minimize the time the company spends under bankruptcy protection. A pre-packaged bankruptcy is arranged when the company and its business franchise are deemed to have significant value, and bankruptcy negotiations can be arranged with a minimum of conflict among stakeholders.
- Also known as PRE-PACK.

PRE-PETITION PHASE A stage of FINANCIAL DISTRESS, such as the VICINITY OF INSOLVENCY, when a company is preparing to file a BANKRUPTCY petition. During this period the rights of creditors often supersede those of shareholders, as DIRECTORS and executives attempt to preserve as much ENTERPRISE VALUE as possible in advance of a REORGANIZATION or LIQUIDATION.

PRE-REFUNDING A new BOND issue floated by a company in order to repay an existing bond issue at the FIRST CALL DATE; proceeds of the pre-refunding are generally invested in low-RISK securities until the original bond can be called and redeemed. Pre-refunding typically occurs in an environment where INTEREST RATES have declined enough to make the refinancing an economically beneficial process.

PRECIPITATION DERIVATIVE An OVER-THE-COUNTER WEATHER DERIVATIVE that provides protection against, or exposure to, snowfall or rainfall based on the amount of solid or liquid precipitation falling in a given location over a set period of time. Precipitation derivatives can be used to HEDGE inputs or outputs that are sensitive to, or impacted by, rainfall or snowfall.
- See also TEMPERATURE DERIVATIVE.

PREFERENCE The transfer of valuable property within 90 days of a company's BANKRUPTCY filing; preference payments made by the company to third parties that prejudice or impair the position of

creditors, or which favor one creditor over others, may be subject to CLAWBACK by the TRUSTEE or RECEIVER.
- Also known as VOIDABLE PREFERENCE.
- See also PREFERENCE PERIOD.

PREFERENCE OPTION See CHOOSER OPTION.

PREFERENCE PERIOD A 90-day period preceding a company's BANKRUPTCY FILING.
- See also PREFERENCE.

PREFERRED RISK An INSURED with a lower probability of generating a loss and CLAIM than a standard applicant; INSURERS attempt to identify such RISKS for inclusion in their PORTFOLIOS in order to maximize UNDERWRITING income and minimize SETTLEMENTS.

PREFERRED STOCK A CAPITAL security issued by a company that pays investors periodic DIVIDENDS, but does not convey voting rights (although consent from two-thirds of preferred investors is often required on any matter that will affect the seniority of their CLAIM). Preferred stock investors rank senior to COMMON STOCK investors in the event of BANKRUPTCY, but junior to BOND investors and LOAN holders. Preferreds can be issued in various forms (with most differences related to the setting, timing, and accumulation of dividend payments), including CUMULATIVE PREFERRED STOCK, NON-CUMULATIVE PREFERRED STOCK, and ADJUSTABLE RATE PREFERRED STOCK.

PREMIUM (1) The payment made by the purchaser to the seller of an EXCHANGE-traded or OVER-THE-COUNTER OPTION. By accepting the premium, the seller is obligated to perform under the terms of the contract when the buyer exercises its rights. Premium is comprised of TIME VALUE and INTRINSIC VALUE, and the premium an option seller charges depends on the price and VOLATILITY of the UNDERLYING reference, the RISK-FREE RATE, and time to expiry. (2) The payment made by an INSURED to an INSURER (or REINSURER) for a future compensatory payment under the terms of an INSURANCE contract. Insurance premiums are determined through ACTUARIAL PRICING based on EXPECTED LOSS ratios and LOADS. (3) The upfront or periodic payment made by an investor to an INSURER for an ANNUITY that will provide a future cash inflow. (4) The MARKET VALUE in excess of PAR VALUE on a FIXED INCOME security. (5) The excess of a TENDER OFFER over a target company's stock price in a corporate MERGER or ACQUISITION. (6) For CONVERTIBLE BONDS, see PREMIUM OVER BOND VALUE.
- (2) Also known as RISK PREMIUM.

PREMIUM CAPACITY The ability for an INSURER or REINSURER to write a large volume of policies on the same LINE or RISK.

PREMIUM LOADING The margin an INSURER requires in order to cover overhead expenses (EXPENSE LOADING) and generate an appropriate profit; premium loading is one of two components, along with PURE PREMIUM, used to determine FAIR PREMIUM.

PREMIUM OVER BOND VALUE The value ascribed to the EQUITY characteristics of a CONVERTIBLE BOND, or the difference between the MARKET VALUE of a convertible and an equivalent STRAIGHT BOND without the EMBEDDED OPTION. In general, the higher the CONVERSION PRICE, the greater the premium over bond value.
  ▪ Also known as PREMIUM.

PREMIUM RAID An attempt by a RAIDER or acquiring company to quickly purchase a block of a target company's COMMON STOCK by offering shareholders a significant PREMIUM to the prevailing stock price.
  ▪ See also DAWN RAID, SATURDAY NIGHT SPECIAL.

PREMIUM SWAP An OVER-THE-COUNTER NON-PAR SWAP where the receiver of fixed INTEREST RATES grants an upfront payment to the floating rate payer in exchange for a higher ongoing fixed rate inflow.
  ▪ See also DISCOUNT SWAP.

PREMIUM TAX A tax payable by an INSURER to a state or jurisdiction based on the amount of PREMIUMS earned from INSURANCE activities. Premium taxes are generally included in EXPENSE LOADING.

PREMIUMS IN FORCE A measure of an INSURER's UNDERWRITING business, measured as PREMIUM earned on all INSURANCE policies that have not lapsed or have not been cancelled.

PREPAYMENT The early repayment of a MORTGAGE by a borrower as a result of the sale of the underlying home/property or a refinancing to take advantage of a lower INTEREST RATE environment.
  ▪ See also PREPAYMENT MODEL, PREPAYMENT SPEED.

PREPAYMENT MODEL An analytic process used to estimate the PREPAYMENT SPEED of MORTGAGES comprising a pool or PASS-THROUGH SECURITY, which can then be used to value the ASSET. Common models include the CONSTANT PREPAYMENT RATE model, which assumes mortgage PRINCIPAL prepayments occur at a constant annual rate that can be estimated from historical mortgage data, and the Public Securities Association standard prepayment model, which assumes mortgage PREPAYMENTS occur at variables speeds (e.g., 0.2%/month for 30 months, then 6% annually).

PREPAYMENT SPEED The rate at which underlying commercial or residential MORTGAGES in a pool or PASS-THROUGH SECURITY are expected to repay (i.e., as rates decline, PREPAYMENTS accelerate as refinancings increase; as rates rise, prepayments decelerate as refinancings slow). Prepayment speed is an essential component of pricing and HEDGING MORTGAGE-BACKED SECURITIES and can be estimated through a PREPAYMENT MODEL or SIMULATION process.

PRESENT EXPECTED VALUE An ACTUARIAL PRICING method of calculating PREMIUM for INSURANCE coverage, generally via:

$$PEV = Prob_{occ} \, (Face_{pol}) \, (PV_{factor})$$

where $Prob_{occ}$ is the probability of loss occurrence, $Face_{pol}$ is the FACE VALUE of the policy, and PV_{factor} is a PRESENT VALUE factor.

PRESENT VALUE A financial computation where future CASH FLOWS are discounted back to current terms through use of an appropriate DISCOUNT RATE or COST OF CAPITAL. The general form of the equation is given as:

$$PV = \sum_{t=1}^{n} \frac{CF_t}{(1+r)^t}$$

where CF_t is the expected cash flow at time t, n is the number of periods, and r is the discount rate.

The present value of an ANNUITY can be computed through an extension of the same equation:

$$PV_A = CF_P \left[\frac{1 - \frac{1}{(1+r)^n}}{r} \right]$$

where CF_P is the periodic cash flow and other terms are as defined above.

- See also DISCOUNTED CASH FLOW, FUTURE VALUE, NET PRESENT VALUE.

PRESETTLEMENT RISK See FRACTIONAL EXPOSURE.

PRESIDING DIRECTOR See LEAD INDEPENDENT DIRECTOR.

PRICE–BOOK RATIO A measure that compares market and accounting values to determine potential undervaluation or overvaluation of a company. Price–book is generally computed via:

$$P/B = \frac{S}{BVPS}$$

where S is the current stock price and $BVPS$ is BOOK VALUE per share.

A high ratio, or an increasing ratio over time, may indicate a growth stock, while a low ratio may suggest an opportunity to purchase the stock of a company that has not realized its valuation potential.

PRICE COMPRESSION A phenomenon where the price of a

CALLABLE BOND remains close to its call redemption price in a declining INTEREST RATE environment since the likelihood of call, redemption, and refinancing increases.

PRICE DISCOVERY A process where buyers and sellers utilize transparent auction or quotation methods to determine a fair price for a reference ASSET.

PRICE/EARNINGS (P/E) RATIO A measure of a company's value and earnings RISK, computed from previously reported earnings (trailing P/E) or earnings forecasts (forward P/E) in the general form of:

$$P/E = \frac{S}{EPS}$$

where S is the stock price and EPS is EARNINGS PER SHARE (historic or forecast).

A company's P/E can be compared against past performance, the market, or a specific industry norm to determine relative value and performance. Alternatively, a target stock price can be imputed by using EPS and an industry or company estimate of the P/E ratio. The higher the P/E, the more investors are paying for the stock, and the greater the expectation of earnings growth. Lower P/E stocks tend to carry less RISK, as earnings expectations are lower; mature companies generally feature lower P/Es than aggressive or start-up firms.

- Also known as MULTIPLE.

PRICE ELASTICITY The ratio of a proportional change in quantity supplied or demanded for a proportional change in price; the greater the price elasticity, the more sensitive supply or demand to changes in price.

- See also ELASTICITY.

PRICE LIMIT A boundary placed on certain EXCHANGE-traded ASSETS (e.g., FUTURES, OPTIONS, COMMON STOCKS) that limits the amount of upward or downward price movement that can occur during a TRADING session. A price limit is one type of CIRCUIT BREAKER that is intended to control excessive VOLATILITY and/or market overreaction.

PRICE SPREAD See BEAR SPREAD, BULL SPREAD.

PRICE TAKER A small investor that has no ability to impact or influence securities prices, and must simply accept the BID or OFFER in the marketplace.

PRIMACY In INSURANCE, a rule that indicates which specific insurance coverage takes precedence when multiple coverage exists, in order to avoid dispute or conflict.

- See also APPORTIONMENT, DIVIDED COVER, OVERLAPPING INSURANCE, PRO RATA.

PRIMARY DEALER A financial institution, officially approved by government authorities, which is permitted to deal in the PRIMARY MARKET for GOVERNMENT BONDS. In order to create an efficient, transparent, and well-controlled process, CENTRAL BANKS and monetary authorities issuing government securities often deal only through a primary dealer network. To qualify as a primary dealer, an institution must generally meet certain minimum standards of financial strength and ethical behavior. In exchange for participating in government securities auctions and acting as a MARKET MAKER, the dealer is generally given full access to ORDER flows.

PRIMARY INSURER See INSURER.

PRIMARY MARKET The general marketplace for the initial flotation of NEW ISSUE securities, including NOTES, BONDS, COMMON STOCK, PREFERRED STOCK, and CONVERTIBLE BONDS, on behalf of corporate or sovereign issuers. Once securities are placed and the UNDERWRITING SYNDICATE is broken the primary market phase is concluded. Any subsequent TRADING activity forms part of the SECONDARY MARKET.

PRIMARY OFFERING The inaugural sale of a corporate or sovereign issuer's securities in the PRIMARY MARKET, including INITIAL PUBLIC OFFERINGS and DEBT NEW ISSUES. Subsequent new issues launched in the primary market are considered SECONDARY OFFERINGS.

PRIME RATE In the United States, a semi-floating INTEREST RATE reflecting the unsecured lending rate that BANKS charge their best corporate customers.

PRIME RATE FUND A MUTUAL FUND or CLOSED-END FUND that invests primarily in corporate LOANS tied to the PRIME RATE. Prime rate funds feature limited LIQUIDITY as a result of the ILLIQUID nature of the SECONDARY MARKET for corporate loans.

PRINCIPAL (1) The primary, or authorizing, party in a transaction or business relationship. (2) The FACE VALUE of a financial transaction, such as a LOAN, BOND, or SWAP.

- (1) See also AGENT, (2) see also NOTIONAL.

PRINCIPAL-ONLY (PO) STRIP A component of a stripped MORTGAGE-BACKED SECURITY or COLLATERALIZED MORTGAGE OBLIGATION that is entitled only to PRINCIPAL payments from the underlying securities; interest COUPONS are redirected to the INTEREST-ONLY (IO) STRIP investors. The price of a PO strip declines as interest rates rise since higher rates slow refinancing and result in slower principal repayments. Since PO strips lack the additional CASH FLOW buffer generated by the coupons, they feature more price VOLATILITY than other FIXED INCOME securities.

PRIOR LIEN BOND A BOND, often issued in a corporate REORGANIZATION, that gives investors a first CLAIM on the issuer's ASSETS, even if the security is equally senior to other outstanding securities.

PRIOR PREFERRED STOCK PREFERRED STOCK that ranks senior to a company's other preferred stock issues. Within the preferred stock class, prior preferreds are entitled to a first CLAIM on DIVIDENDS, and in a BANKRUPTCY and LIQUIDATION scenario, a first claim on the company's ASSETS.
  ▪ See also SECONDARY PREFERRED STOCK.

PRIVATE EQUITY A proprietary investment by a VENTURE CAPITAL fund, INVESTMENT BANK, or MERCHANT BANK in the EQUITY of a private company. Private equity stakes are generally held for several years, and exit is generally arranged through an INITIAL PUBLIC OFFERING or the sale of the company to a third party.

PRIVATE PLACEMENT A DEBT security that is not registered with a securities regulator and can therefore only be sold on a CAVEAT EMPTOR basis to a very limited number of sophisticated institutional investors. Private placements are highly ILLIQUID and are generally only transferable to the original SYNDICATE or other QUALIFIED INSTITUTIONAL BUYERS when regulations permit. In the United States, a SAFE HARBOR RULE is provided by SECURITIES AND EXCHANGE COMMISSION RULE 144A, which allows limited resale of securities that have not been registered.
  ▪ See also PUBLIC SECURITIES, REGISTRATION.

PRIVILEGED SUBSCRIPTION ISSUE See RIGHTS ISSUE.

PRO FORMA [LAT] Literally "as a formality;" in the financial sector it relates to the presentation of hypothetical or projected corporate balance sheet, income statement, and/or CASH FLOW statement data to reflect the potential impact of expected earnings, a NEW ISSUE, or a CORPORATE FINANCE transaction. Pro-forma statements are used by investors considering a CAPITAL investment or BANKS arranging a financing as a gauge of the possible future financial position of a company.
  ▪ See also PRO-FORMA EARNINGS REPORT.

PRO-FORMA EARNINGS REPORT A financial statement that expresses profits by excluding exceptional costs or including exceptional gains; although pro-forma reports are widely used by companies and analysts, they do not typically conform to GENERALLY ACCEPTED ACCOUNTING PRINCIPLES or INTERNATIONAL ACCOUNTING STANDARDS and must be interpreted with care.

PRO RATA [LAT] Literally "proportional allocation;" in the financial sector it reflects an allocation of NEW ISSUE securities to investors in proportion to the ORDERS submitted. In INSURANCE, it relates to a

clause in a contract indicating that any SETTLEMENT to the INSURED will be in proportion to the total amount of insurance in force on the same PERIL.
- See also APPORTIONMENT, DIVIDED COVER, OVERLAPPING INSURANCE, PRIMACY.

PROBABILITY OF RUIN The likelihood that the distribution of average losses exceeds a BENCHMARK SOLVENCY value (i.e., a minimum amount of CAPITAL surplus or tangible net worth), leading to a company's BANKRUPTCY. Probability of ruin is incorporated in certain DEFAULT MODELS.

PROCESS RISK The RISK of loss arising from control/process inadequacies or failures, including DISASTER RECOVERY RISK, BUSINESS RECOVERY RISK, COLLATERAL RISK, KEY MAN RISK, OPERATIONAL ERROR RISK, and REGULATORY COMPLIANCE RISK.
- Also know as OPERATIONAL RISK.

PRODUCER PRICE INDEX An INFLATION measure at the wholesale level based on production components by commodity, industry, and processing stage. In the United States the producer price index measures the prices of underlying goods and commodities, but not associated services; the complete index includes volatile food and energy components, while the core index excludes both.
- See also CONSUMER PRICE INDEX, HARMONIZED INDEX OF CONSUMER PRICES, RETAIL PRICE INDEX.

PROFIT AND LOSS (P&L) EXPLAIN A financial process commonly used by BANKS, INVESTMENT BANKS, and SECURITIES FIRMS following MARK-TO-MARKET accounting rules, where the sources of daily profits and losses are examined in detail. The process involves decomposing profits and losses and relating them to specific daily activities, including TRADING, market-making, commissions, and fee-generating business; this allows an institution to understand how it earns and loses money and assists in the RISK MANAGEMENT control process. P&L explain is also a central component of the BACK-TESTING of VALUE-AT-RISK models.

PROGRAM TRADING See INDEX ARBITRAGE.

PROHIBITED RISK See UNINSURABLE RISK.

PROMISED YIELD See YIELD TO MATURITY.

PROMISSORY NOTE A written promise by one party to pay another party a stated sum on a certain date or upon presentation; the promise represents the maker's LIABILITY. A promissory note may be transferred to another party as a NEGOTIABLE INSTRUMENT through an ENDORSEMENT; the act of endorsing the note allows the BENEFICIARY to convert it into cash.

PROMPT MONTH See NEARBY CONTRACT.

PROOF OF LOSS Documentary evidence an INSURED must present an INSURER when submitting a CLAIM under an INSURANCE policy. Since an insurance contract requires the insured to have an INSURABLE INTEREST, proof of loss is an essential element in ensuring validity.

PROPERTY AND CASUALTY INSURANCE INSURANCE coverage for damage or loss to property. The standard contract specifies PERILS, limits, and duration, and whether coverage includes CONSEQUENTIAL LOSSES or is restricted to DIRECT LOSSES. Certain perils, such as damage or destruction from war, terrorism, or neglect in preserving damaged property from further loss, are often excluded from coverage. Property and casualty insurance generally requires the INSURED to agree to SUBROGATION.
- See also PROPERTY AND LIABILITY INSURANCE.

PROPERTY AND LIABILITY INSURANCE INSURANCE coverage for an INSURED whose property is damaged or destroyed by a PERIL, or whose negligence causes another property to be destroyed.
- See also PROPERTY AND CASUALTY INSURANCE.

PROPERTY PER RISK EXCESS OF LOSS A REINSURANCE agreement providing the PRIMARY INSURER with cover for any loss in excess of the specified retention on each type of RISK.

PROPORTIONAL AGREEMENT A QUOTA SHARE or SURPLUS SHARE REINSURANCE agreement requiring the INSURER and REINSURER to share PREMIUMS, RISKS, losses, and LOSS ADJUSTMENT EXPENSES on the basis of a predefined formula, such as a fixed or variable percentage of policy limits, or a monetary value amount.
- See also EXCESS OF LOSS AGREEMENT.

PROSPECTIVE FINITE POLICY An INSURANCE contract that seeks primarily to shift the timing risk of losses that are expected to occur in the future. In common with other FINITE RISK POLICIES, the prospective agreement is primarily a RISK FINANCING rather than RISK TRANSFER vehicle.
- See also RETROSPECTIVE FINITE POLICY.

PROSPECTUS A REGISTRATION statement filed by an issuer with a securities commissioner or registrar of CORPORATIONS, and distributed in final form to investors. The prospectus conveys particulars regarding a public PRIMARY OFFERING or SECONDARY OFFERING, relevant financial details regarding the issue and issuer, and the nature of potential RISKS arising from a purchase of securities. Core information generally includes form, denomination, and transfer of securities; status (seniority); form of NEGATIVE PLEDGE; interest and payment details; redemption, issuer CALL and investor PUT

features; taxation matters; EVENTS OF DEFAULT; issuer financials and description; and, form of SUBSCRIPTION AGREEMENT.
- Also known as OFFERING CIRCULAR, STATUTORY PROSPECTUS.
- See also RED HERRING.

PROTECTED CELL COMPANY A multi-user CAPTIVE with individual accounts ("cells") that clients hire for SELF-INSURANCE programs. Individual cells are separated by statute, which prevents commingling of ASSETS and RISKS, and ensures the assets of each client remain safe in the event other cell clients encounter FINANCIAL DISTRESS. Protected cell companies are widely used by firms that are interested in self-insurance but do not want to establish and manage a captive of their own.

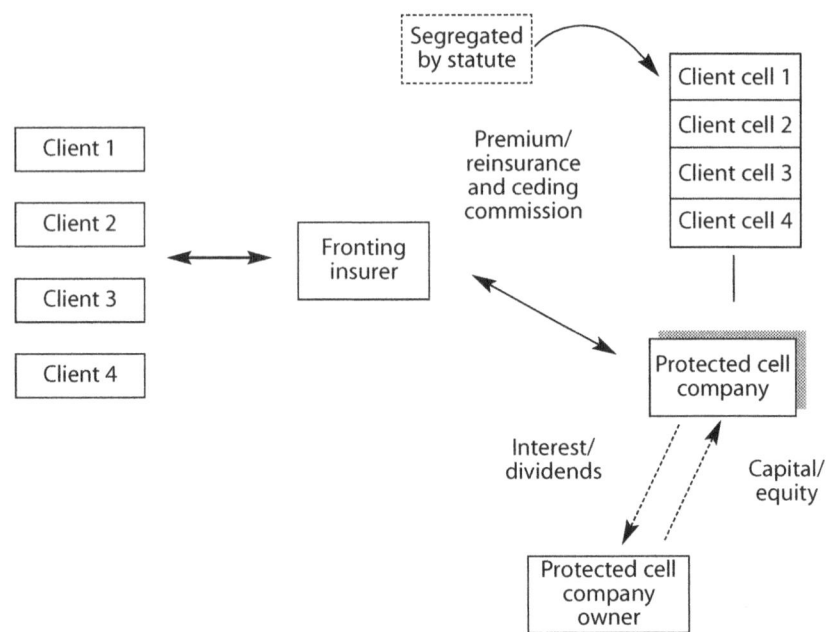

- See also AGENCY CAPTIVE, GROUP CAPTIVE, PURE CAPTIVE, RENT-A-CAPTIVE, CAPTIVE, SENIOR CAPTIVE, SISTER CAPTIVE.

PROXIMATE CAUSE See DIRECT LOSS.

PROXY (1) A document that conveys a COMMON STOCK shareholder's right to vote. (2) A person or institution authorized to vote on behalf of a shareholder.

PROXY CONTEST A HOSTILE TAKEOVER technique where the acquiring company attempts to persuade shareholders of the target company to vote their PROXIES against the incumbent DIRECTORS and in support of a new slate of directors favorably disposed to the takeover. Proxy contests can be lengthy, and the existence of defenses such as STAGGERED BOARDS or DEAD HAND CLAUSES can delay or block the process.

▪ Also known as PROXY FIGHT.

PROXY FIGHT See PROXY CONTEST.

PUBLIC LIMITED COMPANY (PLC) In the United Kingdom a corporate entity with LIMITED LIABILITY, registered under the Companies Act, which is publicly listed and traded.

PUFFERY [COL] A legal, if questionable, sales practice where BROKERS promote the positive aspects/upside of a potential investment while de-emphasizing RISKS/negative points in order to entice clients to invest.

PUKE POINT [COL] A capitulation price, or the price at which a DEALER or trader decides to sell some, or all, of a money-losing position.

PUMP AND DUMP [COL] An illegal practice where a pool of investors circulates positive, but false, news about a company in order to lure new buyers in and drive the stock price up ("pump"); once the price has reached a certain level the pool sells its shares ("dump") at a profit, leaving duped investors with positions in a falling market. This type of scheme is typically targeted at small, thinly traded stocks.

▪ See also DAISY CHAIN, PAINTING THE TAPE, POOP AND SCOOP.

PUNT [COL] (1) A risky or speculative position. (2) The act of SPECULATION.

PUP COMPANY [COL] The subsidiary of an INSURER that writes SPECIAL RISK INSURANCE on behalf of the parent company or other group companies.

PURCHASE GROUP See SYNDICATE.

PURCHASE GROUP AGREEMENT A contract between the members of the SYNDICATE (or PURCHASE GROUP) involved in UNDERWRITING a NEW ISSUE of securities that authorizes formation of the syndicate, designates the LEAD MANAGER, establishes deal allocations, responsibilities, and LIABILITIES, and defines the duration of the syndicate. The issuer is not a party to the purchase group agreement (the relationship between issuer and syndicate is contained in the UNDERWRITING AGREEMENT).

PURCHASE TRANSACTION An accounting methodology used for an ACQUISITION which involves a cash payment to the firm being acquired. The process adds revalued ASSETS, LIABILITIES, and EQUITY to the acquirer's balance sheet, with any difference between the merger price and fair market value reflected in the GOODWILL account, depreciable over a defined number of years.

▪ See also POOLING OF INTERESTS.

PURCHASING POWER PARITY An economic theory indicating that purchasing power across countries should be equal when goods, services, labor, and CAPITAL can be transported without restriction. Since barriers and frictions exist, cross-border purchasing power is not equal, suggesting that FOREIGN EXCHANGE rates need to adjust over the long term to reflect the amount of goods and services that can be purchased with each currency.

PURE ARBITRAGE Any ARBITRAGE strategy that makes use of external, or borrowed, funds rather than internal funds.
- See also QUASI ARBITRAGE.

PURE BOND VALUE See INVESTMENT VALUE.

PURE CAPTIVE A licensed INSURER or REINSURER that is wholly owned by a single sponsor and writes INSURANCE cover solely or primarily for the sponsoring firm. Although the pure captive structure allows for greater management control, tax treatment of PREMIUMS may not be favorable as the amount of true RISK TRANSFER outside the group structure is generally negligible.
- Also known as a SINGLE PARENT CAPTIVE.
- See also AGENCY CAPTIVE, CAPTIVE, GROUP CAPTIVE, PROTECTED CELL COMPANY, RENT-A-CAPTIVE, SENIOR CAPTIVE, SISTER CAPTIVE.

PURE CATASTROPHE SWAP An OVER-THE-COUNTER SWAP transaction that allows INSURERS or REINSURERS to exchange uncorrelated CATASTROPHIC HAZARDS in their PORTFOLIOS in order to improve DIVERSIFICATION.
- See also CATASTROPHE REINSURANCE SWAP.

PURE PREMIUM The amount an INSURER needs to charge to cover EXPECTED LOSSES and LOSS ADJUSTMENT EXPENSES; pure premium is one of two components, along with PREMIUM LOADING, used to determine FAIR PREMIUM.
- See also EXPENSE LOADING.

PURE PREMIUM RATING METHOD A method of determining the PREMIUM on PROPERTY AND CASUALTY INSURANCE that excludes PREMIUM LOADING factors, generally computed as:

$$PP = \frac{(Loss + LAE)}{U}$$

where $Loss$ is the amount of losses per year, LAE is the LOSS ADJUSTMENT EXPENSE per year, and U is the number of exposure units (e.g., policies).

PURE RISK A RISK exposure that can result only in a loss or no loss, but no possibility of a gain.
- Also known as STANDARD RISK.

See also SPECULATIVE RISK.

PURPOSE LOAN A LOAN, collateralized by securities and subject to MARGIN rules, where the proceeds are used to purchase other securities.
- Also known as MARGIN LOAN.
- See also NON-PURPOSE LOAN.

PUT See PUT OPTION.

PUT–CALL PARITY Relationships in OPTION pricing that must hold true in order for no-ARBITRAGE conditions to exist. The primary parity relationship indicates that the sum of the price of a CALL OPTION and the PRESENT VALUE of the STRIKE PRICE must equal the sum of the price of the PUT OPTION and the UNDERLYING ASSET. If parity does not hold, ARBITRAGE opportunities will arise and persist until ARBITRAGEURS force the discrepancy to disappear. Put–call parity is summarized as:

$$c + Xe^{-r_f t} = p + S$$

where c is the price of the call option, X is the strike price, p is the price of the put option, S is the underlying STOCK (or asset) price, r_f is the RISK-FREE RATE, t is the time to maturity, and e is the exponential constant.

PUT ON A CALL A COMPOUND OPTION that grants the buyer the right to sell an underlying CALL OPTION to the seller of the compound.
- See also CALL ON A CALL, CALL ON A PUT, PUT ON A PUT.

PUT ON A PUT A COMPOUND OPTION that grants the buyer the right to sell an underlying PUT OPTION to the seller of the compound.
- See also CALL ON A CALL, CALL ON A PUT, PUT ON A CALL.

PUT ON THE BEST OF N-ASSETS An OVER-THE-COUNTER COMPLEX OPTION that grants the buyer a payoff based on the difference between a predefined STRIKE PRICE and the best performing ASSET in a PORTFOLIO.
- See also CALL ON THE BEST OF N-ASSETS, CALL ON THE WORST OF N-ASSETS, MULTI-INDEX OPTION, OPTION ON THE BEST/WORST OF N-ASSETS, PUT ON THE WORST OF N-ASSETS.

PUT ON THE MINIMUM An OVER-THE-COUNTER COMPLEX OPTION that grants the buyer a payoff based on the difference between a predefined STRIKE PRICE and the lowest price achieved by the UNDERLYING reference ASSET over the life of the transaction.
- See also OPTION ON THE MAXIMUM/MINIMUM, CALL ON THE MAXIMUM, LOOKBACK OPTION.

PUT ON THE WORST OF N-ASSETS An OVER-THE-COUNTER COMPLEX OPTION that grants the buyer a payoff based on the

difference between a predefined STRIKE PRICE and the worst performing ASSET in a PORTFOLIO.
- See also CALL ON THE BEST OF N-ASSETS, CALL ON THE WORST OF N-ASSETS, MULTI-INDEX OPTION, OPTION ON THE BEST/WORST OF N-ASSETS, PUT ON THE BEST OF N-ASSETS.

PUT OPTION A DERIVATIVE contract that gives the buyer the right, but not the obligation, to sell an UNDERLYING ASSET to the seller at a set STRIKE PRICE at, or before, expiry; in exchange, the buyer pays the seller a PREMIUM. Puts, which can be written on a broad range of financial and commodity references, are available as EXCHANGE-traded and

Long put payoff profile

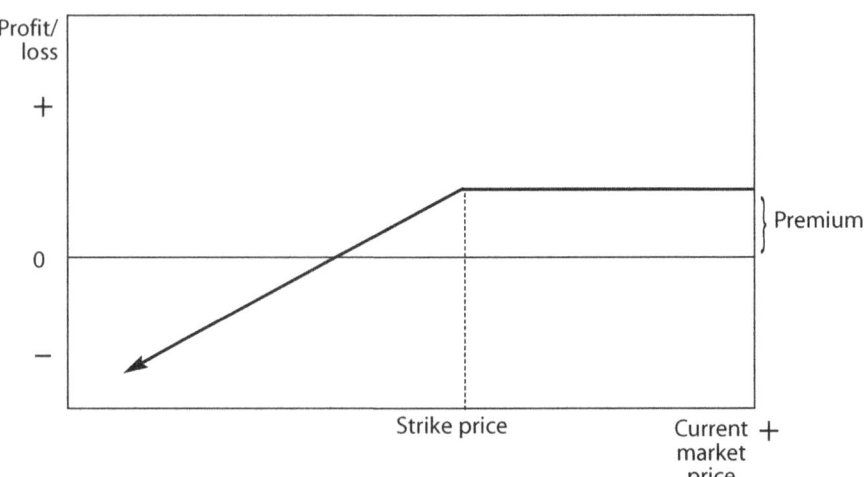

Short put payoff profile

OVER-THE-COUNTER contracts, and can be structured as AMERICAN OPTIONS, BERMUDAN OPTIONS, or EUROPEAN OPTIONS.
- See also CALL OPTION.

PUT PROTECTED EQUITY A CONTINGENT EQUITY facility where a company buys a PUT OPTION on its own COMMON STOCK from an intermediary, generating an economic gain which increases RETAINED EARNINGS if the value of its stock declines (such as in the aftermath of a large loss resulting from a CATASTROPHIC HAZARD).
- See also LOSS EQUITY PUT.

PUT SPREAD An OPTION position created by buying and selling PUT OPTIONS with the same expiry date but different STRIKE PRICES (i.e., the purchaser of a put spread buys a closer-to-the-money put option and sells a farther out-of-the-money put option (a bearish strategy), the seller of a put spread does the reverse (a bullish strategy)). The spread limits the gain/LIABILITY to an area defined by the two strikes.
- See also BULL SPREAD, BEAR SPREAD, CALL SPREAD.

PUTABLE BOND A BOND with embedded PUT OPTIONS which gives investors the right to sell the security back to the issuer at a predetermined price, generally a PREMIUM to PAR VALUE; in exchange for granting investors the put, the issuer obtains a lower COUPON. An investor may choose to put the bond if it can reinvest the capital proceeds in more favorable alternatives or requires the capital for other purposes. From the issuer's perspective, a putable bond can be considered the equivalent of a non-putable bond and a SHORT POSITION in a put option with a STRIKE PRICE equal to the bond's put price.
- See also CALLABLE BOND, HYBRID BOND.

PUTABLE CONVERTIBLE BOND A CONVERTIBLE BOND that contains a PUT OPTION which gives investors the right to sell the securities back to the issuer at a PREMIUM to PAR VALUE on a specific date(s); in exchange for granting investors the put, the issuer obtains a lower COUPON. The putable structure is offered in one of two forms: a single premium put, allowing for a one-time exercise (commonly used in the EUROMARKETS) and a rolling premium put, allowing for multiple exercise opportunities on pre-defined dates.
- See also CONDITIONAL PUT CONVERTIBLE BOND.

PUTABLE SWAP An OVER-THE-COUNTER SWAP structure that gives the institution receiving fixed rates the OPTION to cancel the transaction at a future date.
- See also CALLABLE SWAP, CANCELLABLE SWAP.

Q

QIB See QUALIFIED INSTITUTIONAL BUYER.

QT See QUESTIONED TRADE.

QUALIFIED INSTITUTIONAL BUYER (QIB) An institutional investor that is authorized to purchase and sell to other QIBs and DEALERS PRIVATE PLACEMENTS and other securities that have not been floated in the public markets. The QIB resale mechanism injects additional LIQUIDITY into otherwise unmarketable securities. In the United States, a SECURITIES AND EXCHANGE COMMISSION SAFE HARBOR, RULE 144A, allows QIB resales provided that the number of QIBs and the minimum size of their participation are specified in the selling documents or private placement agreement.

QUALIFIED OPINION An AUDIT OPINION by an external auditor indicating that the accuracy of a company's financial statements cannot be verified because of omissions or lack of information, i.e., the auditor is unable to ascertain tax or legal LIABILITIES associated with certain transactions or is unable to confirm details regarding the company's INVENTORY or ACCOUNTS RECEIVABLE.

- See also ADVERSE OPINION, UNQUALIFIED OPTION.

QUANTITY ADJUSTED OPTION See QUANTO.

QUANTO An OPTION that converts gains from an underlying DERIVATIVE into a target currency at a predetermined FOREIGN EXCHANGE rate. The quanto allows an investor to participate in a foreign market/ASSET while protecting it from exchange rate RISK.

- Also known as GUARANTEED EXCHANGE RATE OPTION, QUANTITY ADJUSTED OPTION.

QUANTO SWAP See DIFFERENTIAL SWAP.

QUASI ARBITRAGE Any ARBITRAGE strategy that makes use of internal, rather than external or borrowed, funds.

- See also PURE ARBITRAGE.

QUESTIONED TRADE See DK.

QUICK ASSETS A measure of a firm's most LIQUID ASSETS, generally taken to include cash, marketable securities (e.g., FIXED INCOME securities, COMMON STOCK, PREFERRED STOCK) and ACCOUNTS RECEIVABLE. The quick asset measure is precisely equal to CURRENT ASSETS less INVENTORY.
- See also QUICK RATIO.

QUICK RATIO A measure of a company's ability to meet obligations that are coming due with its most LIQUID ASSETS, typically computed as:

$$QR = \frac{QA}{CL}$$

where QA is QUICK ASSETS and CL is CURRENT LIABILITIES.

A quick ratio above 1.0 indicates that the company has sufficient CASH FLOW from maturing or saleable assets to meet its short-term obligations; a ratio below 1.0 suggests the possibility of LIQUIDITY RISK pressures. Since the quick ratio only includes truly liquid assets as a potential source of cash, it is a more conservative measure than the CURRENT RATIO.

QUIET PERIOD [COL] The period of time during which a company in the process of registering a NEW ISSUE of securities is prohibited from releasing any public relations material or other sensitive information.

QUOTA SHARE In REINSURANCE, a PROPORTIONAL AGREEMENT where an INSURER and REINSURER agree to split PREMIUMS, RISKS, losses, and LOSS ADJUSTMENT EXPENSES as a fixed percentage of the policy limit rather than a specific monetary amount.
- See also SURPLUS SHARE.

QUOTE-DRIVEN MARKET A marketplace where DEALERS or MARKET MAKERS give prices to BROKERS or traders, who can then buy or sell. Prices are typically adjusted to reflect ORDER flow and supply and demand forces. Most institutional OVER-THE-COUNTER markets are quote driven.
- See also DEALER MARKET, ORDER-DRIVEN MARKET.

QUOTED SPREAD The difference between the BID and the OFFER before a transaction occurs; the quoted spread may be a FIRM QUOTE or an INDICATIVE QUOTE.
- See also EFFECTIVE SPREAD, REALIZED SPREAD.

R

RAIDER [COL] A hostile acquirer that attempts to purchase another company, often to engage in ASSET STRIPPING or receive GREENMAIL payments. Although raiders were active primarily during the HOSTILE TAKEOVER phase of the 1980s, they still exist.
- See also HOSTILE TAKEOVER.

RAINBOW OPTION See MULTI-INDEX OPTION.

RAINMAKER [COL] A financial services professional that is capable of generating a significant amount of new business for an employing BANK or INVESTMENT BANK. The rainmaker generally refers to investment bankers that are capable of winning MANDATES to arrange NEW ISSUES or CORPORATE FINANCE transactions, but can also apply to institutional salespeople, BROKERS, or traders that are extremely successful in their respective areas.

RANDOM VARIABLE An event or observation with an uncertain outcome; a random variable may be discrete (appearing at specified time intervals) or continuous (appearing at any time), and it may be limited to a defined value or carry any value. Samplings of random variables are often used in SIMULATION processes that generate ASSET prices or distributions.

RANDOM WALK A financial theory indicating that ASSET prices move in a random and unpredictable (though not irrational) fashion, suggesting that future prices cannot be predicted by past or current prices; the longer the time period associated with the asset observations, the greater the possible dispersion of prices. More formally, the random walk is a STOCHASTIC PROCESS where asset prices are RANDOM VARIABLES, with each price increment independent and identically distributed.
- See also EFFICIENT MARKET HYPOTHESIS.
- Additional references: Cootner (1964), Samuelson (1965).

RANGE FLOATER See RANGE FLOATING RATE NOTE.

RANGE FLOATING RATE NOTE (FRN) A STRUCTURED NOTE that provides the investor with an enhanced COUPON if the floating INTEREST RATE reference trades within a predefined range; for every day the reference falls outside the band the investor loses one day's interest. The security is effectively a standard FRN with a strip of embedded BINARY OPTIONS.
- Also known as ACCRUAL NOTE, DAY COUNT NOTE, RANGE FLOATER.
- See also CAPPED FLOATING RATE NOTE, INVERSE FLOATING RATE NOTE, PERPETUAL FLOATING RATE NOTE, RANGE KNOCK-OUT FLOATING RATE NOTE.

RANGE KNOCK-OUT FLOATER See RANGE KNOCK-OUT FLOATING RATE NOTE.

RANGE KNOCK-OUT FLOATING RATE NOTE (FRN) A STRUCTURED NOTE that provides the investor with higher COUPONS than a RANGE FLOATING RATE NOTE but ceases paying interest for an entire period (typically one quarter), if the reference trades outside the range for a single day. The security is effectively a standard FRN with a strip of embedded KNOCK-OUT OPTIONS.
- Also known as RANGE KNOCK-OUT FLOATER.
- See also CAPPED FLOATING RATE NOTE, INVERSE FLOATING RATE NOTE, PERPETUAL FLOATING RATE NOTE.

RAROC See RISK-ADJUSTED RETURN ON CAPITAL.

RATCHET OPTION See CLIQUET OPTION.

RATE LOCK A mechanism that guarantees a borrower an underlying INTEREST RATE on a LOAN for a period ranging from 30 to 90 days. The rate lock ensures the borrower faces a known financing cost, as long as the loan is concluded during the effective period.
- Also known as LOCK-IN PROVISION.
- See also DROP LOCK, SPREADLOCK.

RATE MAKING In INSURANCE, the process of establishing PREMIUM rates so that they adequately cover EXPECTED LOSSES and are reasonable and non-discriminatory. When supplemented by relevant LOAD factors, the INSURER obtains the FAIR PREMIUM that it charges INSUREDS.
- See also EXPENSE LOADING, PREMIUM LOADING, PURE PREMIUM.

RATE ON LINE A measure of an INSURER's or REINSURER's gross profitability, generally calculated as:

$$ROL = \frac{Pr}{Line}$$

where *Pr* is PREMIUM and *Line* is the amount of the LINE provided by the insurer or reinsurer.

The higher the rate on line, the more gross profit the insurer earns.

RATE-SENSITIVE ASSETS ASSETS of a financial institution that are exposed to changes in INTEREST RATES (e.g., FIXED INCOME investments, REVERSE REPURCHASE AGREEMENTS, LOANS). Measurement of rate-sensitive assets is an essential component of GAP MANAGEMENT; by determining balance sheet sensitivity to changes in interest rates, a financial institution can manage its exposure to DIRECTIONAL RISK, CURVE RISK, and REPRICING RISK.
- See also ASSET LIABILITY MANAGEMENT, RATE-SENSITIVE LIABILITIES.

RATE-SENSITIVE LIABILITIES LIABILITIES of a financial institution that are exposed to changes in INTEREST RATES (e.g., DEPOSITS, REPURCHASE AGREEMENTS, BONDS). Measurement of rate-sensitive liabilities is an essential component of GAP MANAGEMENT; by determining balance sheet sensitivity to changes in interest rates, a financial institution can manage its exposure to DIRECTIONAL RISK, CURVE RISK, and REPRICING RISK.
- See also ASSET LIABILITY MANAGEMENT, RATE-SENSITIVE ASSETS.

RATIO HORIZONTAL SPREAD See TIME SPREAD.

RATIO SWAP See POWER SWAP.

RATIO VERTICAL SPREAD An OPTION SPREAD that is designed to generate profits from VOLATILITY. Ratio vertical spreads are created through the purchase of a smaller quantity of closer-to-the-money PUT

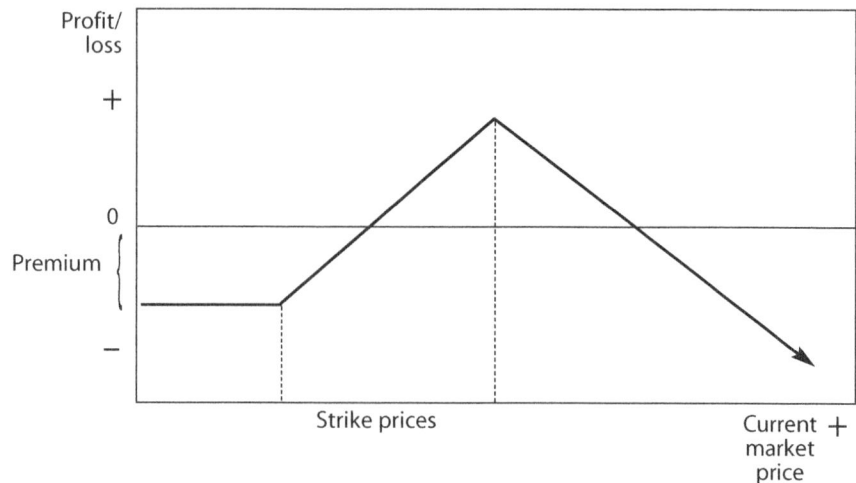

Call ratio vertical spread payoff profile

OPTIONS or CALL OPTIONS and the sale of a larger quantity of farther-from-the-money puts or calls.
- See also BACKSPREAD.

RATIO WRITING An OPTION position where an option writer sells a combination of COVERED OPTIONS and NAKED OPTIONS, in specific quantities or ratios. The RISKS associated with the strategy are lower than they are with a pure naked option strategy, but higher than on a covered option approach.

REACQUIRED STOCK See TREASURY STOCK.

REAL ESTATE INVESTMENT TRUST (REIT) An INVESTMENT COMPANY or INVESTMENT TRUST that raises CAPITAL from investors and invests proceeds on a tax-advantaged basis in income-producing real estate; in the United States, if 95 percent of income generated by the REIT is distributed to investors, earnings are exempt from federal taxation. A REIT may be created as an EQUITY trust, which owns and operates real estate, or a MORTGAGE trust, which lends to developers on a secured basis.

REAL ESTATE MORTGAGE INVESTMENT CONDUIT (REMIC) An investment vehicle that raises funds from investors and uses the proceeds to acquire commercial and residential MORTGAGE-related ASSETS. REMICS, which can be structured as CORPORATIONS, INVESTMENT TRUSTS, or LIMITED PARTNERSHIPS, purchase WHOLE LOANS, COLLATERALIZED MORTGAGE OBLIGATIONS, and/or MORTGAGE-BACKED SECURITIES through the issuance of DEBT in TRANCHES with unique maturities, RISK classes, and levels of SUBORDINATION. Each tranche gives investors an undivided interest in the underlying assets.

REAL INTEREST RATE The core level of INTEREST RATES, excluding the effects of INFLATION, typically computed as:

$$1 + r_{real} = \frac{1 + r_{nom}}{1 + r_{inf}}$$

where r_{real} is the real rate, r_{nom} is the nominal rate, and r_{inf} is the inflation rate.
- See also NOMINAL INTEREST RATE.

REAL OPTION The analysis of corporate investment projects using financial DERIVATIVE pricing theory and techniques. Through this process an investment cost is viewed as a STRIKE PRICE, the PRESENT VALUE of a project as the price of the UNDERLYING, and the maturity horizon of a project as the expiry date. Real option techniques can be applied to decisions related to investment timing and sequencing, plant closure, and resource extraction and conversion.

REALIZED SPREAD The difference between the weighted average of

the BIDS and OFFERS of executed securities transactions over a specific period of time.
- See also EFFECTIVE SPREAD, QUOTED SPREAD.

REALIZED VOLATILITY SWAP An OVER-THE-COUNTER COMPLEX SWAP involving the exchange of realized, or actual, VOLATILITY and IMPLIED VOLATILITY for a given market reference. Realized volatility is the floating volatility of the underlying reference index evident over the life of the transaction, while implied volatility is the fixed volatility rate contracted between buyer and seller at the start of the transaction. Realized volatility swaps are used in the EQUITY and FOREIGN EXCHANGE markets.
- See also VARIANCE SWAP.

RECAPITALIZATION (1) The general process of restructuring the financial CAPITAL of a company, generally by increasing EQUITY and reducing DEBT. Recapitalization can apply to companies that are solvent as well as those that are in the process of REORGANIZATION following filing of BANKRUPTCY protection. (2) The act of converting the nature and voting characteristics of a company's COMPANY STOCK by assigning more or less voting power to individual shares.
- (1) Also known as DELEVERAGING.
- (2) See also DUAL CLASS RECAPITALIZATION.

RECEIVER An institution named by a BANKRUPTCY court to act as AGENT for a bankrupt debtor while maintaining ASSETS for the benefit of creditors.
- See also RECEIVERSHIP.

RECEIVER SWAPTION A SWAPTION granting the buyer the right to enter into an OVER-THE-COUNTER INTEREST RATE SWAP to receive fixed rates and pay floating rates. The buyer is likely to exercise the receiver swaption as floating rates fall below a particular STRIKE PRICE.
- See also PAYER SWAPTION.

RECEIVERSHIP A state where a company has filed for BANKRUPTCY and is being overseen by a RECEIVER until courts decide on LIQUIDATION or REORGANIZATION.

RECIPROCAL EXCHANGE An unincorporated association where INSUREDS amalgamate their RISKS in order to insure one another; existing pool members actively attempt to recruit new members to spread risks even more widely. The affairs of the reciprocal exchange, including collection of PREMIUMS, adjustment of losses, and payment of CLAIMS, are often administered by an ATTORNEY-IN-FACT.
- Also known as RECIPROCAL INSURANCE EXCHANGE.

RECIPROCAL INSURANCE EXCHANGE See RECIPROCAL EXCHANGE.

RECISSION The cancellation of an INSURANCE contract by the INSURED or INSURER within a set time period, or the cancellation by insurer at any time upon the discovery of FRAUD or misrepresentation.

RECOMBINING TREE See LATTICE MODEL.

RECONSTITUTION The process of reassembling the CORPUS (or PRINCIPAL) and interest COUPONS of a security that has previously been decomposed into STRIPS, often to take advantage of ARBITRAGE opportunities. This generally occurs in the US TREASURY BOND market and the UK GILT market, where long-term securities are routinely split into ZERO COUPON BONDS and coupon streams.
- See also STRIPPING.

RECOUPONING The process of MARKING-TO-MARK and settling a PORTFOLIO of DERIVATIVES in order to reduce ACTUAL EXPOSURE between COUNTERPARTIES. A net cash SETTLEMENT is paid to the party holding the contracts with current value and the derivatives are then rewritten, or recouponed, at current market levels. The process is then repeated at a future settlement period.

RECOURSE The ability for a lender to seek repayment from a borrower rather than the ASSET or project that is being financed, or the right to a CLAIM on a contracting party. The greater the degree of recourse, the greater the repayment options to the lender. A contract agreed on a full recourse basis means the original seller of a product, maker of a NEGOTIABLE INSTRUMENT, or borrower under a credit facility is liable for repayment.
- See also FULL RECOURSE LOAN, NON-RECOURSE, NON-RECOURSE LOAN, PARTIAL RECOURSE LOAN.

RECOVERY The amount received by creditors after BANKRUPTCY proceedings have concluded, typically related to the SENIORITY of the CLAIM and/or the amount of COLLATERAL held. Secured creditors typically recover the greater percent of their outstanding claims (i.e., 60–100 percent RECOVERY RATE), followed by senior, unsecured creditors (20–50 percent) and junior, unsecured creditors (10–40 percent); subordinated debt holders, PREFERRED STOCK investors, and COMMON STOCK investors receive the smallest recoveries. The actual amount of recovery is dependent on the value of a company in LIQUIDATION or REORGANIZATION, as well as the total amount of outstanding claims.
- See also LOSS-GIVEN DEFAULT.

RECOVERY RATE The percentage of an obligation or CLAIM recovered by a creditor following a defaulted debtor's BANKRUPTCY proceedings.
- See also LOSS-GIVEN DEFAULT, RECOVERY.

RED HERRING [COL] In the United States, a preliminary REGISTRATION STATEMENT filed by a company with the SECURITIES AND EXCHANGE COMMISSION related to a forthcoming NEW ISSUE of securities. The red herring contains no price or issue size details, and is updated regularly until it becomes the final PROSPECTUS. The document derives its name from the red ink that is used to warn that the circular is not an attempt to sell securities in advance of registration statement approval.

RED-LINING [COL] Refusal by a BANK to provide funds, or an INSURER to supply INSURANCE cover, in particular areas or sectors as a result of previous negative experiences and/or losses. Red-lining that is discriminatory or prejudicial is illegal in many jurisdictions.

REDEEMABLE BOND See CALLABLE BOND.

REDISCOUNT The process of discounting a NEGOTIABLE INSTRUMENT a second time, e.g., a BANK first discounts a BILL OF EXCHANGE, and a CENTRAL BANK then rediscounts the bank's discounted bill when presented. Each act of rediscounting implicitly reflects a charge taken for the obligor's CREDIT RISK.

REFINANCING RISK See REPRICING RISK.

REFUNDING A process where the issuer of a BOND repays investors at a predefined redemption price. Refunding can only occur when a bond issue is CALLABLE, and is generally arranged in a declining INTEREST RATE environment, when a NEW ISSUE of cheaper bonds can be floated to replace the refunded bonds.
- See also REFUNDING PROTECTION.

REFUNDING PROTECTION A clause in an INDENTURE that prohibits an issuer from redeeming a BOND for a stated period of time from proceeds of an issue floated at a lower cost and ranking equal, or senior, to the original bond.
- See also REFUNDING.

REGISTERED SECURITY Any NEW ISSUE of securities that must adhere to requirements set forth by a national securities regulator prior to FLOTATION, listing, and TRADING. Registered securities must generally be supported by a detailed REGISTRATION STATEMENT that provides information on the proposed issue of securities and the issuer.
- See also BEARER SECURITY, PRIVATE PLACEMENT.

REGISTRATION STATEMENT A detailed statement accompanying every NEW ISSUE of public securities that contains details on both the issuer and the issue. In the United States, the SECURITIES AND EXCHANGE COMMISSION requires that all public offerings of securities include information on the proposed issue of securities and associated RISK factors, and the nature and condition of, and prospects

for, the issuer. Small offerings (under $500,000) as well as PRIVATE PLACEMENTS, TREASURY BONDS/NOTES, and AGENCY SECURITIES, are exempt from the registration statement requirement.
- See also PROSPECTUS, RED HERRING.

REGULAR CHOOSER OPTION See CHOOSER OPTION.

REGULATED ELECTRONIC COMMUNICATIONS NETWORK (ECN) An ELECTRONIC COMMUNICATIONS NETWORK that is authorized by regulatory authorities to operate as an EXCHANGE. Regulated ECNs must adhere to financial and reporting requirements imposed by regulators, and may be required to arrange for CLEARING of transactions through an independent CLEARINGHOUSE.
- See also DEALER MARKET ELECTRONIC COMMUNICATIONS NETWORK, HYBRID ELECTRONIC COMMUNICATIONS NETWORK.

REGULATION FAIR DISCLOSURE (FD) In the United States, a SECURITIES AND EXCHANGE COMMISSION rule that requires a company to issue sensitive information to the public broadly rather than selectively. The rule eliminates the information access privileges often granted to research analysts of INVESTMENT BANKS and SECURITIES FIRMS.

REGULATION T In the United States, a FEDERAL RESERVE BOARD regulation related to extensions of credit by BROKER/DEALERS and SECURITIES FIRMS to their clients. Regulation T LOANS must be secured by MARGIN comprised of ELIGIBLE SECURITIES and capped at maximum LOAN-TO-VALUE levels; minimum margin levels must be maintained and supplemented as necessary through the MAINTENANCE MARGIN process.
- See also NON-PURPOSE LOAN, PURPOSE LOAN.

REGULATORY ARBITRAGE The process of taking advantage of internal or external differences in the regulatory treatment of business activities in order to decrease regulatory costs or expand into products or markets normally off limits.
- See also REGULATORY CONSOLIDATION, REGULATORY HARMONIZATION.

REGULATORY CAPITAL CAPITAL resources that financial institutions must allocate to their FINANCIAL RISKS and OPERATING RISKS in order to comply with applicable national regulatory requirements. Regulators often establish minimum thresholds to ensure SOLVENCY under a range of stress loss scenarios.
- See also ECONOMIC CAPITAL, RISK-ADJUSTED CAPITAL, TIER 1 CAPITAL, TIER 2 CAPITAL, TIER 3 CAPITAL.

REGULATORY COMPLIANCE RISK The RISK of loss arising from failure to comply with regulatory rules related to business, TRADING, and lending, authorized dealing personnel, reporting, disclosure, or capitalization. A sub-category of PROCESS RISK.

REGULATORY CONSOLIDATION The process of combining separate regulators with a specific focus under a single "umbrella" in order to unify treatment of markets, products, and forums and eliminate inefficiencies and instances of REGULATORY ARBITRAGE. A fully consolidated regulator might be responsible for banking, securities, INSURANCE, investment management, and listed markets.
- See also REGULATORY HARMONIZATION.

REGULATORY HARMONIZATION The process of ensuring that rules for business and financial activities are generally similar across countries in order to reduce instances of cross-border REGULATORY ARBITRAGE.
- See also REGULATORY CONSOLIDATION.

REINSTATEMENT The reactivation of an INSURANCE contract that has lapsed due to non-payment of PREMIUM by the INSURED. In reinstating a contract an INSURER reserves the right to charge a higher PREMIUM or modify coverage terms.

REINSURANCE A RISK TRANSFER from an INSURER to a REINSURER that provides an insurer with cover for specified INSURANCE exposures. The agreement may be arranged as FACULTATIVE REINSURANCE (i.e., customized, one-off) or TREATY REINSURANCE (i.e., standardized, multiple exposure).

REINSURANCE BROKER A BROKER representing the CEDING INSURER in placing business with a REINSURER.

REINSURANCE CAPACITY (1) The amount of REINSURANCE available to INSURERS from the reinsurance market at large or from an individual REINSURER. (2) The amount of PREMIUM that an individual reinsurer is able to write for specific types of RISKS.

REINSURANCE CREDIT A credit balance on a CEDING INSURER's balance sheet that reflects PREMIUMS CEDED to, and losses recoverable from, REINSURERS. The credit balance, which is a reflection of RISK TRANSFER, permits an insurer to write additional primary INSURANCE coverage for INSUREDS.

REINSURANCE FACILITY See REINSURANCE POOL.

REINSURANCE POOL A group of REINSURERS that agrees to UNDERWRITE RISKS on a joint basis; under a typical pool each member agrees to pay a fixed percentage of any loss, or a percentage of any loss above a defined RETENTION level.
- Also known as REINSURANCE FACILITY.

REINSURED An INSURER that CEDES a particular RISK to a REINSURER through a REINSURANCE agreement.

REINSURER An INSURER that provides REINSURANCE coverage to other insurers through FACULTATIVE REINSURANCE or TREATY REINSURANCE agreements.

REINVESTMENT RISK See REPRICING RISK.

REIT See REAL ESTATE INVESTMENT TRUST.

RELATED-PARTY TRANSACTION A financial transaction conducted between a company and a related entity, such as a parent, holding company, subsidiary, affiliate, SPECIAL PURPOSE ENTITY, or joint venture. Common related-party transactions include paying or receiving DIVIDENDS, accepting or granting LOANS, HEDGING RISKS, and transferring CAPITAL.

RELATIONSHIP MODEL A general corporate system that is characterized by concentrated ownership stakes and cross-shareholdings, moderately LIQUID CAPITAL MARKETS, and a relatively inactive CORPORATE CONTROL MARKET; formal legal dealings are often supplemented by informal negotiation arising from long-term business relationships. Germany and Japan are representative examples of the relationship model.

- See also HYBRID MODEL, MARKET MODEL.

REMIC See REAL ESTATE MORTGAGE INVESTMENT CONDUIT.

RENEGOTIATED LOAN A LOAN where the original terms of contract (i.e., maturity, amount, INTEREST RATE, repayment frequency) are altered to avoid forcing the lending BANK to commence FORECLOSURE proceedings. A renegotiated loan may involve an extension of the maturity, a lowering of the interest rate, or a change in the PRINCIPAL AMORTIZATION schedule. Although the loan may perform under the new terms, the bank may still be required to establish LOAN LOSS RESERVES.

- See also RESCHEDULING, SOFT LOAN.

RENT-A-CAPTIVE A licensed INSURER or REINSURER that makes an account available to a firm that wishes to SELF-INSURE but does not want to administer its own CAPTIVE program. A rent-a-captive prevents account commingling by segregating ASSETS, LIABILITIES, and RISK exposures into individual accounts that are separated through a shareholder's agreement.

- See also AGENCY CAPTIVE, CAPTIVE, GROUP CAPTIVE, PROTECTED CELL COMPANY, PURE CAPTIVE, SENIOR CAPTIVE, SISTER CAPTIVE.

RENT RIGHT The financial benefit granted to an investor through a share of COMMON STOCK, comprised of a PRO RATA share of the discounted future CASH FLOWS of the company (which manifests itself via share price appreciation) and any periodic DIVIDENDS that might be paid.

- See also CONTROL RIGHT.

REOPENING A SECONDARY OFFERING of a new TRANCHE of securities under an existing issue with a defined COUPON and maturity. Frequent issuers often use reopenings in order to concentrate LIQUIDITY in a smaller number of issues and establish more robust BENCHMARKS.

REORGANIZATION A state of corporate BANKRUPTCY that results in an agreement among creditors and the bankruptcy court to restructure, rather than liquidate, an insolvent company. In order for a company to emerge from reorganization, creditors must be willing to accept concessions related to the value of their credit CLAIMS. A TRUSTEE, RECEIVER, or administrator is often appointed to manage the affairs of the company while in reorganization and prepare a reorganization plan for court approval. If no trustee is appointed, the debtor becomes a DEBTOR-IN-POSSESSION (DIP) and must assume the responsibilities. If agreement is not reached on the reorganization plan the bankruptcy judge may order implementation via a CRAMDOWN or may opt for LIQUIDATION.

REORGANIZATION BOND See INCOME BOND.

REPLACEMENT COST (1) From an accounting perspective, the amount required to replace an ASSET based on its BOOK VALUE, accumulated DEPRECIATION, and obsolescence. In some cases replacement cost requires subjective input and judgment, particularly if the asset has become obsolete. (2) See ACTUAL EXPOSURE.

REPO [COL] See REPURCHASE AGREEMENT.

REPO RATE The INTEREST RATE a borrower pays a lender through a REPURCHASE AGREEMENT transaction. The repo rate, which is set according to the specific terms of the transaction (including maturity and underlying COLLATERAL), is generally lower than equivalent bank credit financing rates since the exposure is secured by collateral.

REPRESENTATION (1) A statement of fact that an INSURED provides to the INSURER when applying for INSURANCE coverage. An insurer routinely relies on representations as part of its UNDERWRITING process. (2) A statement of fact that an issuer of securities supplies to the LEAD MANAGER or SYNDICATE conducting DUE DILIGENCE in advance of a NEW ISSUE.
- See also WARRANTY.

REPRICING RISK The RISK that a maturing ASSET or LIABILITY will be reinvested or refinanced at a less favorable rate. Assets that reprice in a lower-rate environment and liabilities that reprice in a higher-rate environment create an opportunity cost or loss.
- Also known as REFINANCING RISK, REINVESTMENT RISK.
- See also NEGATIVE GAP, POSITIVE GAP, RATE-SENSITIVE ASSETS, RATE-SENSITIVE LIABILITIES.

REPURCHASE AGREEMENT A financial transaction involving the sale, and future repurchase, of securities for cash. Through the exchange, the repurchase agreement party effectively borrows money from the REVERSE REPURCHASE AGREEMENT party on a collateralized basis, paying a financing charge (REPO RATE) for doing so. Repurchase agreements carry maturities ranging from overnight to several months, and are generally secured by high-quality COLLATERAL such as TREASURY NOTES, TREASURY BONDS, JAPANESE GOVERNMENT BONDS, or GILTS. Repurchase agreements are generally MARKED-TO-MARKET daily via the reverse party, and MARGIN is called or returned as needed.

- Also known as REPO.
- See also DOLLAR ROLL, GENERAL COLLATERAL, GENSAKI, OPEN REPO, OVERNIGHT REPO, SPECIAL, TERM REPURCHASE AGREEMENT.

RESALE See REVERSE REPURCHASE AGREEMENT.

RESCHEDULING Renegotiating an existing LOAN with new terms and conditions, including those that may be more favorable to the debtor, in order to avoid any instance of non-accrual or FORECLOSURE.
- See also RENEGOTIATED LOAN.

RESERVE CURRENCY A currency featuring full CURRENCY CONVERTIBILITY on the CURRENT ACCOUNT and CAPITAL ACCOUNT, and which is widely used in international trade, finance, and FOREIGN EXCHANGE transactions. Reserve currencies are typically associated with national economies that have strong industrial bases and low INFLATION rates. Dollars, EURO, yen, and sterling are examples of reserve currencies.
- Also known as HARD CURRENCY.
- See also CONVERTIBLE CURRENCY, EXOTIC CURRENCY.

RESERVE REQUIREMENTS A minimum percentage of total ASSETS that financial institutions must hold in highly LIQUID form to ensure sufficient ability to meet DEPOSITS or other demand LIABILITIES as they mature or are presented for repayment. In addition to reinforcing LIQUIDITY, CENTRAL BANKS and monetary authorities often use reserve requirements as a tool of MONETARY POLICY.

RESERVES Funds segregated by an institution to cover future LIABILITIES, CLAIMS, obligations, or uncertainties. Reserves, which are often established as CONTRA-ACCOUNTS on the ASSET side of the balance sheet, may be designated in different forms. In banking these may include legal or regulatory reserves (non-interest bearing DEPOSITS held with a CENTRAL BANK) and LOAN LOSS RESERVES (funds set aside for NON-PERFORMING LOANS). In INSURANCE they may include UNEARNED PREMIUM RESERVES (funds set aside to reflect the timing differences between upfront receipt of PREMIUM and the TAIL of written policies) and EXPECTED LOSS reserves (funds set aside to cover expected claims). In some cases reserves may be hidden or implicit, such as unrealized CAPITAL gains within a securities PORTFOLIO. In many systems accounting rules control the establishment and release of reserves so that firms cannot use them to manipulate their earnings.

RESET BOND A BOND with a provision that allows the INTEREST RATE to be adjusted so that the security always trades at its original value. A reset bond can be beneficial for issuers in a declining rate environment, but can be problematic if rates rise or CREDIT SPREADS widen; the act of keeping the bond trading at PAR VALUE through an upward adjustment in the rate can lead to financial pressures for certain issuers.

- See also RESET PAYMENT IN KIND BOND.

RESET OPTION See PARTIAL LOOKBACK OPTION.

RESET PAYMENT IN KIND (PIK) BOND A PAYMENT IN KIND SECURITY with a requirement that the issuer float additional BONDS to investors in order to keep the original securities trading at PAR VALUE. Reset PIKs are generally issued by weaker companies that are unable to secure better financing terms, and can prove risky: if the issuer's credit deteriorates and the price of the original bonds declines, it will have to issue more bonds, which will increase LEVERAGE, lower credit quality and result in further price declines and more issuance, in a self-fulfilling cycle.

- See also RESET BOND.

RESIDUAL See RESIDUAL SECURITY.

RESIDUAL RIGHT Discretionary powers and authorities delegated by DIRECTORS to executives, allowing them to act as AGENTS and make decisions related to the daily management of the firm, including financing plans, ACQUISITIONS, investments, production and marketing, and employee matters.

RESIDUAL SECURITY (1) A financial instrument that can increase a company's DILUTION if EXERCISED into COMMON STOCK, including CONVERTIBLE BONDS, WARRANTS, RIGHTS, and OPTIONS. (2) The last TRANCHE in a SECURITIZATION to receive cash, payable only after all other tranches have been serviced; the value of the residual is often quite uncertain as CASH FLOWS may be impacted by a number of dynamic market variables that can cause a cash flow deficit or surplus. The issuer of the securitization often retains the residual.

RESIDUAL VALUE The anticipated value of an ASSET at the conclusion of a LEASE; value may be determined through an independent appraisal or prior agreement.
- See also RESIDUAL VALUE GUARANTEE, RESIDUAL VALUE SECURITIZATION.

RESIDUAL VALUE GUARANTEE A contingent FINANCIAL GUARANTEE that provides a company with a CAPITAL infusion if it experiences a shortfall in the RESIDUAL VALUE of ASSETS that have been LEASED.
- See also RESIDUAL VALUE SECURITIZATION.

RESIDUAL VALUE SECURITIZATION An INSURANCE-LINKED SECURITY that protects an issuing firm from the RESIDUAL VALUE RISKS embedded in a variety of fixed ASSET LEASES by shifting exposure to CAPITAL MARKETS investors. If the issuer experiences a shortfall in residual value, it reduces or suspends PRINCIPAL and/or COUPONS payable on the securities, thus protecting itself against the economic shortfall.
- See also CATASTROPHE BOND, LIFE ACQUISITION COST SECURITIZATION, MORTGAGE DEFAULT SECURITIZATION, WEATHER BOND.

RESIDUAL VARIANCE ASSET returns that deviate from the SECURITY MARKET LINE or a security/PORTFOLIO relationship. Residual variance can be computed via:

$$\varepsilon_{j,t} = r_{j,t} - (A + \beta_j (r_{m,t}))$$

where $r_{j,t}$ is the return on security j at time t, $r_{m,t}$ is the return on the market portfolio at time t, β_j is the BETA of security j, and A is the intercept of the security market line or security/portfolio relationship.
- See also ARBITRAGE PRICING THEORY, CAPITAL ASSET PRICING MODEL, CAPITAL MARKET LINE.

RESISTANCE LEVEL A TECHNICAL ANALYSIS charting figure of a security or index price level that withstands repeated bouts of buying pressure. If the price manages to breach the resistance level after several repeated attempts, further upward moves may follow (as in a BREAKOUT).

- See also SUPPORT LEVEL.

RESTORATION PREMIUM The PREMIUM paid by an INSURED to an INSURER to restore an INSURANCE policy to its previous limits after a loss has occurred and a SETTLEMENT has been received.

RESTRICTED RETAINED EARNINGS A portion of the RETAINED EARNINGS account that cannot be used to pay DIVIDENDS. The restriction may arise from the breach of a COVENANT test or an arrears due to CUMULATIVE PREFERRED STOCK investors.
- Also known as RESTRICTED SURPLUS.

RESTRICTED STOCK Shares of a company's COMMON STOCK granted to executives and employees as a form of compensation, which generally vest over a multi-year period; awards may also be granted in the form of CALL OPTIONS. Restricted stock grants result in the creation of new shares and are thus dilutive.

RESTRICTED SURPLUS See RESTRICTED RETAINED EARNINGS.

RETAIL PRICE INDEX (RPI) A UK INFLATION measure based on the retail prices of goods and services (and also including rents, utilities, and MORTGAGE payments); all computations are inclusive of VALUE ADDED TAX. A separate index (RPIX), which excludes mortgage payments, is also tabulated.
- See also CONSUMER PRICE INDEX, HARMONIZED INDEX OF CONSUMER PRICES, PRODUCER PRICE INDEX.

RETAINED EARNINGS The portion of a company's EQUITY CAPITAL account comprised of net earnings generated and kept within the business, after all DIVIDENDS have been paid to COMMON STOCK and PREFERRED STOCK investors.
- Also known as EARNED SURPLUS, UNDISTRIBUTED EARNINGS.
- See also PAID-IN CAPITAL.

RETENTION (1) Any RISK preserved, knowingly or unknowingly, by an individual or an institution. Unknowing retention might arise from misunderstanding the nature of an exposure, while knowing retention is generally the result of a conscious decision to keep a particular amount of exposure for financial or strategic reasons. (2) In INSURANCE, risk retained by an INSURED through a DEDUCTIBLE, EXCLUSIONS, and/or POLICY CAP. Policies with large deductibles, small policy caps and minimal exclusions result in less RISK TRANSFER and more retention. (3) In a NEW ISSUE of securities, the amount allocated to SYNDICATE members less the amount held in the POT.

- (1), (2) Also known as ASSUMPTION OF RISK.
- (1) See also PASSIVE RETENTION, RISK RETENTION.

RETROCEDANT A REINSURER that CEDES RISK to another REINSURER through a RETROCESSION contract.

RETROCEDE The process of transferring RISK from one REINSURER to another reinsurer through a RETROCESSION contract.

- See also CEDE, RETROCEDANT, RETROCESSIONAIRE.

RETROCESSION A form of REINSURANCE contract that allows a REINSURER to transfer designated RISKS to another reinsurer in order to manage and diversify its PORTFOLIO of REINSURANCE exposures.

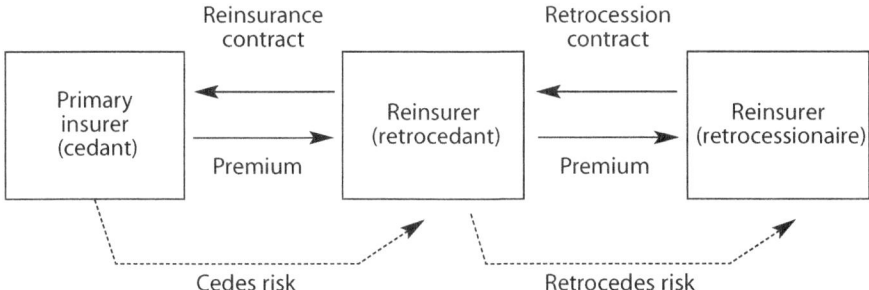

- See also RETROCEDANT, RETROCESSIONAIRE.

RETROCESSIONAIRE A REINSURER accepting RISK from another REINSURER through a RETROCESSION contract.

- See also RETROCEDANT.

RETROSPECTIVE AGGREGATE LOSS COVER A FINITE INSURANCE CONTRACT that allows the INSURED to finance existing losses and losses INCURRED BUT NOT YET REPORTED by paying the INSURER a PREMIUM and ceding its LIABILITIES. The insured must still pay for losses above a specified amount when they are incurred, and thus retains some timing risk.

- See also LOSS PORTFOLIO TRANSFER, RETROSPECTIVE FINITE POLICY.

RETROSPECTIVE FINITE POLICY A FINITE INSURANCE CONTRACT that allows the INSURED to manage the timing RISKS of LIABILITIES that already exist and losses that have already occurred. Common structures include the ADVERSE DEVELOPMENT COVER, LOSS PORTFOLIO TRANSFER, and RETROSPECTIVE AGGREGATE LOSS COVER.
- Also known as a POST-FUNDED POLICY.
- See also PROSPECTIVE FINITE POLICY.

RETROSPECTIVE RATING In INSURANCE, the process of adjusting PREMIUM rates to reflect actual current year losses. The retrospective approach is based on an initial premium plus an adjustment as loss experience is crystallized.

RETROSPECTIVE SCRUTINY A legal review by regulators and other external parties of a bankrupt company's history of financial deterioration, with a focus on the actions of the BOARD OF DIRECTORS during the period leading up to FINANCIAL DISTRESS.

RETROSPECTIVELY RATED POLICY A LOSS SENSITIVE INSURANCE CONTRACT requiring the INSURED to pay an initial PREMIUM to an INSURER and, at some future time, make an additional premium payment (i.e., a retrospective premium) or receive a refund (i.e., a retrospective refund), depending on the size of any losses that occur.

RETURN ON ASSETS (ROA) A measure of the return a firm generates from the average ASSETS it holds during a reporting period. ROA can be computed via:

$$ROA = \frac{NI_n}{ATA_n}$$

where NI_n is net income in period n, and ATA_n is average total assets during period n.

The higher the ratio, the greater the profitability of the assets.

RETURN ON EQUITY (ROE) A measure of the return a firm generates for shareholders that have supplied CAPITAL. ROE, which is not adjusted for the effects of FINANCIAL RISK or OPERATING RISK, can be computed in different forms, including:

$$ROE = \frac{NI_n}{Eq_n}$$

$$ROE = \frac{EPS_n}{BVEqPS_n}$$

where NI_n is net income in period n, Eq_n is equity in period n, EPS_n is EARNINGS PER SHARE in period n, and $BVEqPS_n$ is BOOK VALUE equity per share in period n.

The higher the ratio, the greater the profitability on invested equity.

■ See also RISK-ADJUSTED RETURN ON CAPITAL.

RETURN ON INVESTMENT (ROI) A measure of the operating return a firm generates from a core base of CAPITAL resources, computed as:

$$ROI = \frac{EBIT}{TC}$$

where *EBIT* is EARNINGS BEFORE INTEREST AND TAXES, and *TC* is total capital, or the sum of COMMON STOCK, PREFERRED STOCK and LONG-TERM DEBT.

The higher the ratio, the greater the operating profitability on capital resources.

RETURN PERIOD In INSURANCE, the average time within which an event of a particular magnitude is reached/exceeded. The return period, which is inversely proportional to frequency of occurrence, is commonly used in analyzing CATASTROPHIC HAZARDS; the lower the frequency of occurrence, the longer the return period.

REVENUE BOND A municipal security that pays investors PRINCIPAL and COUPON interest from specific revenue streams generated by the project funded through the bond. A revenue bond is generally a NON-RECOURSE obligation, and is thus backed only by the project and not the credit resources of the municipal issuer.

■ See also GENERAL OBLIGATION bond.

REVERSAL A TECHNICAL ANALYSIS charting pattern that depicts a prolonged change in the upward or downward direction of a security or index.

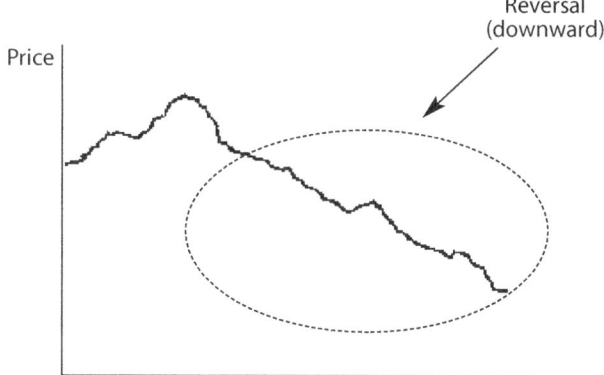

REVERSE [COL] See REVERSE REPURCHASE AGREEMENT.

REVERSE BARRIER OPTION See REVERSE KNOCK-IN OPTION, REVERSE KNOCK-OUT OPTION.

REVERSE CASH-AND-CARRY ARBITRAGE An ARBITRAGE strategy where a profit can be secured by buying a FORWARD or FUTURE, selling the UNDERLYING ASSET, and lending the proceeds until maturity. The arbitrage only works when the forward price is less than the SPOT PRICE plus the COST OF CARRY.

▪ See also CASH-AND-CARRY ARBITRAGE.

REVERSE CONVERTIBLE BOND A BOND that can be exchanged into COMMON STOCK at the OPTION of the issuer rather than the investor. The issuing company might choose to convert if it is attempting to decrease its LEVERAGE and improve its overall creditworthiness.

▪ See also CONVERTIBLE BOND, MANDATORY CONVERTIBLE BOND.

REVERSE FLOATER SWAP See INVERSE FLOATER SWAP.

REVERSE FLOATING RATE NOTE See INVERSE FLOATING RATE NOTE.

REVERSE HEAD AND SHOULDERS [COL] A TECHNICAL ANALYSIS charting formation of a security or index that features a supporting price plateau, followed by a dip, and a reversal to a second supporting price plateau; the formation of a reverse head and shoulders might then lead to a BREAKOUT on the upside or downside.

▪ See also HEAD AND SHOULDERS.

REVERSE INDEX PRINCIPAL SWAP An OVER-THE-COUNTER COMPLEX SWAP with a NOTIONAL PRINCIPAL that increases as a floating INTEREST RATE reference declines through prespecified BARRIER levels. As the notional increases, fixed and floating rate payments associated with the swap become larger. A reverse index

principal swap can be used to HEDGE CASH FLOWS associated with an accreting ASSET.
- See also ACCRETING SWAP, AMORTIZING SWAP, INDEX PRINCIPAL SWAP, VARIABLE PRINCIPAL SWAP.

REVERSE KNOCK-IN OPTION A BARRIER OPTION that creates an underlying IN-THE-MONEY option once the BARRIER is breached, i.e., the barrier is above the STRIKE PRICE in the case of a reverse knock-in CALL, and below the strike in the case of the reverse knock-in PUT.
- Also known as KICK-IN OPTION.
- See also REVERSE KNOCK-OUT OPTION.

REVERSE KNOCK-OUT OPTION A BARRIER OPTION that extinguishes an underlying IN-THE-MONEY option once the BARRIER is breached, i.e., the barrier is above the STRIKE PRICE in the case of a reverse knock-out CALL, and below the strike in the case of the reverse knock-out PUT.
- Also known as KICK-OUT OPTION.
- See also REVERSE KNOCK-IN OPTION.

REVERSE LEVERAGED BUYOUT (LBO) A transaction where a company that has been taken private through a LEVERAGED BUYOUT (LBO) is floated publicly through an INITIAL PUBLIC OFFERING. A reverse LBO generally occurs after the company has been streamlined and operating efficiencies have been created by the LBO management group.

REVERSE MORTGAGE A MORTGAGE where the borrower receives monthly payments from the lender based on accumulated EQUITY in the property. The ultimate source of repayment in a reverse mortgage is the borrower's estate, which is pledged to the lending BANK as COLLATERAL.

REVERSE REPO [COL] See REVERSE REPURCHASE AGREEMENT.

REVERSE REPURCHASE AGREEMENT A financial transaction involving the purchase, and future resale, of securities for cash. Through the exchange, the reverse repurchase agreement party effectively lends funds to the REPURCHASE AGREEMENT party on a collateralized basis, charging a financing rate (REPO RATE) for doing so. Reverse repurchase agreements have maturities ranging from overnight to several months, and are generally secured by high-quality COLLATERAL such as TREASURY NOTES, TREASURY BONDS, JAPANESE GOVERNMENT BONDS, or GILTS. Reverse repurchase agreements are generally MARKED-TO-MARKET daily via the lending party, and MARGIN is called or returned as needed.
- Also known as RESALE, REVERSE, REVERSE REPO.
- See also DOLLAR ROLL, GENERAL COLLATERAL,

GENSAKI, OPEN REPURCHASE AGREEMENT, OVERNIGHT REPO, REVERSE TO MATURITY, SPECIAL, TERM REPURCHASE AGREEMENT.

REVERSE STOCK SPLIT A corporate action that increases the PAR VALUE of a company's COMMON STOCK while reducing the number of shares outstanding. A reverse stock split may be undertaken to improve the optics of the stock price level or reduce the administrative burden of tracking a larger amount of shares and shareholders; although there is no change in the MARKET VALUE of the company, a reverse split is occasionally viewed as a sign of financial weakness.
- See also STOCK SPLIT.

REVERSE TO MATURITY A REVERSE REPURCHASE AGREEMENT with a maturity equal to the maturity of the underlying ASSET being lent; a reverse to maturity often involves collateralization of high COUPON securities that the holder does not want to sell.

REVERSE TYING [COL] A practice where a BANK or INVESTMENT BANK agrees to purchase goods or services from a company in exchange for the company's agreement to award it with lucrative fee-based NEW ISSUE or CORPORATE FINANCE MANDATES. In some jurisdictions the practice is illegal, as it constitutes a violation of fair trading practices.
- See also TYING.

REVERSE W FORMATION See DOUBLE TOP.

REVOLVER [COL] See REVOLVING CREDIT FACILITY.

REVOLVING CREDIT FACILITY A secured or unsecured credit line with a maturity ranging from six months to five-plus years that a borrower can draw down and repay multiple times. A typical facility requires the borrower to pay the lending BANK an annual COMMITMENT FEE on the entire line in order to keep it available for future use; those without a fee may be withdrawn by the lender bank at will. In some instances lending banks require borrowers to repay the facility in full before allowing further draw-downs or renewals (a process known as a CLEANUP CALL).
- Also known as LINE OF CREDIT, REVOLVER.
- See also BANK LINE, COMMITTED FUNDING, EVERGREEN, LOAN COMMITMENT.

REVOLVING UNDERWRITING FACILITY (RUF) A medium-term EURONOTE facility that guarantees the borrower funds through the issuance of NOTES or a draw-down under a credit line. If the TENDER PANEL arranging the RUF on behalf of the issuer is unable to place the notes it supplies funds through a REVOLVING CREDIT FACILITY.
- See also NOTE ISSUANCE FACILITY.

RHO A measure of the change in the value of an OPTION for a change in the RISK-FREE RATE, with all other variables held constant. The rhos of the CALL OPTION and PUT OPTION under the BLACK-SCHOLES MODEL are given by:

$$\rho_c = t\,X\,e^{-r_f t}\,N(d_2)$$

$$\rho_p = t\,X\,e^{-r_f t}\,N(-d_2)$$

where

$$d_2 = \frac{\ln\left(\frac{S}{X}\right) + \left(r_f - \frac{\sigma^2}{2}\right)t}{\sigma\sqrt{t}}$$

S is the stock price, X is the STRIKE PRICE, t is the time to maturity, r_f is the risk-free rate, σ^2 is the VARIANCE, and where the N value of $N(d_2)$ can be obtained from a standard table of probability functions.

The rhos of LONG and SHORT puts and calls are shown as:

	Long call	Long put	Short call	Short put
Rho	+	–	+	–

■ See also DELTA, GAMMA, GREEKS, VEGA, THETA.

RICH [COL] An ASSET that is perceived by market participants to be expensive compared with alternatives (i.e., the SPREAD is too narrow in the case of a risky BOND or the price too high in the case of a COMMON STOCK, currency, or commodity). Those believing the asset is rich will seek to profit by selling it, either directly or through an ARBITRAGE trade.

■ See also CHEAP.

RIDER An ENDORSEMENT to an INSURANCE policy that modifies the provisions of coverage. The terms contained in the rider supersede those contained in the original policy.

RIDING THE CURVE [COL] See ROLLING DOWN THE CURVE.

RIGHT OF SUBSTITUTION The legal ability for a borrower and/or lender to replace COLLATERAL securing a financial transaction with other ASSETS that feature at least the same minimum value and marketability.

RIGHTS ISSUE An offer of new COMMON STOCK to existing shareholders at a discount to the company's current stock price, in an amount proportional to existing holdings; rights that are not exercised or sold to other investors may be taken up by an UNDERWRITING group through a STANDBY COMMITMENT. A rights issue must be arranged if new EQUITY is sought, unless a company has already arranged for a PRE-EMPTIVE WAIVER OF RIGHTS.

- Also known as **PRIVILEGED SUBSCRIPTION ISSUE, RIGHTS OFFERING, SUBSCRIPTION RIGHTS**.
- See also **SUBSCRIPTION WARRANT**.

RIGHTS OFFERING See RIGHTS ISSUE.

RIO TRADE [COL] A large trade executed in an attempt to reverse losses on existing positions; so named as if the strategy fails the trader may be tempted to flee, e.g. take the next plane to Rio.

RISING BOTTOM A TECHNICAL ANALYSIS charting figure of a security or index depicting rising prices and an increasing support level; a rising bottom is generally considered to be a bullish signal.

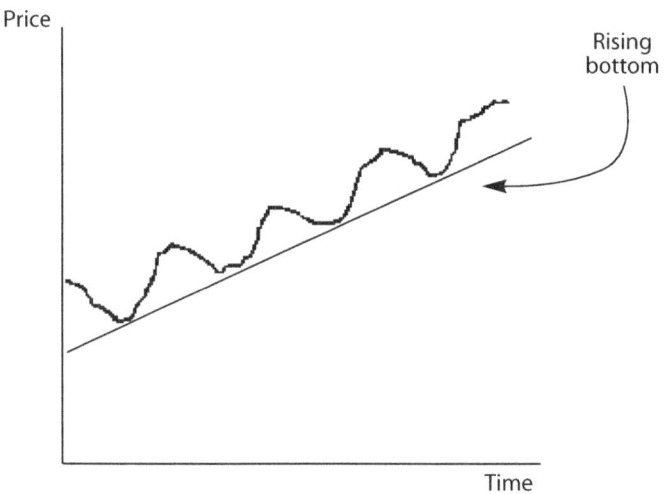

- See also **ASCENDING TOP, DESCENDING BOTTOM, FALLING TOP**.

RISK Uncertainty or unpredictability associated with a future outcome or event. From a corporate and financial perspective, risk can be broadly divided into SPECULATIVE RISK and PURE RISK, and may also be classed as FINANCIAL RISK and OPERATING RISK.

RISK-ADJUSTED CAPITAL ECONOMIC CAPITAL, calibrated for specific dimensions of FINANCIAL RISK and/or OPERATING RISK, which a company allocates internally to support unexpected losses. Riskier activities attract a greater amount of capital since they have the potential of generating larger financial losses; speculative risks that a company assumes or preserves for profit reasons must therefore generate a greater return than those that are less risky. Risk-adjusted capital is often estimated by applying a risk weighting to a class of exposure and then ensuring a minimum level of capital is kept against the risk-weighted exposure at all times.

- See also REGULATORY CAPITAL, RISK-ADJUSTED RETURN ON CAPITAL.

RISK-ADJUSTED RETURN ON CAPITAL (RAROC) The return earned on CAPITAL after adjustments for the effects of FINANCIAL RISK and/or OPERATING RISK. By risk-adjusting returns on CAPITAL, the true costs/earnings of risk can be properly compared. RAROC can be computed via:

$$RAROC = \frac{NI_n}{RAEq_n}$$

where NI_n is net income in period n and $RAEq_n$ is the RISK-ADJUSTED CAPITAL allocated in support of the income producing business in period n. An alternative computation adjusts the returns for riskiness and leaves capital unadjusted.

RISK ARBITRAGE A position taken in a COMMON STOCK, or group of stocks, based on perceived profit opportunities related to a MERGER, ACQUISITION, HOSTILE TAKEOVER, RECAPITALIZATION, SPIN-OFF or other CORPORATE FINANCE transaction. The risk ARBITRAGEUR analyzes possible positive and negative outcomes from a proposed transaction and attempts to profit by establishing LONG or SHORT POSITIONS on a proprietary basis.

RISK AVERSION A characteristic of an individual or institution that prefers less, rather than more, RISK, and is willing to pay a price or accept a lower return for protection/mitigation (through, for example, INSURANCE, DERIVATIVES, or other methods of RISK TRANSFER or HEDGING).

RISK CAPACITY The ability for an institution to accept the transfer of RISK from another party. Risk capacity is generally based on an institution's financial resources, expertise, and operating mandate.

RISK CAPITAL The amount of ECONOMIC CAPITAL financial institutions require in order to support RISK-related activities, such as TRADING, lending, and UNDERWRITING. Risk capital may be allocated through internal processes and/or regulatory measures. For BANKS, risk capital is generally set as a percentage of the exposures arising from MARKET RISK and CREDIT RISK. For SECURITIES FIRMS net capital is allocated primarily against open market risks. For INSURERS risk capital is held in support of net INSURANCE written.
- See also REGULATORY CAPITAL, RISK-ADJUSTED RETURN ON CAPITAL.

RISK EQUIVALENT EXPOSURE See POTENTIAL EXPOSURE.

RISK FINANCING The general class of RISK MANAGEMENT products and mechanisms that seeks primarily to shift the timing of RISK-related losses rather than their permanent transfer to a third

party; an institution engaged in risk financing simply delays funding of losses until a future period.
- See also FINITE INSURANCE CONTRACT, FINITE REINSURANCE.

RISK-FREE RATE The DEFAULT-free BENCHMARK INTEREST RATE accorded to sovereign nations with the strongest CREDIT RATINGS. The risk-free rate is often used as the base reference rate for the pricing of credit-risky LOANS, BONDS, and DERIVATIVES.
- See also DISCOUNT RATE, RISK PREMIUM.

RISK IDENTIFICATION The first stage of the RISK MANAGEMENT PROCESS, where a firm defines its actual, perceived, or anticipated FINANCIAL RISKS and OPERATING RISKS.
- See also RISK MANAGEMENT, RISK MONITORING, RISK QUANTIFICATION.

RISK MANAGEMENT The third stage of the RISK MANAGEMENT PROCESS, where a firm decides whether to control, retain, eliminate, or expand its FINANCIAL RISKS and OPERATING RISKS. This process may be guided by cost–benefit analysis, available financial resources, and corporate operating directives.
- See also RISK IDENTIFICATION, RISK MONITORING, RISK QUANTIFICATION.

RISK MANAGEMENT PROCESS A four-stage process centered on identifying, quantifying, managing, and monitoring FINANCIAL RISK and OPERATING RISK.
- See also RISK IDENTIFICATION, RISK MANAGEMENT, RISK MONITORING, RISK QUANTIFICATION.

RISK MANAGEMENT TECHNIQUES A broad group of methods, including LOSS CONTROL, LOSS FINANCING, and RISK REDUCTION, which companies and sovereign entities often use to manage FINANCIAL RISKS and OPERATING RISKS.

RISK MARGIN See RISK PREMIUM.

RISK MONITORING The fourth stage of the RISK MANAGEMENT PROCESS, where a firm tracks and reports its RISK exposures and communicates them to internal and external STAKEHOLDERS.
- See also RISK IDENTIFICATION, RISK MANAGEMENT, RISK QUANTIFICATION.

RISK PHILOSOPHY A formal expression of a firm's view on RISK, including its corporate goals related to risk, the focus of its risk activities, and STAKEHOLDER expectations regarding risk activities.
- See also RISK TOLERANCE.

RISK POOLING A practical implementation of DIVERSIFICATION, and a fundamental mechanism of the RISK MANAGEMENT markets and the INSURANCE mechanism, based on the concept that inde-

pendent (i.e., uncorrelated) risks can be combined to reduce the overall level of risk.
- Also known as POOLING.

RISK PREMIUM (1) A payment made by a RISK-averse firm to a third party to secure ex-ante protection against financial loss from a specific risk exposure. (2) The margin added to the RISK-FREE RATE to compensate for the risk of DEFAULT; the sum of the two yields the DISCOUNT RATE, or the total rate used to discount the value of future risky cash flows.
- (2) Also known as RISK MARGIN.
- (1) See also PREMIUM.

RISK QUANTIFICATION The second stage of the RISK MANAGEMENT PROCESS, where a firm uses mathematical, statistical, or actuarial techniques to estimate the economic impact of FINANCIAL RISKS and OPERATING RISKS on its operations.
- See also RISK IDENTIFICATION, RISK MANAGEMENT, RISK MONITORING.

RISK REDUCTION A RISK MANAGEMENT TECHNIQUE based on either withdrawal from a business with particular RISK characteristics or DIVERSIFICATION of exposures through RISK POOLING. The intent in either case is to reduce the overall level of FINANCIAL RISK and/or OPERATING RISK to a level consistent with a firm's RISK TOLERANCE.
- See also LOSS CONTROL, LOSS FINANCING.

RISK RETENTION A LOSS FINANCING technique where a company chooses to preserve, rather than transfer or hedge, a portion of its FINANCIAL RISK and/or OPERATING RISK.
- See also HEDGING, RETENTION, RISK RETENTION GROUP, RISK TRANSFER, SELF-INSURANCE.

RISK RETENTION GROUP A RETENTION vehicle, conceptually similar to a GROUP CAPTIVE, where several companies with similar RISKS combine and then spread their exposures via RISK POOLING.

RISK TOLERANCE A quantitative expression of a firm's view on RISK, generally based on the amount it is willing to lose through exposure to FINANCIAL RISK and/or OPERATING RISK, the amount it can earn in assuming or preserving risk or must pay to transfer it, and the financial resources it has at its disposal to support risky activities.
- See also RISK PHILOSOPHY.

RISK TRANSFER A LOSS FINANCING technique where one party shifts an exposure to another party, paying a small, certain cost (such as a PREMIUM or fee) in exchange for coverage of uncertain losses. A standard INSURANCE contract is a common risk transfer mechanism.

- See also RISK RETENTION, HEDGING.

ROA See RETURN ON ASSETS.

ROADSHOW [COL] A series of sales and marketing presentations held for institutional investors by a company or sovereign entity preparing to launch a NEW ISSUE of securities; the focus of such meetings is on the issuer's financial standing and prospects, and on a general review of the planned new issue. Roadshows are typically arranged and managed by the LEAD MANAGER and/or other institutions forming part of the SYNDICATE.
- Also known as DOG AND PONY SHOW.

ROE See RETURN ON EQUITY.

ROI See RETURN ON INVESTMENT.

ROLL DOWN The process of exchanging one OPTION position for a new one with a lower STRIKE PRICE by closing out the original position.
- See also ROLL FORWARD, ROLL UP.

ROLL FORWARD The process of exchanging one OPTION position for a new one with a longer maturity date by closing out the original position.
- See also ROLL DOWN, ROLL UP.

ROLL UP The process of exchanging one OPTION position for a new one with a higher STRIKE PRICE by closing out the original position.
- See also ROLL DOWN, ROLL FORWARD.

ROLLER COASTER [COL] See VARIABLE PRINCIPAL SWAP.

ROLLING DOWN THE CURVE [COL] An investment strategy involving the purchase, and hold, of long-term BONDS in anticipation of capital gains as YIELDS decline.
- Also known as RIDING THE CURVE.

ROLLING HEDGE A HEDGING strategy, generally applied to long-term RISK exposures, that requires the hedger to purchase or sell the NEARBY or NEXT NEARBY DERIVATIVE contract, close it out prior to maturity, re-establish it with the next contract, and so forth, until the final exposure being protected enters the LIQUID part of the market. Through this process the hedger effectively stacks, and then "rolls," the hedge from one contract to the next. Though the strategy reduces or eliminates DIRECTIONAL RISK, it creates CURVE RISK: if the near term FUTURES price is below the expiring contract price (e.g., the market is in BACKWARDATION), stacking and rolling is profitable, otherwise it is unprofitable.
- Also known as a STACK AND ROLL.
- See also STRIP HEDGE.

ROLLOVER (1) The process of renewing or reissuing a REPURCHASE AGREEMENT, REVOLVING CREDIT FACILITY, EVERGREEN,

DEPOSIT, COMMERCIAL PAPER, ACCOUNT PAYABLE, or NOTE coming due. The rollover provides the debtor with continued funding and the investor/creditor with continued returns. (2) The simultaneous sale and purchase of foreign exchange for one-day settlement, as in a SPOT NEXT or TOM NEXT transaction.

ROUND LOT A securities ORDER executed in the standard TRADING size associated with the security marketplace. Round lots typically carry lower commissions or fees than small size ODD LOTS.

ROUND TRIP [COL] The purchase and sale of a security or EXCHANGE-TRADED DERIVATIVE, generally over a short period of time.

RPI See RETAIL PRICE INDEX.

RUF See REVOLVING UNDERWRITING FACILITY.

RULE 144A In the United States, a SECURITIES AND EXCHANGE COMMISSION SAFE HARBOR allowing limited resale of securities that have not been registered (e.g., PRIVATE PLACEMENTS) among QUALIFIED INSTITUTIONAL BUYERS (QIB) and DEALERS, provided the maximum number of QIBs and the minimum size of their participation are specified in the selling documents or private placement agreement. Rule 144A is designed to create LIQUIDITY in securities that otherwise have limited marketability.

RULE 415 REGISTRATION See SHELF REGISTRATION.

RUN-OFF Future CLAIMS that an INSURER expects to pay and which are already covered by RESERVES.

RUNNING YIELD See FLAT YIELD.

S

S&L See SAVINGS AND LOAN ASSOCIATION.

S&P 500 See STANDARD AND POOR'S 500.

SAFE HARBOR RULE [COL] A provision in law or regulation that permits a company to avoid LIABILITY if it is attempting to comply with rules in good faith. Various financial safe harbors exist, such as: the repurchase of TREASURY STOCK is permissible under rules that normally prohibit a company from repurchasing its own securities; the disposal of COLLATERAL upon DEFAULT by a COUNTERPARTY to a DERIVATIVE contract (or REPURCHASE AGREEMENT) is allowed under AUTOMATIC STAY rules that normally forbid disposal; the limited resale of securities that have not been registered is permissible under rules that otherwise ban such sales.

SALE AND LEASEBACK A transaction involving the sale of a real ASSET by one party and an agreement to LEASE the same asset back from the acquirer on a long-term basis. The sale and leaseback allows the seller/LESSEE to inject LIQUIDITY into its balance sheet and the acquirer/LESSOR to obtain the tax and financial benefits generated by the lease.

SAME DAY FUNDS Funds that can be transferred or withdrawn on the same business day they are presented or collected, such as FEDERAL FUNDS transmitted via the FED WIRE or electronic transfers arranged via the CLEARINGHOUSE INTERBANK PAYMENTS SYSTEM or CLEARINGHOUSE AUTOMATED PAYMENT SYSTEM.

SAMURAI [JPN, COL] A BOND, NOTE, or CERTIFICATE OF DEPOSIT issued in Japanese yen in the Japanese markets by a foreign company.

■ See also DAIMYO, GEISHA, SHIBOSAI, SHOGUN.

SATURDAY NIGHT SPECIAL [COL] A sudden TAKEOVER attempt

by one company for another through a rapid and unexpected TENDER OFFER.
- See also DAWN RAID, PREMIUM RAID.

SAVINGS AND LOAN (S&L) ASSOCIATION In the United States, a state or federally chartered DEPOSITORY institution that is primarily involved in accepting retail DEPOSITS and granting residential MORTGAGES. Although S&Ls can also engage in certain commercial banking LOAN transactions, most retain their traditional retail focus.
- Also known as THRIFT.
- See also BUILDING SOCIETY.

SCALPER [COL] (1) A MARKET MAKER or DEALER that charges an excessive SPREAD on a transaction, in contravention of established rules. (2) An INVESTMENT ADVISOR or BROKER that takes a position in an investment before advising clients to do so, and then exits at a profit; such pre-positioning is illegal in certain national systems.

SCENARIO ANALYSIS Hypothetical "what if" computations that reveal the profit or loss impact from any RISK exposures that are subject to a particular market shock, such as a movement in FOREIGN EXCHANGE RATES, a shift in a YIELD CURVE, or a change in VOLATILITY or CREDIT SPREADS. Scenarios are widely used by financial institutions to understand how PORTFOLIOS of MARKET RISKS or CREDIT RISKS react under various low-probability/high-severity stress situations. The most extreme scenarios ignore any benefits obtained from DIVERSIFICATION and can be computed through techniques such as MAXIMUM LOSS.
- Also known as STRESS TESTING.

SCHEDULE RATING A pricing method for INSURANCE that involves modification of a general PREMIUM rate class based on the specific characteristics of the coverage; the adjustment is typically based on charges or credits to a base premium.
- See also EXPERIENCE RATING.

SCHULDSCHEIN [GER] Abbreviated form of Schuldscheindarlehen, or German certificates of indebtedness. Schuldschein represent transferable interests in LOANS between borrowers and lending BANKS; the certificates allow loan interests to be transferred to other investors, creating a certain amount of secondary LIQUIDITY in the contracts.

SCORCHED EARTH DEFENSES [COL] ANTI-TAKEOVER DEFENSES designed to create a significant amount of "corporate destruction" if enacted. A company using scorched earth techniques may convey their existence to would-be acquirers in order to dissuade any potential action.
- See also CROWN JEWEL DEFENSE, DEAD HAND CLAUSE,

LOBSTER TRAP, MACARONI DEFENSE, PAC MAN DEFENSE, POISON PILL.

SCRIP (1) Physical CAPITAL certificates with value, such as a COMMON STOCK certificate or BEARER BOND certificate. (2) Temporary certificates issued for a STOCK SPLIT or a SPIN-OFF that can be used to purchase underlying shares of common stock.

SDR See SPECIAL DRAWING RIGHTS.

SEASONED SECURITY A financial instrument that has been outstanding in the SECONDARY MARKET for a period of at least several months and has a history of prices and volume. The established track record often makes seasoned securities more marketable than newly issued securities that have just completed the PRIMARY MARKET process.

SEAT [COL] A transferable membership on the NEW YORK STOCK EXCHANGE, generally held by an individual (acting for his/her own account or as an officer, partner, or representative of a BANK, INVESTMENT BANK, SECURITIES FIRM, or BROKER/DEALER), which permits dealing on the floor of the EXCHANGE and voting on exchange business matters. Through the millennium the exchange featured more than 1300 seats.

SEC See SECURITIES AND EXCHANGE COMMISSION.

SECONDARY DISTRIBUTION A resale of existing securities on behalf of an existing investor, generally arranged by a BANK or SECURITIES FIRM; the seller, rather than the buyer, is obliged to pay commissions for the redistribution. If the transaction involves COMMON STOCK, no new equity is created and no DILUTION occurs; if it involves DEBT, no new LEVERAGE is added to the issuer's balance sheet.

SECONDARY MARKET The general marketplace for buying and selling a security or ASSET that has already been issued or created. The secondary market for any particular contract varies by level of participation, VOLATILITY, regulation, and market need; some markets are extremely active and LIQUID, while others are ILLIQUID, trading only infrequently.
- Also known as AFTERMARKET.
- See also GRAY MARKET, PRIMARY MARKET, SEASONED SECURITY.

SECONDARY OFFERING Any NEW ISSUE of securities that occurs after an issuer's inaugural PRIMARY OFFERING.
- See also ADD-ON.

SECONDARY PREFERRED STOCK PREFERRED STOCK that is subordinate to an issuer's other preferred stock, including PRIOR PREFERRED STOCK. Such issues, which rank just above COMMON STOCK in seniority, are relatively rare.

SECONDARY RESERVES RESERVES in excess of those that financial institutions are required to hold for regulatory reasons. Secondary reserves are often used as an emergency buffer to meet unexpected obligations; accordingly, they are generally held in the form of very LIQUID, low-RISK securities that can be converted into cash very quickly.

SECTOR OPTION An OVER-THE-COUNTER or EXCHANGE-traded OPTION that references the price or VOLATILITY of an entire industrial or regional sector (e.g. banks, automobile manufacturers, technology companies, emerging markets). Although the sector contract provides DIVERSIFICATION among individual COMMON STOCKS, it still creates a concentration in a broad group.

SECURED DEBT A BOND or LOAN that is collateralized by a CLAIM on the ASSETS of the borrower/issuer. Secured debt holders rank above all other claimholders in the event the borrower/issuer DEFAULTS.
- See also SENIOR DEBT, SUBORDINATED DEBT.

SECURED INTEREST A legal CLAIM of the lender over ASSETS pledged by a borrower to secure an obligation. The security interest grants priority over unsecured creditors and provides the right of FORECLOSURE in the event of DEFAULT.
- Also known as LIEN.
- See also FLOATING LIEN.

SECURITIES AND EXCHANGE COMMISSION (SEC) A US Federal agency created in 1934 that is responsible for regulatory matters related to the public securities markets, including REGISTRATION, issuance, and TRADING of BONDS and EQUITY, oversight of intermediaries participating in the markets, and protection of investors.

SECURITIES FIRM A financial institution that is involved in originating and issuing new DEBT and EQUITY issues, TRADING securities and other financial instruments, and executing trades on behalf of clients. Securities firms that also deal in the broadest range of CORPORATE FINANCE transactions are more appropriately considered INVESTMENT BANKS. Unlike BANKS, securities firms in most countries do not have the benefit of a formal LENDER OF LAST RESORT in the event of a LIQUIDITY crisis.

SECURITIZATION The process of repackaging ASSETS, LIABILITIES, or CASH FLOWS into tradable securities. By selling contracts or cash flows into a securitization CONDUIT, an institution liquefies its balance sheet and transfers RISK exposures. Securitizations are often based on MORTGAGES (MORTGAGE-BACKED SECURITIES), mortgage-backed securities (COLLATERALIZED MORTGAGE OBLIGATIONS), corporate BONDS (COLLATERALIZED

BOND OBLIGATIONS), corporate LOANS (COLLATERALIZED LOAN OBLIGATIONS), ACCOUNTS RECEIVABLE (ASSET-BACKED SECURITIES), and INSURANCE risks (INSURANCE-LINKED SECURITIES).

SECURITY MARKET LINE A financial relationship linking the return and the NON-DIVERSIFIABLE RISK of a LEVERAGED security. The security market line depicts portfolios that maximize return for a given level of borrowing and RISK (reflected through BETA). The expected return is given as:

$$E(r_j) = r_f + \beta_j \lfloor E(r_m) - r_f \rfloor$$

where $E(r_j)$ is the expected return for security j, $E(r_m)$ is the expected return for the market portfolio, r_f is the RISK-FREE RATE, and β_j is the beta of security j.

■ See also ARBITRAGE PRICING THEORY, CAPITAL ASSET PRICING MODEL.

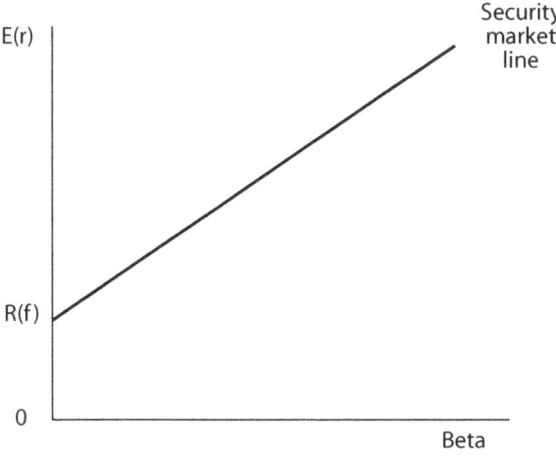

■ Additional references: Jensen (1972), Merton (1973), Roll (1977), Ross (1976).

SELF-FUNDING See SELF-INSURANCE.

SELF-INSURANCE A method of RISK RETENTION where an institution preserves particular types and amounts of RISK and finances EXPECTED LOSSES by creating an internal fund or establishing a CAPTIVE. Self-insurance is generally applied to exposures that are highly predictable and non-catastrophic, or which cannot be covered by traditional INSURANCE contracts as a result of excessive cost.

■ Also known as SELF-FUNDING.

SELF-INSURANCE RETENTION See DEDUCTIBLE.

SELF-LIQUIDATING LOAN A secured or unsecured WORKING

CAPITAL LOAN that is repaid through the sale of the INVENTORY being financed; self-liquidating loans are generally used to finance inventories used to meet seasonal demand for products.
- Also known as ASSET CONVERSION LOAN.

SELF-REGULATORY ORGANIZATION (SRO) An organization that is granted oversight powers by regulators in order to manage daily business affairs. An SRO establishes its own oversight guidelines based on overarching external regulations, approves the admittance of new participants, and supervises the activities of those already active in the marketplace. Many major STOCK and FUTURES EXCHANGE operate as SROs; they are typically divided into separate units, including one to deal with commercial business and the other to ensure that the business unit complies with all relevant rules.

SELF-TENDER A STOCK BUYBACK arranged by a company based on regular open market purchases that increases the TREASURY STOCK CONTRA ACCOUNT and reduces the EQUITY account. A self-tender might be used when a company believes it periodically has excess capital that is not generating an adequate return for shareholders.

SELL DOWN The process of reducing exposure on a new LOAN or BOND, through SYNDICATIONS, participations and sub-UNDERWRITINGS; the sell-down process generally applies to financial intermediaries that are not part of the original SYNDICATE or UNDERWRITING GROUP.

SELL PLUS ORDER An ORDER to execute a securities sale only if the price is higher than the preceding trade.

SELL THE BOOK ORDER An ORDER to sell as much of a current position as possible at the prevailing market price.

SELLER'S OPTION A transaction where the seller of securities has the OPTION to deliver a security at a future time, generally 6 to 60 days after trade date.

SELLING AWAY [COL] An illegal practice where a BROKER at a SECURITIES FIRM or BROKER/DEALER sells clients financial products originated by another securities firm. In the event of problems or losses, clients may not have RECOURSE to the broker's employing firm.

SELLING CONCESSION The discount at which a NEW ISSUE is allocated to SYNDICATE members. The selling concession comprises approximately half the UNDERWRITING SPREAD, or the difference between the price paid to the issuer and the public offering price.

SELLING GROUP See SYNDICATE.

SELLOUT The process of liquidating a MARGIN LOAN or EXCHANGE-TRADED DERIVATIVE when payment is not received for securities or a VARIATION MARGIN call is not met. Sellout leads to *de facto* cancellation of the underlying loan or derivative contract.

SENIOR CAPTIVE A CAPTIVE that functions as an expanded form of the PURE CAPTIVE, writing a sufficiently large amount of third party business that it is generally entitled to greater tax benefits than the pure captive.
- See also AGENCY CAPTIVE, GROUP CAPTIVE, PROTECTED CELL COMPANY, RENT-A-CAPTIVE, SISTER CAPTIVE.

SENIOR DEBT An unsecured BOND or LOAN that ranks higher in CLAIM priority than SUBORDINATED DEBT, but lower than SECURED DEBT.
- Also known as SENIOR UNSECURED DEBT.

SENIOR UNSECURED DEBT See SENIOR DEBT.

SEQUENTIAL PAY BOND A standard COLLATERALIZED MORTGAGE OBLIGATION that pays investors CASH FLOWS from the underlying MORTGAGE-BACKED SECURITIES in strict sequence. Subordinated TRANCHES only receive payments once senior tranches have been paid.
- See also PLANNED AMORTIZATION CLASS BOND, TARGETED AMORTIZATION CLASS BOND.

SERIAL BOND One of a group of BONDS issued by a single company or municipality that matures over a period of successive years.
- See also SERIES BOND.

SERIES BOND One of a group of BONDS issued by a single company or municipality under the same INDENTURE. Each bond in the series may have a unique COUPON and maturity.
- See also SERIAL BOND.

SERVICING The process of collecting PRINCIPAL and interest on LOANS generally, and MORTGAGES specifically. The function is generally performed by a financial institution acting as a TRUSTEE or servicing AGENT. In the mortgage sector the originator of the loan may retain the servicing rights, charging a fee for performing the function, or it may sell the rights to a third party.

SET-OFF A NETTING arrangement where an institution and a COUNTERPARTY in DEFAULT agree to terminate all transactions and net payments due or owed under all existing contracts.
- See also NOVATION, PAYMENT NETTING.

SETTLEMENT (1) A process where two contracting parties complete an exchange of cash for securities, or one currency for a second currency. When settlement is complete, a process that may take several hours to several days for standard financial contracts, the transaction is considered to be concluded. (2) In INSURANCE, the disposition of a CLAIM made by an INSURED under a policy, generally based on the degree of loss and the nature of the coverage.
- (1) See also SETTLEMENT RISK, VALUE DATE.

SETTLEMENT DATE See VALUE DATE.

SETTLEMENT RISK The RISK of loss arising from failure by one party to a contract to receive cash or ASSETS after it has already delivered assets or cash to a second party. Settlement risk is common in the FOREIGN EXCHANGE and international securities markets, where time zone differences and local SETTLEMENT practices can lead to payment and receipt gaps of hours, days, or weeks. A sub-category of CREDIT RISK.
- Also known as CLEAN RISK, DELIVERY RISK.
- See also CONTINGENT CREDIT RISK, CORRELATED CREDIT RISK, DAYLIGHT RISK, DIRECT CREDIT RISK, SOVEREIGN RISK, TRADING CREDIT RISK.

SEVERABILITY CLAUSE A COVENANT in a DIRECTOR AND OFFICERS' LIABILITY INSURANCE policy that permits the INSURER to avoid making a SETTLEMENT payment if a DIRECTOR is found to have committed FRAUD; however, it must still pay legal fees and any judgments against all remaining directors.

SEVERAL BUT NOT JOINT A legal condition where each party to a transaction is liable only for its part of the process and not all others; several but not joint LIABILITY is commonly used in the UNDERWRITING of BONDS, where each SYNDICATE member is only responsible for distributing the portion of bonds it has been allocated.
- See also JOINT AND SEVERAL.

SEVERITY RATE A measure of the expected or potential size of a loss, used by INSURERS to compute appropriate PREMIUM rates.

SHADOW CALENDAR [COL] A listing of NEW ISSUES of securities that are currently in REGISTRATION with a securities commissioner or regulator but have no firm offering date.
- See also PIPELINE.

SHADOW STOCK [COL] See PHANTOM STOCK.

SHARK REPELLENT [COL] See ANTI-TAKEOVER DEFENSE.

SHARPE INDEX A measure of RISK-adjusted PORTFOLIO performance that compares the RISK PREMIUM (or return) of the portfolio with its risk (as measured through STANDARD DEVIATION). The Sharpe index, which uses the CAPITAL MARKETS LINE as a BENCHMARK, can be computed via:

$$SI = \frac{E(r_P) - r_f}{\sigma(r_P)}$$

where $E(r_P)$ is the expected return of the portfolio, r_f is the risk-free rate, and $\sigma(r_P)$ is the standard deviation of the portfolio.

In general, the higher the ratio, the better the investment strategy on a risk–return basis.

- Also known as SHARPE RATIO.
- See also TREYNOR INDEX, JENSEN INDEX.
- Additional reference: Sharpe (1966).

SHARPE RATIO See SHARPE INDEX.

SHELF REGISTRATION A SECURITIES AND EXCHANGE COMMISSION rule that only requires issuers to file securities registrations once every two years; this allows registration in advance for future issues of BONDS, COMMON STOCK, or PREFERRED STOCK. Once the shelf registration is filed, subsequent issuance need only be accompanied by a small amount of updated investor disclosure, allowing launch to occur at very short notice.
- Also known as RULE 415 REGISTRATION.

SHIBOSAI [JPN] A PRIVATE PLACEMENT denominated in Japanese yen, issued by a foreign company in Japan.
- See also DAIMYO, GEISHA, SAMURAI, SHOGUN.

SHIKKO YAKUIN [JPN] The corporate executive officer under the Japanese SINGLE BOARD SYSTEM, responsible for separating the supervisory and executive duties embedded in the BOARD OF DIRECTORS.

SHOCK LOSS A catastrophic loss that is so severe that an INSURER providing INSURANCE coverage related to the loss may suffer FINANCIAL DISTRESS. In practice insurers protect against shock loss by using REINSURANCE mechanisms and DIVERSIFICATION techniques, and establishing internal limits related to maximum UNDERWRITING exposures.
- See also CLASH LOSS.

SHOE [COL] See GREENSHOE.

SHOGUN [JPN, COL] A BOND, NOTE, or CERTIFICATE OF DEPOSIT issued in a foreign currency in the Japanese markets by a foreign company.
- See also DAIMYO, GEISHA, SAMURAI, SHIBOSAI.

SHOKEN [JPN] A Japanese SECURITIES FIRM.

SHORT See SHORT POSITION.

SHORT AGAINST THE BOX [COL] A practice of borrowing securities from a SECURITIES FIRM or BROKER/DEALER and selling them SHORT in order to protect gains embedded in an offsetting LONG POSITION. From a tax perspective, shorting against the box is generally considered a "constructive sale" that generates a capital gains LIABILITY.

SHORT ARBITRAGE An ARBITRAGE strategy employed in the FUTURES market when the FORWARD RATE is higher than the futures rate, indicating that the cash market is underpriced to the futures market; the strategy calls for buying the UNDERLYING ASSET and selling futures.

- See also LONG ARBITRAGE.

SHORT COUPON A COUPON falling between a normal current coupon period, often associated with the first interest payment on a BOND or NOTE; subsequent coupons generally revert to a normal monthly, semi-annual, or annual cycle.

SHORT END [COL] The short maturities of the YIELD CURVE, generally considered to include those less than three years.
- See also BELLY OF THE CURVE, LONG END.

SHORT HEDGE A SHORT POSITION in a DERIVATIVE contract or financial instrument that is used to protect a natural LONG POSITION. As falling prices create a loss on the natural long position, the short hedge produces an offsetting gain; the reverse occurs with rising prices.
- See also LONG HEDGE.

SHORT INTEREST The amount of securities or ASSETS sold SHORT that have not been repurchased or closed out. In general, the greater the level of short interest, the greater the likelihood that investors are expecting a decline in a security or market; however, a large short interest balance lasting for an extended period of time may also lead to buying pressure as short investors and speculators seek to cover their positions.

SHORT POSITION A borrowed and sold position that benefits from price depreciation. In order to neutralize a short, the position has to be repurchased in the market; if the repurchase price is lower than the initial selling price, a profit results. The economics of the short position must take account of the financing costs associated with borrowing the shorted asset.
- Also known as SHORT.
- See also LONG POSITION, NAKED SHORT, SHORT SALE, SHORT SELLER.

SHORT SALE The sale of a borrowed position that establishes a SHORT POSITION. The party selling short expects that the market price of the ASSET, security, or index sold short will decline.
- See also NAKED SHORTING.

SHORT SELLER An investor, hedger, or speculator that engages in SHORT SALES in order to capitalize on expectations that the price of an ASSET, security, or INDEX will decline.

SHORT SQUEEZE [COL] An attempt by one or more institutions to accumulate a sufficient amount of an ASSET so that higher prices can be demanded from those forced to cover (i.e., repurchase) their SHORT POSITIONS. Short covering exacerbates the situation, as more covering drives up the price of the target security, forcing more covering, and so forth, in a continuous cycle. A sustained short squeeze

generally only works with assets that have unique characteristics and/or low TRADING volume.
- See also BEAR TRAP.

SHORT TENDER The process of using borrowed COMMON STOCK to fulfill the terms of a TENDER OFFER.

SHOUT OPTION An OVER-THE-COUNTER COMPLEX OPTION that allows the buyer to locks in any gains when a "shout" is declared (i.e., the buyer formally declares its intention to lock in); gains are not lost if the market subsequently retraces.
- See also CLIQUET OPTION, FIXED STRIKE SHOUT OPTION, FLOATING STRIKE SHOUT OPTION, LADDER OPTION.

SIGHT DRAFT A BILL OF EXCHANGE, DRAFT, or NEGOTIABLE INSTRUMENT that is payable to the holder upon presentation.

SIMPLE BREAKEVEN A measure of the number of years it takes for the YIELD ADVANTAGE of a CONVERTIBLE BOND to cover the initial CONVERSION PREMIUM paid by the bond investor in acquiring the bond, typically computed as:

$$SBE = \frac{Conv_{prem}}{YA}$$

where $Conv_{prem}$ is the conversion premium and YA is the yield advantage.
- See also ADJUSTED BREAKEVEN, EQUIVALENT BREAKEVEN.

SIMPLE YIELD A method of computing the annual YIELD on a BOND, commonly used in the JAPANESE GOVERNMENT BOND market. The standard form of the calculation is:

$$SY = \frac{C + \left[\frac{Par - P}{t}\right]}{P}$$

where C is the annual COUPON, Par is the PAR VALUE of the bond, P is the price of the bond, and t is the number of years until maturity.
- See also BOND EQUIVALENT YIELD, CURRENT YIELD, DISCOUNT YIELD, TAXABLE EQUIVALENT YIELD, YIELD TO CALL, YIELD TO MATURITY.

SIMULATION A statistical process used to estimate the possible price paths of ASSETS over future periods by assuming that prices move randomly over time, but that possible values can be defined in terms of a particular distribution with known MEAN and VARIANCE and associated CONFIDENCE LEVELS. Possible future moves can then be used to value contracts and PORTFOLIOS with dynamic characteristics. Simulation is widely used in SCENARIO ANALYSIS and computation of DERIVATIVE prices and RISKS.

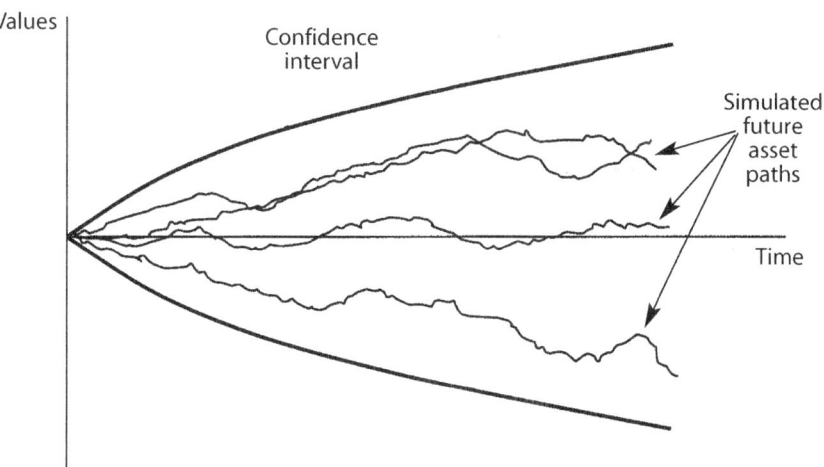

■ See also SIMULATION METHOD.

SIMULATION METHOD A process of estimating the FRACTIONAL EXPOSURE of an INTEREST RATE SWAP through the SIMULATION of future INTEREST RATES. Given a predefined statistical distribution, CONFIDENCE LEVELS, starting interest rate, time intervals, and mathematical relationship of future rate movements, a random generation of an artificial future path can be created, with swap REPLACEMENT COSTS calculated at each interval. Thousands of realizations yield a set of discounted swap replacement costs, and the average can be used as a representation of the discounted replacement cost at each time interval during the life of the swap. The sum of average discounted replacement costs generates a percentage risk factor that can be applied to the NOTIONAL PRINCIPAL to obtain the fractional exposure.

■ See also HISTORICAL METHOD, OPTION METHOD.

SIMULTANEOUS PAY BOND See PLANNED AMORTIZATION CLASS (PAC) BOND.

SINGLE BOARD SYSTEM A corporate system where one BOARD OF DIRECTORS oversees and guides the activities of management. DIRECTORS are generally nominated through an internal committee and/or executive management recommendations, and are formally elected by shareholders via PROXY at the ANNUAL GENERAL MEETING. The board is guided by the chairman (who may or may not also be the chief executive) and ranges in size from 10 to 20 directors, though can grow to more than 30 in some systems.

■ See also DUAL BOARD SYSTEM.

SINGLE PARENT CAPTIVE See PURE CAPTIVE.

SINGLE TEXT METHOD A process where existing, and disparate,

INSURANCE contracts are redrafted into a new master policy so that all covered PERILS are included under a single agreement.
- See also ATTACHMENT METHOD.

SINKER [COL] A BOND that contains a SINKING FUND provision in the INDENTURE.

SINKING FUND (1) Funds that are accumulated in a segregated account in order to retire DEBT on a specific schedule. The sinking fund can be satisfied by direct contributions to the account or by redeeming or repurchasing the debt. (2) A SELF-INSURANCE fund that a company establishes to cover RISKS that it chooses to retain.
- (1) See also DOUBLING OPTION, SINKER.

SISTER CAPTIVE A CAPTIVE formed as a licensed INSURER or REINSURER that acts as an extension of the PURE CAPTIVE, writing INSURANCE cover primarily for other companies forming part of the same "economic family," i.e., subsidiaries or affiliates of the parent or holding-company sponsor. A sister captive may or may not receive the benefit of favorable tax treatment, depending on the nature of the economic relationships between group companies and the amount of true third party business that is conducted.
- See also AGENCY CAPTIVE, GROUP CAPTIVE, PROTECTED CELL COMPANY, RENT-A-CAPTIVE, SENIOR CAPTIVE.

SIZE [COL] A large offering of, or position in, securities or other financial ASSETS.

SLEEPING BEAUTY [COL] A company that is a possible TAKEOVER candidate as a result of large cash holdings, undervalued ASSETS, and/or underperforming operations.

SLOW LOAN A LOAN where the borrower has become delinquent on interest and/or PRINCIPAL payments; a slow loan must generally be reclassified as a NON-ACCRUAL LOAN and LOAN LOSS RESERVES must be allocated in anticipation of a possible write-off.

SMALL CAP STOCK The COMMON STOCK of a company with a small MARKET CAPITALIZATION, typically under $1 billion.
- See also ANKLE BITER, LARGE CAP STOCK, MICRO STOCK, MID CAP STOCK.

SNIF See STANDBY NOTE ISSUANCE FACILITY.

SNOWBALLING [COL] A market phase where the activation of STOP ORDERS leads to additional upward or downward market movements, which trigger more stop orders, and so forth, until a significant sequence of stops and market moves have occurred.
- See also GATHER IN THE STOPS.

SOFT CALL PROTECTION A CALL PROTECTION provision in an INDENTURE that prevents the issuer from calling and redeeming an outstanding security unless a certain price has been reached (for a

standard BOND) or the stock price exceeds the CONVERSION PRICE by a defined percentage (for a CONVERTIBLE BOND).
- See also HARD CALL PROTECTION, NON-CALLABLE BOND.

SOFT DOLLARS Indirect reciprocal payments made by clients to financial institutions for services rendered. In commercial banking a client may be required to keep non-interest-bearing COMPENSATING BALANCES with a BANK in exchange for a LOAN; in securities a client may pay higher BROKER commissions in exchange for research and other FIDUCIARY services.
- See also HARD DOLLARS.

SOFT LANDING A stabilization program enacted by a CENTRAL BANK or monetary authority that attempts to avoid economic recession following a period of excess demand and rising INFLATION. A soft landing may be difficult to achieve; if FISCAL POLICY or MONETARY POLICY are too accommodative inflationary pressures will continue, and if they are too restrictive a sharp slowdown will occur before stability can be regained.
- See also HARD LANDING.

SOFT LOAN A LOAN with favorable terms for the borrower, including below-market INTEREST RATES, long repayment periods, and a continual deferral or ROLLOVER of PRINCIPAL. A bank may grant a soft loan in order to win future business, build a client relationship, or achieve some other relationship-driven goal.

SOFT MARKET An INSURANCE market cycle where excess supply of RISK CAPACITY from the insurance sector leads to lower pricing of PREMIUMS. A soft market arises when loss experience of INSURERS

has been favorable for a period of time and insurers are willing to write new cover and expand business; the excess CAPITAL used to cover risks leads to an extremely competitive environment.
- See also HARD MARKET.

SOFTS [COL] A range of perishable commodities and related DERIVATIVES, originally applied to tropical commodities such as coffee, sugar, and cocoa, but now generally taken to also include GRAINS, cotton, and orange juice.

SOLVENCY A normal state of financial operations for a company functioning as a going concern, where the value of ASSETS exceeds the value of LIABILITIES (i.e., positive EQUITY) and all DEBTS and obligations falling due in the normal course of business are paid on a timely basis.
- See also INSOLVENCY.

SOVEREIGN RISK The RISK of loss arising from an action by a sovereign nation, including DEFAULT, MORATORIUM, EXCHANGE CONTROLS, or currency DEVALUATION. A sub-category of CREDIT RISK.
- See also CONTINGENT CREDIT RISK, CORRELATED CREDIT RISK, COUNTRY RISK, DIRECT CREDIT RISK, SETTLEMENT RISK, TRADING CREDIT RISK.

SPARK SPREAD [COL] A SPREAD in the energy market reflecting the price differential between natural gas and electricity; the spread can be traded through a single FUTURE or OPTION contract on certain EXCHANGES. A hedger or speculator can buy the spark spread (e.g., purchase gas and sell electricity) to take advantage of positive margins in generation, and sell the spread (e.g., sell gas and purchase electricity) to profit from negative margins.
- See also CRACK SPREAD.

SPE See SPECIAL PURPOSE ENTITY.

SPECIAL [COL] COLLATERAL in the REPURCHASE AGREEMENT market that is in tight supply, and which therefore allows a repurchase agreement borrower to obtain a lower borrowing rate.
- See also GENERAL COLLATERAL.

SPECIAL DIVIDEND A mechanism that enables a company to return CAPITAL to its shareholders; by granting a one-time DIVIDEND to current investors, it reduces the RETAINED EARNINGS account by the necessary amount. A company may declare a special dividend when it is consistently unable to identify investment or expansion opportunities that can generate an adequate return for investors.
- See also CUTTING THE MELON, STOCK BUYBACK.

SPECIAL DRAWING RIGHT (SDR) A currency introduced in 1970 by the INTERNATIONAL MONETARY FUND to supplement national

RESERVES and maintain FOREIGN EXCHANGE stability. The SDR is a neutral unit of account allocated in proportion to the GROSS DOMESTIC PRODUCT of each country, and is backed by the credit of participating countries. The SDR is convertible into gold and HARD CURRENCIES.

SPECIAL-PURPOSE ENTITY (SPE) An off balance sheet company, often incorporated as a BANKRUPTCY-remote entity in a favorable tax jurisdiction, which is used to arrange SECURITIZATION, financing, DERIVATIVE, and/or tax-related transactions on behalf of the corporate sponsor. In order to avoid CONSOLIDATION into the corporate operation, an SPE may be established as a charitable TRUST that is nominally owned by a third party. To gain the benefits of particular transactions, the corporate sponsor must generally hold a nominal share of the EQUITY.
- Also known as SPECIAL PURPOSE VEHICLE, VARIABLE INTEREST ENTITY.

SPECIAL-PURPOSE VEHICLE (SPV) See SPECIAL-PURPOSE ENTITY.

SPECIAL RISK INSURANCE Customized INSURANCE coverage that is unique and situation-specific, and which cannot be priced through standard actuarial techniques or managed via RISK POOLING. The INSURER UNDERWRITING the special risk policy generally attempts to price the exposure as conservatively as possible and limit the amount underwritten.
- Also known as SPECIFIC INSURANCE.
- See also PUP COMPANY.

SPECIALIST An individual or firm on an EXCHANGE that acts as a MARKET MAKER in a particular COMMON STOCK. The specialist manages an auction book of BIDS and OFFERS and attempts to maintain a balanced and orderly market at all times. Under certain exchange rules a specialist can deal for its own account as a proprietary DEALER but must adhere to AFFIRMATIVE OBLIGATION (i.e., taking one side of a trade if no offsetting ORDER is available in the market) and NEGATIVE OBLIGATION (i.e., not participating in a trade if an order can be matched).

SPECIFIC EXCESS REINSURANCE An EXCESS OF LOSS (XOL) REINSURANCE contract written on a FACULTATIVE basis that provides cover for a PRIMARY INSURER's policy.

SPECIFIC INSURANCE See SPECIAL RISK INSURANCE.

SPECIFIC STOP LOSS INSURANCE An INSURANCE contract that becomes effective when a CLAIM breaches an INSURED's predefined SELF-INSURANCE threshold.

SPECULATION A strategy that involves taking a position in an ASSET

or market through financial instruments (e.g., STOCK, BONDS) or DERIVATIVES in an attempt to generate profits; resulting gains and losses are not offset by underlying exposures/positions, as in a HEDGE transaction.
- See also ARBITRAGE.

SPECULATIVE RISK A RISK exposure that yields the possibility of either a gain or a loss.
- See also PURE RISK.

SPECULATOR An individual or firm engaged in SPECULATION in order to generate profits. Speculators are an essential driver of market LIQUIDITY, helping balance or support flows arising from parties that are engaged in HEDGING or ARBITRAGE.

SPIN-OFF See CARVE-OUT.

SPINNING [COL] An illegal practice where BANKS, INVESTMENT BANKS, or SECURITIES FIRMS UNDERWRITING a NEW ISSUE grant executives of favored corporate clients allocations in an attempt to win future CORPORATE FINANCE business.

SPLIT-COUPON BOND A BOND that functions as a ZERO-COUPON BOND for a pre-specified period of time and then converts into a standard COUPON-bearing instrument, paying interest on a regular basis.

SPOT A transaction in the current, or cash, market.
- See also SPOT MARKET, SPOT PRICE, SPOT RATE.

SPOT MARKET The current, or cash, market for an ASSET.
- Also known as CASH MARKET.
- See also FORWARD MARKET.

SPOT NEXT The purchase of FOREIGN EXCHANGE for delivery the day after SPOT delivery (which is generally two business days after trade date); the delivery price in a spot next deal is adjusted for the extra day.
- See also TOM NEXT.

SPOT PRICE The price of an ASSET in the current, or cash, market.
- Also known as CASH PRICE.
- See also FORWARD PRICE.

SPOT RATE An INTEREST RATE or FOREIGN EXCHANGE RATE in the current, or cash, market.
- Also known as CASH RATE.
- See also FORWARD RATE.

SPREAD (1) In general, two or more financial instruments that are combined to produce an exposure to, or protection against, price or VOLATILITY references. The spread strategy can be applied to COMMON STOCKS, OPTIONS, YIELDS on FIXED INCOME securities, credit references, or cross-market/ASSET classes. (2) In TRADING and MARKET-MAKING, the difference between the BID and

OFFER. (3) In a NEW ISSUE transaction, see UNDERWRITING SPREAD.
- (1) See also BULL SPREAD, BEAR SPREAD. (2) See also EFFECTIVE SPREAD, QUOTED SPREAD, REALIZED SPREAD.

SPREAD LOSS A form of FINITE REINSURANCE where the CEDING INSURER pays a PREMIUM into an EXPERIENCE ACCOUNT every year of a multi-year contract period; the experience account generates an agreed rate and is used to pay losses as they occur. If a deficit arises in the account at the end of any year, the ceding insurer covers the shortfall through an additional contribution; if a surplus results, the reinsurer returns the excess. If the spread loss account is in surplus at the end of the contract, the ceding insurer and reinsurer share profits on a pre-agreed basis.

SPREAD OPTION A COMPLEX OPTION that grants the buyer a payoff based on the difference between two reference ASSETS versus a predefined STRIKE PRICE; the assets may be drawn from similar or different classes/markets.
- Also known as DIFFERENCE OPTION, OUTPERFORMANCE OPTION, UNDERPERFORMANCE OPTION.
- See also MULTI-INDEX OPTION, YIELD CURVE OPTION.

SPREAD RISK The RISK of loss due to adverse changes between two reference ASSETS with a common link, such as a risk-free asset and a risky asset pegged to the risk-free asset. A sub-category of MARKET RISK.

SPREADLOCK A financial contract that guarantees a BOND issuer or an INTEREST-RATE SWAP party a fixed SPREAD over a reference BENCHMARK for a specific period of time prior to issuance or trade execution. The spreadlock ensures that the issuance or execution price will be a function solely of the reference benchmark rather than the CREDIT SPREAD.
- See also DROP LOCK, RATE LOCK.

SPRING LOADING [COL] A form of financial manipulation where the pre-ACQUISITION earnings of a company to be purchased are understated in order to give the acquiring company an earnings boost and the appearance of financial strength following the acquisition.

SPV See SPECIAL PURPOSE VEHICLE.

SQUARE [COL] (1) A RISK position that has been neutralized, i.e., an offset between a LONG and a SHORT POSITION, or a HEDGE and an UNDERLYING ASSET or exposure. (2) The process of neutralizing the risk of a position.

SQUARE ROOT RULE A statistical property used in financial mathematics indicating that the STANDARD DEVIATION of the changes in a market variable, such as a STOCK or BOND price, is proportional to the square root of time.

SQUEEZE [COL] A lack of sufficient acceptable ASSETS deliverable into an EXCHANGE-TRADED DERIVATIVE contract or as cover for a SHORT POSITION, which can lead to price distortions.
- See also SHORT SQUEEZE.

SRO See SELF-REGULATORY ORGANIZATION.

STACK AND ROLL [COL] See ROLLING HEDGE.

STAG [COL] See FLIPPER.

STAGFLATION An economic condition that is characterized by the simultaneous onset of high INFLATION and high unemployment.

STAGGERED BOARD An ANTI-TAKEOVER DEFENSE tactic where an external TENDER OFFER for a company automatically triggers a change in the company's DIRECTOR re-election policy, from annual to staggered (e.g., only a third of directors re-elected every year, so that the entire board can only be replaced over a three-year period). This means a suitor will be unable to engage in a PROXY CONTEST to remove the board and undo POISON PILLS or other defenses within a one-year time frame.

STAGS Acronym for Sterling Transfer Accruing Government Security, a STRIP security in the UK GILT marketplace.

STAKEHOLDERS From a GOVERNANCE perspective, the group of parties that have a legal, financial, and/or social interest in a company and its success, and are impacted directly or indirectly by the actions a company takes.
- See also DIRECT STAKEHOLDERS, INDIRECT STAKEHOLDERS.

STAMP DUTY A tax levied by authorities on specific types of financial transactions. The duty may be applied to an issuer of securities in the PRIMARY MARKET, a buyer and/or seller of securities in the SECONDARY MARKET, or a borrower of funds through a LOAN or other credit mechanism.

STANDARD AND POOR'S 500 (S&P 500) A BENCHMARK index of the US stock market, comprised of 500 LARGE CAP STOCKS representing the industrial, transportation, financial, and utility sectors; the index is rebalanced periodically as industries and corporate leadership change. The S&P500 can be traded directly through EXCHANGE-TRADED FUNDS and DERIVATIVES.

STANDARD DEVIATION A measure of RISK, variability, or dispersion that indicates the magnitude by which an outcome will differ from the EXPECTED VALUE, or the degree to which an observation deviates from the MEAN of a distribution. It is generally computed via:

$$\sigma = \sqrt{\frac{\sum_{i=1}^{N}(x_i - \mu)^2}{N}}$$

where x_i is an observation, μ is the mean, and N is the number of observations.
- See also VARIANCE.

STANDARD RISK See PURE RISK.

STANDBY AGREEMENT An agreement where the UNDERWRITERS of a RIGHTS ISSUE agree to purchase any unsold shares after shareholders exercise their PRE-EMPTIVE RIGHTS, thereby ensuring the company gains the full amount of anticipated proceeds.
- Also known as STANDBY UNDERWRITING.

STANDBY LETTER OF CREDIT A contingent LETTER OF CREDIT obligation of the issuing BANK that becomes effective only if the drawing customer fails to perform on a specific transaction. If performance does not occur as planned, the bank automatically pays the BENEFICIARY of the letter of credit and then attempts to recover cash flows from the customer.
- See also CONFIRMED LETTER OF CREDIT, DIRECT PAY LETTER OF CREDIT, TRANSFERABLE LETTER OF CREDIT, IRREVOCABLE LETTER OF CREDIT.

STANDBY NOTE ISSUANCE FACILITY (SNIF) A banking facility that guarantees investors payment if the issuer of securities floated under a NOTE ISSUANCE FACILITY DEFAULTS on its obligation. The guaranteeing BANK charges the issuer a fee in exchange for assuming the contingent LIABILITY.

STANDBY UNDERWRITING See STANDBY AGREEMENT.

STANDSTILL AGREEMENT A formal agreement between a RAIDER or acquiring company and a target company, where the acquirer agrees not to purchase any additional shares in the target until further negotiations regarding a possible deal can be conducted.

STAPLED STOCK [COL] See PAIRED SHARES.

STATUTORY BOND A SURETY BOND that a government authority or regulator may require contractors, businesses, or FIDUCIARIES to post for work performance affecting the public interest. The intent of the statutory bond is to ensure adequate third party financial protection in the event the contract party fails to perform as intended.

STATUTORY PROFIT In INSURANCE, a measure of an INSURER's profitability, typically defined as earned PREMIUMS less total expenses and losses paid.

STATUTORY PROSPECTUS See PROSPECTUS.

STATUTORY RESERVE A RESERVE that INSURERS are required to maintain to ensure they can withstand potential losses from RISKS they have underwritten and can remain solvent. Methods of computing the minimum amount of the statutory reserve vary, although most are based on loss frequency calculations.

STATUTORY VOTING The conventional corporate method of assigning one shareholder vote to each share of COMMON STOCK and requiring that each vote be apportioned equally to DIRECTOR nominees.
- See also CUMULATIVE VOTING.

STERILIZATION Action by a CENTRAL BANK or monetary authority to increase or decrease a nation's money supply to offset any changes caused by active intervention in the FOREIGN EXCHANGE markets. If a country has a greater amount of foreign exchange reserves as a result of its intervention activities, its money supply will increase and cause the central bank to sell GOVERNMENT BONDS as an offset; if reserves decline and the money supply contracts, the central bank will purchase government bonds.
- See also DIRTY FLOAT.

STICKY DEAL [COL] See HUNG DEAL.

STOCHASTIC PROCESS A mathematical process used to describe the continuous and dynamic movement of asset prices. Certain OPTION pricing models use a stochastic process to generate values.
- See also MARKOV PROCESS.

STOCK See COMMON STOCK.

STOCK BUYBACK A mechanism for returning CAPITAL to shareholders by repurchasing and retiring a specified amount of outstanding COMMON STOCK. From an accounting perspective the buyback has the effect of increasing the TREASURY STOCK CONTRA ACCOUNT, thus reducing the overall EQUITY account. The buyback may be conducted via direct open market purchases, a general TENDER OFFER to shareholders, or direct negotiation with a major investor; a buyback arranged on a regular basis through a formulaic process is known as a SELF-TENDER.
- Also known as STOCK REPURCHASE.
- See also SPECIAL DIVIDEND.

STOCK DIVIDEND A regular corporate DIVIDEND that is payable to COMMON STOCK shareholders of record in the form of additional shares of stock rather than cash.
- Also known as BONUS ISSUE, BONUS SHARE.

STOCK REPURCHASE See STOCK BUYBACK.

STOCK SPLIT A corporate action that reduces the PAR VALUE of a company's COMMON STOCK while increasing the number of shares

outstanding. A split is often undertaken in order to broaden the investor base by lowering the minimum purchase price of a share; although there is no change in the MARKET VALUE of the company, a stock split is generally viewed as a sign of strength.
- See also REVERSE STOCK SPLIT.

STOCK SWAP (1) A MERGER or ACQUISITION involving the exchange of COMMON STOCK between two companies; the transaction is generally accounted for as a POOLING OF INTERESTS. (2) A tax-motivated transaction where an investor with unrealized losses in a stock PORTFOLIO sells the positions, realizes the losses, and uses the losses to offset capital gains on other securities; excess losses from the stock swap can be carried forward to future periods, subject to certain limitations.
- (2) See also TAX CARRYBACK, TAX CARRYFORWARD.

STOP LIMIT ORDER An ORDER to buy or sell securities at a limit price once the stop level is reached, rather than the market price characteristic of a traditional STOP ORDER.

STOP LOSS ORDER A STOP ORDER to sell a security at the market once a particular price level is reached. The stop loss does not guarantee a specific execution price, it simply invokes an order to sell at the stop level.

STOP LOSS REINSURANCE A REINSURANCE contract that protects the CEDING INSURER against an aggregate amount of CLAIMS in excess of a specified percentage of earned PREMIUMS; stop loss reinsurance effectively protects the insurer against the possibility that the sum of individual losses from the INSURANCE it has UNDERWRITTEN will be greater than expected. In most instances the REINSURER is only liable up to a defined percentage of the losses or a maximum value amount.

STOP ORDER An ORDER to purchase or sell securities once a particular price level is reached on the upside or downside. The stop order does not guarantee specific price execution, simply that the order will become an effective purchase or sale and will then be filled at the best available price. The most common stop order is the STOP LOSS ORDER.
- See also LIMIT ORDER, MARKET ORDER, TIME ORDER.

STOP OUT PRICE The lowest price at which GOVERNMENT BILLS are sold in an AUCTION MARKET process.

STORY PAPER [COL] A security with unusual characteristics that requires detailed explanations or disclosure in order to attract investors. Story paper must occasionally be sold at a higher YIELD (or a larger price discount) than comparable "conventional" securities as a result of its unique or complex qualities.

STRADDLE An OPTION SPREAD designed to take advantage of VOLATILITY rather than market direction. A straddle is created through the purchase or sale of options with identical STRIKE PRICES and expiry dates; a LONG straddle consists of a long PUT OPTION and a long CALL OPTION, while a SHORT straddle consists of a short put and call. The purchaser of the straddle gains on the put or call if there is significant market movement; the seller

Payoff profile of a long straddle

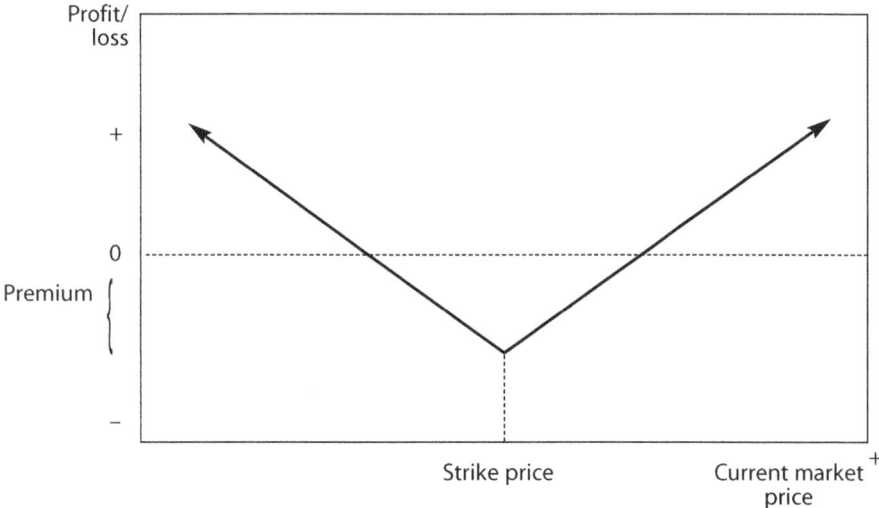

Payoff profile of a short straddle

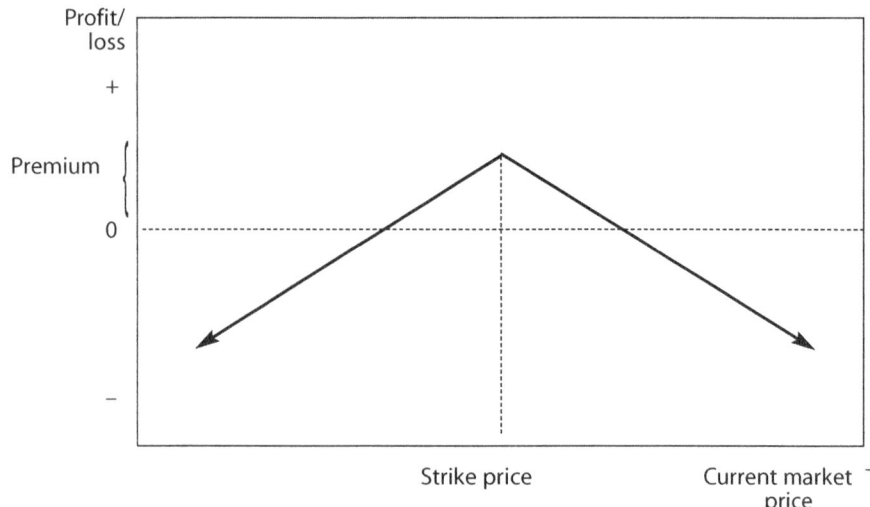

gains if markets remain calm and both options expire OUT-OF-THE-MONEY.

- See also STRANGLE.

STRAIGHT BOND (1) A NON-CALLABLE BOND. (2) In the EUROMARKETS, a bond with a fixed rate COUPON. (3) A GILT with a bullet repayment.

STRAIGHT-LINE DEPRECIATION A DEPRECIATION mechanism that applies equal reductions in value to a depreciable ASSET based on the expected life of the asset. Straight-line methods are commonly applied to fixed assets that are not expected to become obsolete before the end of their economically useful lives.

- See also ACCELERATED DEPRECIATION.

STRANGLE An OPTION SPREAD designed to take advantage of VOLATILITY rather than market direction. A strangle is created through the purchase or sale of options with different STRIKE PRICES but the same expiry dates: a LONG strangle consists of a long PUT OPTION and a long CALL OPTION, each with a different STRIKE PRICE, while a SHORT strangle consists of a short put and call with unique strikes. The purchaser of the strangle gains on the put or call if there is significant market movement; the seller gains if markets remain calm and both options expire OUT-OF-THE-MONEY.

- See also STRADDLE.

Payoff profile of a long strangle

Payoff profile of a short strangle

STRAP An OPTION SPREAD designed to take advantage of VOLATILITY. A LONG strap, which is created through a long PUT OPTION and two long CALL OPTIONS with the same STRIKE PRICE, is characterized by unlimited profit potential and limited downside RISK; the short strap, simply a short put and two short calls with identical strikes, has limited profit potential and unlimited downside risk.
- See also STRIP.

STREET NAME [COL] Client-owned securities that are registered to a BANK, BROKER/DEALER, or third party NOMINEE rather than the client. Securities held in street name eliminate the need to physically deliver securities to the client.

STRESS TESTING See SCENARIO ANALYSIS.

STRICT LIABILITY A LIABILITY motion requiring that the plaintiff need only prove harm in a specific manner in order to collect damages and need not demonstrate the methods, motivations, or intent leading to the damage.

STRIKE See STRIKE PRICE.

STRIKE PRICE The agreed price, rate, or level at which an OPTION begins creating value for the buyer and a LIABILITY for the seller. When the market price exceeds the strike price for a CALL OPTION, or falls below the strike for a PUT OPTION, INTRINSIC VALUE is created.
- Also known as STRIKE, EXERCISE PRICE.

STRIP (1) An OPTION SPREAD designed to take advantage of

VOLATILITY. A LONG strip, which is created through a long CALL OPTION and two long PUT OPTIONS with the same STRIKE PRICE, is characterized by unlimited profit potential and limited downside RISK; the short strip, which is simply a short call and two short puts with the same strikes, has limited profit potential and unlimited downside risk. (2) A security that has been split into CORPUS and COUPONS, enabling each component to be priced and traded separately. In the United States the Treasury Department conducts a stripping program of GOVERNMENT NOTES and GOVERNMENT BONDS to create STRIPS (Separate Trading of Registered Interest and Principal Securities). In the UK the BANK OF ENGLAND operates a GILT stripping program known as the STAGS (Sterling Transfer Accruing Government Securities); similar programs exist in other countries. Individual financial institutions also create their own private-label strips of government bonds and MORTGAGE-BACKED SECURITIES.
- (1) See also STRAP, (2) see also COUPON STRIPPING, INTEREST-ONLY STRIP, PRINCIPAL-ONLY STRIP, RECONSTITUTION, STRIPPING.

STRIP HEDGE A HEDGE based on the use of sequential OVER-THE-COUNTER or EXCHANGE-traded contracts that match or approximate future CASH FLOWS associated with the underlying RISK being hedged. A successful strip hedge can eliminate DIRECTIONAL RISK and CURVE RISK.
- See also ROLLING HEDGE.

STRIPPING The process of separating a BOND's CORPUS and interest COUPONS so that they can be traded separately. Stripping is done by government agencies and financial institutions, often by creating separate TRUST vehicles that hold the original securities and issue new, decomposed securities.
- See also COUPON STRIPPING, RECONSTITUTION, STRIP.

STRIPPING THE YIELD CURVE [COL] The process of deconstructing the PAR YIELD CURVE (i.e., the yield curve observable from coupon instruments trading in the market) to obtain a ZERO-COUPON YIELD CURVE. Stripping the yield curve commences with identifying several coupon instruments traded in the market, converting the first one into a zero coupon rate, using the second coupon instrument and the first derived zero-coupon rate to determine the second zero-coupon rate, and so forth, until an entire zero-coupon curve has been created. The zero-coupon curve is then converted into an IMPLIED FORWARD CURVE in order to value transactions requiring an estimate of FORWARD RATES.
- Also known as BOOTSTRAPPING.

STRIPS Acronym for Separate Trading of Registered Interest and Principal Securities, a STRIP security in the US marketplace

STRONG HANDS [COL] A holder of an EXCHANGE-TRADE DERIVATIVE contract that expects to receive the UNDERLYING ASSET at expiry or EXERCISE.
- See also WEAK HANDS

STRUCTURAL MODEL A form of CREDIT DEFAULT MODEL that defines the probability of COUNTERPARTY DEFAULT in terms of a firm's ASSETS, LIABILITIES, and CAPITAL structure. Default occurs when a boundary value, such as a liability or negative net worth threshold, is reached.
- See also INTENSITY MODEL.

STRUCTURAL SUBORDINATION The relative degree of SUBORDINATION between creditors of a holding company and creditors of an associated operating company. A holding company that has extensive LEVERAGE and is heavily reliant on the operating company for upstreaming of DIVIDENDS to cover its DEBT SERVICE places its creditors in a structurally subordinate position to the creditors of the operating company, which has its own cash generating capabilities.

STRUCTURED NOTE A NOTE or BOND containing EMBEDDED OPTIONS that create a customized payout for investors. The options, which carry varying degrees of potential RISK, allow returns to be linked to a variety of different ASSETS on a leveraged or unleveraged basis. Structured notes may be issued as PRIVATE PLACEMENTS and often feature very limited LIQUIDITY as a result of their unique structural characteristics. Common structured notes include the INVERSE FLOATER NOTE, LEVERAGED NOTE, MULTIPLE INDEX NOTE, RANGE FLOATER NOTE, and RANGE KNOCK-OUT FLOATER NOTE.
- See also COMPLEX STRUCTURED PRODUCT.

STUB [COL] (1) The NEARBY FUTURES contract on EURODOLLARS. (2) A SHORT COUPON on a NOTE or a BOND.

STUCK DEAL [COL] See HUNG DEAL

STYLE DRIFT A phenomenon when a HEDGE FUND or INVESTMENT COMPANY deviates from its original investment focus and expertise in an attempt to find new investment opportunities. Style drift can introduce additional RISK into a fund, as managers may lack the requisite base of knowledge needed to effectively manage the ASSETS.

SUB-INVESTMENT GRADE A CREDIT RATING designation applied to any issuer of securities that is rated between below BBB– by Standard and Poor's or Baa3 by Moody's Investors Services. Sub-investment-grade credits have weaker financial profiles than INVESTMENT-GRADE credits, and thus a greater likelihood of encountering FINANCIAL DISTRESS leading to DEFAULT.

SUBORDINATED DEBT A LIABILITY that ranks below SECURED DEBT and SENIOR DEBT in CLAIMS priority in the event of a DEFAULT by the debtor. Subordinated debt can be issued with varying levels of SUBORDINATION, making a given obligation senior to one liability and subordinate to another one. Subordinated debt holders do not receive any restitution in BANKRUPTCY until all senior debt holders have been compensated; in exchange for accepting the subordinated position, they demand a higher RISK PREMIUM on capital invested.
- Also known as JUNIOR DEBT, MEZZANINE FINANCING.
- See also SUBORDINATED PERPETUAL DEBT.

SUBORDINATED PERPETUAL DEBT A COUPON-bearing BOND that has no PRINCIPAL redemption feature and ranks junior to all other DEBT CLAIMS. The bond functions as permanent financing or quasi-EQUITY (although it ranks senior to equity holders and has no voting rights).
- See also SUBORDINATED DEBT.

SUBORDINATION The ranking of CLAIMS priority of a NOTE, BOND, or LOAN in the event of DEFAULT by the issuer or borrower; the greater the subordination, the lower the claims priority, and the lower the creditor RECOVERY RATE following BANKRUPTCY proceedings. The degree of creditor subordination may also be influenced by an issuer's or borrower's corporate structure, with holding company creditors generally subordinate to operating company creditors as a result of STRUCTURAL SUBORDINATION.
- See also ABSOLUTE PRIORITY RULE.

SUBPRIME LOAN A LOAN granted to a weak COUNTERPARTY, including one that may have had a history of prior loan delinquency or DEFAULT. Subprime loans, which are generally secured against a specific ASSET, typically have much lower LOAN-TO-VALUE ratios than conventional loans in order to protect the lender in the event of default.
- Also known as B & C LOAN, NON-PRIME LOAN.

SUBROGATION (1) The transfer of rights of loss recovery from the INSURED to the INSURER, allowing the insurer to seek its own restitution. The insured, whose rights are transferred, is known as the subrosor; the insurer accepting the subrogated rights is known as the subrosee. (2) The right to substitute one credit for another in settling a CLAIM or transferring ownership.

SUBSCRIPTION An offer to purchase securities, exercisable for a specific period of time.

SUBSCRIPTION AGREEMENT An agreement between the LEAD MANAGER, SYNDICATE members, and an issuer to offer securities at the issue price less an agreed SELLING CONCESSION. The agreement delineates instances where the transaction can be cancelled (through FORCE MAJEURE) and contains details related to taxes, expenses, listing fees, commissions, and STAMP DUTIES. A form of the subscription agreement is often included in the final PROSPECTUS.
- See also SYNDICATE AGREEMENT.

SUBSCRIPTION PRIVILEGE See PRE-EMPTIVE RIGHT.

SUBSCRIPTION RIGHTS See RIGHTS ISSUE.

SUBSCRIPTION WARRANT A WARRANT granted to existing shareholders of a company's COMMON STOCK, giving them the right to purchase shares of an ADD-ON issue, generally in an amount proportional to their current shareholdings, at a price that is below the current market. Subscription warrants may be issued when PRE-EMPTIVE RIGHTS do not exist.
- See also RIGHTS ISSUE.

SUITABILITY RISK The RISK of loss arising from clients claiming financial injury on transactions with characteristics that might be regarded as "unsuitable" (i.e., too speculative, risky, or leveraged, insufficient disclosure, ineffective HEDGE).
- See also ULTRA VIRES.

SUPERMAJORITY VOTE An ANTI-TAKEOVER DEFENSE requiring a supermajority, rather than just simple majority, vote by shareholders on a proposed CORPORATE FINANCE or corporate control action.

SUPERSINKER [COL] A TRANCHE of a MORTGAGE-BACKED SECURITY or COLLATERALIZED MORTGAGE OBLIGATION with an average life that is shorter than other tranches in the series. The tranche is retired at an accelerated rate through early PREPAYMENTS.

SUPERVISORY BOARD The first BOARD OF DIRECTORS in the DUAL BOARD SYSTEM, responsible for appointing, supervising and advising members of the MANAGEMENT BOARD, and developing fundamental corporate strategy. Supervisory board directors are generally nominated through an internal committee and/or executive management recommendations, and are formally elected by shareholders via PROXY at the ANNUAL GENERAL MEETING; in countries following LABOR CODETERMINATION, one or more labor representatives is appointed to the board. Board size can vary from 10 to 30 directors, depending on the national system.

SUPPORT BOND See COMPANION BOND.

SUPPORT LEVEL A TECHNICAL ANALYSIS chart reflecting a security or index price level that withstands repeated bouts of selling pressure. If the price breaches the support level after several repeated attempts, further downward moves may follow (as in a BREAKOUT).

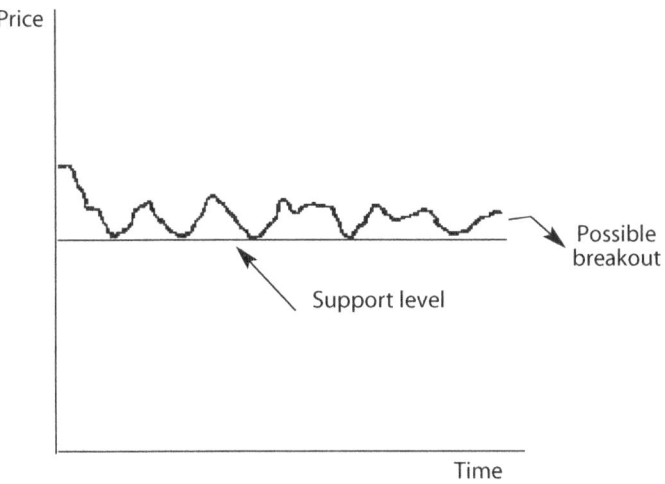

■   See also RESISTANCE LEVEL.

SURETY (1) A guarantee of contract fulfillment. (2) The party responsible for performing under a SURETY BOND should the original contract party DEFAULT on its obligations.

SURETY BOND A financial agreement where an INSURER assumes the role of the contracting party in completing a transaction or project in the event the contracting party DEFAULTS on its performance obligations. A conventional surety bond features three parties: the PRINCIPAL, who is responsible for performing on the underlying contract, task, or transaction; the SURETY, who performs upon the DEFAULT of the principal; and, the obligee, who is owed the right of performance. Surety bonds are commonly used in project financings and municipal/government developments.

■   See also COMPLETION BOND, PERFORMANCE BOND.

SURPLUS LINES INSURANCE INSURANCE cover that cannot be obtained from an ADMITTED INSURER and which must therefore be provided by a NON-ADMITTED INSURER.

■   Also known as EXCESS SURPLUS LINE INSURANCE.

SURPLUS NOTES SUBORDINATED DEBT that functions in a manner similar to CONTINGENT SURPLUS NOTES, except that securities are issued directly by the company rather than through a TRUST. Surplus notes have maturities ranging from 10 to 30 years, and must generally be approved by INSURANCE regulators.

SURPLUS SHARE In REINSURANCE, a PROPORTIONAL AGREEMENT where the REINSURER agrees to accept RISK on a variable percentage basis above the INSURER's DEDUCTIBLE, up to a defined maximum; the amount the CEDING INSURER retains is referred to as a LINE and is expressed in monetary terms.

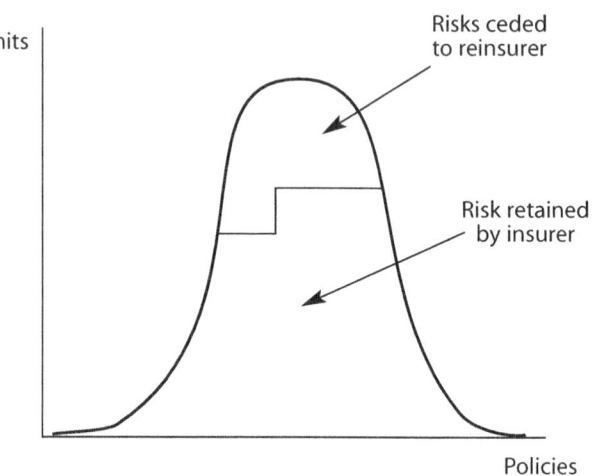

- See also QUOTA SHARE.

SWAP (1) A customized OVER-THE-COUNTER DERIVATIVE involving the periodic exchange of payments between two parties in order to achieve a specific goal related to HEDGING, ARBITRAGING, or SPECULATING. Swaps are defined in terms of a NOTIONAL amount, maturity, and payment/receipt terms; transactions generally have maturities ranging from 1 to 10 years, although longer deals are possible. Swaps are available on various references from the FIXED INCOME, EQUITY, FOREIGN EXCHANGE, commodity, and credit markets; common transactions include INTEREST RATE SWAPS, COMMODITY SWAPS, CURRENCY SWAPS, DEFAULT SWAPS, TOTAL RETURN SWAPS, and EQUITY SWAPS. (2) In the FOREIGN EXCHANGE market, a pair of SPOT and FORWARD transactions, where the spot offsets or unwinds the forward.
- (1) See also BASIS SWAP, CATASTROPHE REINSURANCE SWAP, COMPLEX SWAP, DISCOUNT SWAP, OFF-MARKET SWAP, PREMIUM SWAP, PURE CATASTROPHE SWAP.

SWAP SPREAD The differential between an INTEREST RATE SWAP or CURRENCY SWAP rate (representing the CREDIT RISK of BANK counterparties), and a BENCHMARK GOVERNMENT BOND rate (representing a sovereign RISK-FREE RATE). A widening of swap spreads generally reflects credit deterioration in the FIXED INCOME sector, while a narrowing reflects improvement.

SWAPTION An OVER-THE-COUNTER OPTION on a SWAP, available in the form of a RECEIVER SWAPTION and a PAYER SWAPTION. The purchaser of a swaption has the right, but not the obligation, to enter into an underlying swap transaction at a predetermined rate at a future time.

SWEETENER [COL] See KICKER.

SWING LOAN See BRIDGE LOAN.

SWING TRADING A TRADING strategy based on buying and selling securities for short periods of time (often intra-day) in order to take advantage of perceived overreactions. Swing trading is essentially a form of very short-term MOMENTUM TRADING.
- See also POSITION TRADING.

SWINGLINE A short-term backup LINE OF CREDIT that can be drawn by the borrower when needed. Swinglines are often used by COMMERCIAL PAPER issuers as a backup in the event investors are unwilling to ROLL OVER maturing paper. The swingline may be structured as a REVOLVING CREDIT FACILITY, REVOLVING UNDERWRITING FACILITY, or LETTER OF CREDIT facility.
- Also known as BACKUP LINE.

SYNDICATE (1) A group of financial institutions that UNDERWRITES a NEW ISSUE of securities, typically by purchasing them at a discount from the issuer and reselling them to investors at a fixed price in the PRIMARY MARKET. In some cases the syndicate will act as AGENT, placing securities through a BEST EFFORTS UNDERWRITING. (2) The process of selling or distributing securities or LOANS. (3) A group of INSURERS or REINSURERS that agree to jointly underwrite a RISK exposure.
- (1) Also known as PURCHASE GROUP, SELLING GROUP, UNDERWRITING GROUP.
- (2) See also SYNDICATION, (3) see also POOL.

SYNDICATE AGREEMENT An agreement related to an UNDERWRITING of securities that assigns rights and responsibilities to each participating SYNDICATE member. The agreement designates the LEAD MANAGER, the securities allotment by member, the duration of the syndicate, offering mechanism, and fees; the syndicate agreement generally expires one to two months after the securities placement.
- Also known as UNDERWRITING AGREEMENT.
- See also SUBSCRIPTION AGREEMENT.

SYNDICATE MANAGER See LEAD MANAGER.

SYNDICATED LOAN A LOAN granted by a banking group to a corporate borrower and then sold to smaller banks and hold-to-maturity institutional investors. A syndicated loan is distinct from a

PARTICIPATION LOAN, as the funding banks are known to the borrower.

SYNDICATION A process where a SYNDICATE UNDERWRITING a NEW ISSUE or a BANK arranging a LOAN sells portions of the obligation to other financial intermediaries. Syndication is a common means of distributing PRIMARY or SECONDARY OFFERINGS, and is used to supplement direct sales to investors.

SYNTHETIC CATASTROPHE BOND An OPTION on a CATASTROPHE BOND that permits, but does not obligate, the issuer to launch a bond transaction if needed in order to HEDGE or transfer RISK exposures.

SYNTHETIC COLLATERALIZED DEBT OBLIGATION (CDO) A COLLATERALIZED DEBT OBLIGATION that is created on an unfunded basis through the use of CREDIT DERIVATIVES, including TOTAL RETURN SWAPS, BASKET OPTIONS, and/or BASKET SWAPS. A synthetic CDO may be structured as a BALANCE SHEET CDO or an ARBITRAGE CDO, and may be managed statically or dynamically.
- See also CASH COLLATERALIZED DEBT OBLIGATION.

SYNTHETIC CREDIT FACILITY See SYNTHETIC LENDING FACILITY.

SYNTHETIC GUARANTEED INVESTMENT CONTRACT (GIC) A GUARANTEED INVESTMENT CONTRACT where the investment ASSETS are owned by the GIC plan rather than the INSURER managing the plan, as is common in a standard GIC; the assets of the plan and insurer are thus segregated.
- See also PARTICIPATING GUARANTEED INVESTMENT CONTRACT, NON-PARTICIPATING GUARANTEED INVESTMENT CONTRACT.

SYNTHETIC LENDING FACILITY A FORWARD commitment to purchase REVOLVING CREDIT AGREEMENTS or undrawn LOANS. The facility allows an investor to participate in an unfunded revolver or loan, receiving a COMMITMENT FEE while the facility remains undrawn, and requiring it to provide financing in the event the borrower elects to draw down. The facility is equivalent to a TOTAL RETURN SWAP based on revolvers/loans rather than BONDS.
- Also known as SYNTHETIC CREDIT FACILITY.

SYNTHETIC LONG POSITION A combination of a LONG CALL OPTION and a SHORT PUT OPTION with identical STRIKE PRICES that replicates the economics of a LONG POSITION.
- See also SYNTHETIC SHORT POSITION.

Payoff profile of a synthetic long position

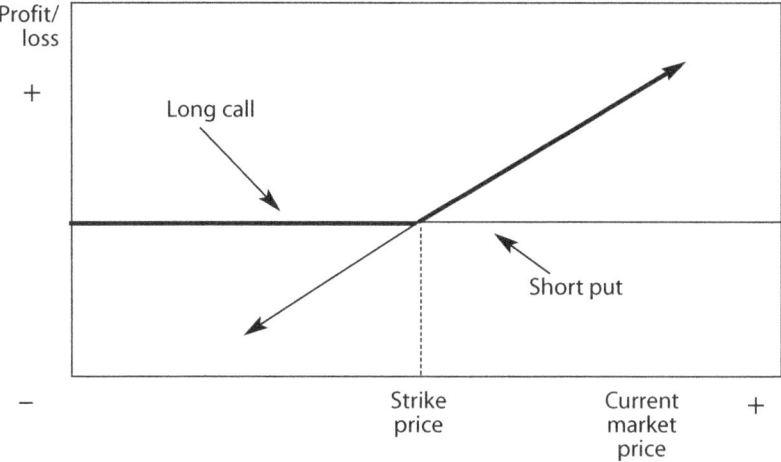

SYNTHETIC OPTION An OPTION position created through the combination of a LONG or SHORT option on an UNDERLYING security and a long or short position in the same underlying security.

Synthetic option =	Underlying +	Option
Long call	Long underlying	Long put
Long put	Short underlying	Long call
Short put	Long underlying	Short call
Short call	Short underlying	Short put

SYNTHETIC SHORT POSITION A combination of a LONG PUT OPTION and a SHORT CALL OPTION with identical STRIKE PRICES that replicates the economics of a SHORT POSITION.

Payoff profile of a synthetic short position

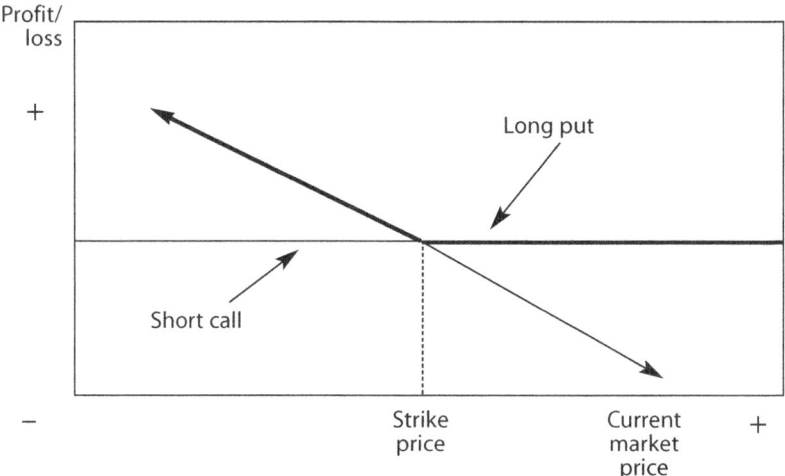

- See also SYNTHETIC LONG POSITION.

SYNTHETIC UNDERLYING An ASSET position created through the combination of two LONG or SHORT OPTIONS on the same UNDERLYING security.

Synthetic underlying =	Option +	Option
Long underlying	Long call	Short put
Short underlying	Short call	Long put

- See also SYNTHETIC LONG POSITION, SYNTHETIC SHORT POSITION.

SYSTEMATIC RISK See NON-DIVERSIFIABLE RISK.

T

TAC BOND See TARGETED AMORTIZATION CLASS BOND.

TAG ALONG RIGHTS [COL] Legal rights designed to protect MINORITY INTERESTS in the event of a TAKEOVER bid. If a bid occurs and majority shareholders tender their shares, then minority holders have the right to join on the same terms. Tag along rights must be specifically negotiated in a CORPORATE FINANCE transaction.
- See also DRAG ALONG RIGHTS.

TAIL [COL] (1) The extreme portion of a statistical distribution (e.g., NORMAL DISTRIBUTION, LOGNORMAL DISTRIBUTION) used to estimate EXPECTED LOSSES, unexpected losses, and associated probabilities of occurrence. Tails, which can be difficult to estimate with accuracy, are important to BANKS and INSURERS attempting to establish extreme loss values. (2) In an auction of securities, the differential between the average COMPETITIVE BID submitted and the highest YIELD (lowest price) accepted (i.e., the STOPOUT PRICE); a long tail indicates a weak auction, a short tail a strong auction. (3) In INSURANCE, the time between the receipt of PREMIUM and the payment of a CLAIM. (4) Price figures quoted after a decimal point.
- (1) See also FAT TAIL, (2) see also BID-TO-COVER, (4) see also PIP, POINT.

TAIL COVERAGE INSURANCE coverage that extends beyond the end of the standard policy. Tail coverage is useful in the case of a CLAIMS MADE BASIS policy, which only provides restitution for claims received during the policy period.

TAILGATING [COL] A practice where a BROKER replicates a client's trade in a proprietary account. Although tailgating is not strictly illegal (as is FRONT RUNNING), it can be regarded as unethical.
- See also COAT-TAILING.

TAILING A HEDGE A process where an EXCHANGE-TRADED

DERIVATIVE HEDGE is discounted using a PRESENT VALUE factor in order to take account of the fact that exchange-traded positions are MARKED-TO-MARKET and settled every day.

TAKE-OUT The replacement of one form of financing with another one, often associated with the replacement of a temporary BRIDGE LOAN with a long-term BOND or LOAN.

TAKE THE OFFER [COL] A buyer's willingness to accept the seller's price on a transaction.
- See also HIT THE BID.

TAKEDOWN (1) An advance or drawing of funds by a borrower under a REVOLVING CREDIT FACILITY. (2) The amount of a NEW ISSUE of securities a SYNDICATE member agrees to purchase and resell to clients.

TAKEOVER A CORPORATE FINANCE transaction where one company offers to acquire another company in order to expand its client, product, or market scope, or achieve some other strategic goal. The transaction may be structured as a FRIENDLY TAKEOVER or HOSTILE TAKEOVER, and may be based on an all cash offer, or a mix of cash and the acquiring company's shares. Hostile takeover attempts may be delayed or thwarted through ANTI-TAKEOVER DEFENSES and ANTI-TAKEOVER LAWS.
- See also TAKEOVER BID.

TAKEOVER BID The price an acquiring company is willing to pay for a target company. The bid value is generally represented as a particular PREMIUM to the target's share price.
- See also ANY-AND-ALL BID, TAKEOVER, TWO-TIER BID.

TAKEOVER VALUE See BREAKUP VALUE.

TAP ISSUE In the UK, an issue of GOVERNMENT BILLS sold directly to governmental entities without using GILT EDGE MARKET MAKERS.

TARGETED AMORTIZATION CLASS (TAC) BOND A TRANCHE of a COLLATERALIZED MORTGAGE OBLIGATION (CMO) that exhibits reasonable price and return stability by deflecting some amount of PREPAYMENT RISK to a COMPANION BOND. The companion bond shields the TAC from accelerating PREPAYMENTS, providing investors with a constant YIELD for a select PREPAYMENT SPEED (rather than a band of speeds, as is characteristic of the PLANNED AMORTIZATION CLASS BOND).
- See also SEQUENTIAL PAY BOND.

TAX CARRYBACK A tax benefit generated by applying eligible losses to a current tax LIABILITY. In the United States, capital or operating losses can be offset against profits for the three prior years.
- See also TAX CARRYFORWARD, TAX UMBRELLA.

TAX CARRYFORWARD A tax benefit generated by applying eligible losses to a future tax LIABILITY. In the United States, losses can be carried forward to offset future profits for five years (capital losses) and 15 years (operating losses).
- Also known as CARRYFORWARD LOSS.
- See also TAX CARRYBACK, TAX UMBRELLA.

TAX SHIELD A tax benefit generated through interest deductibility on LOANS, BONDS, and other DEBT funding instruments (i.e., interest expense is deducted from operating income before a tax rate is applied). In general, the higher the marginal corporate tax rate, the greater the benefits derived from the shield. The PRESENT VALUE of a tax shield is given as:

$$PV_{TS} = TR \left[\frac{D(r_{davg})}{r_{davg}} \right]$$

where TR is the effective tax rate, D is total debt, and r_{davg} is the average cost of the debt.
- See also TAX UMBRELLA.

TAX UMBRELLA Any tax transaction that is intended to decrease a company's effective tax rate, generally considered to include TAX CARRYBACKS, TAX CARRYFORWARDS, and TAX SHIELDS.

TAXABLE EQUIVALENT YIELD The YIELD on a tax-free FIXED INCOME security grossed up to allow comparison with taxable investment alternatives. The taxable equivalent yield is generally computed via:

$$TEY = \frac{y_{TF}}{(1 - TR)}$$

where y_{TF} is the tax-free yield and TR is the effective tax rate.
- See also BOND EQUIVALENT YIELD, DISCOUNT YIELD, SIMPLE YIELD, YIELD TO CALL, YIELD TO MATURITY.

TBA See TO BE ANNOUNCED.

TEAR-UP PRICE The price at which a DERIVATIVES DEALER will close out, or buy out, a client's derivative transaction. The tear-up price is generally a function of the transaction's current MARK-TO-MARKET value and a profit SPREAD.
- Also known as UNWIND PRICE.

TEASER [COL] A below-market INTEREST RATE on a LOAN used to entice an individual or company to borrow funds, or an above-market rate on a DEPOSIT used to attract clients to place funds. The favorable teaser rate generally lasts for up to several quarters, then reverts to normal market levels.

TECHNICAL ANALYSIS Security and market analysis techniques that

are based on the concept that past price formations repeat in particular patterns and can thus be used to forecast future movements. Technical analysts believe that historical price patterns have a bearing on both present and future price movements, suggesting that their views stand in contrast to theories such as the EFFICIENT MARKET HYPOTHESIS and RANDOM WALK. The technical analysis process involves charting techniques such as HEAD AND SHOULDERS, REVERSE HEAD AND SHOULDERS, ASCENDING TOPS, FALLING TOPS, DESCENDING BOTTOMS, RISING BOTTOMS, DOUBLE TOPS, REVERSE DOUBLE TOPS, FLAGS, PENNANTS, TRIANGLES, SUPPORT levels, and RESISTANCE levels, among others. Technical analysis also relies on other statistical tools, such as MOVING AVERAGES and MOMENTUM OSCILLATORS.
- See also FUNDAMENTAL ANALYSIS.
- Additional reference: Edwards and Magee (2001).

TED SPREAD See TREASURY–EURODOLLAR SPREAD.

TEENY [COL] The smallest trading unit in US TREASURY BONDS and AGENCY SECURITIES, e.g., 1/64th of $1.

TEMPERATURE DERIVATIVE An OVER-THE-COUNTER or EXCHANGE-traded WEATHER DERIVATIVE that references the movement of a temperature index, such as cumulative average temperatures, heating degree days, or cooling degree days. A temperature derivative involves the exchange of payments based on the actual movement of the temperature index against a predefined level. Most contracts are traded on a seasonal basis (e.g., the summer cooling season and the winter heating season) and are based on a particular reference city. Since temperature is not a tradable commodity, all contracts feature FINANCIAL SETTLEMENT.
- See also TEMPERATURE-LINKED BOND.

TEMPERATURE-LINKED BOND An INSURANCE-LINKED SECURITY with COUPON interest and/or PRINCIPAL redemption that are contingent on the level of cumulative temperatures in a particular city, group of cities, or region. The bond provides investors with an alternative investment opportunity and the issuer with a HEDGE or RISK TRANSFER mechanism.
- See also TEMPERATURE DERIVATIVE.

TENDER OFFER A publicly announced offer by a company or RAIDER to purchase the COMMON STOCK of a target company at a stated price. The offer price, known as a TAKEOVER BID, is generally made at a PREMIUM to the market in order to induce shareholders to sell (or "tender") their shares.
- See also FRIENDLY TAKEOVER, HOSTILE TAKEOVER, PREMIUM BID, TAKEOVER, TWO-TIER BID.

TENDER PANEL A SYNDICATE of BANKS backing an issuer's REVOLVING UNDERWRITING FACILITY, NOTE ISSUANCE FACILITY, or MULTIPLE OPTION FACILITY. The panel sells NOTES on behalf of the issuer on a BEST EFFORTS basis and purchases any securities that remain unsold, thus providing the issuer with funds.

TERM LOAN A LOAN with a maturity ranging from 1 to 15+ years, generally used to fund medium- and long-term ASSETS such as INVENTORY and plant and equipment. A term loan may be secured or unsecured, carry a fixed or variable INTEREST RATE, and contain general or specific performance COVENANTS.

TERM REPURCHASE AGREEMENT A REPURCHASE AGREEMENT with a final maturity ranging from 7 to 30 days; the opposite side of the transaction is referred to as a term REVERSE REPURCHASE AGREEMENT.
- See also OPEN REPURCHASE AGREEMENT, OVERNIGHT REPURCHASE AGREEMENT.

TERM STRUCTURE The level of INTEREST RATES across time/maturity, generated through the construction of a YIELD CURVE.
- See also EXPECTATIONS THEORY, LIQUIDITY PREFERENCE THEORY, MARKET SEGMENTATION THEORY.
- Additional references: Cox, Ingersoll, and Ross (1981), Hicks (1946), Meiselman (1962).

TERMINAL EXPECTED RISK EXPOSURE POTENTIAL EXPOSURE of an OVER-THE-COUNTER DERIVATIVE that is based on the final maturity of the transaction and the expected movement of the UNDERLYING market reference.
- See also AVERAGE EXPECTED RISK EXPOSURE, AVERAGE WORST-CASE RISK EXPOSURE, TERMINAL WORST-CASE RISK EXPOSURE.

TERMINAL EXPOSURE POTENTIAL EXPOSURE of an OVER-THE-COUNTER DERIVATIVE that is based on the final maturity of the transaction.
- See also AVERAGE EXPOSURE.

TERMINAL WORST-CASE RISK EXPOSURE POTENTIAL EXPOSURE of an OVER-THE-COUNTER DERIVATIVE that is based on the final maturity of the transaction and the worst-case movement of the UNDERLYING market reference.
- See also AVERAGE EXPECTED RISK EXPOSURE, AVERAGE WORST CASE RISK EXPOSURE, TERMINAL EXPECTED RISK EXPOSURE.

TERMINATION OPTION An OPTION embedded in an OVER-THE-COUNTER SWAP that permits one or both parties to terminate the transaction based on the passage of time or the occurrence of a triggering credit event (often a CREDIT RATING downgrade). A firm might employ a termination option to help mitigate the effects of counterparty CREDIT RISK on very long-term transactions.

TEXAS HEDGE [COL] A financial transaction that increases RISK or produces losses under all market scenarios, i.e., it does the opposite of what a properly functioning HEDGE is meant to do.

THEORETICAL FUTURES PRICE The ARBITRAGE-FREE price of a FUTURES contract, equal to the SPOT PRICE plus the COST OF CARRY.

THETA A change in the value of an OPTION for a change in the passage of time, with all other variables held constant. The thetas of the CALL OPTION and PUT OPTION under the BLACK–SCHOLES MODEL are given by:

$$\theta_c = -\frac{\partial C}{\partial t} = -\frac{S\sigma}{2\sqrt{t}} N'(d_1) - r_f X e^{-r_f t} N(d_2)$$

$$\theta_p = -\frac{\partial P}{\partial t} = -\frac{S\sigma}{2\sqrt{t}} N'(d_1) + r_f X e^{-r_f t} N(-d_2)$$

where

$$d_1 = \frac{\ln\left(\frac{S}{X}\right) + \left(r_f + \frac{\sigma^2}{2}\right)t}{\sigma\sqrt{t}}$$

$$d_2 = \frac{\ln\left(\frac{S}{X}\right) + \left(r_f - \frac{\sigma^2}{2}\right)t}{\sigma\sqrt{t}}$$

and S is the stock price, X is the STRIKE PRICE, t is the time to maturity, r_f is the RISK-FREE RATE, σ^2 is the VARIANCE, and where the N values of $N(d_1)$ and $N(d_2)$ can be obtained from standard tables of probability functions.

The thetas of long and short puts and calls are shown as:

	Long call	Long put	Short call	Short put
Theta	−	−	+	+

- Also known as OMEGA.
- See also DELTA, GAMMA, GREEKS, RHO, TIME DECAY, TIME VALUE, VEGA.

THIN MARKET [COL] An ILLIQUID market that features low volume, wide BID–OFFER SPREADS, and high price VOLATILITY; a thin

market may also feature periods of one-way activity and large ORDER IMBALANCES.
- See also TIGHT MARKET.

THIRD MARKET [COL] (1) The general marketplace for TRADING of OVER-THE-COUNTER instruments. (2) EXCHANGE trading between non-member firms, or between a member and non-member firm.

THIRD PARTY ENHANCEMENT Any form of support obtained from a third party credit support provider, such as a GUARANTEE, SURETY BOND, or LETTER OF CREDIT. Such enhancements are used to increase the creditworthiness of a transaction, often in lieu of posting physical or financial ASSETS as COLLATERAL.

THRIFT See SAVINGS AND LOAN.

TIBOR See TOKYO INTERBANK OFFERED RATE.

TICK VALUE The value of a single price increment of an EXCHANGE-TRADED DERIVATIVE contract.

TIDE PROVISION A "three year independent director evaluation" provision included in certain POISON PILL defenses to make them more acceptable to shareholders. The provisions require DIRECTORS to evaluate the nature and status of poison pill defenses every three years to ensure that they remain equitable and appropriate, and do not harm or prejudice shareholder interests.

TIER 1 CAPITAL Core REGULATORY CAPITAL for BANKS, defined by the BANK FOR INTERNATIONAL SETTLEMENTS as COMMON STOCK, RETAINED EARNINGS, PERPETUAL PREFERRED STOCK, and disclosed RESERVES.
- See also ECONOMIC CAPITAL, TIER 2 CAPITAL.

TIER 2 CAPITAL Supplementary REGULATORY CAPITAL for BANKS, defined by the BANK FOR INTERNATIONAL SETTLEMENTS as hybrid DEBT/EQUITY securities (including MANDATORY CONVERTIBLE BONDS), SUBORDINATED DEBT with maturities in excess of five years, PERPETUAL DEBT, PREFERRED STOCK with a stated maturity, LOAN LOSS RESERVES, unrealized gains on investments, and hidden reserves.
- See also ECONOMIC CAPITAL, TIER 1 CAPITAL.

TIGHT MARKET [COL] A LIQUID market that features large volume and strong two-way flows, and narrow BID–OFFER SPREADS. ORDER IMBALANCES and one-way quotations are rare in a tight market.
- See also THIN MARKET.

TIME AND DISTANCE REINSURANCE A FINITE REINSURANCE contract, generally structured as EXCESS OF LOSS (XOL) REINSURANCE, where the REINSURER agrees to pay the CEDING

INSURER an agreed schedule of loss payments in the future, without assuming any LIABILITY for losses in excess of those contained in the schedule. In exchange, the insurer pays the reinsurer a PREMIUM that is equal to the PRESENT VALUE of the loss payments.

TIME DECAY Daily gain or loss impacting the TIME VALUE component of OPTION PREMIUM due to the passage of time; time decay is often used as a practical expression of THETA.

TIME DEPOSIT A non-negotiable DEPOSIT issued by a BANK that pays periodic fixed or variable COUPONS for a period ranging from several months to several years. The deposit can only be redeemed by the depositor on the stated maturity and cannot be transferred on a secondary basis.
- See also CERTIFICATE OF DEPOSIT, INTERBANK DEPOSIT, LOCK-UP CERTIFICATE OF DEPOSIT, NEGOTIABLE CERTIFICATE OF DEPOSIT.

TIME ORDER An ORDER to purchase or sell securities with a specific time constraint, such as at the close or open of a market, or at some future date.
- See also LIMIT ORDER, MARKET ORDER, STOP ORDER.

TIME SPREAD An OPTION SPREAD designed to take advantage of perceived price or VOLATILITY discrepancies in the FORWARD MARKET. Time spreads are created through the purchase or sale of OPTIONS with identical STRIKE PRICES but different expiry dates. A LONG time spread consists of a SHORT POSITION in a near maturity PUT OPTION or CALL OPTION and a LONG POSITION in a far maturity put or call; a SHORT time spread consists of a long position in a near maturity put or call, and a short position in a far maturity put or call. Time spreads can also be established through FUTURES and FORWARDS.
- Also known as CALENDAR SPREAD, RATIO HORIZONTAL SPREAD.

TIME-TO-DECAY RISK See FRACTIONAL EXPOSURE.

TIME VALUE One of two components, along with INTRINSIC VALUE, which comprises the value of an OPTION. Time value measures the remaining economic worth of the contract that is specifically attributable to time, i.e., the time remaining for the UNDERLYING reference to move IN-THE-MONEY (or further in-the-money). Since time is a wasting ASSET, time value declines on a daily basis for the option buyer until it reaches zero at expiry. Longer term options have greater time value than shorter time options, while in-the-money and OUT-OF-THE-MONEY options have less time value than AT-THE-MONEY options.
- See also THETA, TIME DECAY.

TIME VALUE OF MONEY A central financial concept indicating that the FUTURE VALUE of a sum of money invested today, in an interest-bearing ASSET, is worth more than its current value. By extension, the future value of a sum can be discounted at a DISCOUNT RATE to obtain today's PRESENT VALUE.

TIMES INTEREST EARNED A measure of a firm's ability to cover its debt obligations, generally measured as:

$$TIE = \frac{EBIT}{Int}$$

where *EBIT* is EARNINGS BEFORE INTEREST AND TAXES and *Int* is interest expense.

The greater the ratio, the stronger the firm's INTEREST COVERAGE.

TIPS See TREASURY INFLATION PROTECTED SECURITY.

TO BE ANNOUNCED (TBA) The common name given to a MORTGAGE-BACKED SECURITY (issued by the GOVERNMENT NATIONAL MORTGAGE ASSOCIATION, FEDERAL NATIONAL MORTGAGE ASSOCIATION, or FEDERAL HOME LOAN MORTGAGE CORPORATION) that trades as a WHEN ISSUED (WI) SECURITY, i.e., announced but not yet priced or settled. While in the "WI" period informal, but legally binding, GRAY MARKET TRADING occurs between DEALERS. Once the TBA has settled, it trades in the same manner as any other SEASONED SECURITY.

TOBIN'S Q RATIO A corporate valuation measure developed by the economist Tobin, computed as:

$$Q = \frac{MV}{BV}$$

where *MV* is the MARKET VALUE of the firm and *BV* is the BOOK VALUE of the firm (measured on a REPLACEMENT COST basis).

A Q ratio below 1.0 means the firm is earning less than its required rate of return; each marginal dollar invested in ASSETS fails to produce future CASH FLOWS whose PRESENT VALUE is equal to the marginal dollar invested. A ratio above 1.0 means the firm is exceeding the required rate of return.

TOKYO INTERBANK OFFERED RATE (TIBOR) The OFFER side of the yen-based Tokyo INTERBANK DEPOSIT market, or the rate at which prime BANKS are willing to lend funds. TIBOR, which is set every business day, is quoted for deposits in a range of maturities and serves as an important base reference for other financial instruments (e.g., DERIVATIVES, FLOATING RATE NOTES) with a floating rate component.

TOKYO STOCK PRICE INDEX (TOPIX) A BENCHMARK index of

the Japanese stock market comprised of all COMMON STOCKS listed on the first section of the Tokyo Stock Exchange, with further subdivisions by size and industry. The TOPIX can be traded directly through EXCHANGE-TRADED FUNDS and DERIVATIVES.

TOM NEXT [COL] Abbreviated form of "tomorrow-next", referring to FOREIGN EXCHANGE and MONEY MARKET transactions that are executed tomorrow (t+1) for delivery the day after that (t+2).
- Also known as DEALING OVER TOMORROW, ROLLOVER.

TOMBSTONE [COL] An advertisement announcing the completion of a NEW ISSUE of DEBT or EQUITY securities. The tombstone provides details of the transaction, along with the UNDERWRITING GROUP responsible for distributing the issue, and constitutes an informational advertisement rather than a solicitation to sell securities (any explicit advertisement in support of a new issue, apart from the PROSPECTUS, is illegal).

TON [COL] Common reference for one hundred million.
- See also BUCK, YARD.

TOO BIG TO FAIL [COL] A financial institution that is so large and integral to the effective functioning of a local, regional, or global system that its failure would have systemic repercussions that could create instability for a much larger population of institutions. Institutions that are considered too big to fail generally enjoy implicit (though rarely explicit) support from a CENTRAL BANK or monetary authority, and might expect to receive a bailout in the event of FINANCIAL DISTRESS.

TOPIX See TOKYO STOCK PRICE INDEX.

TORPEDO STOCK [COL] A COMMON STOCK that has fallen dramatically and is expected to continue declining, generally as a result of poor financial performance and uncertain prospects.

TORT An intentional or unintentional act of negligence by an individual or company, excluding breach of contract. A party damaged by a tort may seek remedy in court through a damage suit.

TOTAL CONTROL A process or structure where effective corporate control is gained through complete ownership. This exists primarily in the case of family-owned or private companies, where accumulation or retention of a total block of shares is feasible.
- See also LEGAL MECHANISM CONTROL, MAJORITY CONTROL, MANAGEMENT CONTROL, MINORITY CONTROL, VOTING TRUST CONTROL.

TOTAL RATE OF RETURN SWAP See TOTAL RETURN SWAP.

TOTAL RETURN SWAP An OVER-THE-COUNTER SWAP that synthetically replicates the economic flows of a reference ASSET, such as a credit risky BOND or EQUITY index, over a stated maturity (generally ranging from six months to five years). A generic total return swap involves the exchange of a periodic COUPON or upfront CASH FLOW plus any appreciation in the price of the reference for any depreciation in the reference. The contract permits balance sheet exposures or investments to be reproduced off balance sheet, on a LEVERAGED basis.

- Also known as CONTRACT FOR DIFFERENCES, TOTAL RATE OF RETURN SWAP.

TOXIC WASTE [COL] A financial instrument that is considered to be very risky, generally one with high VOLATILITY and significant CREDIT RISK, MARKET RISK, and/or LIQUIDITY RISK. Toxic waste may be developed by design (e.g., a STRUCTURED NOTE with a risky profile) or it may be the by-product of a SYNTHETIC ASSET (e.g. a RESIDUAL, COMPANION BOND, or exotic TRANCHE of a COLLATERALIZED DEBT OBLIGATION or COLLATERALIZED MORTGAGE OBLIGATION) that proves difficult to sell to investors.

TRACKING ERROR A measure of the divergence between the performance of an investment PORTFOLIO and a target or BENCHMARK index, which generally arises as a result of transaction costs, portfolio composition (including a smaller number of securities used in the portfolio), and ASSET pricing differentials. Minimizing tracking error is a central element of successful INDEXING.

- Also known as TRACKING RISK.

TRACKING RISK See TRACKING ERROR.

TRACKING STOCK A COMMON STOCK based on a portion of a company's operations (i.e., a separate subsidiary or business unit). Tracking stocks are priced and traded independently of the company's primary stock and are permitted to pay a DIVIDEND; however, they carry no voting power and have no legal CLAIM on the main company's ASSETS.

TRADING The process of buying and selling ASSETS in order to generate profits from market movements and BID and OFFER spreads. Trading is a common line of business for BANKS, INVESTMENT BANKS, SECURITIES FIRMS, BROKER-DEALERS, HEDGE FUNDS, and certain MUTUAL FUNDS.

TRADING CREDIT RISK The RISK of loss associated with DEFAULT by a COUNTERPARTY on a financial transaction that dynamically changes in value, such as a DERIVATIVE or REVERSE REPURCHASE AGREEMENT. A loss on default is not always certain; when the transaction generates bilateral CREDIT RISK (as in a FORWARD or SWAP), the contract may have value to the counterparty rather than the intermediary at the time of default, indicating that the credit provider sustains no loss. A sub-category of CREDIT RISK.

- See also CONTINGENT CREDIT RISK, CORRELATED CREDIT RISK, DIRECT CREDIT RISK, SETTLEMENT RISK, SOVEREIGN RISK.

TRADING INDEX (TRIN) A measure of stock market strength that compares the number of companies advancing and declining to volume. The general TRIN formula is given as:

$$TRIN = \frac{\left[\left(\frac{Adv_{num}}{Dec_{num}}\right)\right]}{\left[\left(\frac{Adv_{vol}}{Dec_{vol}}\right)\right]}$$

where Adv_{num} is the number of advancing issues, Dec_{num} is the number of declining issues, Adv_{vol} is the volume of advancing issues, and Dec_{vol} is the volume of declining issues.

A TRIN below 1.0 is considered a bullish signal, while a result above 1.0 is a bearish signal.

- Also known as ARMS INDEX.

TRANCHE [FR] A slice or portion of a securities issue or financing that is characterized by unique features related to currency, COUPON payoff, maturity, CREDIT RATING, and seniority. Tranching is commonly used in SECURITIZATION, multi-currency LOANS, and CERTIFICATES OF DEPOSIT in order to create a range of investment selections.

TRANCHETTE A small issue of GILTS issued by the BANK OF ENGLAND, intended primarily for retail investors.

TRANSACTION-SPECIFIC COLLATERAL A COLLATERAL management technique where collateral is taken on an incremental basis in support of each discrete credit-sensitive transaction. Individual pieces of collateral security are thus associated with specific transactions; as transactions mature or are unwound, the specific collateral is released.

- See also CROSS COLLATERAL AGREEMENT, POOLED PORTFOLIO COLLATERAL.

TRANSACTION RISK The RISK of loss arising from adverse FOREIGN EXCHANGE movements on corporate operations; gains or losses from such risks are typically reflected directly through the corporate income statement. Dealings that give rise to transaction risk may be hedged through CURRENCY DERIVATIVES in order to decrease the possibility of loss.

- Also known as CURRENCY TRANSACTION RISK.
- See also TRANSLATION RISK.

TRANSFERABLE LETTER OF CREDIT A LETTER OF CREDIT that gives the BENEFICIARY the option of shifting some, or all, of the facility to a third party, such as a subsidiary or joint venture partner. The transfer must first be approved by the issuing BANK.
- See also CONFIRMED LETTER OF CREDIT, DIRECT PAY LETTER OF CREDIT, IRREVOCABLE LETTER OF CREDIT, STANDBY LETTER OF CREDIT.

TRANSFERABLE REVOLVING UNDERWRITING FACILITY (TRUF) A REVOLVING UNDERWRITING FACILITY giving the original UNDERWRITER the right to transfer its commitment to another BANK.

TRANSITION PROBABILITY The likelihood that a COUNTERPARTY's CREDIT RATING will migrate from one rating class to another; such probabilities are essential components of CREDIT MARK-TO-MARKET MODELS.

TRANSLATION RISK The RISK of loss arising from a restatement of FOREIGN EXCHANGE accounts into the home currency. Gains or losses are typically reflected directly in the corporate EQUITY account.
- Also known as CURRENCY TRANSLATION RISK.
- See also TRANSACTION RISK.

TREASURY BILL A MONEY MARKET instrument issued by the US Treasury as a funding mechanism and a tool for conducting MONETARY POLICY. Treasury bills are issued on a discount, rather than COUPON-BEARING, basis through weekly and monthly auctions, and have maturities extending from 3 to 12 months.
- See also TREASURY BOND, TREASURY INFLATION PROTECTED SECURITY, TREASURY NOTE.

TREASURY BOND A DEBT instrument issued by the US Treasury as a funding mechanism. Treasury bonds are issued on an AUCTION basis through PRIMARY DEALERS as fixed rate, COUPON-BEARING, instruments with maturities extending from 10 to 20 years (issuance in the 30-year LONG BOND was discontinued in the millennium). Select bonds are also issued as INFLATION-LINKED SECURITIES and STRIPS.
- See also TREASURY BILL, TREASURY INFLATION-PROTECTED SECURITY, TREASURY NOTE.

TREASURY–EURODOLLAR (TED) SPREAD The YIELD differential between EURODOLLAR DEPOSITS and TREASURY BILLS of the same maturity. The TED SPREAD provides an indication of the relative credit performance of the banking sector, with a widening of the spread reflecting weakness or deterioration, and a tightening signaling an improvement.

TREASURY INFLATION-PROTECTED SECURITY (TIPS) A US TREASURY NOTE or TREASURY BOND with a return that is linked to the level of INFLATION (as measured by the CONSUMER PRICE INDEX). TIPS are available in a range of medium- to long-term maturities and are sold in small minimum denominations so that they may be purchased by retail investors. TIPS pay fixed COUPONS on a regular cycle and the PRINCIPAL repayment is adjusted at maturity to reflect inflation performance.

TREASURY NOTE A DEBT instrument issued by the US Treasury as a funding mechanism. Treasury notes are issued on an AUCTION basis through PRIMARY DEALERS as fixed-rate, COUPON-BEARING, instruments with maturities extending from 1 to 10 years. Select notes are also issued as INFLATION-LINKED SECURITIES and STRIPS.
- See also TREASURY BILL, TREASURY BOND, TREASURY INFLATION PROTECTED SECURITY.

TREASURY STOCK Outstanding COMMON STOCK that is repurchased by a company, meaning it is classified as stock that is authorized and issued but is no longer outstanding. The repurchase, which is shown as a net reduction in total EQUITY through a CONTRA ACCOUNT, can be arranged through a single STOCK BUYBACK or via a regular, formulaic, repurchase known as a SELF-TENDER. In the United States, a SECURITIES AND EXCHANGE COMMISSION SAFE HARBOR (Rule 10b-18) allows a company to repurchase its own stock without being charged with securities manipulation.
- Also known as REACQUIRED STOCK.

TREATY FACILITY A mechanism allowing a CAPTIVE to access the REINSURANCE markets for large exposures. The facility generally reinsures a small percentage of the captive's exposures and then RETROCEDES the balance through TREATY REINSURANCE.

TREATY REINSURANCE A REINSURANCE agreement where the primary INSURER agrees to CEDE to a REINSURER a portion of all RISKS conforming to pre-agreed guidelines. Since conforming risks must be assumed by the reinsurer, the insurer is assured of necessary coverage; it also means, however, that the insurer cannot retain in its own PORTFOLIO a full share of conforming risks that may be especially profitable.
- See also FACULTATIVE REINSURANCE, QUOTA SHARE, SURPLUS SHARE, TREATY FACILITY.

TRENDLINE A TECHNICAL ANALYSIS charting technique created by connecting the highest or lowest prices of a security or market over time; the resulting line is indicative of an overall directional trend.

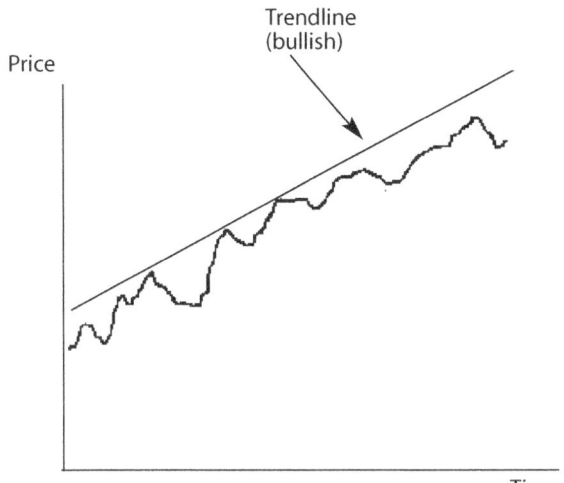

TREYNOR INDEX A measure of RISK-adjusted PORTFOLIO performance that compares the RISK PREMIUM (return) earned by the portfolio with the risk of the portfolio (as reflected through the portfolio BETA). The Treynor index, which uses the SECURITY MARKET LINE as a BENCHMARK, can be computed via:

$$TI = \frac{E(r_P) - r_f}{\beta_P}$$

where $E(r_P)$ is the expected return of the portfolio, r_f is the RISK-FREE RATE, and β_P is the beta of the portfolio.

- See also JENSEN INDEX, SHARPE INDEX.
- Additional reference: Treynor (1965).

TRIANGLE A TECHNICAL ANALYSIS charting technique that depicts the price of a security or index in a formation with two base points and a top that gives the appearance of a triangle; a triangle features multiple rallies and retreats, with each subsequent peak occurring at a lower level than the previous one. A BREAKOUT from a triangle may portend a much larger move to the upside or downside. (See figure on following page.)

TRIGGER (1) A value or event threshold embedded in an INSURANCE contract that determines whether an INSURED (or BENEFICIARY) will receive a compensatory payment in the event of loss. A generic insurance contract has a single trigger, i.e., whether a named PERIL has created a loss. More complex structures, including DUAL TRIGGERS and TRIPLE TRIGGERS, require the onset of additional events (or breach of particular values) before providing loss payments. Similar triggers are found in INSURANCE-LINKED SECURITIES, and provide an indication of whether an issuer's PRINCIPAL and/or COUPON interest payments will be suspended. (2) In BANK credit agreements and BOND INDENTURES see COVENANT.

TRIN See TRADING INDEX.

TRIPLE TRIGGER An INSURANCE mechanism that provides the INSURED with a payout only if three separate TRIGGER events occur; one trigger is often related to a traditional insurance RISK (e.g., destruction in plant and equipment leading to business interruption), while the second and third may relate to insurance or FINANCIAL RISKS (e.g., a decline in operating revenues of a certain amount and a fall in the stock price to a particular level). Since all three events must occur in order for a SETTLEMENT to take place, the PREMIUM is generally lower than it is on a standard insurance contract.

■ See also DUAL TRIGGER, MULTIPLE TRIGGER PRODUCTS.

TRIPLE WITCHING HOUR [COL] A single business day when index FUTURES, index OPTIONS, and individual EQUITY options all settle, which occurs once each quarter (i.e., the third Friday in March, June, September, and December). There is evidence to indicate that volume and VOLATILITY increase during triple witching hour days as investors, HEDGERS, and SPECULATORS rebalance their positions.

TRUST (1) A legal vehicle that permits ownership of property by one party for the express benefit of another party. The TRUSTEE receives title to, but cannot benefit from, the property, and is legally obliged to manage the property in a prudent manner on behalf of the ultimate BENEFICIARY. (2) A monopolistic business entity formed through consolidation or amalgamation of various existing CORPORATIONS, prevalent primarily during the early twentieth century.

TRUST DEED See INDENTURE.

TRUSTEE (1) In general, a party that administers a TRUST. A trustee is typically designated as the legal owner of property being administered on behalf of a BENEFICIARY; all actions taken by the trustee must be done in the best interests of the beneficiary. (2) In a BOND issue, an institution responsible for enforcing terms of the INDENTURE, managing the SINKING FUND, collecting PRINCIPAL and COUPON interest from the issuer for disbursement to investors, investing and disbursing cash balances, and holding COLLATERAL for the ultimate benefit of bond investors.

TRUSTEE IN BANKRUPTCY A FIDUCIARY appointed by a court or creditors to manage the affairs of a company that has filed for BANKRUPTCY. In the United States a trustee in bankruptcy is appointed under Chapter 7 to oversee LIQUIDATION and dispersal of ASSETS. A trustee may or may not be appointed under CHAPTER 11; if no trustee is appointed a DEBTOR-IN-POSSESSION assumes the role and responsibilities of the trustee, including the development of a REORGANIZATION plan.

TURBO OPTION See POWER OPTION.

TURKEY [COL] A bad investment, or a promising deal that has soured.

TWIN-IN BARRIER OPTION An OVER-THE-COUNTER COMPLEX OPTION that is created when an upper or lower BARRIER is breached. The inclusion of two barriers, which increase the probability of triggering, generally makes the structure more expensive than a standard KNOCK-IN OPTION.

- See also BARRIER OPTION, TWIN-OUT BARRIER OPTION.

TWIN-OUT BARRIER OPTION An OVER-THE-COUNTER COMPLEX OPTION that is extinguished when an upper or lower barrier is breached. The inclusion of two barriers, which increases the probability of triggering, generally makes the structure cheaper than a standard KNOCK-OUT OPTION.

- See also BARRIER OPTION, TWIN-IN BARRIER OPTION.

TWIST The process of moving the YIELD CURVE up or down by a different number of BASIS POINTS in the short and long maturities of the curve and recalculating the value of a FIXED INCOME transaction or PORTFOLIO. The curve twist reveals the sensitivity of the fixed income position(s) to unequal changes in the curve and can be used to compute hypothetical profits and losses or the effectiveness of a possible HEDGE strategy. Twists can be created by holding constant short-term rates while raising/lowering long-term rates, holding constant long-term rates while raising/lowering short-term rates, raising short-term rates and lowering long-term rates, or raising long-term rates and lowering short-term rates.

- See also PARALLEL SHIFT.

TWISTING [COL] See CHURNING.

TWO-FACTOR INTEREST RATE MODEL An OPTION pricing model that values BOND options by generating an entire YIELD CURVE through two INTEREST RATE references, i.e., a short-term rate and a long-term rate. Although such models are more complex to calibrate and implement than ONE-FACTOR INTEREST RATE MODELS, they can generate more precise results.

TWO-TIER BID A TAKEOVER BID that features a more attractive price for investors willing to tender their shares by the first cut-off date; those choosing not to tender by a certain date are offered a less favorable deal.

- See also ANY-AND-ALL BID, FAIR PRICE PROVISION.

TYING [COL] A practice where a BANK, INVESTMENT BANK, or SECURITIES FIRM grants a client a low margin LOAN only if the client agrees to award it more lucrative financial business, such as an UNDERWRITING or CORPORATE FINANCE transaction. In some jurisdictions the practice constitutes a violation of fair trading practices and is illegal.

- See also REVERSE TYING.

U–V–W

U

UBERRIMAE FIDEI [LAT] Literally "in utmost good faith;" a characteristic commonly applied to INSURANCE contracts, where the INSURED and INSURER disclose all relevant information and express intention to carry out their respective obligations in good faith.

ULTIMATE NET LOSS A computation performed by an INSURER that reflects the net economic loss sustained in INSURANCE activities, generally calculated via:

$$UNL = -(Cl + LAE) + (Reins + Sal + Sub)$$

where Cl is CLAIMS loss, LAE is LOSS ADJUSTMENT EXPENSE, $Reins$ is recovery from REINSURANCE contracts in force, Sal is recovery from salvage value, and Sub is recovery from SUBROGATION rights.

ULTRA VIRES [LAT] Literally "outside one's jurisdiction;" any action or financial dealing undertaken by a company or municipal authority that is beyond the scope of authorities dictated by CORPORATE CHARTER, municipal by-laws, or state/federal/national laws. *Ultra vires* actions are not generally defensible and leave open the possibility of third party legal proceedings against those committing the actions. Use of DERIVATIVES, STRUCTURED NOTES with embedded LEVERAGE, and other risky instruments have been cited by the courts, in certain instances, to be *ultra vires*.

UMBRELLA POLICY An INSURANCE contract that provides the INSURED with additional coverage for specific LIABILITY and/or various named PERILS. The umbrella policy works in tandem with an insured's existing policies to provide EXCESS LAYER coverage or ensure that any potential gaps that exist are appropriately filled.

UMBRELLA REINSURANCE A REINSURANCE contract that covers MULTIPLE PERIL POLICIES. All treaties written under the umbrella comprise a single block of business, so REINSURERS participating in the agreement cannot select which treaty to reinsure.

UNAUTHORIZED INSURER See NON-ADMITTED INSURER.

UNAUTHORIZED INSURANCE See NON-ADMITTED INSURANCE.

UNCOVERED OPTION See NAKED OPTION.

UNDATED SECURITY See PERPETUAL DEBT.

UNDERBANKED A future NEW ISSUE of securities with few INDICATIONS OF INTEREST, suggesting that the deal may be difficult for the SYNDICATE to place with investors unless pricing or other deal terms are altered.

UNDERFUNDED PENSION PLAN A PENSION PLAN where future LIABILITIES are not fully covered by existing fund resources.
- See also FUNDED PENSION PLAN.

UNDERINSURANCE (1) Insufficient INSURANCE to cover an INSURABLE RISK, leaving the INSURED exposed to financial loss. (2) Failure by the insured to meet COINSURANCE requirements specified by the INSURER.
- (1) See also OVERINSURANCE.

UNDERINVESTMENT PROBLEM A situation where a company in FINANCIAL DISTRESS is urged by creditors to invest in projects with low RISKS and low returns. Such investments are intended to protect the ASSET position of the firm for the benefit of creditors rather than maximize ENTERPRISE VALUE for the benefit of shareholders.

UNDERLYING The ASSET or market reference defining or underpinning a DERIVATIVE contract.

UNDERPERFORMANCE OPTION An OVER-THE-COUNTER COMPLEX OPTION that grants the buyer a payoff based on the underperformance of a market reference or SPREAD against a pre-defined STRIKE PRICE.
- See also OUTPERFORMANCE OPTION, SPREAD OPTION.

UNDERWATER [COL] (1) A market situation where an OPTION is so far OUT-OF-THE-MONEY that it is virtually worthless. (2) An investment position with a MARKET VALUE that is below BOOK VALUE or carrying value, and which will crystallize a loss if sold.

UNDERWRITER (1) A financial institution involved in UNDERWRITING a NEW ISSUE of securities. (2) An INSURER or REINSURER that analyzes, prices, and accepts or rejects INSURABLE RISKS.
- (1) See also SYNDICATE.

UNDERWRITER'S LIABILITY The LIABILITY an UNDERWRITER faces in arranging and issuing securities for a company. If DUE

DILIGENCE has not been performed (or has been performed in error), or if financial disclosure contained in the PROSPECTUS is incorrect, investors holding securities that ultimately DEFAULT may be able to recover their loss from the underwriter.

UNDERWRITING (1) In the securities industry, the process of issuing NOTES, BONDS, CONVERTIBLE BONDS, COMMON STOCK, or PREFERRED STOCK in the PRIMARY MARKET on behalf of an issuer. (2) In the banking and INSURANCE industries, the process of thoroughly evaluating a RISK exposure and determining whether anticipated profitability is commensurate with EXPECTED LOSS. In banking this is often done through credit analysis; in insurance it is accomplished through ACTUARIAL PRICING and analysis.
- (1) See also ALL-OR-NONE UNDERWRITING, BEST EFFORTS UNDERWRITING, BOUGHT DEAL.

UNDERWRITING AGREEMENT See SYNDICATE AGREEMENT.

UNDERWRITING GROUP See SYNDICATE.

UNDERWRITING INCOME In INSURANCE, the net amount earned from core insurance UNDERWRITING activities, typically computed as:

$$UI = Pr - (IL + LAE + UE + Div)$$

where Pr is PREMIUM, IL is INCURRED LOSSES, LAE is LOSS ADJUSTMENT EXPENSES, UE is underwriting expense, and Div is policyholder DIVIDENDS.

UNDERWRITING RISK (1) The RISK that a SYNDICATE of BANKS or SECURITIES FIRMS UNDERWRITING a NEW ISSUE on a BOUGHT DEAL basis will be unable to place securities with investors, indicating that they will be required to fund any shortfall from their own resources. (2) The risk that the PREMIUM an INSURER charges INSUREDS will prove insufficient to cover future losses, and that losses and LOSS ADJUSTMENT EXPENSES will not be properly covered by RESERVES.

UNDERWRITING SPREAD In a NEW ISSUE, the difference between the amount paid by the SYNDICATE to the issuer and the price at which securities are offered to investors. The spread varies by issuer, class of issue, market conditions, and marketplace, and can range from 4–7 percent for COMMON STOCK to less than 1 percent for NOTES and BONDS.
- Also known as GROSS SPREAD, SPREAD.
- See also SELLING CONCESSION.

UNDISTRIBUTED PROFITS See RETAINED EARNINGS.

UNEARNED PREMIUM RESERVE A RESERVE that contains a portion of the advance PREMIUM paid by an INSURED to an INSURER (or a CEDING INSURER to REINSURER) to cover the amount of INSURANCE (or REINSURANCE) that is still in force. Since premiums are normally charged at the inception of a policy but potential LIABILITY exists until the policy terminates, the reserve reflects the amount needed to cover EXPECTED LOSS prior to expiry. The amount of the reserve associated with a specific policy declines as contract expiry draws closer.

UNEXPECTED CREDIT LOSS The difference between EXPECTED CREDIT LOSS and WORST CASE CREDIT LOSS; alternatively, the difference between the MEAN of the credit loss distribution function and a point represented by multiple STANDARD DEVIATIONS from the mean.

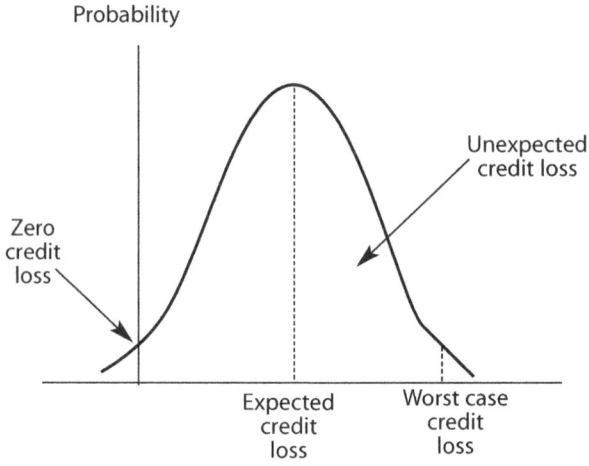

UNILATERAL COLLATERAL A COLLATERAL agreement where only one party to a transaction is required to post security; this generally occurs when one of the two COUNTERPARTIES to a transaction has a materially lower CREDIT RATING than the second party.
■ See also BILATERAL COLLATERAL.

UNINSURABLE RISK A RISK that cannot be covered by INSURANCE as it fails to meet the standard requirements set forth for an INSURABLE RISK, i.e., the risk can produce a loss that is not definable or fortuitous, or the risk is catastrophic and cannot be transferred through payment of an economically reasonable PREMIUM.
■ Also known as PROHIBITED RISK.

UNISSUED STOCK COMMON STOCK that is authorized for issuance through a firm's CORPORATE CHARTER, but has not yet been floated; unissued stock stands in contrast to TREASURY STOCK, which is issued but no longer outstanding.

UNIT INVESTMENT TRUST See CLOSED-END FUND.

UNIT TRUST (1) In the UK, a fund where investors contribute CAPITAL that is used to acquire a PORTFOLIO of earning ASSETS; investors receive a proportional share of any returns generated. A unit trust is legally constructed as a TRUST, with a TRUSTEE appointed as a guardian to hold assets on behalf of the beneficial owners under the terms of a trust deed. A separate investment management company is responsible for managing the portfolios and making investment decisions. Investors purchase individual units in the fund, which can be open-ended; subsequent sales and purchases of units are arranged through the investment manager. (2) See MUTUAL FUND.

UNIVERSAL BANK A BANK that engages in traditional commercial banking activities (i.e., lending, accepting DEPOSITS) and securities activities (i.e., TRADING securities, UNDERWRITING NEW ISSUES, arranging CORPORATE FINANCE transactions, granting investment advice). Europe has featured a system of universal banking for many years; the same has not existed in the United States as a result of regulatory restrictions that were only dismantled in the millennium via the GRAMM–LEACH–BLILEY ACT.
- See also BANCASSURANCE, COMMERCIAL BANK, INVESTMENT BANK.

UNLIMITED LIABILITY A concept and structure where the personal ASSETS of investors, general partners, or sole proprietors are at RISK in the event of a business loss; the extent of financial liability is not bounded as it is in a LIMITED LIABILITY company.
- See also PIERCING THE CORPORATE VEIL.

UNMATCHED BOOK A PORTFOLIO of ASSETS and LIABILITIES (such as the LOANS and DEPOSITS of a BANK, or the REPURCHASE AGREEMENTS and REVERSE REPURCHASE AGREEMENTS of a SECURITIES FIRM), with unequal maturities or DURATIONS. An unmatched book increases an institution's exposure to MARKET RISK and/or LIQUIDITY RISK, but provides for the possibility of a greater return on CAPITAL.
- See also GAP, GAPPING, MATCHED BOOK, MISMATCH, OPEN BOOK.

UNQUALIFIED OPINION An AUDIT OPINION by an external auditor indicating that a company's financial statements present a fair and accurate view of its financial position and conform to accepted accounting principles.
- Also known as CLEAN OPINION.
- See also ADVERSE OPINION, QUALIFIED OPINION.

UNREGISTERED STOCK See LETTER STOCK.

UNSECURED DEBT A BOND or LOAN without any COLLATERAL backing; the sole source of repayment for investors or lenders comes

from the debtor and its financial resources. Unsecured debt is most common among borrowers/issuers with strong CREDIT RATINGS.
- See also SECURED DEBT.

UNWIND PRICE See TEAR-UP PRICE.

UP AND IN OPTION A COMPLEX OPTION that creates a standard EUROPEAN OPTION if the price of the UNDERLYING market reference rises above a predefined BARRIER.
- See also BARRIER OPTION, DOWN AND IN OPTION, DOWN AND OUT OPTION, KNOCK-IN OPTION, REVERSE KNOCK-IN OPTION, UP AND OUT OPTION.

UP AND OUT OPTION A COMPLEX OPTION that extinguishes a standard EUROPEAN OPTION if the price of the UNDERLYING market reference rises above a predefined BARRIER. If the barrier is not breached the European option remains in effect.
- See also BARRIER OPTION, DOWN AND IN OPTION, DOWN AND OUT OPTION, KNOCK-OUT OPTION, REVERSE KNOCK-OUT OPTION, UP AND IN OPTION.

UPFRONT COLLATERAL A process where an institution takes initial COLLATERAL from its COUNTERPARTY in an amount sufficient to cover expected POTENTIAL EXPOSURE for the entire life of the transaction. Under this arrangement no periodic evaluations or collateral calls are required.
- See also PERIODIC COLLATERAL.

UPSTAIRS MARKET [COL] Trades executed within a BROKER/DEALER, or between two broker/dealers, that do not flow through an EXCHANGE. Upstairs market transactions cannot occur at prices that are prejudicial to customers.
- See also CROSSED TRADE.

UPTICK See PLUS TICK.

UPTICK RULE A rule imposed by the SECURITIES AND EXCHANGE COMMISSION that only permits a SHORT SALE in a security or INDEX ARBITRAGE program to be initiated on a PLUS TICK or ZERO PLUS TICK. The rule is intended to halt a self-fulfilling downward spiral, where each downtick leads to further short selling.

UPWARD SLOPING YIELD CURVE See POSITIVE YIELD CURVE.

USURY The practice of charging an excessive INTEREST RATE on any class of DEBT or LIABILITY; in many national systems usury is prohibited by law through the establishment of maximum interest rate ceilings.

UTILIZATION RATE The portion of a REVOLVING CREDIT FACILITY that is drawn down by the borrower, and which must be repaid according to scheduled terms.

V

VALUE ADDED TAX (VAT) An indirect tax applied in certain national systems that is payable by producers and consumers of goods and services. A tax is levied on each incremental stage of the production process that adds value to the good or service being produced.
- See also AD VALOREM.

VALUE-AT-RISK (VAR) A statistical measure that estimates how much a PORTFOLIO of ASSETS and LIABILITIES might lose in a given time period as a result of MARKET RISK. VAR, which can be implemented through the VARIANCE/COVARIANCE, historical, or SIMULATION methods, is based on assumptions related to LIQUIDATION period, shape of the statistical distribution, desired CONFIDENCE LEVEL, and VOLATILITIES and CORRELATIONS between portfolio contracts. Though widely used, the measure has shortcomings related to statistical assumptions and uncertainty regarding the magnitude of potential losses in the TAIL of the distribution.
- See also BACKTESTING, MAXIMUM LOSS, PROFIT AND LOSS EXPLAIN.

VALUE DATE The date on which funds become GOOD MONEY, or a securities or FOREIGN EXCHANGE transaction is settled.
- Also known as SETTLEMENT DATE.

VALUED CONTRACT An INSURANCE contract that provides the INSURED with a stated payout amount, agreed on an ex-ante basis, in the event of a loss. Valued contracts are generally associated with life insurance policies, which specify a sum certain payable to the BENEFICIARY upon the death of the insured.
- See also INDEMNITY CONTRACT.

VANILLA [COL] A standard or conventional financial transaction, rather than one with esoteric or complex parameters, RISKS, or payout profiles. Since vanilla transactions are common, they tend to feature the greatest LIQUIDITY and the narrowest BID–OFFER SPREADS.

VAR See VALUE-AT-RISK.

VARIABLE ANNUITY An ANNUITY where PREMIUMS received from the investor are used to purchase accumulation units with variable value determined by the worth of the securities in the INSURER's investment PORTFOLIO. When the benefits are ultimately paid to the ANNUITANT, units are converted into a fixed number, crystallizing the payout.

VARIABLE INTEREST ENTITY (VIE) See SPECIAL-PURPOSE ENTITY.

VARIABLE LIMIT A provision in a PROPERTY AND CASUALTY INSURANCE contract that automatically increases the size of the

INSURED's limit at each anniversary date, to coincide with increased value attributable to the underlying property being insured. The insured retains the sole right not to increase the limit on each specified date.

VARIABLE PRINCIPAL SWAP The general class of OVER-THE-COUNTER SWAPS with NOTIONAL PRINCIPAL amounts that increase or decrease according to time or the movement of a reference index, generally INTEREST RATES. Payments made or received vary according to the movement of both the market reference and the notional size of the transaction.
- Also known as ROLLER COASTER.
- See also ACCRETING SWAP, AMORTIZING SWAP, INDEX PRINCIPAL SWAP, MORTGAGE SWAP, REVERSE INDEX PRINCIPAL SWAP.

VARIABLE RATE CERTIFICATE OF DEPOSIT (VRCD) See FLOATING RATE CERTIFICATE OF DEPOSIT.

VARIABLE RATE DEMAND NOTE A NOTE issued by a BANK that pays a floating INTEREST RATE based on PRIME RATE or LIBOR, and which is redeemable on demand by the investor.

VARIABLE RATE MORTGAGE See ADJUSTABLE RATE MORTGAGE.

VARIABLE RATE PREFERRED STOCK See ADJUSTABLE RATE PREFERRED STOCK.

VARIABLE STRIKE OPTION See DEFERRED STRIKE OPTION.

VARIANCE A measure of RISK, variability, or dispersion, reflecting the magnitude by which an outcome differs from the EXPECTED VALUE, or the degree to which an observation deviates from the MEAN of a distribution. Variance, which is simply STANDARD DEVIATION squared, can be computed as:

$$\sigma^2 = \left[\frac{\sum_{i=1}^{N} (x_i - \mu)^2}{N} \right]$$

where x_i is an observation, μ is the mean, and N is the number of observations.

VARIANCE SWAP An OVER-THE-COUNTER COMPLEX SWAP involving the exchange of the difference between the square of realized VOLATILITY and the square of IMPLIED VOLATILITY related to a defined market reference. Realized volatility is the floating volatility of the underlying reference index evident over the life of the transaction, while implied volatility is the fixed volatility rate contracted between buyer and seller at the start of the transaction. Since the contract is a NON-LINEAR INSTRUMENT it provides the purchaser with

POSITIVE CONVEXITY (i.e., gains are larger when realized volatility is greater than implied volatility, and losses are smaller when the reverse occurs). Variance swaps are often used in the EQUITY and FOREIGN EXCHANGE markets.
- See also REALIZED VOLATILITY SWAP.

VARIATION MARGIN Incremental security – generally cash, a LETTER OF CREDIT, or high quality BONDS – posted by the buyer or seller of an EXCHANGE-TRADE DERIVATIVE contract once the MAINTENANCE MARGIN level has been breached. If variation margin is not posted with the CLEARINGHOUSE as required, the underlying contract is closed out.
- See also INITIAL MARGIN, CLEARING MARGIN.

VAT See VALUE ADDED TAX.

VEGA The change in the value of an OPTION for a change in VOLATILITY, with all other variables held constant. The vegas of the CALL OPTION and PUT OPTION computed under the BLACK–SCHOLES MODEL (which are equivalent) are given by:

$$V_c = \frac{\partial C}{\partial \sigma} = S\sqrt{t}\, N'(d_1)$$

$$V_p = \frac{\partial P}{\partial \sigma} = S\sqrt{t}\, N'(d_1)$$

where

$$N'(d_1) = \frac{1}{\sqrt{2\pi}} e^{\frac{-d_1^2}{2}}$$

and S is the stock price, t is the time to maturity, σ is the STANDARD DEVIATION, and where the value of $N'(d_1)$ can be obtained from a standard table of probability functions.

The vegas of long and short puts and calls are shown as:

	Long call	Long put	Short call	Short put
Vega	+	+	–	–

- Also known as KAPPA, LAMBDA.
- See also DELTA, GREEKS, THETA, RHO, GAMMA.

VENTURE CAPITAL CAPITAL funds invested in a new, often high-RISK, venture, generally in exchange for a pre-INITIAL PUBLIC OFFERING EQUITY stake. Venture capital specialists, BANKS, and INVESTMENT BANKS actively supply capital to start-up firms in industries such as technology and bio-technology.

■ See also DOWN ROUND, MEZZANINE FINANCING.

VERTICAL LAYERING A practice where different REINSURERS assume the risk of different loss layers under an EXCESS OF LOSS (XOL) REINSURANCE agreement. Each reinsurer becomes liable for its own layer of coverage between a specific ATTACHMENT level and individual POLICY CAP. Under this approach not every reinsurer is susceptible to losses and CLAIMS once the underlying DEDUCTIBLE is exceeded; the higher vertical layers may not be exposed unless the losses are large.

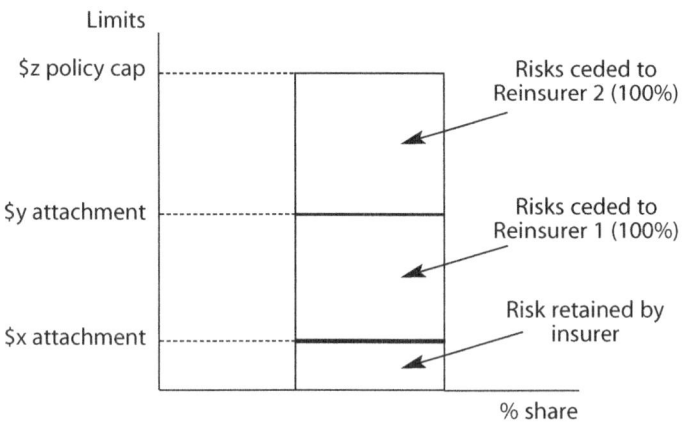

■ See also EXCESS LAYER, HORIZONTAL LAYERING.

VERTICAL MERGER A MERGER between companies that represent different components or stages of the service or industrial process. A vertical merger may be arranged if a company wishes to control or influence the majority of the processes that are used in the production of goods and services, including raw material extraction, processing, production, warehousing, transporting, shipping, and retailing.

■ See also CONGLOMERATE MERGER, HORIZONTAL MERGER.

VERTICAL SPREAD See BEAR SPREAD, BULL SPREAD.

VICINITY OF INSOLVENCY A legal concept where the FIDUCIARY DUTIES of DIRECTORS shift from shareholders to creditors prior to the actual INSOLVENCY of a company. This occurs when a company is almost certain to become insolvent (though has not yet met the technical definition) and is designed to protect the interests of creditors by ensuring actions are taken to protect as much ASSET value as possible.

VIE See VARIABLE INTEREST ENTITY.

VIS MAJOR [LAT] Literally, "overpowering force;" an unavoidable calamity or catastrophic event that can impact the financial profile of a firm, causing it to seek RISK TRANSFER solutions through INSURANCE, REINSURANCE, or DERIVATIVES.

■ See also FORCE MAJEURE.

VISIBLE Any good that is exported from, or imported into, a country. Visibles form a key element of a country's BALANCE OF TRADE and BALANCE OF PAYMENTS accounts.

■ See also INVISIBLE.

VISIBLE SUPPLY See PIPELINE.

VOIDABLE CONTRACT A valid CONTRACT that can be cancelled for cause on the basis of FRAUD or misrepresentation.

VOIDABLE PREFERENCE See PREFERENCE.

VOLATILITY A measure of the price movement of a reference ASSET or market; in general, a reference with high volatility is deemed to be riskier than one with low volatility. Measures of volatility may be backward-looking (HISTORICAL VOLATILITY) or forward-looking (IMPLIED VOLATILITY) and are used in a broad range of financial applications, including pricing of OPTIONS and other DERIVATIVES, computation of CREDIT RISK exposure, and determination of VALUE-AT-RISK.

■ See also STANDARD DEVIATION, VARIANCE, VEGA, VOLATILITY SKEW, VOLATILITY SMILE, VOLATILITY STRATEGY.

VOLATILITY SKEW The difference in VOLATILITY between OUT-OF-THE-MONEY PUT OPTIONS and CALL OPTIONS. In certain markets puts trade at a higher IMPLIED VOLATILITY than calls, reflecting the fact that buyers and sellers value RISK protection more highly on the downside than on the upside.

■ See also VOLATILITY SMILE.

VOLATILITY SMILE A comparison of the IMPLIED VOLATILITY of an OPTION with its STRIKE PRICE. A "conventional" smile attributes greater implied volatility to IN-THE-MONEY OPTIONS and OUT-OF-THE-MONEY OPTIONS, although in some markets out-of-the-money options trade at the highest volatility under the assumption that investors wish to protect against the disaster scenario (which

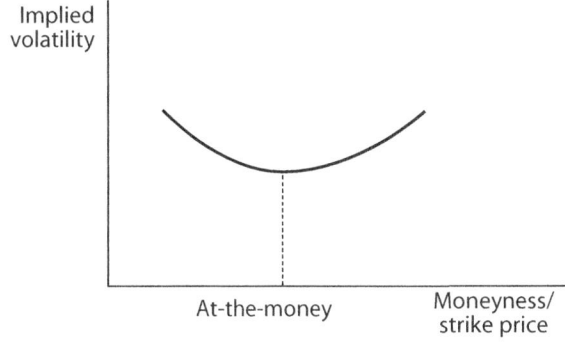

occurs more frequently than financial theory normally suggests, i.e., the FAT TAIL phenomenon) by purchasing less expensive out-of-the-money contracts.
  ▪ See also VOLATILITY SKEW.
VOLATILITY STRATEGY An OPTION strategy that seeks to take advantage of changes in IMPLIED VOLATILITY or historical volatility, rather than market direction. Common volatility strategies include STRADDLES, STRANGLES, BUTTERFLIES, CONDORS, CALENDAR SPREADS, BACKSPREADS, and RATIO VERTICAL SPREADS. Similar strategies can be created through VOLATILITY SWAPS.
  ▪ See also DIRECTIONAL STRATEGY.
VOLATILITY SWAP A general class of OVER-THE-COUNTER SWAPS involving the exchange of realized (actual) VOLATILITY of an UNDERLYING reference for fixed volatility. Volatility swaps provide a mechanism for directly participating in, or protecting against, ASSET or market movement, obviating the need for indirect participation using OPTIONS. Volatility swaps generally have terms ranging from six months to five years, and can be structured in the form of REALIZED VOLATILITY SWAPS and VARIANCE SWAPS.
VOLUMETRIC RISK The RISK of loss from volume imbalances, which can be impacted by changes in both price and quantity. Certain RISK MANAGEMENT structures, such as MULTIPLE TRIGGER PRODUCTS, allow simultaneous management of both dimensions of RISK.
VOLUNTARY BANKRUPTCY A process where a debtor files a petition for BANKRUPTCY protection, invoking an AUTOMATIC STAY. Once filed, the debtor's operations may be placed under the management of a TRUSTEE (or administrator) or they may remain with the debtor itself (who becomes a DEBTOR-IN-POSSESSION).
  ▪ See also INVOLUNTARY BANKRUPTCY.
VOLUNTARY LIQUIDATION LIQUIDATION of a company that has become insolvent, following approval by shareholders, and in some systems creditors. Any proceeds from the liquidation are apportioned to creditors and investors in order of seniority.
VORSTAND [GER] The MANAGEMENT BOARD of a German CORPORATION.
  ▪ See also AUFSICHTSRAT.
VOSTRO [LAT] Literally "your account"; a local account held on behalf of a foreign BANK to accommodate local currency business, e.g., a Japanese bank maintains a US bank's yen vostro account so that the US bank can manage its yen inflows and outflows.
  ▪ See also NOSTRO.
VOTING CAP Corporate or regulatory provisions allowing companies to restrict votes to a particular percentage of a company's stock, regard-

less of the ownership stake held. Voting caps can be used as an ANTI-TAKEOVER DEFENSE or as a method of diffusing the power of control blocks.

VOTING TRUST CONTROL A process or structure where effective corporate control is gained through TRUSTEES who have total, or near total, discretion over how to vote shares. This mechanism represents a true separation of ownership and control, as the trustees do not technically own the stock but exercise the CONTROL RIGHTS embedded in the shares.
- See also LEGAL MECHANISM CONTROL, MAJORITY CONTROL, MANAGEMENT CONTROL, MINORITY CONTROL, TOTAL CONTROL.

VRCD See VARIABLE RATE CERTIFICATE OF DEPOSIT.

VULTURE BID [COL] A deep-discount BID by an investor or investment group for securities or DISTRESSED ASSETS of uncertain worth, or those that must be liquidated by an eager seller.
- See also FIRE SALE, VULTURE FUND.

VULTURE FUND [COL] A LIMITED PARTNERSHIP or private fund that invests in DISTRESSED ASSETS, including securities and real property.
- Also known as a DISTRESSED FUND.

W

W FORMATION See DOUBLE BOTTOM.

WAC See WEIGHTED AVERAGE COUPON.

WAIVER OF PRE-EMPTIVE RIGHTS An investor's agreement to relinquish the affirmative right to obtain new shares of COMMON STOCK when they are issued. Once a waiver is granted, the investor has no further legal ability to take up shares before they are offered in the marketplace at large.
- See also PRE-EMPTIVE RIGHTS, RIGHTS ISSUE.

WAM See WEIGHTED AVERAGE MATURITY.

WAR CHEST [COL] (1) Cash and NEAR CASH held by a company or RAIDER for the express purpose of acquiring another company, often via a HOSTILE TAKEOVER. (2) Funds that can be used by a target company to defend against a possible hostile takeover attempt, i.e., repurchasing shares in the market, declaring a SPECIAL DIVIDEND for existing shareholders.

WAREHOUSE BOND A SURETY BOND guaranteeing that goods or INVENTORY stored in a public warehouse will be delivered upon presentation of authorizing documents.

WAREHOUSE RECEIPT Documentary evidence of INVENTORY placed in storage in a public warehouse. A warehouse provides no guarantee as to the quality or condition of the inventory and does not provide INSURANCE against damage, it simply evidences existence of the inventory. Inventory blocked by a warehouse receipt can only be sold or transferred by the bearer of the receipt, meaning the receipt functions as a mechanism for collateralizing a LOAN.

WAREHOUSING (1) The process of holding ASSETS, such as MORTGAGES, ACCOUNTS RECEIVABLE, or corporate BONDS and LOANS, in a CONDUIT until they are repackaged for SECURITIZATION. The institution warehousing the securities faces full MARKET RISK and CREDIT RISK on the underlying assets. (2) The process of assuming a RISK position (e.g., a block of securities) in advance of a HEDGE or sale to another party.

WARRANT A form of long-term OPTION (i.e., three- to five-year maturity), generally issued as a private instrument and often attached to a BOND issue to lower funding costs (and typically detached and traded separately). Warrants are often issued on a company's COMMON STOCK (e.g., an EQUITY WARRANT), but are also available on FIXED INCOME, FOREIGN EXCHANGE, equity index, and commodity references.
- See also BOND WITH WARRANT, COVERED WARRANT, EX-WARRANT.

WARRANTY A pledge by a company, INSURED, or securities issuer indicating that specific conditions related to the commencement or fulfillment of a contract exist. Warranties may be relied upon by another party to the transaction as an element of the contract, and any breach may lead to cancellation.
- See also REPRESENTATION.

WASH SALE The purchase and sale of a security over a short time frame, which, for non-financial institutions operating in certain national systems, may qualify for tax loss benefits. Wash sales that are done in a coordinated fashion with other parties with the intent of manipulating or PEGGING the price of a security are illegal.
- See also BED AND BREAKFASTING.

WATERED STOCK COMMON STOCK of a company with ASSETS that are overvalued and do not accurately convey the financial position of the firm. Watered stock may also arise from companies that feature significant operating losses, excessive DIVIDEND payments, or overcapitalized operations.

WEAK HANDS [COL] A holder of an EXCHANGE-TRADED DERIVATIVE contract that is not expecting to receive or take delivery of the underlying ASSET, intending instead to close out the position prior to

expiry or exercise. Retail investors and speculators typically have "weak hands."
- See also STRONG HANDS.

WEATHER BOND A SECURITIZATION of a non-catastrophic weather RISK, including temperature and precipitation. Repayment of PRINCIPAL and/or COUPONS is contingent on the occurrence of a defined loss-making weather event; if a specified loss occurs, the issuer of the BOND may delay or cease making payments to investors, meaning that it has HEDGED its exposure.
- See also CATASTROPHE BOND, LIFE ACQUISITION COST SECURITIZATION, MORTGAGE DEFAULT SECURITIZATION, RESIDUAL VALUE SECURITIZATION.

WEATHER DERIVATIVE An EXCHANGE-TRADED DERIVATIVE or OVER-THE-COUNTER DERIVATIVE with an UNDERLYING reference based on the performance of non-catastrophic weather references such as temperature, precipitation, wind, and streamflow. TEMPERATURE DERIVATIVES and PRECIPITATION DERIVATIVES are the two most common forms of weather derivatives.

WEIGHTED AVERAGE COUPON (WAC) The average COUPON on MORTGAGES, LOANS, or other ASSETS forming part of a SECURITIZATION, weighted by value.
- See also WEIGHTED AVERAGE MATURITY.

WEIGHTED AVERAGE MATURITY (WAM) The average maturity of MORTGAGES, LOANS, or other ASSETS forming party of a SECURITIZATION, weighted by value.
- See also WEIGHTED AVERAGE COUPON.

WEINER PROCESS A STOCHASTIC PROCESS that is normally distributed with EXPECTED VALUE of 0 and VARIANCE of 1 at each time interval t. Under a Weiner process, values at time t and $t+1$ are independent (i.e., they have a CORRELATION COEFFICIENT of 0), meaning that a Weiner process is also a MARKOV PROCESS. The Weiner process is used in certain OPTION pricing models.

WET BARRELS [COL] Physically delivered, rather than financially settled, crude oil. Traders dealing in wet barrels generally have need of the physical commodity for production, refining, or supply purposes.

WHEN-IN-THE-MONEY OPTION See CONTINGENT PREMIUM OPTION.

WHEN-ISSUED (WI) SECURITY Any security that has been announced but not yet priced or settled. While in the "WI" period informal, but legally binding, GRAY MARKET TRADING occurs between dealers. Once the WI security has settled, it trades in the same manner as all other SEASONED SECURITIES.
- See also TO BE ANNOUNCED, WHEN-ISSUED TREASURY.

WHEN-ISSUED TREASURY (WIT) A US TREASURY NOTE or TREASURY BOND that has been announced but not yet priced or settled. While in the "WI" period informal, but legally binding, GRAY MARKET TRADING occurs between dealers. Once the WIT has settled, it trades in the same manner as all other seasoned Treasury issues.
- See also TO BE ANNOUNCED, WHEN-ISSUED SECURITY.

WHIPSAW [COL] A fall in the price of a security, triggering a STOP LOSS ORDER and sale, followed by a price rebound. Alternatively, a rise in the price, triggering a buy order and purchase, followed by a price decline.

WHISPER NUMBERS [COL] The release of projected corporate earnings guidance by a company's management in advance of a full public announcement. In the United States this has been limited though SECURITIES AND EXCHANGE COMMISSION Regulation FD, which prohibits selective disclosure to specific parties such as BANK research analysts.

WHISPER STOCK [COL] The COMMON STOCK of a company that is rumored to be the target of a potential TAKEOVER transaction. A whisper stock may exhibit unusual price and volume patterns as a result of the rumors.

WHISTLEBLOWER [COL] An employee who reports internal infractions to senior levels of management in order to reveal or contain a problem. A whistleblower often comes in contact with information that might not be apparent or available to other control functions and is thus an additional element of the GOVERNANCE process.

WHITE KNIGHT [COL] A company that assumes the role of a friendly partner by acquiring a controlling stake in a company that is the subject of a HOSTILE TAKEOVER.
- See also BLACK KNIGHT, GRAY KNIGHT, WHITE SQUIRE.

WHITE SQUIRE [COL] A company that assumes the role of a friendly partner by acquiring a substantial, though not controlling, stake in a company that is the subject of a HOSTILE TAKEOVER.
- See also BLACK KNIGHT, GRAY KNIGHT, WHITE KNIGHT.

WHOLE LOAN A commercial or residential MORTGAGE sold to an investor complete with servicing rights (e.g., collection of principal and interest). Whole loans are periodically sold to CONDUITS for subsequent private label SECURITIZATION.

WI See WHEN-ISSUED SECURITY.

WIDOWS AND ORPHANS [COL] An individual or institution that is considered to be an unsophisticated investor. Certain securities laws exist to protect widows and orphans from being financially damaged through bad financial advice or FRAUD.

- See also AUNT MILLIE.

WILLINGNESS TO PERFORM A COUNTERPARTY's intent to perform on its financial obligations, unrelated to its financial capability of doing so. In some instances a company may choose not to perform on its contracts if it believes it has been mistreated by a financial intermediary or its AGENT.
- See also ABILITY TO PERFORM.

WINDING-UP [COL] See LIQUIDATION.

WINDOW DRESSING [COL] The practice of altering the appearance of corporate financial statements through various short-term transactions, with the primary goal of presenting an improved financial position during reporting periods. Although such alterations may be legal from a strict accounting and regulatory standpoint, they may be ethically questionable.

WIRE TRANSFER An electronic ORDER for the payment of funds from one party to another. Various wire mechanisms exist to accommodate such transfers, including the Fed Wire, CLEARINGHOUSE AUTOMATED PAYMENT SYSTEM, and the CLEARINGHOUSE INTERBANK PAYMENT SYSTEM.

WIT See WHEN-ISSUED TREASURY.

WITHOUT [COL] An indication that only a one-way quote is available on a particular security; rather than quoting a standard BID and OFFER, a MARKET MAKER or DEALER may quote a "bid without" or an "offer without."

WORKING CAPITAL A measure of a company's short-term operating resources, i.e. CURRENT ASSETS and CURRENT LIABILITIES.
- See also GROSS WORKING CAPITAL, NET WORKING CAPITAL, WORKING CAPITAL LOAN.

WORKING CAPITAL LOAN A short-term business LOAN used to purchase short-term ASSETS, often INVENTORY used for production and resale. The credit may be unsecured or secured on the assets being financed, and is generally payable within 60 to 90 days.
- See also WORKING CAPITAL.

WORKOUT AGREEMENT An agreement between a borrower and lender to restructure existing LOAN terms, including repayment schedule, maturity, and/or rate, in order to avoid any act of DEFAULT and FORECLOSURE. A loan subject to a workout agreement is likely to be fully covered by a lender's LOAN LOSS RESERVES.
- See also NON-PERFORMING LOAN, SLOW LOAN.

WORLD BANK See INTERNATIONAL BANK FOR RECONSTRUCTION AND DEVELOPMENT (IBRD).

WORLD TRADE ORGANIZATION (WTO) A supranational organization, created in 1994 as a successor body to the GENERAL

AGREEMENTS ON TARIFFS AND TRADE (GATT), that manages functions and negotiations related to multilateral trade in goods and services.

WORST-CASE CREDIT LOSS A potential extreme credit loss represented by a point multiple STANDARD DEVIATIONS from the MEAN value of the credit LOSS DISTRIBUTION function. Financial institutions allocate CAPITAL in support of worst-case credit losses.

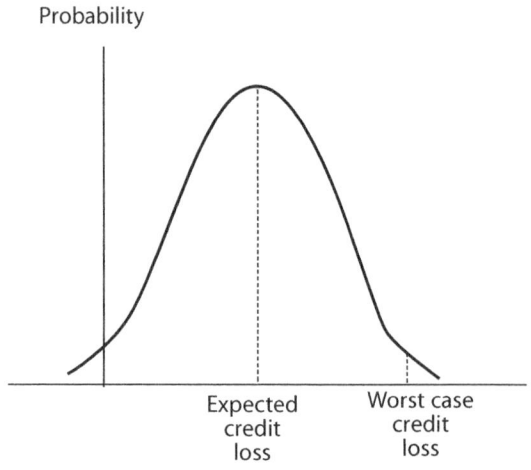

- See also EXPECTED CREDIT LOSS, UNEXPECTED CREDIT LOSS.

WRAP-AROUND INSURANCE An INSURANCE contract covering various aspects of SOVEREIGN RISK, including embargo, sanction, loss, abandonment, control, and expropriation.
- See also POLITICAL RISK INSURANCE.

WTO See WORLD TRADE ORGANIZATION.

X–Y–Z

X

XD See EX-DIVIDEND.
XOL AGREEMENT See EXCESS OF LOSS AGREEMENT.
XR See EX-RIGHTS.
XW See EX-WARRANT.

Y

YANKEE [COL] A BOND, NOTE or CERTIFICATE OF DEPOSIT issued in US dollars in the US markets by a foreign company.

YARD [COL] Common reference for billion.
- See also BUCK, TON.

YIELD The percentage return derived from an investment, typically determined by dividing the earnings from the investment by the initial amount invested. Yield is a relevant return measure for FIXED INCOME instruments, as well as DIVIDEND-paying COMMON STOCK and PREFERRED STOCK.
- See also BOND EQUIVALENT YIELD, CURRENT YIELD, DISCOUNT YIELD, DIVIDEND YIELD, SIMPLE YIELD, TAXABLE EQUIVALENT YIELD, YIELD TO CALL, YIELD TO MATURITY.

YIELD ADVANTAGE The additional SPREAD an investor gains from holding a CONVERTIBLE BOND instead of the equivalent COMMON STOCK, typically computed as:

$$YA = FY - DY$$

where FY is the FLAT YIELD and DY is the DIVIDEND YIELD.

- See also SIMPLE BREAKEVEN.

YIELD BURNING [COL] An illegal practice in MUNICIPAL BOND refinancings where UNDERWRITERS charge excessive prices for TREASURY BONDS purchased and held in escrow before retirement of existing bonds. The high Treasury prices result in a "burning" down of the YIELD.

YIELD CURVE A plot of INTEREST RATES against maturities that results in the creation of a TERM STRUCTURE. In a normal interest rate environment the yield curve is upward sloping (i.e., POSITIVE YIELD CURVE), meaning it costs more to borrow long-term funds than short-term funds, or the investment yield on long-term securities is higher than it is on short-term securities. Other market scenarios include the NEGATIVE YIELD CURVE, which features short-term rates that are higher than long-term rates, and the KINKED YIELD CURVE, which features medium-term rates that are higher than both short- and long-term rates. The shape of the yield curve is influenced by economic, LIQUIDITY, and monetary factors, as well as general market expectations. Yield curves are widely used in financial RISK MANAGEMENT to price and hedge securities and DERIVATIVES.

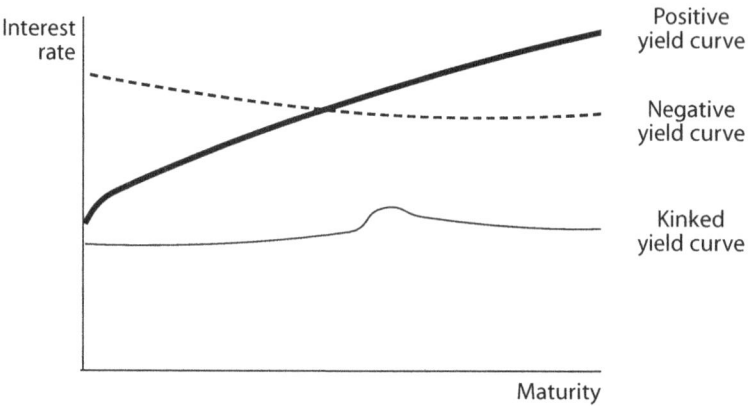

- See also EXPECTATIONS THEORY, IMPLIED FORWARD CURVE, LIQUIDITY PREFERENCE THEORY, MARKET SEGMENTATION THEORY, PAR YIELD CURVE, TERM STRUCTURE, ZERO COUPON YIELD CURVE.

YIELD CURVE OPTION A SPREAD OPTION that grants the buyer a payoff based on the difference between two points on a YIELD CURVE against a predefined STRIKE PRICE. By embedding the two references in a single option contract, the purchaser gains cost and efficiency advantages.

YIELD ENHANCEMENT A financial strategy designed to increase an

investor's core returns; most yield-enhancing techniques, such as SPREAD trades and COVERED CALL and COVERED PUT strategies, are intended to be low RISK, i.e., limited downside with moderate upside.
- See also ARBITRAGE, SPECULATION, HEDGING.

YIELD TO CALL A method of measuring the YIELD of a CALLABLE BOND, computed as the percentage annualized return on a BOND to the FIRST CALL date. The general formula is given as:

$$YTC = \sum_{t=1}^{n^*} \frac{C}{(1+y)^t} + \frac{M^*}{(1+y)^n}$$

where C is COUPON interest, y is the yield, n^* is the number of periods until the first call date, and M^* is the callable bond price.
- See also YIELD TO MATURITY.

YIELD TO MATURITY A common method of measuring the YIELD on a COUPON-bearing security, computed as the percentage annualized return on a BOND until its final maturity. The general formula is given as:

$$YTM = \sum_{t=1}^{n} \frac{C}{(1+y)^t} + \frac{M}{(1+y)^n}$$

where C is the COUPON interest, y is the yield, n is the number of periods, and M is the redemption value of the bond at maturity (generally PAR VALUE).
- Also known as PROMISED YIELD.
- See also YIELD TO CALL.

Z

Z-BOND See ACCRUAL BOND.

Z SCORE A measure used to predict the likelihood of BANKRUPTCY. The model is based on a weighted average of five key financial ratios:

1.2 * WORKING CAPITAL/Total ASSETS +
1.4 * RETAINED EARNINGS/Total Assets +
3.3 * EARNINGS BEFORE INTEREST AND TAXES/Total Assets +
0.6 * MARKET VALUE of EQUITY/BOOK VALUE of DEBT +
1.0 * Sales/Total Assets

A z-score less than 2.675 is indicative of impending bankruptcy. The original z-score measure has been updated (though not supplanted) by a modified Zeta™ model with proprietary parameters.
- Additional reference: Altman (1968).

ZAIBATSU [JPN] A Japanese corporate conglomerate with a central company controlling the ownership and activities of other companies. The zaibatsu structure was banned in the mid-1940s and replaced by the KEIRETSU.

ZAITECH [JPN] Financial SPECULATION undertaken by many Japanese companies in order to boost non-operating income. The practice was very widespread during the late 1980s and early 1990s, although it continues to some degree in the millennium. Transactions involving STRUCTURED NOTES and DERIVATIVES, often with LEVERAGED EQUITY and FOREIGN EXCHANGE RISKS, are popular vehicles for zaitech activities.

ZERO COST COLLAR An OPTION SPREAD consisting of a LONG POSITION in a CAP or CALL OPTION and a SHORT POSITION in a FLOOR or PUT OPTION, or vice versa. The sale of one option offsets the PREMIUM payable on the second option, resulting in "zero cost."

- See also COLLAR.

ZERO COUPON BOND A deep-discount BOND that is sold and traded at a discount to PAR VALUE and pays no periodic COUPON interest during the life of the issue. The difference between the discounted value and the par redemption value generates an implicit return to the investor. The price of a coupon bond is typically computed as:

$$P = \frac{M}{(1 + r)^n}$$

where r is the DISCOUNT RATE, n is the number of periods, and M is the redemption value of the bond at maturity (generally par value).

ZERO COUPON CONVERTIBLE BOND A discounted CONVERTIBLE BOND exchangeable into the issuer's COMMON STOCK, often issued with a CONVERSION PREMIUM of 15–25 percent and used primarily in the US markets. Since the security is structured as a ZERO COUPON BOND it pays no current COUPON while it remains a bond, but accrues interest. The zero coupon convertible is often PUTABLE by the investor back to the issuer at the current redemption price (i.e., accreted value).

ZERO COUPON INFLATION SWAP An OVER-THE-COUNTER SWAP involving the exchange of floating and fixed INFLATION at maturity, with no intervening payments during the life of the transaction. Zero coupon inflation swaps, which generally reference an inflation index of consumer prices, are often structured as long-term transactions, with maturities extending to 10+ years.

- See also ANNUAL INFLATION SWAP, INFLATION SWAP.

ZERO COUPON SWAP An OVER-THE-COUNTER SWAP involving

the exchange of periodic interim payments by one party in return for receipt of a single bullet payment at maturity. A zero-coupon swap acts as a *de facto* LOAN for the party contracting to pay at maturity.

ZERO COUPON YIELD CURVE A YIELD CURVE representing DISCOUNT RATES across maturities, starting from the present. The zero coupon curve is generally constructed from an observable PAR YIELD CURVE through a process known as STRIPPING THE YIELD CURVE (or BOOTSTRAPPING). The zero coupon curve is then used to construct the IMPLIED FORWARD CURVE, which is used to price instruments requiring a forward estimate of rates.

ZERO MINUS TICK Sale of a security at the same price as the last transaction, but lower than the transaction prior to that one. A SHORT SALE cannot be initiated on a zero minus tick.

■ See also MINUS TICK, PLUS TICK, ZERO PLUS TICK.

ZERO PLUS TICK Sale of a security at the same price as the last transaction, but higher than the transaction prior to that one. A SHORT SALE can be initiated on a zero plus tick.

■ See also MINUS TICK, PLUS TICK, ZERO MINUS TICK.

ZOMBIE [COL] A company that is in technical INSOLVENCY but continues to operate, pending the finalization of a restructuring, REORGANIZATION, or bailout.

Numeric

8-K In the United States, a report filed by a company with the SECURITIES AND EXCHANGE COMMISSION containing details on an event that may impact the company's financial statements or MARKET VALUE; the 8-K must be filed within 30 days of the event.

10-K In the United States, an audited annual report filed by a company with the SECURITIES AND EXCHANGE COMMISSION. All issuers of REGISTERED SECURITIES, all companies listed on an EXCHANGE, and companies with more than 500 shareholders, must file a 10-K.
- See also 10-Q.

10-Q In the United States, an audited/unaudited quarterly report filed by a company with the SECURITIES AND EXCHANGE COMMISSION. All issuers of REGISTERED SECURITIES, all companies listed on an EXCHANGE, and companies with more than 500 shareholders must file a 10-Q.
- See also 10-K.

12b–1 MUTUAL FUND A MUTUAL FUND that charges investors for its annual marketing and promotion expenses (which can range from under 25 BASIS POINTS to a maximum of 8.5 percent). 12b–1 funds are generally sold through BROKERS or financial planners, who require the additional compensation in order to distribute fund shares.

Selected References

Altman, E. (1968) "Financial ratios, discriminatory analysis, and the prediction of corporate bankruptcy," *Journal of Finance*, September.

Berle, A. and Means, G. (1991) *The Modern Corporation and Private Property* (rev. edn of 1932 original), New Brunswick, NJ: Transaction.

Black, F. and Scholes, M. (1973) "The pricing of options and corporate liabilities," *Journal of Political Economy*, May–June, pp. 637–59.

Cootner, P. (1964) *The Random Character of Stock Market Prices*, Boston: MIT Press.

Cox, J., Ingersoll, J., and Ross, S. (1981) "A re-examination of traditional hypotheses about the term structure of interest rates," *Journal of Finance*, September.

Cox, J., Ross, S., and Rubinstein, M. (1979) "Option pricing: a simplified approach," *Journal of Financial Economics*, Vol. 7, pp. 229–63.

Cox, J. and Rubinstein, M. (1985) *Options Markets*, Englewood Cliffs, NJ: Prentice Hall.

Edwards, R. and Magee, J. (2001) *Technical Analysis of Stock Trends*, 8th edn, St Lucie Press.

Fama, E. (1970) "Efficient capital markets: a review of theory and empirical work," *Journal of Finance*, Vol. 25, pp. 383–417.

Graham, B. and Dodd, D. (1962) *Security Analysis*, 4th edn, New York: McGraw-Hill.

Hicks, J. (1946) *Value and Capital*, 2nd edn, Oxford: Oxford University Press.

Jensen, M. (1969) "Risk, the pricing of capital assets, and the evaluation of investment portfolios," *Journal of Finance*, April.

Jensen, M. (1972) *Studies in the Theory of Capital Markets*, New York: Praeger.

Lintner, J. (1956) "Distribution of incomes of corporations among dividends, retained earnings, and taxes," *American Economic Review*, Vol. 46, pp. 97–113.

Lutz, F. and Lutz, V. (1951) *The Theory of Investment in the Firm*, Princeton: Princeton University Press.

Markowitz, H. (1952) "Portfolio selection," *Journal of Finance*, March, Vol. 7, pp.77–91.

Meiselman, D. (1962) *The Term Structure of Interest Rates*, Englewood Cliffs, NJ: Prentice-Hall.

Merton, R. (1973) "An intertemporal capital asset pricing model," *Econometrica*.

Miller, M. and Modigliani, F. (1958) "The cost of capital, corporation finance, and the theory of investment," *American Economic Review*, June, Vol. 48, pp. 261–97.

Miller, M. and Modigliani, F. (1961) "Dividend policy and growth: the valuation of shares," *Journal of Business*, October, Vol. 34, pp. 411–33.

Rendleman, R. and Bartter, B. (1979) "Two state option pricing," *Journal of Finance*, Vol. 34, No. 5.

Roll, R. (1977) "A critique of the asset pricing theory's tests," *Journal of Financial Economics*, March.

Roll. R. and Ross, S. (1980) "An empirical investigation of arbitrage pricing theory," *Journal of Finance*, December.

Ross, S. (1976) "The arbitrage theory of capital asset pricing," *Journal of Economic Theory*, Vol. 13, pp. 341–60.

Samuelson, P. (1965) "Proof that properly anticipated prices fluctuate randomly," *Industrial Management Review*, Vol. 6, No. 2, pp. 41–9.

Sharpe, W. (1964) "Capital asset prices: a theory of market equilibrium," *Journal of Finance*, September.

Sharpe, W. (1966) "Mutual fund performance," *Journal of Business*, January.

Sharpe, W. (1971) *Portfolio Theory: Capital Markets*, New York: McGraw-Hill.

Treynor, J. (1965) "How to rate management investment funds," *Harvard Business Review*, January–February.

CPSIA information can be obtained at www.ICGtesting.com
Printed in the USA
LVOW020008120213

319676LV00007B/67/A